TRACING
BRITISH BATTALIONS
ON THE SOMME

Other books by the same author

Collecting Metal Shoulder Titles
(Leo Cooper, 1980)

British Regiments at Gallipoli
(Leo Cooper, 1996)

British Battalions in France & Belgium 1914
(Leo Cooper, 1997)

TRACING
BRITISH BATTALIONS
ON THE SOMME

by

RAY WESTLAKE

Pen & Sword
MILITARY

First published in Great Britain in 1994
Reprinted in 1995 and 1998 by Leo Cooper
Republished in 2004 by Pen & Sword Select

Republished in this format in 2009 by
Pen & Sword Military
An imprint of
Pen & Sword Books Ltd
47 Church Street
Barnsley
South Yorkshire
S70 2AS

ISBN 978 184415 885 0

A CIP catalogue record for this book is
available from the British Library

Printed and bound in England
By CPI UK

Pen & Sword Books Ltd incorporates the Imprints of Pen & Sword Aviation,
Pen & Sword Family History, Pen & Sword Maritime, Pen & Sword Military,
Wharncliffe Local History,
Pen & Sword Select, Pen & Sword Military Classics, Leo Cooper, Remember
When, Seaforth Publishing and Frontline Publishing

For a complete list of Pen & Sword titles please contact
PEN & SWORD BOOKS LIMITED
47 Church Street, Barnsley, South Yorkshire, S70 2AS, England
E-mail: enquiries@pen-and-sword.co.uk
Website: www.pen-and-sword.co.uk

for
Keith Enright
who hopefully will never know war.

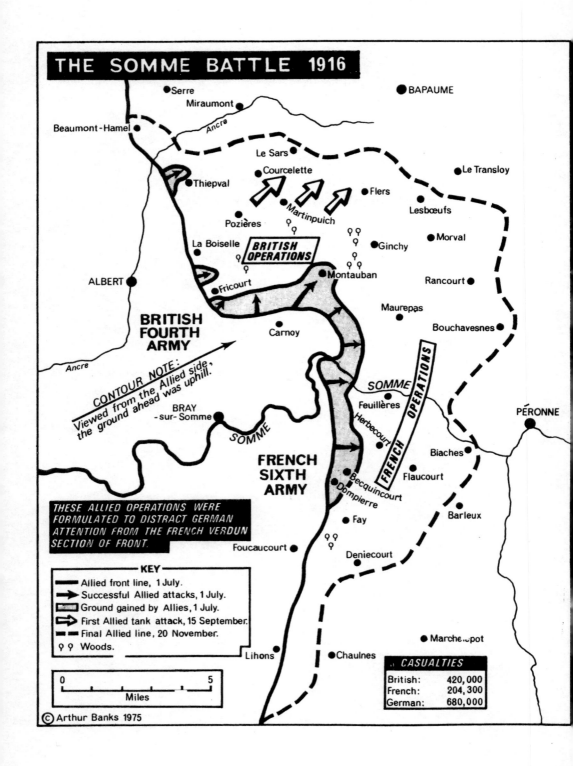

THE SOMME BATTLE 1916

●Serre
Miraumont●
●BAPAUME
Beaumont-Hamel●
Ancre
Le Sars●
●Le Transloy
Courcelette●
●Thiepval
●Flers
Martinpuich
Lesbœufs●
Pozières●
BRITISH OPERATIONS
●Ginchy
●Morval
La Boiselle●
●Montauban
●Rancourt
ALBERT●
Fricourt●
Maurepas●
●Bouchavesnes
BRITISH FOURTH ARMY
Carnoy●
Ancre
SOMME
FRENCH OPERATIONS
CONTOUR NOTE:
Viewed from the Allied side,
the ground ahead was uphill.
Feuillères●
PÉRONNE●
BRAY -sur-Somme●
SOMME
Herbecourt●
FRENCH SIXTH ARMY
●Biaches
Flaucourt●
Becquincourt●
Dompierre●
THESE ALLIED OPERATIONS WERE FORMULATED TO DISTRACT GERMAN ATTENTION FROM THE FRENCH VERDUN SECTION OF FRONT.
●Fay
●Barleux
Foucaucourt●
Deniecourt●
●Marchelepot

KEY
— Allied front line, 1 July.
➤ Successful Allied attacks, 1 July.
▓ Ground gained by Allies, 1 July.
⇨ First Allied tank attack, 15 September.
- - - Final Allied line, 20 November.
♀ ♀ Woods.

Lihons●
●Chaulnes

CASUALTIES
British:	420,000
French:	204,300
German:	680,000

0 _____ 5
Miles

© Arthur Banks 1975

Introduction

The idea behind this book evolved as a result of many years of enquiries from historians and researches. There has also been in recent times a welcome interest shown by many who simply wish to know where their relatives served during the Great War. I hope this work will provide help, at least as far as the 1916 Battle of the Somme is concerned, and literally enable any visitor to France to follow in the footsteps of their grandfathers, fathers, uncles, etc.

British Battalions of the Somme 1916 is not intended to be a history of the battle. Other and more knowledgeable authors having already covered this important period of British military history adequately. What has been provided is an account of some 616 infantry battalions belonging to regiments of the British Army and the 63rd (Royal Naval Division) during their service in the Somme area, battles and engagements, along with movements out of the line, being dealt with at battalion level rather than on a larger and less detailed divisional scale.

The period covered by this work is that generally accepted as 'The Battle of The Somme' – viz: 1 July–18 November, 1916. Movements of battalions are generally dealt with while each remains within the area designated as *Departement de la Somme*. Consequently, locations out of the battle area, such as those around Amiens, Abbeville and Doullens appear in the records of each. Geographically, positions in the vicinity of the Gommecourt sector (Pas de Calais) would not qualify. However, the importance of this part of the line and the fighting that went on there necessitates their inclusion.

Normally, locations given are those where the majority of the battalion bivouacked or billeted. Often small parties (or single companies) moved away for temporary attachment to other formations, or on work detail, and this has been mentioned where known. Trench names are as given in war diaries. Casualty figures, where given, are generally those recorded in war diaries and are made up from killed, wounded and missing lists.

Notes on Infantry Organization

In 1914 infantry battalions of the British Army were those contained within the 4 regiments of foot guards (Welsh Guards raised Feb. 1915) and some 69 Line regiments. There were also several regiments made up entirely from members of the Territorial Force.

Each Line regiment contained Regular battalions (usually 2) and a number of Reserve battalions (the old Militia). In the case of English, Scottish and Welsh regiments, these also had Territorial Force battalions intended for home defence. At the outbreak of war Lord Kitchener created a 'New Army' and these battalions were added and numbered on from those Regular, Reserve and Territorial battalions of Line regiments already in existence.

Regular battalions (usually numbered 1st and 2nd) are referred to by number only. In the main, Reserve battalions did not go overseas as such. Those that did are listed as '(Extra Reserve)'. The titles of Territorial Force battalions are followed by the letters '(T.F.)', while those of Kitchener's New Army include the word '(Service)'. A number of non-combatant battalions '(Labour)' were also raised and numbered within regiments.

A Division (in 1916) comprised 3 infantry brigades (each containing 4 battalions) and a pioneer battalion. In the case of the 9th (Scottish) Division, 1 brigade was made up entirely from South African battalions, while in the 29th the 88th Infantry Brigade included the Newfoundland Regiment.

Sources of Information

The main source of information for this book has been war diaries and unit histories. The latter amounts to some 250 volumes, making a list impractical. War diaries are held at the Public Records Office under W.O.95 classification. References drawn from published memoirs, diaries, etc, have been acknowledged in the text. My own files (RAY WESTLAKE UNIT ARCHIVES) have also been put to good use – the 6,000-plus files formed over the last twenty-five years providing in many cases hitherto unpublished information.

The following works have been essential:

History of The Great War – Order of Battle of Divisions, Major A.F. Becke.

Part 1 – Regular British Divisions
Part 2A – 1st Line Territorial Force Divisions
Part 2B – 2nd Line Territorial Force Divisions
Part 3A – New Army Divisions (9th–26th)
Part 3B – New Army Divisions (30th–41st) and 63rd (R.N.)
H.M.S.O. 1935, 1936, 1937, 1938, 1945.

History of The Great War – Military Operations France and Belgium 1916.

Two volumes, Brigadier-General Sir James E. Edmonds, Macmillan, 1932, 1938.

British Regiments 1914–18, Brigadier E.A. James. Samson Books 1978.

When The Barrage Lifts, G. Gliddon, Gliddon Books, 1987.

The V.C. and D.S.O, Sir O'Moore Creagh, V.C. and Miss E.M. Humphris. Standard Art Book Co. Ltd, 1924.

Monthly Army List, June, 1916, War Office.

Acknowledgements

The help given by the following individuals and organizations has made this book possible – Major P.J. Ball (Duke of Edinburgh's Royal Regiment Museum), Stuart Barr, Malcome Baxter, Mike Beckett, Bedfordshire Records Office, Major M. Beedle, Christine Beresford (Regiments of Gloucestershire Museum), John Bodsworth, Dr Stephen Bull, Canterbury City Council, Major J. Carroll (Dorset Military Museum), Terry Carter, Ann Clayton, Gillian Cooke (Thameside Local Studies Library), Colonel J.S. Cowley (King's Own Yorkshire Light Infantry Museum), Geoffrey Crump (Cheshire Regiment Museum Researcher), Brigadier J.M. Cubiss (The Prince of Wales's Own Regiment of Yorkshire Museum), Colonel C.D. Darroch (Royal Hampshire Regiment Museum), Pete Duckers, Stuart Eastwood, Lieutenant-Colonel Clive Elderton, Billy Ervine (Somme Association), Charles Fair, Nick Forder, Bob Gregory, Captain C. Harrison (Gordon Highlanders Museum), Hertfordshire Records Office, Norman Holme (Royal Welch Fusiliers Museum), I. Hook (Essex Regiment Museum), Les Hughes, Jim Kellerher, Peter Lead, Leicestershire Records Office, Lincolnshire County Council, Major R.D.W. McLean (Staffordshire Regiment Museum), Major C.D. Miller (Duke of Wellington's Regiment Museum), Laurie Milner, National Museums and Galleries on Merseyside, Fred Perry, Earnie Platt, Public Records Office, Queen's Lancashire Regiment Museum, Queen's Own Highlanders Museum, R.A. Rayner, Paul Reed, Lieutenant-Colonel D.R. Roberts (Devonshire and Dorset Regiment Museum), Royal Scots Museum, Royal Sussex Regiment Museum, Royal Warwickshire Regiment Museum, Stephen Shannon (Durham Light Infantry Museum), South Wales Borderers Museum, Alan Stansfield, Margaret Stansfield, Graham Stewart, Suffolk Regiment Museum, Sussex Combined Services Museum, Welch Regiment Museum, Lieutenant-Colonel L.Wilson, John Woodroff.

Families also play an important part in the writing of books. Thanks to my wife Barbara for not only putting up with me during the two years that the Somme Battalions have been living in the house, but for tolerating rooms of dusty books and every flat surface covered with maps. Our son Paul's help with the day-to-day running of RAY WESTLAKE-MILITARY BOOKS is now essential.

Grenadier Guards

1st Battalion. 3rd Guards Brigade, Guards Division: Arrived Halloy (30/7). To Bus-lès-Artois (1/8). Regimental history by Sir Frederick Ponsonby records that later 2 days were spent in trenches at Beaumont-Hamel. Entrained for Méricourt (25/8) and from there to Ville-sous-Corbie. Moved forward to reserve at Bernafay Wood (8/9). One company sent forward to Arrow Head Copse in support of 4th Grenadier Guards (10/9) and another to 1st Welsh Guards – the latter coming into action against enemy attack. Rest of Battalion moved forward to Guillemont. Attack on Ginchy Telegraph and The Quadrilateral (12/9) – assault checked with heavy casualties. Relieved and to Happy Valley (13/9). To Trônes Wood via Carnoy (14/9). Advanced to positions south-west of Ginchy (15/9) – in support of attack towards Lesbœufs. Moved forward to trenches in front of Ginchy (16/9) – on right of attack – advance as far as high ground west of Lesbœufs – heavy casualties by machine gun fire from church tower. *Official History of The Great War* records advance as being without artillery support and against accurate machine gun fire. Battalion dug-in about 250 yards from objective. Withdrew to Carnoy (17/9). To trenches west of Lesbœufs (20/9), Trônes Wood (21/9), assembly trenches for attack (24/9). Attack on Lesbœufs (25/9) – in support – passed through leading waves to take final objective by 3.30 p.m. Relieved and to Carnoy (26/9). Casualties for Ginchy/Lesbœufs operations – 611. To Fontaine-le-Sec (1/10), Sandpit Camp (10/11). From there, via Trônes Wood moved to front line trenches east of Gueudecourt.

2nd Battalion. 1st Guards Brigade, Guards Division: Arrived St Pol (30/7) and from there in motor lorries to Bouquemaison. Later marched to Neuvillette. To Sarton (1/8), Bertrancourt (10/8). Later to front line Beaumont-Hamel sector. Relieved and to Bertrancourt (14/8). To Courcelles-au-Bois (16/8), Beauval (23/8). Entrained for Méricourt (25/8) and from there to Méaulte. To Carnoy (31/8) - dug trenches in rear of the 20th Division. Relieved and to Méaulte (3/9). To Carnoy (9/9), front line Ginchy sector (12/9). Successful operation carried out at the orchard just outside Ginchy (13/9) – British line being straightened out in readiness for forthcoming attack. Relieved and to bivouacs just behind Ginchy (14/9). Attack towards Lesbœufs (15/9) – followed 2nd and 3rd Coldstream into action through heavy bombardment, shells, according to one source, said to be dropping at 1 per second. Battalion's right on Ginchy-Lesbœufs Road – cleared enemy trenches at point of bayonet – holding first and second objective by evening. Relieved and to Citadel Camp (16/9). Casualties – 378. To Bernafay Wood (20/9), assembly trenches in front of Ginchy (24/9). Regimental historian – Sir Frederick Ponsonby records that trenches were so narrow that the men were unable to sit or lie down, and had to remain standing shoulder to shoulder. Attacked 12.35 p.m. (25/9) – with Ginchy-Lesbœufs Road on right moved forward – assault held up by uncut wire, 4 officers preceded to cut gaps by hand, Battalion then charged through to take objective. Regimental history records high losses among officers and assault on second objective almost totally led by N.C.Os. Relieved from captured line (26/9) and via Bernafay Wood to Citadel Camp. Casualties – 351. Later to Morlancourt and from there Aumont. To Citadel Camp (10/11), camp near Montauban (12/11), Trônes Wood (15/11), front line between Lesbœufs and Gueudecourt (16/11).

3rd Battalion. 2nd Guards Brigade, Guards Division: From Le Souich took over trenches Beaumont-Hamel sector (13/8). To Sailly-au-Bois (17/8), Bus-lès-Artois (21/8), Amplier (23/8), Naours (24/8). Entrained for Méricourt (25/8) and from there to Morlancourt. To Happy Valley (9/9), Carnoy (12/9), assembly positions east of Ginchy (14/9). Attack towards Lesbœufs (15/9) – advanced 6.20 a.m. – heavy casualties before first objective reached and cleared. Relieved (16/9) and to Bernafay Wood. Casualties – 412. To Carnoy (20/9). In reserve for attack (25/9). Later to Heucourt. To Méaulte (11/11), Mansell Camp (15/11).

4th Battalion. 3rd Guards Brigade, Guards Division: Arrived Halloy (30/7). Later to camps at Arquèves, Mailly-Maillet before taking over line Beaumont-Hamel sector. To Vauchelles-lès-Authie (20/8), Gézaincourt (22/8), Vigna-court (24/8). Entrained for Méricourt (25/8) and from there to Ville-sous-Corbie. To Carnoy (8/9). Worked on road running from village to Wedge Wood. Later to huts near Talus Boisé. To line between Guillemont and Leuze Wood midnight (9/9). In support of failed attack on The Quadrilateral (12/9). Relieved and to Happy Valley. To Carnoy (14/9) and from there to the copse eastern side of Trônes Wood. Attack towards Lesbœufs (15/9) – from reserve advanced on right passing over first objective. Regimental history notes heaps of dead Germans as evidence of recent fighting. Dug in 500 yards north of Ginchy and consolidated gains. In support of attack (16/9). Withdrew to Carnoy during evening. To line in front of Lesbœufs (20/9) – dug communication and assembly trenches for forthcoming attack. Relieved and to Bernafay Wood (22/9). Moved forward (24/9). Attacked 12.35 p.m. (25/9) - Regimental history notes over 150 Germans killed with the bayonet before rushing on to clear first objective. Second objective taken. Relieved 10 p.m. (26/9) and to Carnoy. Casualties since (18/9) – 458. To Sandpit Camp (30/9). Morlancourt (1/10). From there via Amiens to Epaumesnil. To Sandpit Camp (10/11), Carnoy (12/11), trenches in front of Lesbœufs and Gueudecourt (13/11), Carnoy (17/11).

Coldstream Guards

1st Battalion. 2nd Guards Brigade, Guards Division: From Ypres sector arrived Lucheux area end July. Via Bois de Warnimont began duty in forward area Auchonvillers sector second week August. To Bus-lès-Artois (21/8), Amplier (23/8), Naours (24/8). Entrained for Méricourt (25/8) and from there to Morlancourt area. To Happy Valley (9/9), Bernafay Wood (12/9). Attack towards Lesbœufs (15/9) – assembled south-east of Ginchy-Lesbœufs Road. On left of Brigade advanced in line with 2nd Coldstream to left and 3rd to the left of 2nd (all three Coldstream battalions going forward together). Hard fighting crossing 2 forward lines – the enemy, according to Lieutenant-Colonel Sir John Ross of Bladensburg's Coldstream history, defending these with great bravery to the last man. Commanding Officer Lieutenant-Colonel Hon. G.V. Baring killed. Relieved and to Citadel Camp (16/9). Casualties – 360. In reserve during attack on Lesbœufs (25/9) – later moved forward to support line. To front line beyond Lesbœufs (29/9) – attack on Rainy Trench driven back by machine gun fire and strong barrage. Dug in and new line established 200 yards in advance of original line. Relieved and to Carnoy (30/9). Guards Division relieved (1/10) and to Amiens area. Casualties since (18/9) – 129. Arrived Méaulte (11/11).

2nd Battalion. 1st Guards Brigade, Guards Division: From Ypres sector arrived Bouquemaison area end July. Moved forward, arriving Bertrancourt (10/8) and began duty in Beaumont-Hamel sector. Relieved and to Beauval (23/8). Entrained for Méricourt (25/8) and from there to Méaulte. Moved forward via Bernafay Wood to Ginchy sector (12/9). Attack towards Lesbœufs (15/9) – on right of Brigade received heavy casualties from enemy machine guns in sunken Ginchy-Flers Road. Position stormed and advance continued to German first line. Next objective taken by 11.15 a.m. Relieved and to Citadel Camp (16/9). Casualties – 440. To forward area during night (20/9). In support for attack on Lesbœufs (25/9) – bombers cleared cellars in village. Relieved during evening and to Carnoy. Guards Division relieved and to Amiens area (1/10). Casualties since (18/9) – 145. Arrived Citadel Camp (10/11). Later moved forward via Montauban and Trônes Wood to forward area Gueudecourt.

3rd Battalion. 1st Guards Brigade, Guards Division: From Ypres sector arrived Bouquemaison area end July. Moved forward, arriving Bertrancourt (10/8) and began duty in Beaumont-Hamel sector. Relieved and to Beauval (23/8). Entrained for Méricourt (25/8) and from there to Méaulte. Moved forward via Bernafay Wood to Ginchy sector (12/9). Attacked towards Lesbœufs (15/9) – advance of 1st Guards Brigade towards first objective soon met by strong machine gun fire from Ginchy-Flers sunken road. Most officers becoming casualties before they had gone forward more than 100 yards. Lieutenant-Colonel John Campbell, D.S.O. (commanding 3rd Battalion) soon rallied the survivors and then with a blast from his hunting horn, took the men on. In a fierce charge the Guardsmen poured into the sunken road and cleared the enemy by hand-to-hand fighting. Advance continued and German first line taken. In next assault – heavy casualties from machine gun fire from right. Colonel Campbell once again collected his men and led attack onto next objective. Enemy cleared from position by 11.15 and posts established 600 yards in front. Colonel Campbell awarded Victoria Cross. Relieved and to Citadel Camp (16/9). Casualties – 361. To forward area during night (20/9). In support for attack on Lesbœufs (25/9) – bombers in action clearing dug-outs and cellars in village. Relieved during evening and to Carnoy. Guards Division relieved and to Amiens area (1/10). Casualties since (18/9) – 131. Arrived Citadel Camp (10/11). Later, via Montauban, to forward area Gueudecourt.

4th Battalion (Pioneers). Pioneers, Guards Division: From Ypres sector concentrated with Guards Division in Doullens area end July. Began work Hébuterne and Beaumont-Hamel sectors second week of August. Began move to Méaulte area (21/8). Worked on defences. Detachment joined tunnelling companies for mining operations. Moved forward to Ginchy sector beginning September. Attack towards Lesbœufs (15/9) – operated as signallers and carried ammunition to forward area. In action during attack on Lesbœufs (25/9). Remained in forward area until (6/11).

Scots Guards

1st Battalion. 2nd Guards Brigade, Guards Division: Arrived Lucheux from Ypres sector (26/7). To Bois de Warnimont (2/8). Took turns in trenches - Auchonvillers sector facing Beaumont-Hamel (9/8)–(16/8) – resting between tours at Bertrancourt. To Sailly-au-Bois (16/8) and tours in trenches - Hébuterne sector. To Bus-lès-Artois (21/8), Amplier (23/8), Naours (24/8). Entrained for Méricourt-l'Abbé and marched to Morlancourt (25/8). To Happy Valley (9/9), Bernafay Wood (12/9). Moved up to assembly positions in front of Ginchy (14/9). War Diary notes moving up of the 'Armoured Creepers' (Tanks) which was brought to a standstill by heavy fire. Attacked towards Lesbœufs 6.20 a.m. (15/9) – in support behind 3rd Grenadier Guards – fighting on record as being of the severest kind – hand to hand combat encountered by most, and all ranks performing in a gallant and heroic manner. One Guardsman, Lance-Sergeant Fred McNess was to receive the Victoria Cross for his gallantry and leadership while organizing a bombing attack on the enemy – although severely wounded in the neck and jaw he continually brought supplies of bombs up to his men until falling exhausted from loss of blood. Relieved and to Citadel Camp (16/9). Casualties – 288. To Carnoy (20/9), Trônes Wood (25/9) - returning to Carnoy same evening. Later one company sent forward to support 2nd Scots Guards during attack on Lesbœufs. Relieved 2nd Battalion in line at Lesbœufs (26/9). To Fricourt-Carnoy Road (30/9). Entrained at Dernancourt for Airaines (2/10) and from there marched to Warlus. To Méaulte (11/11), camp on Carnoy-Montauban Road (12/11).

2nd Battalion. 3rd Guards Brigade, Guards Division: Entrained at Cassel for Frévent (30/7) and from there marched via Lucheux to Halloy. To Bus-lès-Artois (1/8), Bertrancourt (10/8) and began tours in front line Auchonvillers. To Bus (19/8), Sarton (20/8), Hem-Hardinval (22/8). Entrained at Vignacourt for Méricourt-l'Abbé (25/8) and from there marched to Ville-sous-Corbie. To bivouacs just north of Carnoy (9/9), Bernafay Wood (10/9) – 2 companies moved forward to line north and north-east of Ginchy and assisted in capture of the orchard. Rest of Battalion moved up to Ginchy (11/9). To Happy Valley (12/9). At 5 p.m. marched to Carnoy and from there took up assembly positions east of Trônes Wood. Moved forward 9 a.m. (15/9) for attack on Lesbœufs – heavily shelled and forced to dig in between Guillemont and Ginchy – later provided defensive flank left of 1st (Guards) Brigade. To Carnoy (16/9). Casualties – 164. Moved to forward line facing Lesbœufs (20/9), 2 companies to Trônes Wood (22/9)–(24/9).

Attack on trenches north-west and north of Lesbœufs (25/9). Relieved by 1st Scots Guards and to Trônes Wood (26/9). Casualties – 325. To camp just south of Fricourt (29/9), Vergies (1/10), Via Treux to Sandpit Camp (10/11), Trônes Wood (11/11), reserve trenches (12/11), Montauban (15/11).

Irish Guards

1st Battalion. 1st Guards Brigade, Guards Division: Moved towards Somme from Ypres sector end of July – reaching Bouquemaison (1/8). To Vauchelles-lès-Authie (4/8), via Louvencourt and Bertrancourt to Mailly-Maillet Wood (11/8). Took over reserve positions east of Englebelmer. To Louvencourt (12/8), front line opposite Serre (16/8). – Rudyard Kipling in his history of the Irish Guards records the dead of 1st July still laying around in large numbers. Some 200 being buried by the Battalion. To Bois de Warnimont (20/8), Beauval (23/8). Entrained at Canaples for Méricourt (25/8) and from there marched to Méaulte. Moved forward to Bernafay Wood and trenches near Ginchy (10/9). Formed up north-west of Ginchy (15/9) and in attack towards Lesbœufs at 6.20 a.m. Rudyard Kipling notes advance as being through a haze of flying dirt – No.1 Company behind the Coldstream saw a platoon 'crumped out of existence in one flash and roar.' Withdrew via Bernafay Wood to Citadel Camp (17/9) Casualties – 342. To copse on eastern edge of Trônes Wood (20/9). Led attack left of 1st Guards Brigade on Lesbœufs (25/9). Relieved by 2nd Irish Guards in village (26/9) and withdrew via Bernafay Wood to Citadel Camp. Casualties – over 250. To Hornoy (1/10), camp near Carnoy (10/11), near Montauban (11/11), front line between Lesbœufs and Gueudecourt (13/11). Relieved and via camp between Carnoy and Montauban to Méaulte (16/11).

2nd Battalion. 2nd Guards Brigade, Guards Division: Left Ypres sector end of July – reaching Lucheux (30/7). To Mailly-Maillet Wood (1/8), Bois de Warnimont (6/8), front line Auchonvillers sector (13/8). Relieved and to Mailly-Maillet Wood (15/8), Couin (17/8). Rudyard Kipling in his Regimental history records that at Couin men of the Battalion witnessed the tragic death of music hall artist Basil Hallam ('Gilbert the Filbert') who fell to his death from an observation balloon (20/8). To Bus-lès-Artois (21/8), Amplier (23/8), Naours (24/8). Entrained for Méricourt (25/8). To Happy Valley (9/9), Bernafay Wood (12/9). Moved forward to line at Ginchy. Attack towards Lesbœufs (15/9). Withdrew to Citadel Camp (16/9) – Rudyard Kipling noting that just 88 men made the journey with some 78 arriving later. To Carnoy (20/9), Trônes Wood (25/9). Relieved 1st Irish Guards at Lesbœufs (26/9). To Trônes Wood (28/9), Carnoy (30/9), Méricourt-en-Vimeu (2/10), Méaulte (11/11). Rudyard Kipling recalls the journey to Méaulte as being in French buses driven by Senegalese. An experience, he notes, almost as deadly as warfare itself and justifying the award of a medal. Moved forward to Trônes Wood (18/11).

Welsh Guards

1st Battalion. 3rd Guards Brigade, Guards Division: Left Ypres sector (27/7) – reaching Halloy (30/7), Bus-lès-Artois (1/8), Arquèves (6/8), Mailly-Maillet (9/8). Took over line between Beaumont-Hamel and Serre (10/8). Relived by 2nd Scots Guards and to Colincamps (14/8). To front line (17/8), Bus-lès-Artois (19/8), Vauchelles-lès-Authie (20/8), Gézaincourt (22/8), Vignacourt (24/8), Méricourt-l'Abbé (25/8), Ville-sur-Ancre (7/9). Took part in operations at Ginchy (9/9)–(11/9). Relieved and to Bernafay Wood. To Happy Valley (12/9), trenches west of Trônes Wood (14/9). Attacked towards Lesbœufs just after midday (15/9) – Regimental historian Dudley Ward recording 'hard and confused fighting' during the attack. Relieved and to Carnoy (17/9). To Trônes Wood (20/9), Lesbœufs sector (25/9). Capture of Gueudecourt (26/9). Relieved and to Trônes Wood. To Mansell Camp (29/9), Fricourt (30/9), St. Maulvis (1/10), Mansell Camp (6/11), Montauban (14/11) and from there front line due east of Gueudecourt.

Royal Scots (Lothian Regiment)

2nd Battalion. 8th Brigade, 3rd Division: Arrived Candas (2/7) and from there marched to Bernaville. To Flesselles (3/7), Allonville (4/7), Vaux-sur-Somme (5/7). Less 'A' Company to Celestines Wood (6/7), via Bronfay Farm into trenches near Montauban (7/7). 'A' Company to Bronfay Farm (6/7) – digging and laying cables in front of Carnoy (7/7)–(8/7). Moved forward to reserve positions (13/7). Attack on Bazentin-le-Grand (14/7) – gains held and consolidated. Relieved and to Montauban Alley (19/7). Took over captured German positions between Waterlot Farm and Trônes Wood (20/7). Attacked towards Guillemont – failed assaults taking place (22/7) and (23/7). Relieved and to Happy Valley (25/7). To Méaulte (26/7), Talus Boisé (16/8), Maltz Horn Trench in support (18/8). Relieved and to Talus Boisé (19/8), Sandpit Camp (20/8), Méaulte (21/8). Entrained at Méricourt for Candas (23/8) and from there marched to Prouville. Began journey to Hulluch sector (25/8). Entrained at St. Pol (7/10) – arrived Acheux (8/10) and took over huts in Acheux Wood. Provided working parties to line near Serre. To Vauchelles-lès-Authie (18/10). Began tours in front line Serre sector (23/10). Relieved by 8th East Yorkshire and to Courcelles-au-Bois (1/11). To Vauchelles-lès-Authie (4/11), front line (12/11). Attacked (13/11) – War Diary records left flank of 'A' Company withdrew finding no gaps in enemy wire – supporting companies crawled to the wire and attempted to cut their way through but found it impossible. Relieved at nightfall (14/11) and to Bus-lès-Artois. Casualties – 274. To Courcelles-au-Bois (15/11). Relieved 7th K.S.L.I. in front line (17/11)

5th/6th Battalion (T.F.). 14th Brigade, 32nd Division: Arrived Beauval (18/10). To Warloy (21/10), brickfields on Bouzincourt-Albert Road (23/10), Harponville (26/10), Aveluy (9/11), Mailly-Maillet (15/11). Provided carrying parties for units in front line. Waited in positions near Serre Road, but was not used in an attack carried out by 14th Brigade against Frankfort and Munich Trenches (18/11).

1/8th Battalion (T.F.). Pioneers, 51st (Highland) Division. Arrived Bouque-maison by motor lorry from Monchy-Breton (15/7). To Candas (16/7). Entrained for Méricourt-l'Abbé (20/7) and from there marched to Ribemont. Made ready in Mametz Wood for attack on High Wood (21/7). To Happy Valley (22/7) and awaited orders to consolidate any positions gained. More than 100 casualties sustained from shell fire. Work later included digging of Thistle Alley. To bivouacs on Albert-Amiens Road (6/8). Entrained at Méricourt-l'Abbé for Longpré (9/8) and from there marched to Pont-Remy. Entrained for Armentières sector (12/8). Entrained at Bailleul and Merville for Doullens and Candas (1/10). From there to billets at Hem-Hardinval. To Thièvres (2/10), Louvencourt (3/10). Less 'B' Company to Courcelles-au-Bois and Colincamps (4/10). Began work on communication trenches and railways. To Mailly-Maillet (18/10). Work in Beaumont-Hamel area – included construction of large numbers of dug-outs, maintenance of existing trenches and setting up of dressing-station at White City. Engaged throughout 51st Division's operations on the Ancre (13/11)–(18/11) – playing important role during capture of Beaumont-Hamel.

1/9th (Highlanders) Battalion (T.F.). 154th Brigade, 51st (Highland) Division; From Arras sector reached Beaumetz (16/7). Entrained at Candas for Méricourt-l'Abbé (20/7) and from there marched to Méaulte. Moved forward via Fricourt and Mametz to trenches near Bazentin-le-Grand Wood (21/7). Attack at High Wood (23/7) – War Diary records assaulting companies subjected to heavy shell fire while crossing open ground – also to machine gun fire on reaching first objective (fire was from eastern end of Intermediate Trench, western tip of wood). Relieved during evening and to Mametz Wood. Casualties - 175. To Bécordel-Bécourt (25/7), Mametz Wood (1/8), bivouacs near Dernancourt (6/8). Entrained at Méricourt-l'Abbé for Longpré (9/8) and from there marched to Erondelle. Entrained at Pont-Remy for Steenbecque (11/8). From Armentières sector arrived Candas (30/9). To Famechon (3/10), Bus-lès-Artois (4/10), Colincamps (8/10), Louvencourt (12/10), Forceville (17/10), Léalvillers (18/10), Mailly-Maillet Wood (22/10). Relieved 1/7th Argyll and Sutherland in trenches east of Auchonvillers (26/10). Relieved and to Léalvillers (30/10). To Mailly-Maillet Wood (5/11), front line east of Auchonvillers (8/11), Mailly-Maillet Wood (12/11). Moved into assembly positions along railway line south of Auchonvillers (13/11) – later forward to St. John's Road and in action at Beaumont-Hamel. Relieved and to Mailly-Maillet Wood (19/11).

11th (Service) Battalion. 27th Brigade, 9th (Scottish) Division: In Corps reserve at Copse Valley (1/7). Moved forward and relieved 17th Manchester at Montauban (2/7). Took part in operations at Bernafay Wood. Relieved and to Billon Wood (8/7). To assembly positions Caterpillar Valley (13/7). In action at Longueval (14/7)–(17/7). Relieved and to Talus Boisé. Casualties – 321. To Citadel Camp (19/7). Entrained at Méricourt-l'Abbé for Hangest-sur-Somme (23/7) and from there marched to Bellancourt. Entrained at Pont-Remy for Diéval (25/7). Arrived Neuvillette from Penin (5/10). To Baizieux (7/10), Laviéville (8/10), bivouacs near Mametz Wood (10/10). Moved forward to Bazentin-le-Grand (19/10) and in evening to support positions east of Martinpuich. To front line Le Sars sector (20/10). 'B' Company in action at The Nose (21/10) – War Diary notes some 300 German dead laying about The Nose. A wounded South African was found who had been out in the open for 6 days – another had crawled down into a dug-out; he was found lying at the bottom of the steps with a pick through his skull. Relieved and to Mametz Wood (24/10). To Bécourt (25/10), Franvillers (26/10), Molliens-au-Bois (27/10), Talmas (28/10), Héricourt (29/10).

12th (Service) Battalion. 27th Brigade, 9th (Scottish) Division: At 12.30 a.m. (1/7) arrived in Billon Valley – moved forward 10.30 p.m. to assist 18th Division in consolidation at Pommiers line. War Diary records Battalion returned at 7.30 a.m. (2/7) having been misled by guides and no useful work was carried out. To Montauban (2/7). Attack and capture of Bernafay Wood 9 a.m. (3/7) – with 6th K.O.S.B., only six casualties recorded during advance over 500 yards of open ground. Lewis guns assisted 90th Brigade in attack on Trônes Wood (8/7). War Diary records – 'No. 23433 Pte. J. Stevenson here showed conspicuous gallantry in engaging enemy sniper with his Lewis gun. He advanced across the open and having fired off all his ammunition he sat down and cleaned his rifle until more could be obtained. He was wounded in both arms, but nevertheless later on when one of his team was wounded he went to fetch stretcher for him.' Relieved and to Billon Valley (8/7). To Caterpillar Valley (13/7) and in operations at Longueval. War Diary once more notes the bravery of Pte. J. Stevenson who was recommended for the Victoria Cross and subsequently received the Distinguished Conduct Medal. Relieved and to Talus Boisé (16/7). To front line (18/7), Talus Boisé (19/7). Casualties for period (14/7)–(19/7) – 312. To Citadel Camp (21/7). Entrained at Méricourt-l'Abbé for Hangest-sur-Somme (23/7). To Francieres (24/7). Entrained at Pont-Remy for Diéval (25/7). Arrived Neuvillette (5/10). To Baizieux (7/10), Laviéville (8/10), Mametz Wood (10/10). Moved forward to south-east corner of High Wood (19/10) – later relieved 8th Black Watch in front line Le Sars sector. Relieved and to Mametz Wood (24/10), Bécourt (25/10), Franvillers (26/10), Pierregot (27/10), Talmas (28/10), Ecoivres (29/10).

13th (Service) Battalion. 45th Brigade, 15th (Scottish) Division: Moved from Hulluch sector end of July – arriving Prouville (28/7). To Vignacourt (31/7), Molliens-au-Bois (3/8), Bresle (4/8), Peake Wood via Albert (8/8), support positions at Contalmaison (9/8), front line (10/8). Relieved and via Contalmaison to Peake Wood (12/8). To Bécourt Wood (14/8), front line Martinpuich (19/8), reserve positions on Fricourt Road (22/8), front line (27/8), Villa Wood (29/8), Fricourt Road (30/8), front line Intermediate Trench (3/9), bivouacs east of Albert (4/9), north-east of Laviéville (5/9), east of Albert (12/9), near Shelter Wood (13/9). To front line east of Pozières (15/9) – attack and capture of Martinpuich. War Diary records men went over under heavy bombardment at 6.20 a.m. – there was practically no hostile fire from trenches – 'enemy apparently taken by surprise.' High casualties from British artillery noted. Relieved and to Millencourt (18/9). To Baizieux Wood (19/9), Baizieux (25/9), Bresle (5/10), Scots Redoubt (8/10) and from there into support positions around Destremont Farm – Le Sars sector. To front line (10/10), support (12/10). Relieved at midnight (13/10) and to Martinpuich. To Contalmaison (14/10), Martinpuich (17/10), support line (18/10). Work carried out on Scotland Trench (20/10)–(30/10). Relieved and to Martinpuich (1/11), Albert (3/11), Baizieux (5/11), Lahoussoye (13/11).

15th (Service) Battalion (1st Edinburgh). 101st Brigade, 34th Division: Attack at La Boisselle (1/7) – War Diary notes 1st and 2nd waves forming up in No Man's Land just before zero hour (7.30 a.m.) – the men leaving 'with great heart and in grand form.' Heavy casualties among 3rd and 4th waves when leaving front line parapet – mostly from machine guns; one in a bank south end of La Boisselle; another further up Sausage Valley. News of Scots Redoubt being taken received 7.48 a.m. – 'C' Company in Peake Trench 3 p.m. Relieved and to Long Valley (4/7). To Hénenecourt Wood (6/7). Such tremendous losses had occurred (628) that links with Edinburgh were almost completely wiped away. The City being unable to provide sufficient recruits for the necessary drafts required to bring battalion back to strength. To Bécourt Wood (30/7), trenches north end Mametz Wood (31/7). Provided carrying parties to front line – salvage work – burying dead. Relieved 16th Royal Scots in front line Bazentin-le-Petit (4/8) – bombers assisted 10th Lincolnshire in unsuccessful attack on Intermediate Line. Renewed attack (5/8). Relieved (6/8) and to Quadrangle Trench. War Diary notes – position in midst of many batteries which fire day and night and are constantly shelled – new German phosphorus shells seen for first time. To Bécourt Wood (10/8), front line (13/8), Bécourt Wood (15/8), Franvillers (16/8). Entrained at Méricourt for Longpré (18/8) and from there marched to Liercourt. Entrained at Pont-Remy for Armentières sector (19/8).

16th (Service) Battalion (2nd Edinburgh). 101st Brigade, 34th Division: Left Bécourt Wood for assembly positions 5 a.m. (1/7). Followed 15th Royal Scots into attack at La Boisselle 7.35 a.m. – heavy machine gun and shell fire before reaching British front line. Report in War diary records No Man's Land crossed with few casualties – battalions on left (10th Lincolnshire and 11th Suffolk) suffering heavily with very few reaching enemy lines – some of 16th said to have reached Contalmaison. Messages received – Peake Wood reached 8.45 a.m., German support line 5.40 p.m. Direction somewhat lost owing to exposed flank – enemy counter attacked in neighbourhood of Peake Wood. Scots Redoubt taken and consolidated (2/7). Relieved midnight (4/7) and to

Bécourt Château. To Long Valley 8 a.m. Casualties – 472. To Hénencourt Wood (5/7), Bécourt Wood (30/7). Took over front line (eastern end Intermediate Line) (1/8) – 5 separate bombing attacks made by 'D' Company on German portion of Intermediate Line during night. Attacked 9.20 p.m. (2/8) – 'D' Company taking 150 yards of German trench – later forced to withdraw 30 yards – position held and consolidated. Unsuccessful attack (4/8). Relieved by 15th Royal Scots and to Mametz Wood. To Bécourt Wood (7/8). Relieved 15th Royal Scots in Quadrangle Trench (10/8). To Intermediate Line (11/8). Withdrew to support line (12/8), Bécourt Wood (14/8), Franvillers (15/8). Entrained at Méricourt for Pont-Remy (18/8) and from there marched to Bailleul. Entrained at Pont-Remy for Armentières sector (19/8).

17th (Service) Battalion (Rosebury). 106th Brigade, 35th Division: Entrained at Chocques for Frévent (2/7). To Bois de Warnimont (5/7), Varennes (10/7), Bresle (12/7), Celestines Wood (13/7), Talus Boisé (14/7). Working parties digging trenches at night around Waterlot Farm. To Caftet Wood (19/7). Working party dug trench south end Trônes Wood during night (20/7). Under orders of 8th Brigade 'W' and 'X' Companies to Breslau Trench (23/7) – remainder at Montauban. 'W' and 'X' to northern end of Bernafay Wood (24/7) – later to Longueval Alley. Battalion relieved and to Caftet Wood (25/7). Moved forward to front line (Silesia Trench) and support line (26/7). Relieved and to Caftet Wood (27/7). Moved forward to Casement Trench (29/7). To positions near Maltz Horn Farm (30/7). Held in support of 89th Brigade but was not used and that evening returned to Caftet Wood. To Morlancourt (1/8). Entrained at Méricourt-l'Abbé for Saisseval (5/8). To Morlancourt (10/8), Sandpit Valley (16/8), Contour Wood (20/8). Provided working party at Maltz Horn Farm (21/8). Relieved 16th Cheshire in Silesia Trench (22/8). To Happy Valley (26/8), Bernaville (30/8), Sus-St. Léger (31/8).

Queen's (Royal West Surrey Regiment)

1st Battalion. 100th Brigade, 33rd Division: Arrived Saleux (9/7) and later marched via Dreuil and Agrœuves to St. Sauveur. Via Amiens to Daours (10/7), Morlancourt (11/7), Bécordel-Bécourt (12/7), Fricourt (14/7) and later assembly positions south of the Mametz-Fricourt main road. That evening forward to Flatiron Copse and from there took up positions between High Wood and Bazentin-le-Petit. Attacked towards German Switch Line in front of Martinpuich (15/7). To northern side of Mametz Wood (16/7), High Wood in reserve (20/7), Bécordel-Bécourt via Mametz Wood (21/7). Casualties since (15/7) – 384. To bivouacs just west of Dernancourt-Albert railway line about 1 mile from Albert (23/7), support trenches rear of High Wood (7/8), bivouacs between Bécordel-Bécourt and Méaulte (13/8), Pommiers Redoubt (19/8). In support of attack west of Delville Wood (21/8). Returned to Pommiers but later back in support (22/8). Attack between Wood Lane and Flers Road (Tea Trench) (24/8). To Fricourt Wood (25/8), Bécordel-Bécourt (27/8), Ribemont (30/8), Mirvaux (31/8), Talmas (1/9), Heuzecourt (2/9). Moved to St Pol area (4/9). From Souastre took over front line Gommecourt sector (12/9). To Humbercamps (26/9). Left Somme area (28/9). Arrived Méricourt (19/10). To Méaulte (21/10), Mansell Camp (22/10), bivouacs between Bernafay and Trônes Woods (25/10), Guillemont in reserve (30/10). Moved forward via Ginchy (2/11). Attack on Boritska Trench (3/11). To Carnoy (6/11), Citadel Camp (7/11). Entrained at Buire for Airaines and marched to Liercourt (10/11).

2nd Battalion. 91st Brigade, 7th Division: From Bois des Tailles advanced into assembly positions for attack towards Mametz (1/7) – moving forward at 9.50 a.m. 'A' and 'C' Companies came under heavy fire from Danzig Alley before entering Bucket Trench and Bulgar Alley – 'B' and 'D' following on later cleared Fritz Trench. Cliff and White Trenches taken (2/7). Relieved from Queen's Nullah and to Minden Post (4/7). Casualties – 307. To Buire (5/7), Citadel Camp (11/7), Mansell Copse (13/7). Dug in at head of Mametz Wood and FlatIron Copse Valley (14/7). Moved forward early evening for attack on High Wood – final objective at north-eastern edge of wood taken at 8.45 p.m. Further attacks failed and ordered to evacuate positions at 2.20 a.m. (16/7). To Mansell Copse. Casualties – 305. Latter moved via Méricourt, Hangest-sur-Somme, Picquigny, Ailly-sur-Somme to St. Sauveur – billets taken over there (22/7). To Vignacourt (11/8). Entrained for Méricourt and from there marched to camp just north of Dernancourt (12/8). To Delville Wood (31/8) – taking over Folly, Devil, Diagonal and Angle Trenches. In action until relieved (3/9) and to camp just west of Citadel. To Montauban Alley (5/9) – moved forward into Delville Wood via Diagonal Trench. Attack on eastern edge of Wood 5.30 p.m. – heavy casualties from machine guns situated at north-east corner. In action until relieved during night (7/9) and to camp west of Citadel. Entrained at Albert for Oisemont (11/9) and from there marched to Huppy. Entrained at Abbeville for Ypres Sector (17/9).

6th (Service) Battalion. 37th Brigade, 12th (Eastern) Division: Arrived Millencourt from Bresle 9 a.m. (1/7) – moved forward during evening to trenches north-west of Albert and later front line opposite Ovillers (Hen Trench-Rivington Street). Took part in unsuccessful attack towards Ovillers (3/7) – 'B' Company moved forward 3.15 a.m. – held up by uncut wire and machine gun fire from Mash Valley. 'C' Company on left of attack – War Diary notes 1st Platoon moved too far to their left – just 8 men reaching German wire – bombers entered trench. Supporting waves also held up by strong fire. Casualties – 304. Withdrew to Donnet Post and Ribble Street (4/7). To front line (6/7). Provided covering fire and smoke barrage during 36th Brigade's attack (7/7). To Warloy (9/7), Louvencourt (11/7), Bertrancourt (21/7), Louvencourt (24/7), Bouzincourt (25/7), front line north of Ovillers (27/7). Martinsart Wood (31/7), Ribble Street (4/8) and from there trenches north of Ovillers – took part in successful attack on Ration Trench. To Martinsart Wood (7/8), Bouzincourt (9/8), Ribble Street (11/8), Forceville (13/8), Léalvillers (14/8), Bus-lès-Artois (15/8), Halloy (16/8), Sombrin (17/8). Arrived Grouches from Wanquetin (26/9). To Shelter Camp (29/9). Moved forward via Montauban and Bernafay Wood to support line behind Gueudecourt (Pioneer Trench, Gird Trench, Bulls Road Trench) (1/10), front line (3/10), support line (6/10). In support for attack on Rainbow Trench (7/10) – held front line until relieved (9/10). To trenches near Bernafay Wood (11/10), bivouacs between Montauban and Pommiers Redoubt (16/10), Ribemont (20/10), Albert-Amiens Road (21/10) and there boarded buses for Arras sector.

7th (Service) Battalion. 55th Brigade, 18th (Eastern) Division: Attacked 7.30 a.m. (1/7) west of Montauban – heavy fire at first held up advance in front of Breslau support Trench – later fought on through Back Trench and Train Alley to Montauban Alley. War Diary records that after 12 hours fighting the final objective was reached and consolidated on a front of about 200 yards. Casualties – 532. Relieved and to Back Trench (2/7), Bronfay Wood (3/7), Celestins Wood (7/7). To reserve line north-west of Maricourt (11/7), support (Dublin Trench) (12/7). Attack on Trônes Wood 7 p.m. (13/7) – War Diary records that owing to heavy casualties from bombardment on the way up, only about 1½ platoons arrived in time for assault – attack checked by heavy rifle, machine gun and shell fire. Withdrew to Longueval Alley. Official History of The Great War notes that no drafts had been received to replace losses of (1/7) and that the strength of 7th Queen's stood at just 280. Casualties for (13/7) given as 200. To Grove Town Camp (14/7), Ailly-le-Haut-Clocher (20/7). Entrained at Méricourt for Longpré (21/7). Entrained at Pont-Remy for St. Omer (22/7). Arrived Lucheux from Houvin-Houvigneul (10/9). To Puchevillers (11/9), bivouacs in Blighty Valley (24/9). Attack on Schwaben Redoubt (28/9) – attached to 53rd Brigade – took and held southern side – War Diary records continuous fighting at close quarters until relieved by 8th East Surrey (29/9). To North Bluff near Authuille, casualties – 395. To Forceville (2/10), Acheux (3/10), Longuevillette (15/10), Hérissart (16/10), Albert (17/10), front line – Regina and Hessian Trenches (22/10), support line – Fabeck Trench, east of Mouquet Farm (25/10), Albert (26/10), Regina and Hessian (3/11), Fabeck (6/11), Albert (8/11), Warloy (9/11), Albert (13/11), Ovillers (14/11). Attack on Desire Trench 6.10 a.m. (18/11) – 'C' and 'D' leading incurred high losses from machine gun fire from Stump Road.

8th (Service) Battalion. 72nd Brigade, 24th Division: Arrived Longueau from Bailleul (24/7). Later to Fourdrinoy, Ailly-sur-Somme and Méricourt. Arrived Morlancourt (31/7). To Sandpit Camp (1/8), front line near Guillemont (10/8), Talus Boisé (13/8), front line (17/8), craters at Carnoy (18/8), front line (20/8). Unsuccessful bombing attack on the Quarry near Guillemont 4.30 p.m. (21/8). Relieved and to craters. To Citadel Camp (22/8), positions on Albert-Amiens Road (25/8), Ribemont (27/8). Moved forward via reserve camp near Fricourt to support line Bernafay Wood (31/8). Relieved 8th Royal West Kent in front line Delville Wood (1/9) – under almost continues bombardment for next 3 days. Relieved (5/9). Casualties from shelling – 143. Entrained at Edgehill for Longpré (8/9) and from there to Buigny-l'Abbé. Entrained at Abbeville for St. Pol area (19/9).

10th (Service) Battalion (Battersea). 124th Brigade, 41st Division: Arrived Pont-Remy (23/8) and from there marched to billets at Buigny-l'Abbé. Entrained at Longpré for Ribemont (7/9) and from there marched to Dernancourt. To camp ½ mile north of Méaulte (9/9), Pommiers Redoubt (13/9) and from there to trenches north-east side Delville Wood. Attacked (15/9) – War Diary records 4 lines enemy trenches immediate front assaulted – Flers taken – trenches north-east of village occupied. Official History of the Great War notes – leading waves formed up in No Man's Land before zero hour – little resistance at first – Switch Line captured by 7 a.m. – Flers Trench taken 7.30 a.m. Two enemy counter attacks repulsed (16/9). Withdrew to support line on right of Flers Road (17/9). To Dernancourt (19/9). Casualties – over 300. Moved forward beginning October – via Pommiers Redoubt to Gird Lines. Regimental history by Colonel H.C. Wylly records Battalion under tremendous fire from its front beyond Thilloy

Road (4/10). With 21st K.R.R.C. reinforced 26th and 32nd Royal Fusiliers in front line after attack on Bayonet Trench (7/10) – Official History notes strength of whole brigade less than the establishment of a single battalion. Relieved and to Bécordel (10/10). To Buire (13/10). Entrained for Airaines (15/10) and from Longpré to Méteren (18/10).

11th (Service) Battalion (Lambeth). 123rd Brigade, 41st Division: Entrained at Bailleul for Longpré (23/8) and from there marched to Bussus-Bussuel. Entrained at Longpré for Méricourt (6/9) and from there to bivouacs near Méaulte. War Diary notes Commanding Officer Lieutenant-Colonel H.B. Burnaby killed while reconnoitring front line trenches near Delville Wood (8/9). To Fricourt Camp (9/9). Relieved 9th King's at Carlton Trench, Tea Lane, Flers Road, Tea Trench, Orchard Trench (10/9). Withdrew to Montauban Alley (13/9). In reserve for attack towards Flers (15/9) – moved forward from Carlton Trench 11.30 p.m. to consolidate positions gained north-east of Flers. Relieved and to Méaulte (17/9). To Montauban (27/9), Gird Lines, Factory Corner (28/9). 'C' and 'D' Companies advanced some 100 yards during night (29/9). Relieved and to bivouacs near Pommiers Redoubt (1/10), Mametz Wood (2/10). Moved forward to Flers Trench (Turk Lane-Goose Alley) (7/10). Relieved and to Mametz Wood (10/10), Dernancourt (13/10). Entrained for Oisemont (17/10) and from there marched to Limeux. Entrained at Pont-Remy for Godewaersvelde (19/10).

Buffs (East Kent Regiment)

1st Battalion. 16th Brigade, 6th Division: Arrived Amplier from Poperinghe (2/8). To Puchevillers (4/8), Acheux (7/8), front line trenches south of Beaumont-Hamel (9/8), Beaussart (14/8), front line (20/8), Bertrancourt (27/8), Amplier (28/8), Naours (29/8), Rainneville (6/9), Corbie (7/9), Bois des Tailles (8/9), German Wood and Wedge Wood (11/9). Attack on The Quadrilateral (15/9) – in support of 8th Bedfordshire advanced at 6.35 a.m. – heavy machine gun fire checked both battalions. To Morlancourt (19/9), trenches west of Morval (21/9). German attack repulsed (24/9). In action during successful operation between Morval and Lesbœufs (25/9). To La Briqueterie (26/9), Méaulte (1/10), Trônes Wood (7/10), Ginchy (8/10), Méaulte (21/10), Daours (22/10), Huppy (23/10). Entrained at Pont-Remy for Béthune (23/10).

6th (Service) Battalion. 37th Brigade, 12th (Eastern) Division: At Millencourt (1/7). To trenches facing Ovillers (2/7). Attacked (3/7) – 2 companies moved forward in support about 3.30 a.m. – German line bombed - withdrew after supplies of bombs ran out. Casualties – 274. To Warloy (9/7), Louvencourt (11/7), Bertrancourt (21/7), Louvencourt (24/7), Bouzincourt (25/7). Took over trenches Ovillers sector. Attacked (3/8) – several strongpoints including part of Ration Trench gained. Relieved and to Martinsart Wood. To trenches in front of Ovillers (7/8), Bouzincourt (10/8), Hédauville (13/8), Léalvillers (14/8), Bus-lès-Artois (15/8), Halloy (16/8), Grand Rullecourt (Arras sector) (17/8). Arrived Albert (30/9). Took over trenches at Gueudecourt (3/10). Attack on Rainbow Trench (7/10) – reached objective but after heavy casualties could not hold. Withdrew at midnight and to Longueval. Regimental historian Colonel R.S.H. Moody records that Battalion came out of action just 40 strong and were led away by the Adjutant Captain Page, the only remaining officer. Casualties – 367. To Pommiers Redoubt (13/10), Ribemont (20/10), Arras sector (22/10).

7th (Service) Battalion. 55th Brigade, 18th (Eastern) Division: Moved forward from La Pree Wood 7 a.m. (1/7) – in Brigade support 'B' Company (less 2 platoons) sent to clear enemy from the craters (2 mines blown 7.27 a.m.), this operation taking some 6 hours to complete. Remainder moved forward towards western edge of Montauban – objectives taken – in Montauban Alley by 5.15 p.m. Relieved from Pommiers line (4/7) and to Bronfay Farm. To Celestines Wood (7/7), Maltz Horn Farm area (12/7). In action at Trônes Wood (13/7) – 'B' Company sustaining heavy casualties while attached to 7th Queen's. Part of 'D' Company in bombing attack down Maltz Horn Trench – line cleared and held. To Grove Town Camp

(18/7). Entrained at Méricourt-l'Abbé for Longpré (21/7) and from there marched to Huppy. Entrained for Racquinghem near St. Omer (23/7). Arrived Puchevillers from Le Souich (11/9). To Hedauville (25/9), Crucifix Corner (27/9), front line Thiepval sector (29/9). In action at Schwaben Redoubt (30/9)–(5/10). Relieved and to Hédauville (6/10). To Candas (7/10), Gézaincourt (15/10), Hérissart (16/10), Albert (17/10), front line (Fabeck Trench) (22/10), Albert (26/10), Fabeck Trench (3/11), Regina Trench (6/11), Albert (8/11), Warloy (9/11), Albert (13/11), Ovillers (14/11), front line (16/11). Attack on Desire Trench (18/11).

8th (Service) Battalion. 17th Brigade, 24th Division: Arrived Longueau (25/7) and from there marched to Le Mesge. To Bois des Tailles (31/7), Sandpit Camp (1/8). Via Carnoy to Bernafay Wood (8/8). Attack near Waterlot Farm (18/8) – 'A' Company took Machine Gun House – 'C' northern end of ZZ Trench. Casualties – 358. In support of 3rd Rifle Brigade during failed attack (21/8). To Bray (23/8), Buire-sur-l'Ancre (25/8), Pommiers Redoubt (31/8), support line Delville Wood (1/9). 'D' Company moved forward on loan to 72nd Brigade (2/9) and in support of 9th East Surrey sustained high casualties from shell fire. Attack on Wood Lane Trench noon (3/9) – assault failed. Renewed attempt 4 p.m. also checked. To Fricourt (5/9), Yaucourt-Bussus (6/9). To Vimy sector (19/9).

King's Own (Royal Lancaster Regiment)

1st Battalion. 12th Brigade, 4th Division: Left Bertrancourt 10.05 p.m. (30/6) for assemble area – Green Trench and Bow Street. Attack between Beaumont-Hamel and Serre (1/7) – War diary records leading sections advanced 8.46 a.m. and heavy casualties before British front line was reached – further losses in No Man's Land from both machine gun and shell fire – few men reached German line. Withdrew to support trenches Elles Square. To Mailly-Maillet (7/7), Bertrancourt (9/7), trenches east of Auchonvillers (17/7), Louvencourt (21/7), Authieule (22/7). Marched to Doullens 10.55 p.m. and entrained for Cassel. Entrained at Houpoutre for Saleux (17/9) and from there marched to Poulainville via Amiens. To Allonville (25/9), Corbie (26/9), Citadel Camp (8/10), Bernafay Wood (9/10) and from there to trenches between Ginchy and Lesbœufs. To Bernafay Wood (10/10), trenches in front of Le Transloy (13/10). 'B' Company attacked German held section of Spectrum Trench (14/10) – 60 yards gained and consolidated. Further action until withdrawn to Bernafay Wood (19/10). To front line (22/10). Attack on Spectrum Trench (23/10) – 'C' and 'D' Companies advanced 2.30 p.m. – passed through objective to sunken road – subjected to heavy fire from the right and fell back to Spectrum. Casualties – 193. Relieved and to Bernafay Wood (24/10), Citadel Camp (25/10). To Ville-sur-Ancre (26/10). Entrained at Méricourt-l'Abbé for Airaines (29/10) and from there marched to Allery.

1/4th Battalion (T.F.). 164th Brigade, 55th (West Lancashire) Division: Arrived Berneuil from Sombrin (22/7). Entrained at Candas for Méricourt (25/7) and from there marched to Méaulte. To Happy Valley (26/7), positions between Trônes Wood and Guillemont (30/7). 'B' Company attacked advanced German strong-point 8.30 p.m. (2/8) – forced to retire due to severe shelling. Renewed attack later more successful. Withdrew to reserve line – Dublin and Casement Trenches. To bivouacs south of Carnoy and west of Bronfay Farm (4/8). To trenches near Arrow Head Copse (7/8). Attack on Guillemont 3.45 a.m. (8/8) – assault driven back by bombs and machine gun fire. Casualties – 271. Relieved and to bivouacs south-west of Carnoy (9/8). War Diary notes observation balloon broke away towards enemy lines – occupant parachuted. To Méricourt (14/8). Entrained for Abbeville (19/8) and from there marched to Limercourt. Entrained at Pont-Remy for Méricourt-l'Abbé (30/8) and from there marched to bivouacs near Dernancourt. To positions near Albert on Amiens Road (31/8), east of Bécordel-Bécourt (6/9), Montauban (7/9), Montauban Alley (8/9), reserve line Crucifix Alley (9/9) – 1 company attached to 1/8th King's Liverpool in support. Moved forward to Delville Wood (10/9). Attack on Hop Alley and Ale Alley 5.20 a.m. (11/9) – withdrew after strong machine gun and rifle fire. Relieved and to Bécourt

(12/9), Ribemont (13/9). One officer and 120 other ranks sent to guard German prisoners in Corps cage at Mametz (15/9). To Buire (16/9), Bécourt (17/9), York Trench (18/9) – moving to Mametz at midnight. Working parties around Longueval. To trenches in front of Delville Wood (Green Trench, King's Walk) (24/9). Moved forward to trenches east of Flers (26/9). In support of 1/8th King's Liverpool for attack on Gird Lines (27/9) – took over captured positions (28/9). Relieved and via Mametz to Dernancourt (29/9). Entrained for Longpré (1/10) and from there marched to Bouchon. Entrained at Longpré for Poperinghe (2/10).

1/5th Battalion (T.F.). 166th Brigade, 55th (West Lancashire) Division: Moved from Sombrin to Bouquemaison (20/7). To Boisbergues (21/7). Prouville (22/7). Entrained at Candas for Méricourt-l'Abbé (25/7) and from there marched to Ville-sur-Ancre. To bivouacs near Sandpit Camp (27/7), Wellington Redoubt (30/7), Reserve line Talus Boisé (1/8) – working parties digging communication trenches near Trônes Wood. To Citadel Camp (6/8). 'A' Company moved forward to La Briqueterie (7/8) – providing carrying parties and supervising prisoners during operations at Guillemont. To Dublin and Casement Trenches (8/8), front line and support trenches (9/8). Relieved and to bivouacs south-east of Citadel (10/8), Talus Boisé (13/8) – working parties digging new fire trenches near Guillemont. War Diary records that men were ordered to dig in a kneeling position as to stand would have been impossible due to enemy snipers. To bivouacs east of Citadel (14/8), Méaulte (15/8). Entrained at Edgehill for Martainneville (19/8) and from there marched to Chépy. To Béhen (29/8). Entrained at Pont-Remy for Méricourt-l'Abbé (30/8) and from there marched to bivouacs south-west of Albert. To bivouacs near Bécordel-Bécourt (31/8). Moved forward to trenches north of Delville Wood (5/9). Relieved and to Montauban (8/9), bivouacs south-west of Fricourt (10/9), near Dernancourt (11/9). To Pommiers Redoubt (17/9) and from there positions north of Delville Wood (King's Walk Trench). To front line Flers sector (18/9). Relieved and to Pommiers Redoubt (23/9), Ribemont (28/9). Entrained at Méricourt-l'Abbé for Longpré (30/9) and from there marched to Epagne. Entrained at Abbeville for Proven (2/10).

7th (Service) Battalion. 56th Brigade, 19th (Western) Division: Moved forward from Hénencourt Wood (30/6) and at 7.30 a.m. (1/7) took over support positions in Tara-Usna Line for attack on Ovillers. Took over line at La Boisselle (3/7). Attacked 8.30 a.m. (4/7) – moving forward up 3 communication trenches, assault held up by strong machine gun fire from positions north-east of village. New line taken up and consolidated about 300 yards in advance. Relieved and to Tara-Usna Line (5/7). To support line (6/7). Attacked 8 a.m. (7/7) – War Diary records that whole battalion charged across the open and carried its objective. Over 400 prisoners taken. Casualties – 156. Relieved and to Albert (8/7), Hénencourt Wood (9/7). To support trenches south-western edge of Bazentin-le-Petit Wood (19/7). Working parties digging new forward trench. To Mametz Wood (23/7), bivouacs north of Bernafay Wood (27/7). Took over front line north-east of Bazentin-le-Petit (29/7). In action (30/7). Relieved from captured positions in Intermediate Trench and to bivouacs south of Bécourt Wood (31/7). To Franvillers (1/8). Entrained at Fréchencourt for Longpré (3/8) and from there to Ailly-le-Haut-Clocher. Entrained at Longpré for Bailleul (6/8). Entrained at Bailleul for Doullens (5/10) and from there marched to Rossignol Farm, Coigneux. To Sailly-au-Bois (7/10) – working parties with Royal Engineers and Corps and Divisional Signals. To Couin (11/10), Harponville (17/10), the Brickworks near Albert (21/10). Relieved 11th and 13th Royal Sussex in recently captured Stuff Trench north-east of Thiepval. New front line consolidated. Relieved and to Brigade reserve at Wood Post and Leipzig Redoubt (24/10). To Aveluy (27/10), Stuff Trench (30/10) – War Diary notes average depth of mud 2 foot. Relieved by 7th East Lancashire (1/11) – War Diary records relief as 'difficult' owing to heavy shelling and state of trenches. Relief began at 10.30 a.m. and was not complete until 6 p.m. – 1 man being stuck in mud for 7 hours. To Wood Post and Leipzig Redoubt. Relieved 9th Royal Welsh Fusiliers in Regina Trench (5/11). Relieved and to Ovillers Post (8/11). To Leipzig Redoubt and Wood Post (11/11), Schwaben and Bainbridge Trenches (12/11). In close support for attack on St. Pierre Divion and Hansa Line (13/11) – providing carrying parties. Hansa Line taken over (14/11). Relieved and to Marlborough Huts (17/11).

8th (Service) Battalion. 76th Brigade, 3rd Division: Entrained at St. Omer for Doullens (1/7) and from there marched to Autheux. To Naours (3/7), Coisy (4/7), Franvillers (5/7), Celestines Wood (6/7), Bronfay Farm (8/7), Carnoy (13/7), Caterpillar Wood (14/7). In support of 1st Gordon Highlanders during operations at Longueval and Delville Wood (18/7). Relieved and to Bund Trench near Carnoy (19/7). To trenches south-west of Longueval (22/7). Withdrew to Bund Trench (23/7). To Montauban Alley (24/7) – 'A' Company sent forward in support at Delville Wood. Relieved and via Bund Trench to Bois des Tailles (25/7). To Méricourt (28/7), Sandpit Camp (11/8), Talus Boisé (14/8). Attack on Lonely Trench 5.40 p.m. (16/8) – War Diary records heavy casualties from machine gun and rifle fire as soon as assault was launched. Renewed attack met similar result – all officers and N.C.Os of 'B' and 'C' Companies becoming casualties. Attack by 'D' Company failed (18/8). Later relieved via Citadel to Carnoy. To Happy Valley (19/8). Casualties for period (16/8)–(18/8) – 271. To Morlancourt (21/8). Entrained at Méricourt for

Candas (23/8) and from there marched to Autheux. To Fortel (25/8). Began march to St. Pol area (26/8). Entrained at St. Pol for Acheux (7/10) and from there marched to Raincheval. To Bertrancourt (8/10), Louvencourt (17/10), front line Serre sector (19/10), Courcelles (21/10) – provided working and carrying parties to front line during nights. To front line (25/10), Courcelles (27/10), Bus-lès-Artois (30/10), Courcelles (12/11) and from there to assembly area – Holland, Monk, Campion Trenches. Attack on Serre (13/11) – in support 'D' Company attempted to enter German front line but withdrew under strong machine gun and rifle fire. Held front line until relieved and to Bus-lès-Artois (19/11).

11th (Service) Battalion. 120th Brigade, 40th Division: Arrived Prouville from Noeux (5/11). To Doullens (12/11), Souastre (13/11), Hébuterne (14/11) – relieving 1/5th York and Lancaster in right sub-sector.

Northumberland Fusiliers

1st Battalion. 9th Brigade, 3rd Division: Detrained at Candas (2/7) and marched via Bernaville to Prouville. To Vignacourt (3/7), Poulainville (4/7), Lahoussoye (5/7), Morlancourt (6/7), Carnoy (8/7). Provided carrying parties to forward positions. Attack on Bazentin-le-Grand (14/7) – in support of 13th King's Liverpool and 12th West Yorkshire objective taken by 9.30 a.m. Casualties – 211. Relieved and to Talus Boisé (19/7). Moved forward to assembly positions at Pont Street (23/7) and from there attacked Piccadilly at northern edge of Longueval. Assault failed. Withdrew to bivouacs near Albert (26/7). To Ville-sur-Ancre (28/7), Sandpit Camp (13/8). Provided working party of 400 men from Brigade reserve positions at Great Bear (15/8). Moved up via Carnoy to positions north-east of Maricourt (16/8). Series of attacks on Lonely Trench failed (18/8). To Citadel Camp (20/8), Ville-sur-Ancre (21/8). Entrained at Méricourt for Candas (23/8) and from there marched to Fienvillers. Moved to Hulluch sector (25/8). Entrained at St. Pol for Puchevillers (7/10) and from there marched to Bertrancourt. To Mailly-Maillet (8/10). Relieved 4th Royal Fusiliers in line opposite Serre (12/10). Relieved and to Louvencourt (19/10). To front line (26/10), Courcelles (28/10), front line (30/10), Louvencourt (31/10), front line (8/11), Courcelles (12/11). Moved to Colincamps and forward to front line in support of attack (13/11) withdrew during evening. To Louvencourt (14/11), Bus-lès-Artois (15/11).

1/4th Battalion (T.F.). 149th Brigade, 50th (Northumbrian) Division: Entrained at Bailleul for Doullens (11/8) and from there marched to Fienvillers. To Naours (15/8), Pierregot (16/8), Hénencourt Wood (17/8), Bécourt Wood (9/9). War Diary notes death of 149th Brigade Commander Brigadier-General H.F.H. Clifford while inspecting Eye Trench (11/9). To Mametz Wood (13/9) – moving forward at 9.30 p.m. to assembly trenches west of High Wood – Headquarters in Clark's Trench. Attack (15/9) – moved forward on right of 149th Brigade's assault at 6.20 a.m. – first objective (Hook Trench) gained without much opposition by 7 a.m. War Diary notes all officers of 'C' Company hit and attack on second objective (Starfish Line) led by a corporal. Stokes mortars and Lewis guns assisted 47th Division on right at High Wood. Relieved from Hook trench in afternoon (16/9) and to Mametz Wood. Casualties – 499. To Clark's and Hook Trenches (20/9). Attack on Starfish Line and Prue Trench 10.15 p.m. (21/9) – objectives taken by 5 a.m. with little opposition. To support positions Bazentin-le-Petit (23/9), reserve Mametz Wood (24/9), Bazentin-le-Petit (29/9), Prue and Starfish Trenches (1/10), front line (2/10), Mametz Wood (3/10), Albert (4/10) – billets in Rue de Péronne. To Millencourt (5/10), Mametz Wood (17/10). Working parties provided for road repairs around Bazentin-le-Petit, Bottom Wood and Caterpillar Valley. Moved forward to Flers Line in support (24/10), front line near the Butte de Warlencourt – Snag and Abbaye Trenches (27/10). To Bazentin-le-Grand (31/10), Flers Line between Drop Alley and Pioneer Alley (4/11). In reserve for attack on Bute de Warlencourt (5/11) – War Diary records good view of attacking troops (1/6th, 1/8th, 1/9th D.L.I.) also Australians advancing towards Gird Line on right of 1/8th D.L.I. Relieved and to Bazentin-le-Grand (6/11). To front line (Snag Trench) (11/11), withdrew to Hexham Road and Flers Line (13/11). In action at Gird Trenches (14/11)–(15/11). Relieved and to Bazentin-le-Grand (17/11), Albert (18/11). Casualties for November – 129.

1/5th Battalion (T.F.). 149th Brigade, 50th (Northumbrian) Division: Entrained at Bailleul for Doullens (11/8) and from there marched to billets at Candas and Fienvillers. To Naours (15/8), Pierregot (16/8), Hénencourt Wood (17/8), Lozenge Wood (8/9), front line west of High Wood (9/9). Attack (15/9) – in Brigade Reserve and ordered forward to support advance by 12 noon. To Bazentin-le-Petit in reserve (16/9), Clark's Trench (20/9), Starfish and Prue Trenches occupied (21/9), withdrew to Clark's Trench (23/9), Quadrangle Trench (24/9). To Clark's Trench (29/9). Attack on Le Sars (1/10) – Flers Lines captured. Withdrew to The Quadrangle (3/10), Albert (4/10) – War Diary notes that German helmets and other trophies were very much in evidence. To Millencourt (5/10), Albert (8/10) – work parties provided for road repairs. To Millencourt (11/10), 'A', 'C', 'D' Companies to Fricourt Farm for work on Contalmaison-Fricourt Road, 'B' Company to Bécourt to help with hut building (19/10). Headquarters to Albert (23/10), Battalion to reserve trenches at Bazentin-le-Grand (24/10), support line (31/10). To camp behind High Wood (3/11), Prue and Starfish Trenches (6/11), High Wood (9/11), Flers Line (11/11), front line (13/11). Attack on Gird Trench (14/11) – 'D' Company reached objective – heavy casualties from own barrage and machine gun fire from extreme right – all officers in 'C' company lost – part of 'A' Company on Butte de Warlencourt. Relieved and to Flers Line (15/11). Casualties – 264. To Albert (18/11).

1/6th Battalion (T.F.). 149th Brigade, 50th (Northumbrian) Division: Entrained at Bailleul for Doullens (11/8) and from there marched to Candas. To Naours (15/8), Mirvaux 16/8), Hénencourt Wood (17/8), Quadrangle Trench (9/9), Mametz Wood (10/9), front line west of High Wood (12/9). Attack (15/9) – 2 companies moved forward to Clark's Trench in support – later formed defensive flank in Hook Trench (first objective). Withdrew (16/9). Casualties – 279. To Clark's Trench (22/9) – took over Prue and Starfish Trenches with no opposition. Withdrew to reserve positions (23/9). To Prue and Starfish (30/9). In support for attack on Flers Line (1/10), relieved 1/5th Northumberland Fusiliers in front line (3/10), later withdrew to Mametz Wood. To Albert (4/10), Millencourt (5/10), 'D' Company to Ozy for work at ammunition siding (17/10) and to Albert (22/10). Battalion to Bazentin-le-Petit (23/10), front line facing Butte de Warlencourt (25/10), relieved by 1/4th Northumberland Fusiliers and to High Wood (27/10). To Flers Line (4/11), High Wood (6/11), support trenches (11/11).

1/7th Battalion (T.F.). 49th Brigade, 50th (Northumbrian) Division: Entrained at Bailleul for Doullens (10/8) and from there marched to Candas. To Naours (15/8), Mirvaux (16/8), Hénencourt Wood (17/8), Quadrangle Trench west of Mametz Wood (10/9). Battalion historian Captain F. Buckley recalls that while in the area notification was given of a demonstration at Albert of 'the new tanks' and that as this was thought to be something to do with the water supply 'we did not bother to go.' Assembled in Clark's Trench west of High Wood (14/9). Attack (15/9) – leading waves reached first objective (Hook Trench) soon after going forward at 6.20 a.m. During advance towards second objective (Starfish Trench) there would be enfilade fire from High Wood and confused fighting through dust and smoke. On reaching the sunken road south of Bow Trench, one company commander recalled how his men literally fell into the road taking the enemy by surprise. Many prisoners were taken (more in number than the Northumberland) and these were taken to the rear in the charge of Private Martin. He is said to have cut off the German's trouser buttons and moved off smoking a souvenir cigar and mumbling 'Ha' way, you blinking beggars.' Withdrew to positions near Mametz Wood (16/9). Casualties – 344. To front line (20/9), reserve at Mametz Wood (24/9), support and close support (Prue, Starfish, Flers, Spence Trenches) (29/9)–(3/10). Withdrew to positions south-west of Mametz Wood (3/10), Albert (4/10), Millencourt (5/10), Albert (14/10) – work parties provided for hut building at Bécourt. To Millencourt (19/10), Albert (23/10), bivouacs near High Wood (24/10), support line (Cough Drop, Drop Alley, Flers Line) (27/10), front line (Snag Trench) (31/10), Flers Line (2/11), High Wood (3/11), Prue and Starfish Trenches (9/11), Flers Line (11/11). Attack on Gird Lines and Hook Sap (14/11) – Official history of The Great War notes that the advance appeared to have been a success, but fire from Butte Trench made communication impossible and nothing more was heard of the leading companies. Relieved at 10 p.m. (15/11). Entrained at Bazentin-le-Petit for Albert (18/11). Casualties since (13/11) – 229.

8th (Service) Battalion. 34th Brigade, 11th (Northern) Division: Entrained at Frévent for Puchevillers (3/9). To Bouzincourt (8/9). Provided carrying parties to forward positions. To reserve line at La Boiselle (17/9), Englebelmer (22/9). Relieved 6th York and Lancaster during night in trenches opposite

Mouquet Farm (25/9). Attack on Zollern and Stuff Redoubts 12.35 p.m. (26/9) – War Diary notes the assault being made under heavy barrage and machine gun fire from Mouquet Farm and Zollern – many men being killed within 40 yards of their own front line. Zollern reached but by this time all officers, with one exception, had been hit and casualties were high. Withdrew to Ovillers Corner (29/9). Casualties given in War Diary as 449 (approximate). To Acheux (30/9). Entrained at Varennes for Candas (1/10) and from there marched to Berneuil. To St Ouen (3/10), Domqueur (4/10), St Ouen (14/11), Halloy (15/11), Vadencourt (16/11), Puchevillers (17/11).

9th (Service) Battalion. 52nd Brigade, 17th (Northern) Division: Moved from Bois des Tailles to Morlancourt (2/7) – in reserve during operations at Fricourt. To Méaulte (3/7). Relieved 8th South Staffordshire between Bottom Wood and Shelter Wood (4/7). During a successful attack on Quadrangle Trench (5/7) Battalion historian Captain C.H. Cooke records that 'bayonets were busy and no prisoners were taken.' At midnight (6/7) 'B' and 'C' Companies assembled for an attack on Quadrangle Support – while crossing the 800 yards to their objective heavy losses were incurred from enfilade fire from both flanks – Contalmaison on the left and Mametz Wood on the right as well as from the front. Trapped out in the open and on the enemy's wire, the attackers were now being shelled to the rear and withdrawal was difficult. Moved back to Méaulte during evening. To Ville-sous-Corbie (8/7). Entrained at Méricourt for Ailly-sur-Somme (10/7) and from there marched to Riencourt. To Vauchelles-lès-Domart (15/7). Entrained at Hangest-sur-Somme for Méricourt (23/7) and from there to camp near Dernancourt. Moved up through Fricourt to trenches between High Wood and Delville Wood (1/8). Failed attack on Orchard Trench (4/8). Relieved and to Pommiers Redoubt (5/8). To Fricourt (8/8). Relieved 7th Lincolnshire in Delville Wood (10/8). Relieved by 10th Durham Light Infantry and to Pommiers (12/8). To bivouacs at the side of Albert-Amiens Road near Dernancourt (13/8). Entrained at Méricourt for Candas (15/8) and from there marched to Fienvillers. To Grouches (17/8), Souastre (19/8), Foncquevillers (27/8). Began duty in front line (28/8). Relieved and to Mondicourt (21/9). To Barly (22/9), Hiermont (23/9), Millencourt-en-Ponthieu (24/9), Conteville (9/10), Barly (10/10), Mondicourt (11/10), Le Souich (19/10), Coisy (22/10), Daours (23/10), Sandpit Camp (27/10), Bernafay Wood (30/10). Relieved 12th Manchester in line between Gueudecourt and Lesbœufs (1/11). Relieved and to Carnoy (4/11). To front line (7/11), Carnoy (10/11), Citadel Camp (12/11). Entrained at Dernancourt for Hangest-sue-Somme (14/11) and marched from there to Breilly.

10th (Service) Battalion. 68th Brigade, 23rd Division: From Poulainville marched to Franvillers (1/7). To Millencourt (2/7). Took over reserve trenches along railway outside Albert (3/7). To Bécourt Wood (5/7) and in support of 69th Brigade's attack on Horseshoe Trench. Relieved 8th Green Howards at Scots Redoubt (6/7). War diary records that work parties carried some 20,000 bombs forward during divisional attack. To Bécourt Wood (9/7), Albert (10/7), Tara-Usna Line in support of attack by 34th Division (15/7). Moved forward in support of operations around Pozières (17/7). Relieved and to Albert (19/7), Franvillers (21/7). Moved forward to trenches between Pozières and Bazentin-le-Petit (26/7) – War Diary notes that owing to a bombing fight in Munster Alley, relief of 2nd Welsh was not complete until 3 a.m. (27/7). To Scots Redoubt (27/7), Albert (28/7). Relieved 11th West Yorkshire at Contalmaison (1/8). Work parties supplied during night for digging of Yorkshire Alley. Took over front line opposite Intermediate Line (3/8). Relieved and to Contalmaison (4/8), Albert (5/8). Heavy shelling on Albert during night – moved out to bivouac in Tara Valley. To Lahoussoye (8/8). Entrained at Fréchencourt for Longpré (11/8) and from there marched to Gorenflos. Entrained at Longpré for Bailleul (12/8). Arrived Longueau (10/9) and from there marched to Molliens-au-Bois. To Millencourt (12/9), Bécourt Wood (15/9), forward positions around Martinpuich (18/9), Peake Wood (20/9). Failed attack on 26th Avenue (25/9). Relieved and to Scots Redoubt (26/9). To Shelter Wood (2/10), forward trenches in front of Le Sars (3/10). Relieved and to Prue Trench and Starfish Line east of Martinpuich (7/10). Provided carrying parties for attack on Le Sars. To Bécourt (8/10). Entrained for Longpré (11/10) and from there marched to Gorenflos. To Oneux (13/10). Transferred to Ypres sector (14/10).

11th (Service) Battalion. 68th Brigade, 23rd Division: From Poulainville marched to Franvillers (1/7). To Millencourt (2/7), bivouacs along the railway embankment south of Albert (3/7), Albert (5/7), Bécourt Wood (6/7) – relieved 12th Durham Light Infantry in front line. Attack on Bailiff Wood (7/7) – heavy machine gun fire from Contalmaison accounting for approximately 264 casualties. Relieved and to Bécourt Wood (8/7). To Scots Redoubt (9/7), Albert (10/7), Dernancourt (14/7), Bécourt Wood in support of operations around Pozières 15/7). Moved forward to line between La Boisselle and Bailiff Wood (16/7). In support during attack on Pozières (17/7). Relieved and to bivouacs along railway crossing at Albert (19/7). To Franvillers (20/7), Peake Wood (26/7), trenches east of Bécourt Wood (28/7), support line near Mametz and Bazentin-le-Petit Woods (1/8), front line opposite Intermediate Line (5/8). Attack by 'A' Company repulsed (7/8). Relieved and to Bécourt. To Béhencourt (8/8). Entrained at Fréchencourt for Longpré (11/8) and from there marched to Ailly-le-Haut-Clocher. Entrained at Longpré for Bailleul (13/8). Arrived Longueau (10/9) and marched to Molliens-au-Bois. To Millencourt (12/9), Bécourt Wood (15/9), support lines behind Martinpuich (18/9). Two companies to Contalmaison (20/9). Took over front line (22/9). With 10th Northumberland Fusiliers in attack on 26th Avenue (25/9). Relieved and to bivouacs near Fricourt (26/9). To the Cutting at Contalmaison (2/10), forward trenches in front of Le Sars (3/10). 'A' Company attacked and seized The Tangle (6/10) – forced to withdraw due to heavy shell fire. To Bécourt Wood (8/10). Entrained at Albert (11/10), arrived Longpré and marched to Ailly-le-Haut-Clocher (12/10). To St. Riquier (13/10). Entrained for Proven (15/10).

12th (Service) Battalion. 62nd Brigade, 21st Division: From assembly positions north of Bécordel-Bécourt moved to reserve line at Empress Support and Queen's Redoubt 7.30 a.m. (1/7). In attack on Shelter Wood (3/7). Later withdrew to railway sidings at Dernancourt. Entrained for Ailly-sur-Somme (4/7) and from there marched to billets at St. Sauveur. To Molliens-Vidame (6/7). Entrained at Ailly-sur-Somme for Corbie (10/7) and from there via Ville-sur-Ancre to billets at Méaulte. To Mametz Wood (11/7). In action (12/7) – clearing wood northwards and digging new trench 30 yards beyond. Relieved and to Méaulte (17/7), Buire-sur-l'Ancre (18/7). War diary at this point records total casualties for Somme operations to date as 30 officers and 507 other ranks. Entrained at Dernancourt for Saleux (20/7) and from there marched to Molliens-Vidame. By buses to the Rifle Range at Amiens (22/7). Entrained at Longueau for Arras sector (23/7). Entrained at Frévent for Albert (13/9) and from there marched to positions just north of Dernancourt. To Bécordel-Bécourt (15/9), Pommiers Redoubt via Fricourt (16/9). At 9 p.m. moved up to relieve battalions of 43rd Brigade in forward positions east of Flers (Switch and Gap Trenches). Relieved by 9th K.O.Y.L.I. and to bivouacs just north-west of Bernafay Wood (22/9). To Fricourt Camp via Montauban and Mametz (23/9), Bernafay Wood position in reserve (25/9). Under orders of 64th Brigade moved forward to trenches east of Flers (26/9). Relieved and to Bernafay Wood position (30/9). To Buire (1/10). Entrained at Dernancourt for Longpré (3/10) and from there marched to L'Etoile. Entrained at Longpré for Loos sector (7/10).

13th (Service) Battalion. 62nd Brigade, 21st Division: Took part in operations at Fricourt (1/7)–(3/7). Casualties – 158. Entrained at Dernancourt for Ailly-sur-Somme (4/7) and from there marched to Agrœuves. To Molliens Vidame (7/7). Entrained at Ailly-sur-Somme for Corbie (9/7) and from there marched to Méaulte. To Mametz Wood (11/7) – in action until (18/7). Casualties – 272. Relieved and to Buire. Entrained at Dernancourt for Saleux (20/7) and from there marched to billets at Molliens-Vidame. To bivouacs west of

Amiens (22/7). Entrained at Longueau for Arras sector (23/7). Entrained at Frévent for Albert (12/9) and from to bivouacs outside Dernancourt. To Bécordel-Bécourt (15/9). War diary records 'hundreds' of German prisoners marching back from forward area. To Pommiers Redoubt (17/9) and from there moved forward to front line east of Flers. Relieved and to Fricourt Camp (22/9). To front line (26/9), divisional reserve trenches north-west of Longueval (Savoy and Carlton) (30/9). To Buire (1/10). Entrained at Dernancourt for Longpré (3/10) and from there marched to L'Etoile. Entrained at Longpré for Loos sector (7/10).

14th (Service) Battalion (Pioneers). Pioneers, 21st Division: Moved from Ville into assemble positions at Queen's Redoubt (1/7). Divided to assist 63rd and 64th Brigades during attack on Fricourt. Entrained at Dernancourt for Ailly-sur-Somme (4/7) and from there marched to billets at Picquigny. To Montagne (7/7). Entrained at Ailly-sur-Somme for Corbie (10/7) and from there marched to Ville. In position at Queen's Redoubt by 11.30 p.m. Work in area included digging of trench along southern edge of Mametz Wood, construction of strong points in Bazentin-le-Petit Wood, and repair work on Mametz-Contalmaison Road. To bivouacs southern edge of Fricourt Wood (14/7). Took part in operations at Bazentin Ridge. To camp between Méaulte and Dernancourt (18/7). Entrained at Dernancourt for Saleux (20/7) – arrived 6.15 a.m. (21/7) and marched to billets just east of Picquigny. To Longueau that evening. Entrained for Magnicourt-sur-Canche, west of Arras (22/7). Arrived Dernancourt (13/9). To Pommiers Redoubt via Fricourt Camp (15/9). Work in area included repairs on Longueval-Flers Road and forward positions at Gas Alley, Gap and Switch Trenches, Bulls Road and Cocoa Lane. To bivouacs on north side of Bernafay Wood (17/9). Took part in Morval operations. Began work wiring 21st Divisional front at Gueudecourt (27/9). To Dernancourt (2/10). Entrained for Longpré (4/10) and from there to Eaucourt. Entrained at Abbeville for Chocques (8/10).

16th (Service) Battalion (Newcastle). 96th Brigade, 32nd Division: Moved forward via Martinsart and Aveluy Wood for assault on Thiepval (1/7). According to The Official History of The Great War a football was followed into battle at zero. Within moments leading waves hit by machine gun fire – survivors forced to lay down and await any chance of returning to their lines. Battalion historian – Captain C. H. Cooke records that the enemy stood upon their parapet inviting the men to come forward – then 'picking them of with accurate rifle fire.' One report noted that Battalion had advanced in perfect formation – the dead being later found in straight lines as if 'dressed' for parade. Relieved (2/7) – just 8 officers and 279 other ranks marched to North Bluff. Casualties – 378. To Aveluy Wood during evening. To Warloy via

Bouzincourt (3/7), Varennes (5/7), Hédauville (7/7), Senlis (8/7), Bouzincourt (9/7). Relieved 2nd Manchester in trenches Ovillers sector (11/7). Captain Clarke noted Ovillers as non existent 'it had been disintegrated.' Attacked 14/7). Relieved during night and to Bouzincourt. To Warloy (15/7), Beauval (16/7). Transferred to Béthune sector (17/7). Arrived Harponville (21/10) via Vadencourt, Warloy, Hénencourt and Millencourt. To bivouacs in brickfields just north of Albert (23/10), Warloy via Bouzincourt and Senlis (26/10), Hérissart via Vadencourt and Contay (31/10), Warloy (13/11), front line Schwaben Redoubt (14/11). Captain Clarke records that the men in the Redoubt were waist-deep in mud and with no overhead cover of any sort – 'but made no murmer.' From German machine gun positions of 1st July at Thiepval, note was made of the British attack – bodies still hanging in what was left of the German barbed wire. Relieved and to Mailly-Maillet (17/11).

17th (Service) Battalion (N.E.R. Pioneers). Pioneers, 32nd Division: During attack on Thiepval (1/7) occupied in digging communication trenches – including Sanda Sap which was put to good use by 97th Brigade at the Leipzig Salient. Also involved in tramway extension in Authuille Wood and keeping essential support routes open. For coming weeks each company worked independently on the maintenance of trenches, roads and strong-points – camps being at Authuille, Bouzincourt, Aveluy, Contay and Senlis. Relieved by 1/5th Royal Sussex (16/7) and to Loos sector. In 1916 it was found that the existing railway system was not coping with troop movements and the vast amounts of war material required for operations on the Somme. With much work required on existing line, and the necessity of new railways, the Battalion moved back down to the Somme late in September and subsequently transferred (19/10) to G.H.Q Railway Construction Troops. With Battalion Headquarters at Acheux, companies operating from billets near to the work they were on (Mailly-Maillet Wood, Martinsart Wood, Englebelmer), carried out much work on railway improvements in the Somme area. Battalion was to convert from metre to standard gauge the track between Beaussart and Aveluy and in November extend this line to Mouquet Farm. Other work included construction of a line between Mesnil and the cross-roads near Aveluy.

18th (Service) Battalion (1st Tyneside Pioneers). Pioneers, 34th Division: Took active role during attack at La Boisselle (1/7) – at the Glory Hole just off the Albert-Bapaume Road and in front of the village, 'C' Company assisted Tyneside Scottish Brigade (102nd) during their costly assault. Just south remainder of Battalion were in Bécourt Wood and from there rendered great assistance to the Royal Scots, Lincolnshire and Suffolk of 101st Brigade on the right of 34th Division's attack. Relieved and via Albert to Millencourt (6/7). Later to Pas-en-Artois and the 37th Division then holding line in the Gommecourt sector. Battalion had been included in the transfer of the weakened 102nd and 103rd Brigades (20th-27th Northumberland Fusiliers) from the forward zone. Later returned to 34th Division at Armentières. Moved with 103rd Brigade down to the Somme (25/8). From Albert reached Bécourt Wood (28/8). At Martinpuich relieved units of 15th Division which had been withdrawn for rest and preparation for its assault of 15th September. Rested between tours in line near Contalmaison. Relieved and to Albert (12/9), Laviéville (13/9). To front line (15/9) – consolidating positions taken by 15th Division. Returned to Armentières sector via Albert (18/9).

19th (Service) Battalion (2nd Tyneside Pioneers). Pioneers, 35th Division: Arrived Doullens (3/7). To Acheux Wood (5/7). Attached to 29th Division until (12/7). To Mailly-Maillet Wood (6/7). Work began on a new trench 1000 yards or so in length and situated about 100 yards in front of existing front line. Battalion historian Captain C.H. Cooke describes the scene in No Man's Land as appalling – the dead lay in three parallel lines . . . 'three waves of Inniskillings and Newfoundlanders lay there as if on manoeuvres, the dressing of the lines was perfect.' Help was given to a wounded Inniskilling who dragged himself into the new trench having spent 6 days and nights out in the open. To Harponville (9/7), Albert (10/7). Began work on road through La Boisselle. Heavy shelling (11/7) – Captain Cooke records heavy casualties and the shells destroying more road than could be made. Via Morlancourt to Happy Valley (13/7). Later to bivouacs at Copse Valley and work on positions around Arrow Head Copse. Then to valley east of Carnoy – work carried out at Trônes Wood, Bernafay Wood, Maltz Horn Farm. To Morlancourt (1/8). Entrained at Méricourt-l'Abbé for Saleux (5/8) and from there marched to Riencourt. Entrained at Hangest-sur-Somme for Méricourt-l'Abbé (10/8) and marched to Citadel Camp. Work carried out on Daniell Alley (named after Commanding Officer) and communication trenches during operations around Falfemont Farm. Relieved from line (1/9) and later moved via Morlancourt and Talmas to Arras sector.

20th (Service) Battalion (1st Tyneside Scottish). 102nd Brigade, 34th Division: Moved forward with 23rd Northumberland Fusiliers up Mash Valley north of La Boisselle 7.30 a.m. (1/7) – advance being across widest part of No Man's Land saw Battalion almost completely destroyed within minutes of leaving start positions. In his history of The Tyneside Scottish (102nd Brigade) Brigadier-General Trevor Ternan records situation at night – 20th and 23rd lying dead in No-Man's Land – remnants holding short length of our front trench north of La Boisselle. The tremendous casualties suffered by the Tyneside Scottish were among the worse ever recorded on the Somme. The following details are taken from Brigadier-General Ternan's history – of the 80 officers that went into action only 10 returned, losses including all 4 commanding officers (killed) and all second in commands and adjutants. Of the men, some 80 per cent became casualties. There were 940 all ranks killed and some 1,500 wounded, the 20th Battalion loosing every officer and sergeant. Brigadier-General Ternan notes that not one man was taken prisoner and expresses the opinion that losses in killed were unnecessarily high owing to the fact that the Germans deliberately fired at and killed any wounded lying helpless in front of their trenches that made the slightest movement or showed any sign of life. Brigade collected on ridge between Tara-Usna Line and Albert (4/7) then marched through the town and on to Millencourt. Here, Brigadier-General Ternan noted that when the whole brigade was formed up it barely occupied the space of one battalion. Subsequently 102nd Brigade was removed from the 34th Division and transferred on (6/7) and (7/7) to the 37th then to the north at Pommier.

21th (Service) Battalion (2nd Tyneside Scottish). 102nd Brigade, 34th Division: Under Brigadier-General Trevor Ternan 102nd Brigade was positioned astride Albert-Bapaume Road and facing La Boisselle (1/7). Attacked 7.30 a.m. south of the village – heavy casualties from machine gun and shell fire (see 20th Battalion). Situation at night – about 150 men holding German trenches. Remnants of Brigade collected behind Tara-Usna Line (4/7) and from there marched through Albert to Millencourt. Later transferred to 37th Division at Pommier.

22nd (Service) Battalion (3rd Tyneside Scottish). 102nd Brigade, 34th Division: Attacked south of La Boisselle 7.30 a.m. (1/7) – moved forward with 21st Battalion – high casualties – just 150 men located in German line at nightfall. (Brigade casualties see 20th Battalion). Withdrew from positions behind Tara-Usna Line through Albert to Millencourt (4/7). Later transferred to 37th Division at Pommier.

23rd (Service) Battalion (4th Tyneside Scottish). 102nd Brigade, 34th Division: Attacked (1/7) – moved forward with 20th Battalion up Mash Valley to the north of La Boisselle – heavy casualties while crossing No Man's Land – Battalion almost completely lost. Withdrew with 102nd Brigade through Albert to Millencourt (4/7). Later transferred to 37th Division at Pommier.

24th (Service) Battalion (1st Tyneside Irish). 103rd Brigade, 34th Division: Attack on La Boisselle (1/7) – advanced from assembly positions in Tara-Usna Line 7.40 a.m. in support of 101st Brigade. Heavy casualties moving forward to British front line and in attack up Sausage Valley. War Diary notes enemy's intense machine gun fire – few reached objective – 1 officer with handful of men almost reaching Contalmaison but forced to retire to German second line. Relieved from forward area and to Long Valley. Casualties 650. To Hénencourt Wood (5/7), Humbercamps (6/7). From Armentières sector entrained at Merville for longueau (26/8) and from there marched to Cardonnette. To Laviéville (27/8), Black Wood (28/8). Attached to 15th Division, relieved 7th Cameron Highlanders in support trenches Contalmaison (30/8). To front line (1/9). War Diary notes heavy and accurate shelling – several groups buried. Relieved and to support line (3/9) and later to reserve at Scots Redoubt. To support trench in front of Mametz Wood and The Cutting, Contalmaison (5/9), front line (6/9), Mametz Wood (9/9), Albert (10/9). Working parties to front line. To Laviéville (13/9), Bécourt Wood (15/9). Relieved 8th York and Lancaster in trenches around Contalmaison (16/9). Carrying parties to dumps in front of Martinpuich. To Bécourt Wood (17/9), Franvillers (18/9), Bouchon (20/9). Entrained at Longpré for Merville (22/9).

25th (Service) Battalion (2nd Tyneside Irish). 103rd Brigade, 34th Division: Attack on La Boisselle (1/8). War Diary notes advance at 7.45 a.m. – heavy fire and casualties from moment assembly trenches were left – La Boisselle found to be strongly held. Advance maintained until 'only a few scattered soldiers were left standing, the discipline and courage of all ranks being remarkable.' Survivors collected in trenches near Keats Redan. Relieved and to Belle Vue Farm (2/7). Casualties – 487. To Long Valley (4/7), Hénencourt Wood (5/7), Humbercamps (6/7). From Armentières sector entrained at Merville for Longueau (26/8) and from there marched to Allonville. To Laviéville (27/8), Bécourt (28/8). Attached to 15th Division relieved 8th/10th Gordon Highlanders in front line opposite Martinpuich (30/8). Relieved and to Round Wood (1/9). To Peake Wood (3/9), The Cutting, Contalmaison (4/9), front line (5/9), The Cutting (7/9), front line (10/9), Albert (12/9), Laviéville (13/9). To positions east of Albert in reserve for attack on Martinpuich (15/9). Worked on road at Contalmaison. To Franvillers (18/9). L'Etoile (20/9). Entrained at Longpré for Merville (22/9).

26th (Service) Battalion (3rd Tyneside Irish). 103rd Brigade, 34th Division: Attack on La Boisselle (1/7) – moved forward from assembly trenches near Tara Redoubt. War Diary notes 'A' and 'B' companies in front, 'B' and 'D' in reserve – 'men advanced as if on parade under heavy machine gun and shell fire.' Owing to high casualties attack held up – small parties holding out in shell holes in No Man's Land. Relieved and to Belle Vue Farm (2/7). Casualties 489. To Long Valley (4/7), Hénencourt Wood (5/7), Humbercamps (6/7). From Armentières sector, entrained at Merville for Longueau (26/8) and from there marched to Allonville. To Laviéville (27/8), billets 1 mile south-west of Albert (28/8), Scots Redoubt (30/8). Attached to 15th Division.

To support trenches in front of Contalmaison (1/9), front line (4/9), support line (6/9). Constructed new trench in No Man's Land during night (7/9). To front line (9/9), support line (10/9), Albert (12/9), Laviéville (13/9), positions east of Albert in reserve for attack on Martinpuich (15/9), Franvillers (18/9), L'Etoile (20/9). Entrained at Longpré for Merville (22/9).

27th (Service) Battalion (4th Tyneside Irish). 103rd Brigade, 34th Division: Attack on La Boisselle (1/7) – assembled in Tara-Usna Line on right in support of 15th and 16th Royal Scots. Moved forward 7.40 a.m. – War Diary notes few casualties until crossing Chapes Spur – advance continued (battalion on left held up) – about 70% casualties before German front trench reached. Small parties reached Contalmaison but were forced to retire. Relieved and to Bouzincourt (4/7). Casualties – 550. To Hénencourt Wood (5/7), Humbercamps (6/7). From Armentières sector, entrained at Merville for Longueau (26/8) and from there marched to Allonville. To Laviéville (27/8), Albert (28/8). Moved forward to trenches around Contalmaison (30/8). Attached to 15th Division. To Peake Wood in support (1/9). Began tours in front line. New trench constructed in No Man's Land (9/9). Relieved and to Contalmaison (10/9). To Albert (12/9), Laviéville (13/9), Albert (15/9), Franvillers (18/9), L'Etoile (20/9). Entrained at Longpré for Merville (22/9).

Royal Warwickshire Regiment

1st Battalion. 10th Brigade, 4th Division: Held support positions in sunken Beaumont-Sere road just outside of Auchonvillers (1/7). Advanced at 9.10 a.m. to British front line. To Mailly-Maillet (8/7), front line (15/7), camp north-west of Bertrancourt (18/7), Beauval (21/7). Transferred to Ypres sector (24/7). From Poperinghe reached Coisy (18/9). To Corbie (25/9), Méricourt-l'Abbé (26/9), Daours (1/10), Méaulte (8/10), Mansell Camp (9/10), front line trenches east of Lesbœufs (10/9) – advanced almost 500 yards and dug new positions (Antelope Trench) south of Hazy Trench. Enemy attack in evening repulsed. Relieved and to Guillemont (14/10). To Bernafay Wood (17/10). Provided salvage and working parties. To front line east of Lesbœufs (22/10). In attack (23/10) – hand-to-hand fighting at Boritska Trench. Relieved and to Mansell Camp (26/10), Corbie (28/10), Huppy (31/10), Tours-en-Vimeu (3/11).

2nd Battalion. 22nd Brigade, 7th Division: Took part in operations at Mametz (1/7) – moving forward towards Shrine Alley during afternoon. Relieved and to Heilly (5/7). To Mametz Wood (11/7), Citadel Camp (12/7), front line (13/7). Attack on Bazentin-le-Petit (14/7). Relieved and to Dernancourt (21/7). To Yzeux (22/7), Dernancourt (13/8), support at Montauban Alley (26/8). In action at Ginchy (3/9). Relieved and to Buire (4/9), Forceville (9/9), Méteren (18/9).

1/5th Battalion (T.F.). 143rd Brigade, 48th (South Midland) Division: In front line south-east of Hébuterne (1/7) – with 1/7th Royal Warwickshire discharged smoke along front just before zero hour. Battalion historian Lieutenant C.E. – Carrington, M.C. notes the London Scottish (1/14th London) vanishing into the smoke during the attack on Gommecourt to the left. There would be a German counter-attack in the mid afternoon and by 4. p.m. all the British had been driven back to their own lines. To Couin (5/7) – working parties marching each day to the front line. Moved by bus to Bouzincourt (13/7) and from there marched through Albert to forward positions at La Boisselle. Attack on Ovillers (16/7) – attached to 25th Division leading companies ('A' and 'B') reached Ovillers-Mouquet Farm Road and came under machine gun fire from the village. Moved forward and took German second line. Lieutenant Carrington notes close range sniping – 'A' Company losing all its officers, and heavy losses in 'C' Company – its position being held against 5 or 6 counter attacks. Relieved and to bivouacs just outside Albert (17/7). Dug new trench along Bapaume Road towards Pozières (19/7). Battalion history notes only 1 casualty from shelling and compares this to the 300 of a battalion 200 yards away across the road (see 1/8th Worcestershire). To Bouzincourt (19/7), Ovillers (22/7).

In action at Pozières (23/7) – attempt to link up with Australians failed. To Usna Redoubt (25/7), Coulonvillers (27/7), Longuevillette (10/8), Arquèves (11/8), Varennes (14/8), Bouzincourt (15/8), Ovillers (16/8). Attack on Leipzig Redoubt (18/8) – 'A' Company took first line – 'B' and part of 'C' followed on and cleared second. To bivouacs near Bouzincourt (20/8), Ovillers (Skyline Trench) (22/8), Ovillers Post (25/8), Varennes (28/8), Bois de Warnimont (29/8), Sarton (2/9), Gézaincourt (11/9), Heuzecourt (18/9), Halloy (29/9), Souastre (30/9), Hébuterne (1/10) – took over trenches at Foncquevillers. To St. Amand (6/10), Grand Rullecourt (20/10), Franvillers (25/10), Bécourt (26/10), Contalmaison (2/11), front line Le Sars sector (9/11), Martinpuich (11/11), Contalmaison Villa Camp (14/11).

2/5th Battalion (T.F.). 182nd Brigade, 61st (2nd South Midland) Division: Moved towards Somme beginning of November, reaching Mezerolles (6/11), Candas (15/11), Halloy (16/11), Hérissart (17/11), Warloy (18/11).

1/6th Battalion (T.F.). 143rd Brigade, 48th (South Midland) Division: Attached to 11th Brigade (4th Division) followed 1/8th Royal Warwickshire into attack on The Quadrilateral (1/7) – to the left machine gun fire swept advance and, according to the Battalion historian, reduced it to a strength of 2 weak platoons. Passed through objective and consolidated ground beyond. Withdrew to Mailly–Maillet during night and from there to Couin. To bivouacs just east of Albert (13/7), trenches south of Ovillers (16/7), Bouzincourt (19/7), Maison-Roland (28/7), Gézaincourt (9/8), Léalvillers (10/8), Bouzincourt (14/8), trenches north of Ovillers (16/8). Successful attack on Leipzig Redoubt (18/8) – moving forward with 1/5th Royal Warwickshire at 5.p.m. and taking some 250 prisoners. To Bouzincourt (20/8), support line (24/8), front line (Skyline Trench) (25/8), Bois de Warnimont (29/8), Vauchelles (2/9), Gézaincourt (11/9), Prouville (18/9), Bayencourt (28/9), later St. Amand. Took over line at Hébuterne (12/10). To St. Amand (16/10), Grand Rullecourt (20/8), Baizieux (25/10), Bécourt (26/10), bivouacs west of Mametz Wood (27/10). Work carried out on roads. To Albert (1/11), Peake Wood (3/11). Working parties to forward positions at Le Sars. To Martinpuich (9/11), front line Le Sars (12/11), Fricourt (15/11).

2/6th Battalion (T.F.). 182nd Brigade, 61st (2nd South Midland) Division: Arrived Bernaville from Bonnières (15/11). To Berteaucourt (16/11), Rubempré (17/11), Warloy (18/11).

1/7th Battalion (T.F.). 143rd Brigade, 48th (South Midland) Division: In front line south-east of Hébuterne (1/7) – with 1/5th Royal Warwickshire discharged smoke along front just before zero hour. War Diary notes No Man's Land to the right (31st Division's attack on Serre) 'strewn with bodies after the attack, many wounded try to crawl back and are sniped at by Germans opposite.' Relieved and to bivouacs between Couin and St. Léger (4/7). Found working parties for front line trenches (12/7). Moved by motor lorries via Bouzincourt to positions in a field near Albert (13/7). Attack on Ovillers (14/7) – 'A' and 'B' Companies led assault at 7.30 a.m. – objective reached and held for 7 hours. Withdrew on account of heavy enfilade fire. Casualties estimated at 150. Renewed attack (15/7) – leading waves cut down by machine gun fire upon leaving trenches. Relieved and to Albert. To front line (18/7), Bouzincourt (19/7), support lines just east of Albert (22/7). Provided carrying parties during operations around Pozières. To front line (24/7) – in action until relieved in afternoon (26/7). To Bouzincourt (27/7), Mesnil and Domqueur (28/7), Gézaincourt (9/8), Léalvillers (10/8), bivouacs near Bouzincourt (14/8), front line Ovillers sector (16/8) – War Diary notes German aeroplane brought down in flames in Battalion's lines (17/8). In action at Leipzig Redoubt (18/8) and (19/8). Relieved and to Bouzincourt (22/8). To trenches north of Ovillers (26/8), Bois de Warnimont (28/8), Authie (2/9), Gézaincourt (11/9), Bernaville (18/9), Prouville (23/9), Halloy (29/9), Sailly-au-Bois (30/9). Provided working parties Hébuterne sector. To St. Amand (4/10), front line Hébuterne sector (6/10), St. Amand (7/10), Sombrin (19/10), Franvillers (25/10), Bécourt (26/10), Albert (2/11), camp on Fricourt-Contalmaison Road (3/11), Peake Wood (5/11), front line Le Sars (10/11), support line (12/11), Bazentin-le-Petit Wood (15/11).

2/7th Battalion (T.F.). 182nd Brigade, 61st (2nd South Midland) Division: Arrived Remaisnil from Sibiville (6/11). To Fienvillers (15/11), Pernois (16/11), Hérissart (17/11), Warloy (18/11).

1/8th Battalion (T.F.). 143rd Brigade, 48th (South Midland) Division: Moved forward from Mailly-Maillet (1/7). Attached to 4th Division for attack at Redan Ridge. Right of assault took The Quadrilateral, passed through and gained support trench beyond. On left, German front line entered under heavy fire from Serre. No further progress made. Withdrew to Mailly-Maillet (2/7). Casualties – 563, Including Commanding Officer Lieutenant-Colonel E.A. Innes. Rejoined 48th Division at Couin (4/7). To bivouacs near Albert (13/7). Relieved 3rd Worcestershire in front line (18/7). Relieved by 1/7th Royal Warwickshire and to Usna Redoubt (19/7). To Bouzincourt (20/7), Aveluy (23/7), support trenches La Boisselle (24/7). Took over front line (26/7). Bombing parties in action early morning (27/7) – advancing to position just short of Ovillers-Courcelette track. Relieved and to La Boisselle. To Bouzincourt (28/7), Coulonvillers (29/7), Longuevillette (8/8), Arquèves (10/8), Varennes (14/8), Bouzincourt (15/8). To Ovillers Post (18/8) – 'A' and 'C' Companies in dug-outs Ovillers. To Ration Trench (20/8),

Skyline Trench (21/8). Relieved and to Bouzincourt (22/8). To Aveluy (25/8), Ovillers (27/8). Attacked Constance Trench 7 p.m. – Official History of The Great War records that Battalion ran into its own barrage and swerved to the flanks. On right – parties entered objective, but counter-attacked from Pole Trench and down Constance were forced to retire. To Bouzincourt (28/8) and from there in buses to Bois de Warnimont. To Thièvres (2/9). War Diary notes trench attacks practised and on (6/9) – every man to fire live rifle grenade plus 10 rounds. To Gézaincourt (11/9), Beaumetz (18/9), Montigny-les-Jongleurs (28/9), Halloy (29/9), St. Amand (30/9). Relieved 1/4th Suffolk in Yankee and Welcome Trenches Hébuterne sector (2/10). Relieved and to St. Amand (5/10). To Sombrin (19/10), Franvillers (25/10), Bécourt (26/10), Mametz Wood (27/10). War Diary records whole battalion repairing roads and then moved to camp south-west of wood. 200 men working at The Cutting, Contalmaison (29/10). To Bécourt (1/11), Shelter Wood (2/11). Worked on repairs Martinpuich-Bazentin Road (9/11). To reserve positions at Martinpuich, Destremont Farm and 26th Avenue (10/11). Relieved 1/7th Royal Warwickshire in forward trenches Le Sars (12/11). Relived and to Acid Drop Camp, Contalmaison (16/11).

2/8th Battalion (T.F.). 182nd Brigade, 61st (2nd South Midland) Division: Arrived Mezerolles from Séricourt (6/11). To Candas (15/11), Halloy (16/11), Hérissart (17/11), Warloy (18/11).

10th (Service) Battalion. 57th Brigade, 19th (Western) Division: From Corps reserve moved forward to Millencourt (1/7) – later to positions in Tara-Usna line. In action at La Boisselle (3/7)–(5/7). Relieved and to Albert (6/7). To Millencourt (9/7), Hénencourt (10/7), Millencourt (11/7), Mametz Wood (20/7), Bazentin-le-Petit (23/7). Relieved 10th Worcestershire in front line. To Bécourt Wood (24/7), front line (29/7). Attack on Intermediate Trench (30/7). Relieved and to Bécourt Wood (1/8), Bresle (2/8), Vauchelles-les-Domart (4/8). Transferred to Flanders front (7/8). Arrived Sarton (7/10). To Bois de Warnimont (8/10), Warloy (18/10), brickfields north-west of Albert (22/10), Crucifix Corner (27/10), reserve trenches (Hessian, Regina) (31/10), front line (Zollern Redoubt) (2/11), Ovillers Post (6/11), Zollern Redoubt (9/11), Cromwell and Wellington Camps (13/11). Forward to Battery Valley and in action at Grandcourt (18/11).

11th (Service) Battalion. 112th Brigade, 37th Division: At Hannescamps (1/7) – the 37th Division's role that day being to provide a defensive flank and fire smoke bombs along the front of 46th Division's attack at Gommecourt. To Bienvillers (3/7), Halloy (4/7), Millencourt (6/7). Marched through Albert to the Tara-Usna Line (7/7), later 2 companies moved forward and occupied old German section known as 'Heligoland.' To forward positions between Contalmaison and La Boisselle (8/7). Relieved and to Tara-Usna line (11/7). Casualties from shelling since (8/7) – 170. To support trenches (13/7). Attack on Pozières (15/7) – advanced east of Contalmaison Wood behind 8th East Lancashire and 6th Bedfordshire. Casualties – 275. To Albert (16/7), Heligoland trenches (18/7) – planned attack cancelled and returned to Albert. To Bresle (19/7), Lahoussoye (20/7), Bresle (30/7), Bécourt Wood (31/7), positions between Bazentin-le-Petit Wood and Mametz Wood (6/8). Relieved 6th Bedfordshire in front line north of Bazentin-le-Petit (10/8). Here Battalion faced the German Intermediate Line, its wire being at distances varying from 150-230 yards away. Unsuccessful attack 10.30 p.m. (12/8) – 'A' and 'C' Companies leading sustained around 150 casualties after hand-to-hand fighting. Withdrew to Mametz Wood (14/8), Bécourt Wood (15/8), via Albert to Lahoussoye (16/8). Entrained at Fréchencourt for Longpré (18/8). Total casualties for Somme operations noted by Battalion historian Brevet-Colonel C.S. Collision, D.S.O. as 758 all ranks. Entrained for Béthune sector (19/8). Arrived Bertrancourt (23/10). Moved to Doullens area for training (25/10). Arrived Mailly-Maillet via Louvencourt and Bertrancourt (13/11) and from there took over part of line between Beaumont-Hamel and Serre. Attack on Frankfort Trench (14/11) – heavy machine gun fire from Munich Trench forced withdrawal to Waggon Road. to Englebelmer during night (16/11).

14th (Service) Battalion (1st Birmingham). 13th Brigade, 5th Division: Left Magnicourt for Boisbergues (13/7), to Hérissart (14/7), Franvillers (15/7), Méaulte (18/7), captured trenches between Bazentin-le-Grand and Longueval (19/7), new line running from southern corner of High Wood towards Longueval (20/7). Attack on Wood Lane (22/7) – 'A' and 'B' Companies leading assault soon cut to pieces by fire from High Wood. Casualties – 485. To Pommiers Redoubt (23/7), trenches at Longueval (29/7), attack on strong-points north-west of the village repulsed (30/7). Casualties – 171. Relieved by 15th Royal Warwickshire and to Pommiers Redoubt (31/7). War Diary notes that upon relief 16th Royal Warwickshire were in the same trenches and consequently all three Birmingham City battalions were in line at same time. To camp about 2 miles north-east of Dernancourt (1/8). Entrained at Edgehill for Airaines and from there marched to Laleu (4/8). To Etréjust (5/8). Entrained at Airaines for Edgehill and to bivouacs north-west of Dernancourt (24/8). To Happy Valley (25/8), Maricourt in support positions (26/8), front line facing Falfemont Farm (29/8). Attack at Falfemont Farm (3/9) – gun pits in the valley south-west from Wedge Wood taken – severe casualties on advance to second objective. Withdrew to Dublin Trench on the Maricourt-Montauban Road. Casualties – 303. To Citadel

Camp (6/9), Leuze Wood (10/9), Falfemont Farm (12/9), Billon Wood (13/9), Méricourt (14/9). At one halt on the journey the Battalion historian – J.E.B. Fairclough records that H.R.H. the Prince of Wales rode past on a bicycle. To Waterlot Farm (18/9), Chimpanzee Valley (20/9), support trenches north of The Quadrilateral (22/9), trenches near Gillemont (24/9). In support for attack on Morval (25/9) – dug in on slope west of village that night. To Oxford Copse (26/9), Citadel Camp (27/9). Entrained at Grove Town (28/9) arriving Longpré (29/9) and marching to Caumont. Entrained at Abbeville for Lillers (1/10). Casualties given in Battalion History for period (19/7)–(25/9) – 36 officers and 1,047 other ranks.

15th (Service) Battalion (2nd Birmingham). 13th Brigade, 5th Division: Left Moncheaux for Le Meillard (13/7). To Hérissart (14/7), Franvillers (15/7), Dernancourt (17/7), reserve trenches at rear of Montauban (19/7), support line Bazentin-le-Grand (20/7). Attack on Wood Lane (22/7) – heavy losses due to machine gun fire from High Wood – withdrew to start position. Casualties – 143. Battalion historian Major C.A. Bill recalls a lucky escape while moving up for the attack on (22/7) – dropping to his hands and knees, a shell passed between his arms, underneath his body and hit the ground between his feet. The burst knocking the officer into a trench with a number of burns. To Pommiers Redoubt (24/7), positions between Mametz and Montauban (28/7) – carrying parties for operations at Longueval. To Longueval (29/7), relieved 15th Royal Warwickshire in front line west of village (31/7), to Mametz (1/8), bivouacs north-west of Dernancourt (2/8). Entrained at Edgehill for Airaines and from there marched to Métigny (4/8). To Avesnes-Chaussoy (5/8), Villers-Campsart (9/8). Entrained at Airaines for Edgehill and marched to camp near Dernancourt (24/8). To Happy Valley (25/8), took over trenches between Angle Wood and Falfemont Farm (26/8). To Casement Trench on Maricourt-Briqueterie Road (29/8), Angle Wood (2/9), in support of failed attack on Falfemont Farm (3/9). Casualties – 231. To Casement Trench (4/9), Citadel Camp (6/9), positions near Leuze Wood (10/9) – no accommodation found, returned to Angle Wood. Later to Chimpanzee Trench. To Billon Farm (13/9), Méricourt (14/9), War Diary notes that billets were in cinema hall. To positions west of Billon Farm then forward to Waterlot Farm (18/9), Chimpanzee Trench (20/9), The Quadrilateral (22/9), trenches between Wedge Wood and Guillemont (24/9), Quadrilateral and Warwick Trench (25/9), Oxford Copse (26/9), Citadel Camp (27/9). Entrained at Edgehill for Longpré (28/9), to Villers-sur-Mareuil (29/9). Entrained at Abbeville for Lillers (1/10).

16th (Service) Battalion (3rd Birmingham). 15th Brigade, 5th Division: Arrived Fienvillers (13/7). To Puchevillers (14/7), Lahoussoye (15/7), Ville-sur-Ancre (17/7), bivouacs near Pommiers Redoubt (19/7), reserve trenches north-east of Montauban (23/7), Longueval and in close support of action north of the village and western edge of Delville Wood (27/7). Casualties – 275. To Pommiers Redoubt (28/7), Longueval (30/7), Pommiers Redoubt (1/8), bivouacs near Dernancourt (2/8). Entrained at Méricourt for Hangest-sur-Somme and from there marched to Le Quesnoy (4/8). Entrained at Longpré for Méricourt and from there to camp north of Dernancourt (24/8). To Sandpit Camp (25/8), Billon Wood (26/8), front line near Angle Wood (31/8). Attack on Falfemont Farm (3/9)–(5/9). To Billon Farm (5/9), Citadel Camp (7/9), Morlancourt (9/9), via Citadel to Waterlot Farm (16/9), positions between Ginchy and Morval (18/9) – new trenches dug. To trenches between Guillemont and Wedge Wood (20/9). Attack on Morval (25/9) – moved forward at 6 p.m. and dug new line about 450 yards east of village, left resting on the sunken road. To Oxford Copse (26/9), Citadel Camp (27/9). Entrained at Happy Valley for Longpré (29/9). Entrained for Béthune sector (1/10).

Royal Fusiliers (City of London Regiment)

1st Battalion. 17th Brigade, 24th Division: Arrived Longueau (25/7). To Riencourt (26/7), Bois des Tailles (1/8), Sandpit Camp (2/8), front line between Delville Wood and Trônes Wood (HQ Waterlot Farm) (8/8), Bernafay Wood (14/8). In support for attack towards Guillemont (17/8). Attack on Hill Street and Brompton Road (21/8) – Official History of The Great War records 'good shooting at close range' but the ground gained could not be held. Casualties – 403. To Happy Valley (22/8), Thunderstorm Camp (25/8), camp near Fricourt (30/8), near Mametz (31/8), Carlton Trench between High Wood and Delville Wood (1/9), Montauban (2/9), Dernancourt (5/9), Bussus-Bussuel (7/9). Transferred to Vimy Ridge sector (20/9).

2nd Battalion. 86th Brigade, 29th Division: Moved forward from assembly positions in Mailly-Maillet Wood for attack towards Hawthorn Ridge (1/7) – leading waves swept by machine gun fire soon after leaving front trenches – some men reached and fought at Hawthorn Ridge mine crater – others entered enemy's front line but these were soon killed. Casualties – 561. Relieved from forward area and to Mailly-Maillet (5/7), Acheux (6/7), Mesnil (12/7), Beauval (25/7). Transferred to Ypres sector (27/7). Arrived Dernancourt (11/10). To Mametz Wood (14/10), Delville Wood (20/10), front line Flers sector (24/10), Trônes Wood (26/10), Bernafay Wood (27/10), Mametz (31/10), Corbie (1/11), Méaulte (17/11).

4th Battalion. 9th Brigade, 3rd Division: Moved from Beaumetz to Vignacourt (4/7). To Poulainville (5/7), Lahoussoye (6/7), Morlancourt (7/7), Carnoy (9/7), into reserve positions south of Marlborough Wood (13/7). In support during operations at Bazentin-le-Grand (14/7)–(15/7). To Marlborough Wood (16/7), Carnoy (19/7), Delville Wood (20/7) – some 40 casualties during move forward. Enemy attacked positions (21/7). Relieved and to Sandpit Camp (25/7). Regimental records show that although no attack had been made at this point there had been some 352 casualties since (13/7). To Ville-sur-Ancre (28/7), Sandpit Camp (13/8), Carnoy (14/8), trenches south of Guillemont (15/8). Unsuccessful assault on village (16/8) – 2 companies led attack – their commanders being hit as they crossed the parapet. All other officers later became casualties along with 160 other ranks. Relieved and to Carnoy (18/8), Ville-sur-Ancre (21/8). Entrained at Méricourt for Candas (23/8). To Berneuil (24/8) and from there moved to the Hulluch sector. Took over part of line near Serre (8/10). To Mailly-Maillet (13/10), Courcelles (18/10), Vauchelles (21/10), front line (5/11), Courcelles (8/11). In reserve during attack on Serre (13/11). To Redan sector (14/11), Bus-lès-Artois (16/11), Courcelles (19/11).

7th Battalion (Extra Reserve). 190th Brigade, 63rd (Royal Naval) Division: Arrived Acheux from Ligny-Saint-Flochel (3/10). To Mailly-Maillet (8/10). Relieved 24th Royal Fusiliers in front line Redan sector. To Mailly-Maillet Wood (13/10). Provided working parties for forward area. To Raincheval (16/10), Léalvillers (17/10), Puchevillers (18/10), Hédauville (20/10), Englebelmer (30/10) and from there front line Hamel sector. To Englebelmer (6/11), Hédauville (7/11), Puchevillers (8/11), Hédauville (11/11), Englebelmer (12/11) and from there front line east of Hamel. Attack on Beaucourt (13/11) – 344 casualties. To Englebelmer (16/11), Beauval (18/11).

8th (Service) Battalion. 36th Brigade, 12th (Eastern) Division: Moved forward from Fréchencourt and took over line in front of Albert (1/7). To Ovillers Post (6/7). Attack on Ovillers (7/7) – heavy barrage accounted for great losses while forming up in assembly areas – with 9th Royal Fusiliers and 7th Royal Sussex went on – Soon carried first 3 German lines – footing gained in Ovillers. Survivors could not hold gains – forced to fall back and consolidate in former German second line. Relieved (8/7). Casualties – 640. To Albert (9/7), Senlis (10/7), Forceville (11/7), Bus-lès-Artois (12/7), Mailly-Maillet (20/7), trenches north of Auchonvillers, Bois de Warnimont (25/7), Hédauville (26/7), Bouzincourt (27/7). Took over line in front of Albert (left of Pozières). Attack on 4th Avenue (3/8) and Ration Trench (4/8) – Both successful. Counter attack repulsed (6/8). To Bouzincourt (7/8), Puchevillers (13/8). Transferred via Sarton to Arras sector (16/8). Arrived Neuvillette (28/9). To Pommiers Redoubt (30/9). Took over trenches west of Gueudecourt and near Flers (2/10). Heavy losses during attack on Bayonet Trench (7/10). To Bernafay Wood (9/10), Fricourt (19/10), Buire (22/10). Transferred to Arras sector (23/10).

9th (Service) Battalion. 36th Brigade, 12th (Eastern) Division: Moved from billets at Fréchencourt to Nab trenches in support (1/7). To line at Ovillers (5/7). Heavy losses during attack on Ovillers (7/7). To Senlis (9/7), Forceville (10/7), Bus-lès-Artois (11/7), Mailly-Maillet (20/7), Bois de Warnimont (24/7), Bus-lès-Artois (25/7), Hédauville (26/7), Bouzincourt (27/7), Albert (29/7). Successful attacks on 4th Avenue and Ration Trenches (3/8) and (4/8). To Varennes (9/8), Puchevillers via Léalvillers and Toutencourt (12/8), Vauchelles-les-Authie (15/8). Transferred to Arras sector (16/8). Arrived Neuvillette (28/9). To Pommiers Redoubt (30/9), trenches west of Gueudecourt (2/10). In reserve west of Gueudecourt (6/10). To Gird support line (7/10) – heavy losses during attack on Bayonet Trench. To Bernafay Wood (8/10), front line Gueudecourt (16/10), Fricourt Camp (19/10), Buire (20/10).

Transferred to Arras sector (22/10).

10th (Service) Battalion. 111th Brigade, 37th Division: From Arras sector reached Bresle (6/7). To front line near La Boisselle (8/7), Sausage Valley (9/7). Advanced to Contalmaison Road at La Boisselle and attack launched on Pozières (15/7) – fought way through to the Orchard south-west of village. To Tara-Usna Hill (16/7), Bresle (20/7), Albert via Hénencourt (30/7), Mametz Wood (31/7), trenches west of Mametz Wood (1/8), support line Bazentin-le-Petit (3/8), Windmill line (4/8), High Wood (6/8), Mametz Wood (8/8), Belle Vue Farm via Lozenge Wood (15/8), Bresle (16/8), Allery (18/8). Transferred to Béthune sector (19/8). Arrived Puchevillers (22/10). To Hem-Hardinval (30/10), Varennes via Puchevillers (12/11), Englebelmer (13/11) – moved forward through Hamel to positions in the original British front line. For period (14/11)–(16/11) War Diary gives location as 'redoubt.' Attacked Munich and Frankfort Trenches and Leave Avenue (16/11), later in day occupying Muck Trench. Attacked The Triangle (17/11). Relieved and to Englebelmer.

11th (Service) Battalion. 54th Brigade, 18th (Eastern) Division: With 7th Bedfordshire lead attack up southern face of Mametz spur (1/7) – making rapid advance, stormed Pommiers Trench and later would be involved in fierce hand-to-hand fighting at Maple Trench and during capture of Pommiers Redoubt, Beetle Alley and White Trench. Relieved and to Carnoy (2/7). Casualties – 227. To Bois des Tailles (7/7), positions near Maricourt and in support during 54th Brigade's assault on Trônes Wood (14/7). To Bois Des Tailles (18/7), Grove Town Camp (21/7). Transferred to Armentières sector (22/7). Arrived Raincheval (10/9). To Hédauville via Arquèves, Léalvillers, Acheux and Forceville (23/9), trenches Leipzig sector (24/9). Attack and capture of Thiepval (26/9). To Martinsart (27/9), Martinsart Wood (28/9), Mailly-Maillet Wood (30/9), Senlis (4/10). Via Candas, Fienvillers and Bernaville to Domesmont ('A','B' Companies) and Ribeaucourt ('C', 'D' Companies) (5/10). Via Candas to Beauval (15/10), Warloy (17/10), Bouzincourt (18/10), Albert (20/10), forward positions – Regina Trench (24/10), Albert (6/11), Ovillers (13/11), Regina Trench (14/11), Ovillers (18/11).

12th (Service) Battalion. 17th Brigade, 24th Division: Arrived Bois des Tailles (31/7). To Sandpit Camp (2/8), the craters at Carnoy (8/8), Bernafay Wood (9/8), craters (12/8), trenches between Guillemont and Delville Wood (14/8). In reserve during Guillemont operations – covering attack (16/8) with a smoke barrage. Carrying parties also provided and communication trench dug. To Bernafay Wood (19/8), trenches near Gillemont (22/8), Happy Valley (23/8), camp near Dernancourt (26/8), near Fricourt (31/8), Carlton Trench between High Wood and Delville Wood (1/9) – heavily bombarded with gas shells in Caterpillar Valley on way forward. To Orchard Trench (2/9), Fricourt Camp (5/9), Dernancourt (6/9), Bussus-Bussuel (7/9). Entrained at Pont-Remy for Vimy Ridge sector (19/9).

13th (Service) Battalion. 111th Brigade, 37th Division: Arrived Humbercourt (4/7). To Bresle (5/7), Albert (7/7). Attached to 56th Brigade in successful assault northern end of Ovillers (8/7). To Tara-Usna Hill (11/7), trenches opposite Pozières (16/7), Bresle (22/7), Albert via Hénencourt and Millencourt (30/7), The Quadrangle (2/8), Mametz Wood (3/8), High Wood (8/8), Mérélessart via Fréchencourt (18/8). Entrained at Longpré for Bailleul (19/8). Arrived Gézaincourt (20/10). To Puchevillers and line opposite Beaumont-Hamel (22/10), Gézaincourt (30/10), Puchevillers (11/11), Hédauville (12/11). Moved forward through Hamel and took part in 63rd Division's operations at Beaucourt (13/11) – took Beaucourt Trench (14/11). Positions given in War Diary (19/11) as Beaumont, Mild and Munich Trenches.

17th (Service) Battalion (Empire). 5th Brigade, 2nd Division: Arrived Vaux-sur-Somme (21/7). To Happy Valley (24/7), support positions between Trônes Wood and Longueval Alley (25/7). In action at Delville Wood (27/7). Casualties – 118. To Bernafay Wood (28/7), Longueval Alley (29/7), Angle Trench (30/7), support trenches (1/8), reserve line between Montauban and Carnoy (2/8), Waterlot Farm area (3/8), Sandpit Camp (8/8), Ville-sur-Ancre (11/8), Picquigny (14/8), Flesselles (16/8), trenches at La Signy Farm Beaumont-Hamel sector (20/8), Bus-lès-Artois (23/8), Coigneux (24/8), Board and Wolf Trenches (30/8), Courcelles (6/9), front line (10/9), Coigneux (17/9), Vauchelles (19/9), Bus-lès-Artois (2/10), Mailly-Maillet (3/10), trenches Serre Sector (7/10), Léalvillers (9/10), Mailly-Maillet (18/10), Arquèves (1/11), Mailly-Maillet via Bertrancourt (11/11), trenches Redan sector (12/11). In support line during attack along Redan Ridge (13/11) – later attacked Frankfort Trench, but driven back – held Waggon Road and Crater Lane until relieved. To Mailly-Maillet (17/11), Bertrancourt (18/11).

20th (Service) Battalion (3rd Public Schools). 19th Brigade, 33rd Division: From Givenchy area arrived Poulainville (10/7). To Vecquemont (11/7), Buire-sur-l'Ancre (12/7), Méaulte (14/7), Mametz Wood (15/7) and from there occupied trenches between Bazentin-le-Petit and High Wood. Attack on High Wood (20/7) – 390 casualties during fierce close quarter fighting. Relieved at midnight and to Mametz Wood. To Buire-sur-l'Ancre (22/7), Mametz Wood (13/8), High Wood (22/8). In action near Delville Wood (24/8). Dug communication trenches in the area. To Mametz Wood (26/8), Montauban Alley (27/8), Fricourt Wood (29/8), Ribemont (31/8), Molliens-au-Bois (2/9),

Bernaville (3/9). To St. Pol area (5/9). Arrived Bienvillers (11/9) – began tours in line Hannescamps sector. To Doullens (1/10), Lucheux (11/10), Ville-sur-Ancre (18/10), Citadel Camp (21/10), Bernafay Wood (22/10), trenches north of Morval (28/10) – in support at Hogs Back. Relieved and to Albert. To Carnoy (1/11), front line (3/11). In action between Lesbœufs and Le Transloy (6/11). To La Briqueterie (8/11), Méaulte (9/11). Entrained at Edgehill for Airaines (11/11) and from there marched to Mérélessart.

22nd (Service) Battalion (Kensington). 99th Brigade, 2nd Division: Entrained at Diéval for Longpré (20/7) and from there marched to Morlancourt. To Sandpit Valley (23/7), Montauban (24/7). While at Montauban Christopher Stone, brother-in-law of Compton Mackenzie and junior officer with 22nd Royal Fusiliers, described in a letter to his wife the former German dug-out that he occupied. Although infested with flies the position was typical of many the enemy had constructed for almost permanent use – having wallpaper, an electric bell, cheval glass, cupboards, curtains and a well ventilated deep sleeping area. To Bernafay Wood (25/7). In action at Delville Wood (27/7)–(4/8). Withdrew to Bund Trench and later Citadel Camp. Ccasualties over 250. To Méricourt (11/8). Entrained for Saleux (13/8) and from there marched to Vauxen-Amiénois. To Naours (16/8), Gézaincourt (17/8), Vauchelles-les-Authie (18/8), Bus-lès-Artois (20/8), front line Hébuterne sector (21/8), Couin (25/8), front line (29/8), Couin (4/9), front line (10/9), Couin (16/9), Authie (20/9), Bertrancourt (30/9) – began duty in line Redan sector. To Mailly-Maillet (6/10), Arquèves (8/10), Mailly-Maillet Wood (16/10), trenches Redan sector (17/10), Mailly-Maillet Wood (20/10), Acheux Wood (22/10), Redan sector (30/10), Mailly-Maillet (2/11), Redan sector (5/11), Bertrancourt (7/11), Acheux Wood (9/11), Bertrancourt via Mailly-Maillet and into assembly positions (12/11). Operations on Redan Ridge – moving up into captured positions and making assault on The Quadrilateral (15/11). Relieved and to Mailly-Maillet (16/11), Terramesnil (17/11), Gézaincourt (19/11).

23rd (Service) Battalion (1st Sportsman's). 99th Brigade, 2nd Division: Entrained at Diéval for Longpré (20/7) and from there marched to Morlancourt. To Sandpit Valley (23/7), Bernafay Wood, Montauban Alley (24/7), Delville Wood (Campbell Street – westwards) (26/7). In action (27/7) – passed through Princess Street and on to final objective just inside northern edge of Delville. Regimental historian H.C. O'Neill records 288 casualties and the Battalion coming out of Delville Wood smoking German cigars. Withdrew to Bund support trench (29/7), Citadel Camp via Longueval Alley and Montauban (4/8). To Sandpit Camp (8/8), Méricourt (11/8), Fremont, via Amiens (13/8), Naours (16/8), Longuevillette (17/8), Authie (18/8), Bus-lès-Artois (20/8), front line Hébuterne sector (21/8), Sailly-au-Bois (25/8), front line (29/8), Couin (1/9), front line (16/9), Authie (20/9), Coigneux (30/9), Basin Wood (2/10), trenches in Redan-Serre sector (3/10), Mailly-Maillet (6/10), Raincheval (9/10), Mailly-Maillet (17/10), Redan-Serre sector (18/10), Mailly-Maillet (21/10), Acheux Wood (22/10), front line (30/10), Mailly-Maillet (2/11), front line (5/11), Bertrancourt (8/11). Moved forward 2.10 a.m. (13/11), assembling at Ellis Square, Fort Hoysted and View Trench. Later 'A' and 'C' Companies sent to 5th Brigade at White City. Provided carrying parties to forward area during operations at Redan Ridge. In support for attack on Munich Trench. Relieved and to Mailly-Maillet (17/11), Sarton (18/11), Gézaincourt (19/11).

24th (Service) Battalion (2nd Sportsman's). 5th Brigade, 2nd Division: Arrived Corbie (21/7). To Bernafay Wood (25/7), Trônes Wood (28/7), trenches between Delville Wood and Waterlot Farm (29/7). In action (30/7) – 'C' Company advanced towards German positions around Guillemont Station – heavy casualties in front of uncut wire – just 1 wounded officer and 11 other ranks returning out of attacking force of 117. To reserve line south-west of Montauban (31/7), Longueval Alley (1/8), Breslau Trench in support (5/8), Ville-sous-Corbie (11/8). Entrained at Méricourt for Saleux (13/8) and from there marched to Ailly-sur-Somme. To Flesselles (16/8), Candas (17/8), Bus-lès-Artois (18/8), support line south of Hébuterne (19/8), Green Street Trench (20/8), front line Beaumont-Hamel sector (23/8), Coigneux (30/8), front line (4/9), Green Street (10/9), Courcelles (11/9), front line Redan sector (17/9), Bus-lès-Artois (20/9), Thièvres (21/9), Bus-lès-Artois (2/10), Mailly-Maillet (3/10), front line (6/10), Léalvillers (9/10), Arquèves (16/10), Mailly-Maillet (22/10), front line (23/10), Mailly-Maillet (26/10), Arquèves (30/10), front line (3/11), Mailly-Maillet (10/11), front line (12/11). Attack on Beaumont Trench (13/11) – at 5.15 a.m. moved out in thick fog into No Man's Land – operation succesful – 5th Brigade taking all of its objectives along with many prisoners. Relieved and to Bertrancourt (15/11), Amplier (19/11).

26th (Service) Battalion (Bankers). 124th Brigade, 41st Division: Arrived Vauchelles-les-Quesnoy (31/8). Via Longpré, Méricourt to Fricourt (7/9), Bécordel-Bécourt (10/9), Montauban (14/9) and from there moved to forward trenches north-east of Delville Wood. Attack on Switch Line and Flers Trench (15/9). Casualties 264. In support line (16/9). To Dernancourt (18/9), Pommiers Redoubt (2/10), Thistle Dump (3/10), Gird Lines (5/10). Attacked (7/10) – came under heavy machine gun fire during assault on Bayonet Trench – some gains made and held until relieved by 21st K.R.R.C. and 10th Queens. Casualties – 254. To Caterpillar Wood (9/10), Bécordel-Bécourt (10/10), Buire-sur-l'Ancre (13/10). Entrained at Edgehill for Airaines (15/10). Entrained at Longpré for Méteren (18/10).

32nd (Service) Battalion (East Ham). 124th Brigade, 41st Division: Arrived Bellancourt from Ploegsteert area (24/8). To Ailly-le-Haut-Clocher (31/8), Bellancourt (1/9). Arrived Edgehill Station (8/9) and from there to Fricourt Camp. Via Montauban to trenches north-east of Delville Wood (15/9) – with 26th Battalion took part in attack. Casualties – 293. To Edgehill (18/9), Pommiers Redoubt (3/10), Gird Lines (4/10). Attack on Bayonet Trench (7/10). To Mametz Wood (11/10), Bécordel-Bécourt (12/10), Buire-sur-l'Ancre (14/10). Entrained at Méricourt for Longpré (16/10). Entrained at Longpré for Méteren (20/10).

37th (Labour) Battalion. Arrived Heilly (14/7) and from there to billets at Ville-sur-Ancre. Began work Fricourt, Mametz, Guillemont, Longueval areas.

King's (Liverpool Regiment)

1st Battalion. 6th Brigade, 2nd Division: Entrained at Bryas for Longueau (20/7) and from there marched to billets at Sailly-le-Sec. To Bois des Tailles (23/7). Moved up through Fricourt to trenches outside Carnoy (25/7). 'A' and 'B' Companies to Montauban (26/7). Stood by during attack on Delville Wood (27/7). Prqvided carrying parties to Longueval. Moved up to close support in Montauban Alley (28/7). To Bernafay and Trônes Woods (29/7). In action at Delville Wood (30/7) – War Diary records 'A' Company clearing out German snipers at point of bayonet. Relieved 13th Essex in Delville Wood (31/7). Relieved by 22nd Royal Fusiliers and to Mine Alley just north of Carnoy (1/8). To trenches east of Trônes Wood (7/8). Attack on Guillemont (8/8) – moved forward at 4.20 a.m. – War Diary records conditions as misty and very hard to see more than 10 yards. First objectives – (German front line, Guillemont Station, High Holborn) all carried. Relieved and via Mine Alley to Happy Valley (9/8). Casualties – 250. To Méaulte (12/8). Entrained at Méricourt for Saleux (13/8) and from there moved in buses to Yzeux. To Bernaville (17/8), Bois de Warnimont (18/8), Couin (20/8). Relieved 17th Middlesex in front line Serre sector (26/8). Relieved and to Couin (30/8). To front line (3/9), Couin (8/9), front line (11/9). 'A' Company carried out raid on enemy listening post (15/9). To Couin (16/9), Courcelles-au-Bois (17/9), Bus-lès-Artois (19/9), left sub section Hébuterne sector (1/10), Bertrancourt (4/10), Puchevillers (7/10), Bertrancourt (18/10), Mailly-Maillet (22/10), front line Serre sector south (24/10), Mailly-Maillet Wood (26/10), Aucheux (30/10), Bertrancourt (6/11), front line (9/11), Mailly-Maillet (11/11). Moved at night into front line (12/11) and took part in attack through The Quadrilateral (13/11). In action until relieved (16/11). After almost 4 days fierce fighting and some 255 casualties, entry in War diary dated (16/11) reads 'Relieved early in the morning – marched to Mailly-Maillet and picnicked in wood.' Later to Léalvillers and from there in buses to Vauchelles.

4th Battalion (Extra Reserve). 98th Brigade, 33rd Division: Entrained at Chocques for Longueau (8/7) and from there marched to Rainneville. To Ville-sur-Somme (11/7), Ville-sur-Corbie (12/7), Méaulte (13/7), old German line south of Fricourt (14/7), reserve positions just west of Bazentin-le-Petit Wood (15/7). Relieved 1st Middlesex in front line after attack between High Wood and Martinpuich (15/7). To valley east of Caterpillar Wood (17/7). Moved forward in support and dug in between Flatiron Copse and Sabot Copse (18/7) – enemy counter attacking at Delville Wood. To front line (cross roads north of Bazentin-le-Petit to quarry) (19/7). Relived and to Caterpillar Wood (20/7) – Dernancourt at 11.15 p.m. Relieved 1/9th Royal Scots south-east side of Mametz Wood (6/8). To Fricourt Wood (7/8), front line south corner of High Wood (13/8), Bazentin-le-Grand (14/8) – 2 companies in trenches north-east of village. To front line (17/8). 'B' and 'D' Companies attacked (18/8) – 'C' company in support – 'A' in reserve. Objective Wood Lane – War Diary records 'survivors came in at dusk.' Casualties – 227. War Diary entry for (18/8) also records 'One man to base under age.' Relieved by 1st Cameronians and to Mametz Wood (19/8). Later to position south of Fricourt Wood. To Mametz Wood in divisional reserve (24/8), Carlton Trench north of Bazentin-le-Grand (25/8). In support of 1st Middlesex and 2nd Argyll and Sutherland at front line – working party dug communication trench to join up battalions. Relieved and to bivouacs north of Dernancourt (30/8). By bus to Allonville (1/9) and from there marched to Cardonnette. To Candas (2/9), Barly (4/9), Nuncq-Hautecôte (5/9), Sus-St.Léger (8/9), Coullemont (10/9), Humbercamps (13/9), Bayencourt (19/9), front line Hébuterne sector (20/9), Bayencourt (25/9), Ivergny (1/10), Wanquetin (17/10), Ivergny (18/10), Daours (19/10), Méaulte (21/10), Trônes Wood (23/10), front line Lesbœufs sector (24/10). Attack and capture of Dewdrop Trench (28/10). Relieved and via Trônes Wood to Carnoy (29/10). To Trônes Wood (31/10), front line (1/11), La Briqueterie (4/11), Sandpit Camp (5/11). Entrained at Edgehill for Longpré (9/11) and from there marched to Huppy.

1/5th Battalion (T.F.). 165th Brigade, 55th (West Lancashire) Division: Arrived Longuevillette from Halloy (22/7). Entrained at Candas for Méricourt (25/7). To Bois des Tailles (28/7), Citadel Camp (30/7), Caftet Wood (1/8). Working parties to front line. To reserve line – Dublin and Casement Trenches (4/8), front line – Maltz Horn Farm area (5/8). War Diary notes trenches as very primitive – line irregular and confusing. 'B' company in support of attack on strong-point along Guillemont Road 8.30 p.m. – position consolidated and held. Attack on Guillemont 4.20 a.m. (8/8) – 'A' and 'B' Companies forced to dig in under heavy fire about 130 yards from start line – 'C' and 'D' made further advance south of village but also held up. 'A' Company dug trench through to its right and reached Cochrane Alley. War Diary records the wearing of bright tin discs on backs of jackets – purpose being to inform aerial observers of infantry's progress. Relieved and to Talus Boisé (9/8). Casualties – 311. To front line Maltz Horn Farm area (12/8). Relieved and to Caftet Wood (13/8). To Ville-sur-Ancre (14/8). Entrained at Méricourt for Pont-Remy (19/8) and from there marched to St. Maxent. Entrained at Pont-Remy for Méricourt (30/8) and from there marched to Dernancourt. To support line - Carlton and Savoy Trenches (4/9). Relieved 1/6th King's in front line (7/9). In action around Wood Lane and Tea Trench until relieved during night (10/9). To Buire (11/9), Dernancourt (16/9). War Diary records that film 'Battle of the Somme' was seen at Dernancourt. To Pommiers Redoubt (17/9) and from there to trenches Flers sector. To Green Trench north-east of Delville Wood (18/9), Pommiers Redoubt (19/9), Green Trench (23/9), Fosse Way, Flers Trench, Switch Trench (24/9). Moved forward to front line in support of 1/6th, 1/7th, 1/9th King's attack on Gird Lines (25/9). Objectives gained. 'D' Company with 1/4th South Lancashire dug communication trench to Gird Trench during night. Relieved and to Green Dump (26/9). To Pommiers Redoubt (28/9) and from there to Buire. Entrained at Méricourt for Longpré (1/10) and from there marched to Francieres. Entrained at Pont-Remy for Ypres sector (2/10).

1/6th (Rifle) Battalion (T.F.). 165th Brigade, 55th (West Lancashire) Division: Arrived Gézaincourt from Halloy (22/7). Entrained at Candas for Méricourt (25/7). To Bois des Tailles (28/7), Citadel Camp (30/7), Caftet Wood (1/8). Working parties to Trônes Wood and La Briqueterie. To support lines – Dublin and Casement Trenches (5/8), trenches in front of Maltz Horn Farm (7/8). 'C' Company dug new trench in advance of front line. Attack on Guillemont (8/8) – bombers in action down Cochrane Ally. Relieved and to Talus Boisé (12/8). 'C' Company attacked 4.30 a.m. (13/8) – War Diary notes advance to within 10 yards of German front line – heavy machine gun fire and bombs forced withdrawal. Rejoined Battalion. To Ville-sur-Ancre (14/8). Entrained at Méricourt for Martainneville (19/8) and from there marched to Oisemont. Entrained at Pont-Remy for Méricourt (30/8) and from there marched to bivouacs near Dernancourt. Relieved 12th Royal Fusiliers in trenches between High Wood and Delville Wood (Worcester, Orchard, Carlton) (4/9). Bombers attacked down Worcester Trench and 'C' Company assaulted strong-point at junction of Wood Lane and Orchard Trench 7 p.m. (6/9). Fighting continued to early morning – some ground gained. Relieved and to reserve at Montauban Alley (7/9). To front line (9/9) – successful attack on Wood Lane 4.45 p.m. Relieved and to bivouacs near Bécordel-Bécourt (10/9). To Buire (11/9), Dernancourt (16/9). Moved forward to support at Fosse Way just east of Flers (17/9). Withdrew to York Trench in front of Montauban (18/9), Pommiers Redoubt (20/9). To Fosse Way, Switch Trench, Flers Avenue (23/9). Moved forward in front of Flers (24/9). Attack on Gird Lines 12.35 p.m. (25/9) – War Diary records advance as 'completely successful' – enemy resistance easily dealt with – gains consolidated by nightfall. Casualties 153. Relieved and to York Trench (26/9). To Buire (28/9). Entrained at Méricourt for Longpré (1/10) and from there marched to Bellancourt. Entrained at Pont-Remy for Ypres sector (2/10).

1/7th Battalion (T.F.). 165th Brigade, 55th (West Lancashire) Division: Arrived Gézaincourt from Barly (21/7). Entrained at Candas for Méricourt (25/7). To Bois des Tailles (28/7), bivouacs near Fricourt (30/7), Caftet

Wood (1/8). Moved forward to support trenches near Talus Boisé (7/8). Relieved 1/5th King's in front line Maltz Horn Farm sector (9/8). Withdrew to Caftet Wood (13/8). Casualties since (8/8) – 158. To Ville-sur-Ancre (14/8). Entrained at Méricourt for Pont-Remy (19/8) and from there marched to Oisemont. Entrained at Pont-Remy for Méricourt (30/8) and from there to bivouacs near Dernancourt. To trenches between High Wood and Delville Wood (4/9). Bombing attack on Tea Tench (6/9). Relieved and to Buire (11/9). To Dernancourt (16/9), front line trenches Flers sector (17/9). Relieved and to support line – Carlton and Savoy Trenches (18/9). To Pommiers Redoubt (20/9), front line (23/9). Attacked and gained possession of Goat Trench, Gird Lines, sunken road (Gueudecourt-Factory Corner) (25/9). Withdrew to Carlton and Savoy Trenches (26/9). Casualties since (23/9) – 279. To Buire (28/9). Entrained at Méricourt for Longpré (1/10) and from there marched to Buigny-l'Abbé. Entrained at Pont-Remy for Ypres sector (2/10).

1/8th (Irish) Battalion (T.F.). 164th Brigade, 55th (West Lancashire) Division): Moved from Ivergny to Gézaincourt (21/7). To Fienvillers (22/7). Entrained at Candas for Méricourt (25/7) and from there marched to Méaulte. To Happy Valley (26/7), trenches east of Trônes Wood (30/7). Attacked along sunken road to Guillemont (2/8). Relieved and to Bronfay Farm (4/8). To forward trenches (7/8). Attack on Guillemont (8/8) – advanced over first line trenches and into village without great loss. To the right and left assault was not successful and subsequently enemy closed in to the rear. Relieved by 1/5th North Lancashire (9/8) and to Bronfay Farm. Casualties – 570. To Méricourt (14/8). Entrained for Pont-Remy (19/8) and from there marched to Bouillancourt ('A' and 'B' Companies) and Miannay ('C' and 'D'). Entrained at Abbeville for Méricourt (30/8) and from there to bivouacs just north-west of Dernancourt. To huts off main Albert-Amiens Road (31/8), Montauban defences (7/9), support line (8/9). Took part in attack on Hop and Ale Alley east of Delville Wood (9/9). Held gains until relieved (12/9). To Ribemont (13/9), Buire (16/9), camp just outside Bécordel-Bécourt (17/9), reserve line Delville Wood (18/9), Mametz (19/9), Savoy and Carlton Trenches (21/9), support positions near Flers (25/9), front line (26/9). Attack on Gird lines (27/9) – objective from Factory Corner (Gueudecourt Road) to Ligny-Thilloy Road. Relieved and to Mametz (28/9), Dernancourt (29/9). Entrained at Edgehill for Longpré (1/10) and from there marched to L'Etoile. Entrained at Longpré for Poperinghe (2/10).

1/9th Battalion (T.F.). 165th Brigade, 55th (West Lancashire) Division: From Halloy to Autheux (22/7). Entrained at Candas for Méricourt (26/7). To Bois des Tailles (28/7), Citadel Camp (30/7), bivouacs just south-west of Caftet Wood (1/8). Relieved 1/8th King's near Trônes Wood (4/8). Battalion historian E.H.G. Roberts notes Death Valley to the right littered with corpses of men and horses. Relieved 2/5th Lancashire Fusiliers in front line Arrow Head Copse (5/8). E.H.G. Roberts records 60 casualties from shelling during short journey forward. To Talus Boisé (7/8), trenches Maltz Horn Farm area (10/8). Conditions in this position are noted – feet, hands and faces of the dead protruded from sides of trenches – corpses covered with flies rotted in the heat – smell nauseating. In action at Cochrane Alley (12/8) – 'A' and 'B' Companies attacked at 5.15 p.m. – objective reached by 5.45 p.m. – bombers advanced up Cochrane Alley. War Diary records withdrawal under heavy fire at 11.45 p.m. – block in Cochrane held. Relieved by 1/10th King's and to Caftet Wood (13/8), Ville-sur-Ancre (14/8). Entrained at Méricourt for Martainneville (19/8) and from there marched to Ramburelles. E.H.G. Roberts records this village as possibly the most insanitary the Battalion had ever visited. Entrained at Pont-Remy for Méricourt (30/8). To Dernancourt (31/8), reserve trenches Montauban Alley (4/9), front line between Delville Wood and High Wood (7/9). In action Wood Lane and Tea Trench. Relieved (10/9). To Buire (11/9), camp just outside Dernancourt (16/9). War Diary notes heavy shelling and camp moved to new location. E.H.G. Roberts records cinema show in evening – programme 'The Battle of The Somme.' To front line Flers sector (17/9). Relieved and to York Trench (18/9), Pommiers Redoubt (20/9). Relieved 1/5th King's Own in front line (23/9). In action – Goat Trench, Gird lines, Grove Alley (25/9). Relieved and to York Trench (26/9), Buire (28/9). Entrained at Méricourt for Longpré (1/10) and from there marched to Cocquerel. Entrained at Pont-Remy for Ypres Sector (2/10). Somme casualties recorded in Battalion history as 650.

1/10th (Scottish) Battalion (T.F.). 166th Brigade, 55th (West Lancashire) Division: Moved from Sombrin to Bouquemaison (20/7). To Bernaville (21/7). Entrained at Candas for Méricourt (25/7) and from there marched to Ville-sur-Ancre. To Sandpit Camp (27/7), Mansell Copse (30/7). Here, Battalion historian A.M. McGilchrist records – bombardment by German aeroplanes. Moved forward to Machine Gun Copse south of Montauban (31/7). In reserve at Talus Boisé (1/8)–(7/8). Carried out work digging communication trenches and cable trenches in Bernafay and Trônes Woods. To bivouacs at Great Bear (7/8), trenches in front of Guillemont (8/8). Attacked at 4.20 a.m. (9/8) – left boundary being Trônes Wood-Guillemont Road. Four separate charges made – each driven back. Withdrew to support trenches and Great Bear (10/8). Casualties – 280. Always associated with the attack at Guillemont will be the heroism of Captain Noel Chavasse, medical officer of 1/10th King's. During (9/8) he tended wounded out in the open throughout attack. The following night searched for and brought in many casualties. He later, and always in range of the enemy, personally led stretcher parties. For his gallantry at Guillemont Noel Chavasse was awarded the Victoria Cross. A Bar being posthumously received for his action in front of Wieltje between 31st July and 2nd August 1917. To Talus Boisé (12/8), front line (13/8), Great Bear (14/8), Méaulte (15/8). Entrained at Edgehill for Martainneville (19/8) and from there marched to billets in Valines and St. Mard: To Moyenneville (29/8). Entrained at Pont-Remy for Méricourt (30/8). To bivouacs near Belle Vue Farm (31/8). Casualties for August given in War Diary as 89 killed, 214 wounded, 32 missing. Relieved 1st North Staffordshire in reserve trenches Montauban (5/9). Began work on new front line north of Delville Wood (7/9). New line taken over (8/9). Relieved by 23rd Middlesex and to Ribemont (11/9). To bivouacs near Albert (16/9), Pommiers Redoubt (17/9), Switch Trench (18/9) and in evening relieved 1/6th Battalion in Fosse Way and Flers Avenue. Relieved and to Pommiers (23/9), Ribemont (28/9). Entrained at Méricourt for Longpré (30/9) and from there marched to Pont-Remy. Casualties for September – 124. Entrained at Abbeville for Proven (2/10).

11th (Service) Battalion (Pioneers). Pioneers, 14th (Light) Division: Arrived Outrebois and Frohen-le-Grand from Arras sector (29/7). To Beaumetz (1/8). Entrained at Candas for Méricourt (7/8) and from there marched to camp just south-west of Albert. To Fricourt (12/8). Work carried out throughout operations at Delville Wood until relieved (30/8). To camp just south-east of Heilly. Entrained at Méricourt for Airaines (31/8) and from there marched to Tailly. Entrained at Airaines for Dernancourt (11/9) and from there to Fricourt Wood. Work began in vicinity of Delville Wood and on Bernafay Wood to Longueval Road. To camp Albert-Amiens Road north of Buire (17/9), Ivergny (22/9).

12th (Service) Battalion. 61st Brigade, 20th (Light) Division: Arrived Doullens from Ypres sector (25/7) and marched via Halloy, Thièvres and Authie to Bois de Warnimont. To Bus–les–Artois (26/7), bivouacs between Mailly–Maillet and Colincamps (27/7). Relieved 15th Royal Welsh Fusiliers in front line south–west of Serre (28/7). Relieved and to Mailly–Maillet (3/8), Couin (7/8). Relieved 12th Rifle Brigade facing Serre (14/8). To Couin (16/8), Authie (17/8), Gézaincourt (18/8). Entrained at Candas for Méricourt (20/8) and from there marched to Morlancourt. To Happy Valley (21/8). Relieved 1st Royal Fusiliers in support Bernafay Wood (22/8). To front line near Trônes Wood (25/8). Relieved and to old British line north–east of Carnoy (27/8). To support line facing Guillemont (31/8), craters at Carnoy (2/9). Moved forward to assembly trenches east of Bernafay Wood (3/9) and in action at Guillemont. Relieved and to craters (5/9). Casualties – 187. To

Sandpit Camp (6/9). War Diary notes that upon relief (complete by 5.30 a.m.) Sergeant D. Jones with two Lewis gun teams remained in the line – the incoming battalion (9th Border) having brought no Lewis guns. With most of his party killed, Sergeant Jones held his position against several strong attacks until relieved next morning, arriving at Sandpit Camp at 9.10 a.m. For his gallantry and leadership Sergeant Jones was awarded the Victoria Cross. To Méricourt–l'Abbe (8/9), Ault (10/9), Sandpit Camp (12/9), Citadel Camp (14/9). Assembled at Talus Boisé (15/9) and moved via Montauban and Bernafay Wood to positions south of Delville Wood. Entrenched along Waterlot Farm–Longueval Road. Moved forward east of Ginchy (16/9) and in attack on Lesbœufs. Relieved and via Dummy Trench between Bernafay and Trônes Woods to Carnoy craters (17/9). To line opposite Lesbœufs (19/9), Carnoy craters (20/9), camp near Citadel (21/9), Meaulte (22/9), Citadel (25/9). Moved forward to Maltz Horn Valley (26/9) and later to line west of Morval. Relieved and to Maricourt (28/9). To Longueval (29/9) and into support line near Gueudecourt. To front line (2/11). Relieved and to bivouacs east of Bernafay Wood (4/11). To front line (6/11). Attack on Rainbow and Cloudy Trenches (7/11) – both objectives taken. Casualties – 215. Relieved by 11th Essex and to Montauban (8/11). To Meaulte (9/11), Corbie (15/11), Allonville (19/11), Fremont and Vaux (20/11).

13th (Service) Battalion. 9th Brigade, 3rd Division: Arrived Doullens (2/7) and from there marched to Bernaville. To Vignacourt (4/7), Bertangles (5/7), Lahoussoye (6/7), Morlancourt (7/7), trenches north of Carnoy (9/7). In attack at Bazentin–le–Grand (14/7). Held captured positions until relieved (19/7) and to bivouacs east of Talus Boisé. To Delville Wood (22/7). In action (23/7). To Sandpit Camp (24/7), Ville–sur–Ancre (27/7), Sandpit Camp (11/8), forward positions Guillemont (14/8). Attack on German lines south of village (16/8) – forced to fall back to start positions. Casualties – 389. Relieved and to Citadel Camp (18/8), Ville–sur–Ancre (21/8). Entrained at Méricourt for Candas (23/8). To Barly (25/8). Transferred to Béthune sector (27/8). Entrained at St Pol for Puchevillers (7/10) and from there marched to Bertrancourt. To Mailly–Maillet Wood (8/10), front line (HQ in Legend Trench) (13/10). Relieved and to Louvencourt (19/10). Employed on road cleaning. Relieved 1st Royal Scots Fusiliers in left sub section Serre sector (4/11). To Courcelles (7/11), reserve positions at Jerimiah Trench (12/11), right sub sector (Legend Trench) (14/11). Relieved and to Bus Wood (15/11).

17th (Service) Battalion (1st City). 89th Brigade, 30th Division: On right of 89th Brigade for attack at Montauban (1/7). From trenches north of Maricourt took objectives – Casement and Dublin Trenches. Gains held until relieved.

To Bois des Tailles (4/7), Trigger Wood (8/7), old British line north of Maricourt (9/7). Took part in operations at Trônes Wood (10/7)–(12/7). From Trigger Wood to Bois des Tailles (13/7). To Corbie (14/7), Happy Valley (19/7), Citadel Camp (20/7). Moved forward to assembly positions (29/7). Attack on Guillemont (30/7) – in support of 19th and 20th King's. Relieved and to Citadel (31/7). Casualties – 296. Entrained at Dernancourt for Longpré (2/8) and from there marched to Doudelainville. Entrained at Pont–Remy for Merville (3/8). Arrived Doullens (19/9) and marched to Gézaincourt. To Vignacourt (21/9), Dernancourt (4/10), assembly tenches north–east of Eaucourt l'Abbaye (10/10). Attacked (12/10) – unsuccessful due to uncut enemy wire, heavy machine gun fire and bombardment. Casualties – about 273. Relieved and to positions just west of Montauban (13/10). To brigade reserve at Crest Trench (20/10), Mametz Wood (22/10), Buire (24/10). Entrained at Edgehill for Doullens (25/10) and from there marched to Halloy.

18th (Service) Battalion (2nd City). 21st Brigade, 30th Division: Attack at Montauban (1/7) – War Diary records assault as being pressed with great spirit and determination in spite of heavy shelling and machine gun fire. Whole system of German trenches including – Glatz Redoubt captured. Casualties estimated at just over 500. Withdrew to original line east of Talus Boisé (2/7). To Bois des Tailles (4/7), assembly trenches at Oxford and Cambridge Copse (7/7), Train Alley (8/7). In support during operations at Trônes Wood. Relieved and to Trigger Wood (9/7), Morlancourt (11/7), Welcome Wood (13/7), Fourdrinoy (14/7). Entrained at Ailly–sur–Somme for Méricourt (18/7) and from there to Morlancourt. To bivouacs near Mansell Copse (20/7), moved forward to positions around – Glatz Redoubt and La Briqueterie (22/7). Relieved and to Happy Valley (23/7), Talus Boisé (30/7), Happy Valley (31/7). Entrained at Méricourt for Longpré (2/8) and from there marched to Mérélessart. Entrained at Longpré for Berguette (3/8) and from there marched to Robecq – Givenchy sector. Entrained at Fouquereuil for Doullens (18/9) and from there marched to Amplier. To Naours (21/9), Ribemont (5/10), Pommiers Redoubt (6/10), Flers support trenches (11/10), front line (14/10), support trenches west of Goose Alley (16/10). Assembled for attack (17/10). Assaulted Gird Lines 3.40 a.m. (18/10) – advanced checked by German barrage – right of line met by uncut wire and heavy machine gun fire – attack came to a standstill. Withdrew to support west of Goose Alley. To front line (19/10), Pommiers Redoubt (21/10), Dernancourt (25/10), Lucheux (26/10), Bailleulmont (29/10).

19th (Service) Battalion (3rd City). 89th Brigade, 30th Division: Acted as Brigade carriers during operations at Montauban (1/7)–(4/7). Relieved and to Bois des Tailles. To Billon Valley (7/7), Talus Boisé (8/7). Took part in operations at Trônes Wood (9/7)– (12/7). Relieved and to Trigger Wood. To Bois des Tailles (13/7), Welcome Wood (14/7), Happy Valley (19/7), bivouacs north of Citadel Camp (20/7), Maltz Horn Trench (29/7). On left of 89th Brigade's attack towards Arrow Head Copse 4.45 a.m. (30/7) – War Diary records objectives reached but with heavy losses – gains had to evacuate owing to no reinforcements. At 12 noon roll call was 7 officers and 43 men. Relieved and to Citadel (31/7). Casualties – 436. Entrained at Edgehill for Longpré (2/8) and from there marched to Huppy. Entrained at Pont–Remy for Merville (4/8). Entrained at Lillers for Doullens (18/9) and marched to Gézaincourt. To Vignacourt (21/9). Moved by motor buses to Ribemont (4/10) and from there marched to Dernancourt. To support trenches north–west of Flers (10/10). In reserve Flers Trench (11/10), support during attack (12/10), reserve at Switch and Crest Trenches (13/10)–(16/10). To front line – Gird Trench (16/10). Relieved and to bivouacs west of Caterpillar Wood (19/10), Mametz Wood (22/10), Buire (24/10). Entrained for Doullens (26/10) and from there marched to Halloy.

20th (Service) Battalion (4th City). 89th Brigade, 30th Division: From positions just north of Maricourt advanced on left of 89th Brigade's attack at Montauban (1/7) – War Diary records – after 65 minutes intensive bombardment Battalion advanced 7.30 a.m. – "lines advanced through enemy's artillery fire as though on parade in quick time." With first and second objectives taken (Casement and Dublin Trenches) – No.4 Company went on at 12.20 p.m. to take La Briqueterie. Relieved and to Bois des Tailles (4/7). To Trigger Wood Valley (8/7), Maricourt (9/7). Relieved 2nd Royal Scots Fusiliers at Maltz Horn Trench (10/7). Bombers attacked German held section of Maltz Horn Trench (11/7) – objective taken and held against strong counter attacks. Relieved and to Maricourt (12/7). To Bois des Tailles (13/7), Welcome Wood (14/7), Vaux–sur–Somme (18/7), Happy Valley (19/7), bivouacs north of Citadel Camp (20/7), Maltz Horn Trench (29/7). On right of 89th Brigade's attack between Arrow Head Copse and Maltz Horn Farm (30/7) – moved forward at 4.45 a.m. War Diary records thick mist reducing visibility down to not more than 10 yards. German front trenches overran – Hardecourt–Guillemont Road reached – all gains held and consolidated. Relieved and to bivouacs north of Citadel (31/7). Casualties – 373. Entrained at Edgehill for Longpré (2/8) and from there marched to Huppy. Entrained at Pont–Remy for Merville (4/8). Entrained at Lillers for Doullens (18/9) and from there to Gézaincourt. To Vignacourt (21/9), Dernancourt (4/10), bivouacs near Marlborough Wood (10/10), assembly trenches near Eaucourt l'Abbaye (11/10). In support during 89th Brigade's attack on Gird Lines (12/10) – War Diary records British aeroplane crashing on Battalion lines at 2.40 p.m. Relieved and to Crest Trench (13/10), bivouacs near Marlborough Wood (14/10). Moved forward to Flers support (16/10), front line – Factory Corner (19/10). Relieved and to bivouacs near Mametz Wood (22/10), Buire (24/10). Entrained at Edgehill –for Doullens (26/10) and marched to Halloy.

Norfolk Regiment

1st Battalion. 15th Brigade, 5th Division: Reached positions near Montauban (16/7). Moved forward for operations at High Wood (21/7). To Pommiers Redoubt (25/7), front line (26/7). In action at Longueval (27/7)–(29/7). Came under heavy bombardment while forming up for attack – Lieutenant-Colonel P.V.P. Stone (Commanding Officer) noting that 'A' Company could hardly muster 1 platoon, most of the rest having been buried by the shelling. Official History of The Great War records that nevertheless – attack started punctually and the Norfolk on the right pushed well forward inside western edge of Delville Wood. Relieved and to Pommiers Redoubt (29/7). Casualties since (21/7) – 429. To front line and support positions Longueval (31/7). Relieved and to Le Quesnoy south-east of Abbeville (3/8). Returned to forward area (24/8) – reaching bivouacs near Bronfay Farm (26/8). In reserve to 95th Brigade's attack towards Leuze Wood (3/9). Moved opposite Falfemont Farm and attacked 3.10 p.m. (4/9) – 'A' and 'B' Companies led assault on front of 500 yards – few men of 'A' Company reached south-west corner of farm – but soon bombed out. All but 2 officers were killed or wounded – progress only possible by crawling from one shell hole to another. Objective taken by 3 a.m. (5/9). Withdrew to trenches north of Hardecourt 3.15 p.m. – in evening to Billon Farm. Casualties – 369. To Citadel Camp (7/9), Morlancourt (9/9), Waterlot Farm (16/9), positions between Guillemont and Wedge Wood (18/9). Attack on Morval (25/9). In his history of the Norfolk Regiment F. Loraine Petre records that Lieutenant-Colonel Stone had received permission to lead the attack in person. Due to the fact that his battalion had recently received large drafts from other regiments, and that the new men had not yet settled down. The C.O. is said to have accounted for quite a number of the enemy – treating the attack as a pheasant shoot with his servant acting as loader. Relieved and to Citadel Camp (27/9). Entrained at Dernancourt for Longpré (29/9). Entrained for Béthune area (1/10).

7th (Service) Battalion. 35th Brigade, 12th (Eastern) Division: Marched to Hénencourt Wood (1/7) and in evening in reserve behind embankment of Albert-Arras railway. Moved into assembly trenches for attack on Ovillers (2/7). In reserved during attack (3/7) – taking over and holding Brigade front from Dorset Road to Barrow Road. Relieved and to Albert-Bouzincourt line (6/7). To Albert (8/7), Varennes (10/7), Bois de Warnimont (11/7). Attached to 4th Division at Authie. Rejoined 12th Division at Bertrancourt (21/7). Later to Bouzincourt and Varennes. Moved forward to support positions Ovillers sector (7/8), front line (9/8). Attack on Skyline Trench 10.30 p.m. (12/8) – strong-points established and held. Relieved and to Bouzincourt

(13/8), Bois de Warnimont (16/8). Transferred to Arras sector (17/8). Returned to Somme and reserve positions at Bernafay Wood (2/10). To front line Gueudecourt (10/10). Attack on Bayonet and Scabbard Trenches (12/10) – advance met with heavy machine gun fire from both flanks and later uncut wire. Withdrew to trenches near Flers. Casualties – 221. To Mametz Wood (19/10), Dernancourt (22/10) and moved by buses to Arras sector.

8th (Service) Battalion. 53rd Brigade, 18th (Eastern) Division: Assembled just north of Carnoy for attack south-west of Montauban (1/7) – 'C' and 'D' Companies took Mine Trench, Mine Support and Bund Support without difficulty by 8.40 a.m. Regimental historian F. Loraine Petre records the advance as 'not so easy.' Casualties – 'D' Company on left reduced to about 90 men and commanded by R.S.M. Raven – 'C' had only 2 subalterns left and not more than 100 men. Pommiers Trench, The Loop and Montauban Alley later taken. Relieved and to Carnoy (3/7). Casualties – 385. Working parties clearing battlefield and digging communication trench between Montauban Alley and Caterpillar Wood. To camp south of Bronfay Farm (7/7), Grove Town Camp (8/7), Trigger Valley (14/7), Talus Boisé (18/7). Attack on Delville Wood (19/7) – advanced from south-western edge of Longueval about 7.15 a.m. – after hard fighting cleared southern end of wood – captured positions held against heavy bombardment until relieved (less 'A' Company) (22/7). Withdrew to Grove Town Camp. Casualties – 293. 'A' Company rejoins (23/7) and then entrained for Longpré. Transferred to Armentières sector (26/7). Arrived Acheux from Halloy (11/9). To Léalvillers (12/9), Bouzincourt via Acheux (17/9), Forceville (18/9). Moved forward to Authuille Wood in Brigade support for operations at Thiepval and Schwaben Redoubt (25/9). Withdrew to Forceville (29/9) – 'B' Company remaining at Crucifix Corner on burial detail until (30/9). To North Bluff, Authuille (2/10). Attack and capture of Schwaben Redoubt (5/10). Relieved and later to Candas. To Albert (16/10). Successful attack on Regina Trench (21/10) – gains held until relieved (23/10). From Albert took turns in trenches north of Pozières. To Warloy (5/11), Albert and trenches north of Pozières (8/11), Ovillers (13/11).

9th (Service) Battalion. 71st Brigade, 6th Division: Arrived Candas (3/8) and from there marched to Mailly-Maillet. To front line trenches (14/8), Mailly-Maillet (20/8), Louvencourt (26/8), Beauval (28/8), Flesselles (29/8), Méricourt (5/9), Sandpit Camp (8/9). Moved forward to positions south of Trônes Wood (11/9). Took up line on Ginchy-Leuze Wood Road for attack on The Quadrilateral (15/9). Advance is recorded as being with insufficient artillery support – barrage having gap of 200 yards just in front of The Quadrilateral to allow advance of tanks. Leading waves held up by uncut wire and forced to retire. Relieved at midnight and via trenches south of

Guillemont to Trônes Wood. Casualties – 431. To Ville-sur-Ancre (19/9), bivouacs north of Carnoy (24/9), Bernafay Wood (25/9), trenches north east of Ginchy (26/9), bivouacs north of Carnoy (1/10). Moved forward into line near Gueudecourt (16/10). Attack on Mild Trench (18/10) – objective taken after hard fighting. Commanding Officer Lieutenant-Colonel Prior later went forward and recorded the garrison holding gained positions as being in good spirits – 'they had been heavily shelled, sniped at, machine gunned and at least once counter-attacked.' Second-Lieutenant Cubitt (in a letter) mentions that thick mud had rendered some rifles useless and captured German weapons were used. He also describes how a periscope was hit at both ends while in use and another occasion when a helmet was held up to attract enemy sniper fire. A bullet having hit the helmet then ricochetted and went through a sergeant's cheek just below the eye. The N.C.O was later seen laughing and joking and peering through the hole that had been made in the helmet. Relieved during night (19/10) and to Corbie, casualties – 248. Transferred to Béthune sector (24/10).

Lincolnshire Regiment

1st Battalion. 62nd Brigade, 21st Division: In reserve at Méaulte during opening of attack on Fricourt (1/7). Moved forward 8 a.m. – carrying parties began taking ammunition to forward line. Later consolidated captured positions at Crucifix Trench. Attack on Birch Tree and Shelter Woods 9 a.m. (3/7) – 'B' Company reached objective without serious loss – 'A' on right came under heavy fire from both flanks suffering high casualties. Commanding Officer Lieutenant-Colonel D.H.F. Grant, D.S.O. led attack and was seriously wounded in the head. Objectives cleared by 4.30 p.m. War Diary notes capture of 700 prisoners and losses of 243 all ranks. Entrained at Dernancourt for Ailly-sur-Somme (4/7) and from there marched to Argœuves. To Oissy (7/7). Entrained at Ailly-sur-Somme for Corbie (10/7) and from there marched to Méaulte. To Mametz Wood in reserve (11/7). Heavy shelling noted during night (12/7). Casualties – 121. Relieved midnight (17/7) and to Buire. Casualties since (11/7) – 161. War Diary notes the Bermuda Volunteer Rifle Contingent (attached to battalion) was busily employed carrying for 62nd Trench Mortar Battery. Entrained at Dernancourt for Saleux (20/7) and from there marched to Oissy. Entrained at Longueau for Arras sector (23/7). Entrained at Frévent for Albert (14/9) and from there marched to Dernancourt. To Bécordel-Bécourt (15/9), Pommiers Redoubt (16/9) – moved forward 9.30 p.m. and took over reserve trenches north end of Bernafay Wood. 'A' and 'B' Companies to support at Gap Trench (17/9) and later took over front line facing Lesbœufs. Relieved (19/9). Bombers sent forward for attack down Gas Alley towards Gird Trench (20/9) – enemy driven back about 100 yards. To camp a mile south-west of Fricourt (22/9). Moved forward via Pommiers Redoubt to Gap and Switch Trenches (24/9). Attack on Gird Lines (25/9) – attached to 64th Brigade – 'A' and 'C' Companies advanced from support line at 12.35 p.m. – halted by heavy shelling after 50 yards. On right – War Diary notes that the men bayoneted and bombed their way up Gas Alley until thinned in numbers by heavy casualties – advance of 'B' and 'D' Companies recorded as over distance of 1,500 yards – 'as if on parade without in any way having their morale shaken.' Withdrawn to sunken road between Lesbœufs and Flers. Casualties – 174. To Switch Trench early morning (26/9) and from there bivouacs north of Bernafay Wood. Moved forward to support lines (Gird and Pioneer Trenches, dug-outs in Bulls Road) (29/9), Bernafay Wood (1/10), camp north of Dernancourt (2/10). Entrained at Edgehill for Longpré (4/10) and from there marched to Vauchelles. Entrained at Longpré for Loos Sector (8/10).

2nd Battalion. 25th Brigade, 8th Division: Attack on Ovillers (1/7) – War

Diary records – in positions by 3.30 a.m – wire along whole of front reported cut. Leading waves moved into No Man's Land 7.25 a.m. – German front line reached under heavy fire – 200 yards taken by 7.50 after fierce fighting. Commanding Officer Lieutenant-Colonel Reginald Bastard records that after 2–3 hours fighting in German front line only he and 1 other officer were left – 'and we had bullet holes in our clothing.' Counter attacks forced withdrawal after 9 a.m. Relieved by 6th Royal West Kent at midnight and to Long Valley. Casualties – 471. Entrained at Dernancourt for Ailly-sur-Somme (2/7) and from there marched to St. Sauveur. To Fourdrinoy (5/7). Entrained at Longueau for Béthune sector (8/7). Arrived Pont-Remy from Lillers (14/10) and from there marched to Airaines. To Ville in motor buses (16/10) and from there marched to Citadel Camp. Moved forward to Trônes Wood (19/10) and from there relieved 8th Bedfordshire in front line trenches near Lesbœufs. Attack on Zenith Trench 2.30 p.m. (23/10) – War Diary notes 'gallant' German officer leading his men down parapet – assault held up by strong rifle fire. Withdrew to Rose Trench in Brigade support. Casualties – 272. To Trônes Wood (27/10), Citadel Camp (29/10), Méaulte (3/11), La Briqueterie (8/11). War Diary notes enemy aircraft dropped 2 bombs about 8 p.m. – 5 casualties. Relieved 1st Notts and Derby in trenches near Lesbœufs (9/11). To Guillemont (11/11), front line (14/11), Carnoy (16/11), Sandpit Camp (17/11). Entrained at Edgehill for Airaines (19/11) and from there marched to Heucourt.

1/4th Battalion (T.F.). 138th Brigade, 46th (North Midland) Division: Dug shallow trench in front of British line facing Gommecourt Park during night (30/6). Positioned between attacking divisions (56th and 46th) for attack on Gommecourt (1/7) – this activity intended to draw enemy's fire. Withdrawn to Foncquevillers and later to Hannescamps sector. Arrived Mézerolles from Mondicourt (1/11). To Maison Ponthieu (2/11), Agenvillers (3/11), Neuilly-l'Hôpital (11/11).

1/5th Battalion (T.F.). 138th Brigade, 46th (North Midland) Division: At 8.30 a.m. (1/7) moved from positions 1,000 yards east of Souastre to reserve line at Midland Trench. Advanced through Foncquevillers and Roberts Avenue to front line 9.30 p.m. – War Diary notes trenches full of dead bodies, badly battered by shell fire – wounded coming in from No Man's Land. Sent forward at midnight to assist Sherwood Foresters of 139th Brigade then fighting in enemy's front line at Gommecourt Park – direction lost in darkness – withdrawal forced under heavy fire. Relieved and to Foncquevillers (3/7) and from there moved to Hannescamps sector. Arrived Béalcourt from Halloy (1/11). To Coulonvillers (2/11), Agenvillers (3/11).

6th (Service) Battalion. 33rd Brigade, 11th (Northern) Division: Entrained at Frévent for Acheux (2/9) and from there marched to Léalvillers. To Bouzincourt (5/9). Took over trenches north of Ovillers (12/9). 'C' Company captured and consolidated Constance Trench during night (15/9). Bombing attack on Joseph Trench driven back 10 a.m. (17/9). Enemy counter attack on Constance Trench repulsed during evening. Relieved and to Donnet Post during night (19/9). Moved forward to Ration Trench in support of attack on Thiepval (26/9). Later to Constance Trench. Two companies moved up to Schwaben Trench in support of 7th South Staffordshire 12 a.m. (27/9). Relieved 6th Border in Hessian, Zollern and Schwaben Trenches (29/9) – in support during 32nd Brigade's attack on Stuff Redoubt. Relieved and to Hédauville (30/9). To Léalvillers (1/10), Heuzecourt (2/10), Cramont (3/10), Fieffes (14/11), Vadencourt (15/11), Hédauville (16/11).

7th (Service) Battalion. 51st Brigade, 17th (Northern) Division: Moved forward from Heilly to Bécourt Wood (1/7) and from there relieved 6th Dorsetshire in front line at Fricourt. Attacked towards village 12.15 p.m. (2/7) – first objective reached by 12.50 p.m. – held up at second by machine gun fire from Fricourt Wood. In support (3/7) – Railway Alley taken. Relieved and to Ville during night (4/7). Casualties – 214. Moved forward to Quadrangle Trench (7/7) – withdrew to old front line at Fricourt same evening. To Quadrangle Trench (8/7). Bombers and 'B' company in action at Pearl Alley (9/7). Relieved and to Méaulte (11/7). To Foudrinoy (12/7). Casualties since (1/7) – 337. To Yaucourt (14/7). Entrained at Hangest for Méricourt (23/7). To Pommiers Trench (1/8), Montauban Alley (4/8), support positions Longueval and Delville Wood (7/8). Dug trench eastwards from Piccadilly (9/8). Relieved and to bivouacs near Fricourt (10/8). Casualties since (1/8) – 188. To bivouacs near Dernancourt (12/8). Entrained at Méricourt for Candas (15/8) and from there marched to Gézaincourt. To Bouquemaison (16/8), St. Amand (17/8). Relieved 1/16th London in trenches Foncquevillers sector (19/8). To St. Amand (27/8), front line (4/9), Mondicourt (11/9), Halloy (12/9), Bayencourt (15/9). Began duty in line Hébuterne sector (16/9). Relieved and to Gaudiempré (20/9). To Halloy (22/9), Barly (23/9), Maison-Ponthieu (24/9), Remaisnil (2/10), Halloy (4/10), Sailly-au-Bois (5/10), front line Hébuterne sector (8/10), Sailly-au-Bois (11/10), Souastre (14/10), Lucheux (19/10), Méricourt (22/10), Citadel Camp (27/10), Montauban (31/10). Relieved 7th Border in support lines between Lesbœufs and Gueudecourt (1/11). To front line (Zenith Trench) (2/11). Enemy counter attacks repulsed (3/11) – 'A' Company and bombers attacked and captured enemy held section of Zenith Trench 5 p.m. – held against counter attacks. Relieved and to camp south side Montauban-Carnoy Road (5/11). To support positions German Dump and Needle Trench (9/11). 'A' and 'C' companies to front line (Monsoon and Zenith Trenches) (10/11). Relieved (12/11). To Trônes Wood (13/11), Mansell Camp (14/11), Méaulte (15/11). Entrained at Edgehill for Hangest (16/11) and from there marched to Crouy-St. Pierre. To Picquigny (17/11).

8th (Service) Battalion. 63rd Brigade, 21st and 37th Divisions: In support of 21st Division's attack at Fricourt (1/7). Advanced 8.40 a.m. – heavy casualties while crossing No Man's Land – reinforced 8th Somerset Light Infantry on left of assault – bombing attacks gained further ground. By evening holding positions from Dart Alley to Lozenge Alley. Casualties – 251. Entrained at Dernancourt for Ailly-sur-Somme (4/7) and from there marched to Vaux-en-Amiénois. To Talmas (7/7) and there transferred with 63rd Brigade to 37th Division. To Mondicourt (8/7). Relieved 1/5th Lincolnshire in trenches Hannescamps sector (11/7). Relieved and to Humbercamps (14/7). Began move away from Somme area. Arrived Raincheval from Amplier (22/10). To Beauval (30/10), Lucheux (8/11), Acheux Wood (12/11). Moved forward to Martinsart (14/11) and during evening took over captured positions around Beaucourt. In action (18/11) – gained ground in Muck Trench, west to Leave Avenue. Relieved (20/11) and to Mailly-Maillet. Casualties – 175.

10th (Service) Battalion (Grimsby). 101st Brigade, 34th Division: Attack south of La Boisselle (1/7) – mine exploded south-west corner of village 7.28 a.m. – crater (Lochnagar) formed about 100 yards in diameter. Moved forward on left of 101st Brigade's assault – first objective The Bloater 800 yards ahead. Soon machine gun fire from La Boisselle and Heligoland Redoubt swept through leading waves – War Diary notes advance as 'with the utmost steadiness and courage, not to be surpassed by any troops in the world.' Small parties consolidated and held crater – bombers entered German line to left and formed block. Relieved and to Albert (4/7). Casualties given in War Diary as 502 out of an attacking force of 842. To Long Valley (5/7), Hénencourt Wood (6/7), Bécourt Wood (30/7), trenches around Bazentin-le-Petit Wood (31/7). Relieved 11th Suffolk in support and front line north-east of Bazentin-le-Petit (4/8) – took part in unsuccessful bombing attack on Intermediate line. Relieved and to positions west of Mametz Wood (6/8). Casualties since (31/7) – over 200. To Bécourt Wood (10/8), Mametz Wood (13/8), Bazentin-le-Petit (14/8), Bécourt (15/8), Franvillers (16/8). Entrained at Méricourt for Longpré (18/8) and from there marched to Fontaine. Entrained at Pont-Remy for Bailleul (19/8).

Devonshire Regiment

1st Battalion. 95th Brigade, 5th Division: Moved from Ivergny to Candas (14/7). To Hérissart (15/7), Bresle (16/7), Bécordel-Bécourt (17/7), old German line at Montauban (19/7). From there held reserve positions south-west of Longueval. Later in support during operations around Longueval and Delville Wood. Relieved and to Pommiers Redoubt (29/7). Casualties – over 250. To bivouacs near Albert (1/8). Entrained at Méricourt for Airaines (4/8) and from there marched to St. Maulvis. Entrained at Airaines for Edgehill (24/8). Relieved 17th West Yorkshire in trenches south-east of Guillemont (26/8). To Billon Wood (31/8), former positions near Guillemont (2/9). In support for attack towards Leuze Wood (3/9). Assaulted south-west edge of wood 6.55 p.m. (4/9) – objectives taken and held until relieved by 7th Royal Irish Fusiliers at 6.10 p.m. (5/9). To Happy Valley. Casualties – 194. To Citadel Camp (9/9), reserve trenches near Angle Wood and running south-east from Falfemont Farm (10/9), front line Leuze Wood (12/9). Withdrew to Billon Wood during night (13/9). To Ville-sur-Ancre (14/9), Sandpit Camp and via La Briqueterie took over reserve line Morval sector (18/9). To Oxford Copse (22/9), front line Morval (24/9). In attack on Morval (25/9) – over 40 per cent casualties during assault on Bovril and Mince Trenches. Large supplies of German bombs captured and used up against the enemy. Regimental history by C.T. Atkinson records that the bayonet was put to good use throughout operation. To Oxford Copse (26/9), Citadel Camp (27/9). Entrained at Grove Town for Longpré (29/9) and from there marched to Pont-Remy. Entrained for Chocques (1/10) and from there marched to Béthune.

2nd Battalion. 23rd Brigade, 8th Division: Attack at Ovillers spur (1/7) - advancing along Mash Valley towards Pozières soon came under heavy fire. In the Regimental history of the Devonshire Regiment – C.T. Atkinson records how onlookers from the British trenches were at first to think that the leading waves were lying in No Man's Land awaiting another chance to move forward. It was soon realized, however, that the men were almost entirely casualties. Withdrew to Millencourt. Casualties – 431. Entrained at Méricourt for Ailly (2/7). To La Chaussée (3/7), Soues (4/7). Entrained at Longueau for Diéval (6/7) and marched to Barlin south of Béthune. Entrained at Chocques for Pont-Remy (15/10). To Méaulte (17/10), reserve trenches south-east of Flers (22/10). In support during 23rd Brigade's assault on Le Transloy (23/10). Relieved 1st Notts and Derby in front line (Misty Trench) (28/10). To Mansell Camp (31/10), Méaulte (1/11), Citadel Camp (3/11), La Briqueterie (6/11), front line (Autumn Trench) Le Transloy (7/11). Dug new forward trench (Fall Trench) during night

(9/11). Withdrew to Flers Line (10/11), Carnoy Camp (13/11), Citadel Camp (15/11).

8th (Service) Battalion. 20th Brigade, 7th Division: In support during attack at Mametz (1/7) – following 9th Devonshire and 2nd Gordon Highlanders through Mansell Copse and losing heavily on entering No Man's Land. 'B' Company moving forward at 10.30 a.m. took cover in the hollow of Fricourt Road and would not move again until 4.0 p.m. – all of its officers being casualties and led by the Company Sergeant Major. Clearing the deep dug-outs in Danzig Trench and moving on to Hidden Wood – all objectives would be taken. Further advance made up Orchard Trench North (2/7) and strong-point established in the Orchard. Casualties – 207. War diary records that on (4/7) the dead of the Devonshire Regiment (8th and 9th Battalions) were buried at Mansell Copse. To Treux (5/7), Minden Post (11/7). In action at Bazentin-le-Grand Wood (14/7) – War Diary notes leading wave crept forward into No Man's Land during bombardment and at zero hour (3.25 a.m.) were within 25 yards of enemy's line. First objective entered at 3.26 a.m. – second taken by 3.45 a.m. – patrols cleared north-east side of wood. Relieved and to White Trench (15/7). Casualties – 171. To assembly positions south of High Wood (19/7). In action (20/7) – attacked 3.15 a.m. – many casualties from British artillery firing short. Casualties – 201. Relieved 11 p.m. by 14th Royal Warwickshire and to Dernancourt. Entrained at Méricourt for Hangest (22/7) and from there marched to Ailly-sur-Somme. Entrained at Vignacourt for Buire (12/8). To Mametz and later Montauban (3/9). Took part in operations around Ginchy until (7/9). Relieved and to camp near Citadel. To Buire (8/9). Entrained at Albert for Airaines (9/9) and from there marched to Allery. Entrained at Longpré for Bailleul (18/9).

9th (Service) Battalion. 20th Brigade, 7th Division: Attack on Mametz (1/7). The prophecy by Captain D.L. Martin (9th Devonshire) that a machine gun hidden in a shrine at Mametz Cemetery would inflict great casualties on his battalion is one of the many fascinating stories of the Somme. When the 9th attacked through Mansell Copse the weapon situated exactly where the officer had said was indeed to account for many of the Battalion's losses. Captain Martin being one of the first to fall. From captured positions in Danzig Trench withdrew to Citadel Camp (3/7). Casualties – 464. To Ribemont (5/7). Via Méaulte and Fricourt took up forward positions around Marlborough Wood, Caterpillar Valley, Montauban Alley and White Trench (11/7). Engaged in operations at Bazentin-le-Grand Wood (14/7)–(16/7). Relieved and to Willow Avenue. In support of 8th Devonshire and 2nd Gordon Highlanders north of Bazentin-le-Grand Wood (19/7)–(20/7). Relieved and to Dernancourt. Casualties for period (14/7)–(20/7) – 112. Entrained at

Méricourt for Hangest (22/7) and from there marched to Breilly. To Ailly-sur-Somme (23/7). Entrained at Vignacourt for Méricourt (12/8) and from there marched to Buire. To Mametz (3/9) – forming up at the cross roads and moving into adjacent field. To Montauban and forward to positions at Ginchy (4/9). Engaged in operations in area until (7/9). Casualties – 425. To Buire (8/9). Entrained at Albert for Airaines (9/9) and from there marched to Béttencourt. To Longpré (12/9). Entrained for Bailleul (18/9).

12th (Labour) Battalion. Entrained at Bailleul for Heilly (2/9). To camp at Fricourt Wood (3/9). Worked mainly on roads – Fricourt, Mametz, Montauban, Longueval areas. To Montauban (4/10).

Suffolk Regiment

2nd Battalion. 76th Brigade, 3rd Division: Arrived Doullens from St. Omer (2/7) and from there marched to Longuevillette. To Naours (3/7), Coisy (4/7), Franvillers (5/7), Celestines Wood (6/7), Carnoy (8/7). Began tours in trenches around Bernafay Wood. Two companies to Mine Support and Breslau Trench (12/7). Worked on filling in Mine Alley – improving Montauban-Carnoy Road – dug new communication trench to Caterpillar Valley. To positions southern end of Caterpillar Wood (14/7). Two companies in support of 1st Gordon Highlanders during attack at Longueval (18/7). Attack on Longueval (20/7) – advanced from Pont Street 3.35 a.m. – Official History of The Great War recording that the 2 leading companies – 'with their right flank exposed, pressed on with great resolution and were almost entirely lost.' War Diary notes heavy mist on left caused second line to lose direction – machine gun fire from junction of Duke Street and Piccadilly made movement across open impossible. Dug in along Duke Street. Relieved and to Breslau Trench (21/7). To Bois des Tallies (25/7), Méricourt (28/7). Battalion celebrated Regimental Day (Minden Day) (1/8). War Diary records Bantam drafts (160 received on 28th July) 'a hindrance to others in the ranks.' To Sandpit Camp (11/8), trenches south-west of Trônes Wood and near Maltz Horn Farm (15/8). Successful attack carried out 5.40 p.m. (16/8) – part of enemy's line at Cochrane Alley running as far as the Hardecourt-Gillemont Road taken. Withdrawn after further operations to Happy Valley (18/8). Casualties – 281. To Morlancourt (21/8). Entrained at Méricourt for Candas (23/8) and from there marched to Le Meillard. Began move to Béthune sector (25/8). Entrained at St. Pol (8/10) and via Arquèves took over billets at Bertrancourt. To Louvencourt (17/10), Courcelles (19/10). Two companies to Colincamps. Began tours in line Serre sector (23/10). To Bus-lès-Artois (29/10), front line (12/11). Attacked on Serre (13/11). In his history of the Suffolk Regiment Lieutenant-Colonel C.C.R. Murphy notes the advance as through mist which hung about the low ground – thickened as the smoke of the barrage increased, and making direction extremely difficult to maintain. Commanding Officer Lieutenant-Colonel C.C. Stubbs records failure of attack in War Diary as due to loss of direction in mist – high casualties among officers (11) – muddy state of ground near German line – rifles becoming caked with mud and 'concertina' type German wire. Relieved and to Courcelles (14/11). Casualties – 272. To front line (15/11).

1/4th Battalion (T.F.). 98th Brigade, 33rd Division: From Béthune area passed through Bécordel-Bécourt (14/7) and at night bivouacking between Fricourt and Mametz. In support during attack on Switch Trench (15/7) – ground taken and held immediately in front of Bazentin-le-Petit. Casualties

– over 200. In Reserve at Shell Valley (16/7). To front line Bazentin-le-Petit (17/7), Shell Valley and in support during attack at High Wood (20/7). To Mametz Wood (21/7), Dernancourt (22/7). Casualties for July fighting – 354. Commemorated Minden Day (1/8) by visit to 2nd Suffolk then at Méricourt. To Fricourt Wood (6/8). Working party of 440 men provided to help dig Thistle Alley communication trench (7/8). In support at Bazentin-le-Grand (13/8). To front line High Wood (14/8). Attack on Wood Lane (18/8) – 2 companies occupying objective until relieved (19/8) – all officers having become casualties. Withdrew to Fricourt Wood. Casualties – 196. To camp north-east of Méaulte near Albert Road (20/8), Fricourt Wood (24/8), trenches around Bazentin-le-Grand (25/8). In line Orchard Trench and Wood Lane (29/8). Enemy bombing attacks repulsed (30/8). Relieved and to Méaulte (31/8). Via Dernancourt to Allonville (1/9), Candas (2/9), Remaisnil (4/9). Transferred to Arras sector (5/9). Arrived Sailly-au-Bois (19/9). To front line Hébuterne sector (26/9), St. Amand (2/10), Sus-St.Légar (3/10), Corbie (19/10), Méaulte (21/10), La Briqueterie (23/10), Trônes Wood (24/10), front line near Lesbœufs (28/10). Later made several attacks on Dew Drop Trench. To Flers Line (2/11), huts on the Montauban-Carnoy Road (3/11), Méaulte (6/11), Huchenneville (9/11).

7th (Service) Battalion. 35th Brigade, 12th (Eastern) Division: Moved into support trenches from Hénencourt Wood during early hours (3/7). With 5th Royal Berkshire led attack on Ovillers – first four waves under heavy fire cleared enemy's positions as far as third line – part of assaulting force entered village. After severe fighting in which all company commanders were killed – assault brought to a standstill and survivors forced to re-tire. Casualties – over 450. Remained in forward area. To Albert (8/7), La Boisselle (9/7), Bois de Warnimont (10/7). Later carried out short tour in trenches near White City in front of Beaumont-Hamel. To trenches west of Pozières (3/8). Enemy attacked and took part of Ration Trench, then held by 7th Suffolk and 5th Royal Berkshire (8/8). Ground regained during evening. Regimental historian Lieutenant-Colonel C.C.R. Murphy records that 'Captain Isham's company' made the attack – taking an additional 200 yards of enemy trench. Relieved and to Bouzincourt. Transferred to Arras sector (17/8). Moved by bus to Brévillers and Bécordel-Bécourt (27/9). To reserve positions at Bernafay Wood (2/10), trenches near Flers (10/10). With 7th Norfolk and from positions in sunken road leading to Gueudecourt Wood made assault on Bayonet Trench (12/10) – advanced at 2 p.m. under heavy cross-fire – held up near German trenches by machine-guns and wire and forced to take cover in shell-holes. Lieutenant-Colonel Murphy notes acts of 'remarkable bravery' at this point. Withdrew with over 500 casualties. To Mametz Wood (19/10). By bus to Lattre St. Quentin (22/10).

8th (Service) Battalion. 53rd Brigade, 18th (Eastern) Division: In Brigade reserve west of Carnoy Road during 18th Division's attack south-west of Montauban (1/7). Provided carrying parties to forward areas throughout the day. Moved forward and took over 53rd Brigade front (2/7). Relieved and to Grove Town Camp (7/7). To positions on eastern edge of Bernafay Wood (14/7), later supporting 54th Brigade during its attack on Trônes Wood. Relieved and to camp near Carnoy (17/7). For assault on Delville Wood (19/7) Regimental historian Lieutenant-Colonel C.C.R. Murphy records that the Battalion was brought forward hurriedly – un fed and with no time for reconnaissance. The advance through Longueval brought strong resistance from the enemy – heavy casualties noted around the church. Line in village later advanced about 300 yards. Casualties – 238. Relieved and to Grove Town (21/7). Transferred to Armentières sector (24/7). Returned to Somme during second week of September - billeting at Halloy, Acheux, Bouzincourt and Forceville before taking over part of line south of Thiepval (24/9). Attacked (26/9) – on right of 53rd Brigade – Official History of The Great War recording advance as moving and fighting 'with great precision.' German front-line cleared and many prisoners taken. With first and second objectives (Schwaben and Zollern Trenches) taken and consolidated, advance was then checked at Medway Trench and the Schwaben Redoubt. 'B' and 'C' Companies heavily engaged while taking Bulgar Trench and part of Schwaben (28/9). Relieved and to Forceville. Casualties – over 200. Entrained for Candas (5/10) and from there marched to Heuzecourt. Arrived Albert (14/10) and from there to trenches near Courcelette. Relieved by 8th Norfolk and to Albert (21/10). Rest of October and November spent in and out of line – (Fabeck, Regina Trenches) while resting at Albert and Warloy.

9th (Service) Battalion. 71st Brigade, 6th Division: Entrained at Proven for Candas (2/8) and from there marched via Beauval and Léalvillers to Mailly-Maillet Wood. These positions, with the exception of a week spent at Louvencourt, held until (28/8). Duties in the area included clearing 36th (Ulster) Division's 1st July dead from the battlefield. Via Beauval to Montonvillers (29/8). Later to Cardonnette, Méricourt-l'Abbé and Sandpit Camp. Took over trenches from 4th Grenadier Guards south-east of Ginchy (11/9). With 2nd Notts and Derby attacked The Quadrilateral (13/9) – assault soon checked by machine gun fire. Further attempts made throughout day, but no gains made. Dug in about half a mile in front of start point. Casualties (both battalions) – 21 officers and some 500 other ranks. In support of 9th Norfolk during its attempt at The Quadrilateral (15/9) – Regimental historian

Lieutenant-Colonel C.C.R. Murphy notes 'the trying experiences of the 13th were repeated.' Heavy fire inflicting high losses and withdrawal ordered. In support during 6th Division's capture of The Quadrilateral (17/9)–(18/9). Relieved and to Ville-sur-Ancre (19/9). To reserve at Bernafay Wood (25/9), front line north-east of Ginchy (26/9). In support during 6th Division's operations at Le Transloy (12/10) – holding positions at Misty and Cloudy Trenches were not required to move forward. Relieved and to Corbie (21/10). Transferred Béthune area (28/10).

11th (Service) Battalion (Cambridgeshire). 101st Brigade, 34th Division: Moved up from Bécourt Wood early morning (1/7) to position behind 10th Lincolnshire. To the front, and just left of the Lincolnshire, mine blown (Lochnagar Crater) at 7.28 a.m. The tremendous casualties of 34th Division have been noted in the records of its other battalions – 15th and 16th Royal Scots, 10th Lincolnshire and the two Tyneside Brigades (20th-27th Northumberland Fusiliers). In 11th Suffolk the same situation arose whereas men were cut down within moments of leaving their assembly positions – 'soon men were spun round and dropping everywhere' the historian of the Suffolk Regiment Lieutenant-Colonel C.C.R. Murphy records. One company commander who was wounded wrote – 'my very last memory of the attack is the sight of Gibson in front of me, and C.S.M. Brooks on my right, both moving as if on parade, and both a minute or two later to be mortally hit.' Relieved (4/7) and via Bécourt Wood to Long Valley. Casualties – 691. To Hénencourt Wood (5/7), Bécourt Wood (30/7). Took over part of line a little north of Bazentin-le-Petit Wood (31/7). 'B' Company in assault on Intermediate Trench (4/8) – Lieutenant-Colonel Murphy records assault 'Gallantly led and skilfully handled' by Captain O.H. Brown – objective taken, consolidated and held. Relieved and to bivouacs around Bazentin-le-Petit Wood and Mametz Wood. Another attempt on Intermediate Line by party of bombers (with those of 15th Royal Scots) (5/8). 34th Division relieved from forward area and transferred to Armentières sector (15/8).

12th (Service) Battalion (East Anglian). 121st Brigade, 40th Division: Arrived Berneuil from Barly (5/11). To Villers-l'Hôpital (15/11), Bouquemaison (17/11), Sus-St. Léger (18/11).

Prince Albert's (Somerset Light Infantry)

1st Battalion. 11th Brigade, 4th Division: From Mailly-Maillet at 10 p.m. (30/6) marched to assembly positions on right of Serre Road, Redan Ridge sector. Attacked (1/7) – War Diary records that the men advanced in magnificent style – having entered enemy's first line devastating fire came from The Quadrilateral – desperate fighting with bomb and bayonet followed and soon losses were mounting up. At one point while holding The Quadrilateral – only 2 officers remained. These were later wounded and command then passed to C.S.M. Chappell. Withdrew to British line after dark and ordered back to Mailly-Maillet at 10 p.m. Casualties (including Commanding Officer Lieutenant-Colonel J.A. Thicknesse) – 464. To Bertrancourt (4/7), front line (10/7), support line (Ellis Square, View Trench) and Mailly-Maillet (15/7). Entrained at Doullens for Ypres sector (22/7). Arrived Longueau from Esquelbecq (17/9) and from there marched to Cardonnette. To Corbie (25/9), Méaulte (7/10), Citadel Camp (8/10), La Briqueterie (9/10), support line Lesbœufs sector (17/10). In reserve at start of attack (18/10) – later moved forward – 'A' Company supporting 1st Rifle Brigade – 'B' company entering and consolidating Frosty Trench. Counter attack repulsed (19/10). To Gillemont (21/10). In his history of the Somerset Light Infantry Everard Wyrall records the trying conditions at Frosty Trench – the men working throughout to improve the shallow line were exhausted and soaked to the skin. The mud was knee deep – upon arrival at Guillemont some 68 men were ordered to hospital suffering from trench feet and exhaustion, while 83 were sent to the transport lines for rest and attention. Later in the day the Senior Medical Officer would evacuate more men. Battalion, about 300 strong remained in Brigade Reserve. To Trônes Wood (24/10), Mansell Camp (25/10). Here War Diary records – 'all ranks who had had no sleep for 8 nights enjoyed the luxury of tents.' Entrained at Méricourt for Airaines (30/10) and from there marched to Citerne.

6th (Service) Battalion. 43rd Brigade, 14th (Light) Division: Left Arras sector end July – arriving Prouville (1/8). Entrained at Candas for Méricourt (6/8) and from there marched 5 miles to camp on a hill overlooking Albert. To front line Delville Wood (12/8). Enemy attack repulsed during night (14/8). To support trenches in front of Montauban Alley (15/8) – working parties sent up to dig in Delville Wood during nights (15/8) and (16/8). Moved forward to assembly positions south-east corner of Delville Wood 3 a.m. (18/8) – attacked 2.45 p.m. – assaulting companies in German trenches by 2.50 p.m. – 'A' Company supported by 'D' taking Beer Trench – 'C' on left occupying Hop Alley – gains held against counter attacks and under heavy bombardment. Relieved at midnight (19/8) and to Fricourt. Casualties – 280.

To reserve trenches in front of Bernafay Wood (26/8), 1 company to Delville Wood (27/8). To Fricourt (30/8). Entrained at Méricourt for Selincourt (31/8). Entrained for Méricourt (12/9) and from there marched to bivouacs just south of Albert. To camp near Méaulte (14/9), Pommiers Redoubt (15/9) and from there positions between Delville Wood and the Switch Line. Took over front line (16/9) – carried out attack on Gird Trench north-east of Flers 9.25 a.m. – under heavy fire from Gas Alley assault failed – all 17 officers that went into action and some 387 other ranks becoming casualties. Withdrew just before daybreak (17/9) – first to Pommiers Redoubt and then to Fricourt Camp. To Ribemont (18/9), Arras sector (27/9).

7th (Service) Battalion. 61st Brigade, 20th (Light) Division: Arrived Doullens from Ypres sector (25/7) and from there marched to Bois de Warnimont. To Bus-lès-Artois (26/7), Mailly-Maillet (27/7), front line (28/7) – same trenches held by 1st Somerset Light Infantry at beginning of its 1st July attack on the Redan Ridge. Regimental historian Everard Wyrall records that still laying all around were the unburied corpses of their comrades. Periods out of the line spent around Couin, Authuille and Sailly Dell. Began to move south (16/8), reaching Morlancourt (20/8), Happy Valley (21/8). Took over line opposite Guillemont (25/8), The Quarries (26/8). To Carnoy craters (27/8) – the withdrawal being noted as through trenches knee-deep in mud and full of half-buried corpses (Everard Wyrall). Headquarters, 'A' and 'B' Companies to La Briqueterie in support of 59th Brigade (31/8). Returned to craters at Carnoy midnight (2/9). Assembled on western edge of Trônes Wood (3/9) – attacked 12 noon – 'A' and 'D' Companies leading took objective – the Wedge Wood-Ginchy Road south of the Guillemont cross roads. Later, 'B' company assisted 47th Brigade north of Guillemont-Combles Road – consolidating and holding their position until rejoining Battalion at midnight. Relieved and to Carnoy craters (5/9). Casualties for Guillemont operations – 166. To Sandpit Camp (6/9), Maricourt (8/9), Sandpit Camp (12/9), Citadel Camp (14/9), Talus Boisé (15/9) and from there moved forward to positions near Waterlot Farm. Attached to Guards Division moved up through Ginchy at midnight to line facing Lesbœufs. When Battalion attacked at 9.35 a.m. (16/9) it would be under the command of a second-lieutenant – all other officers having become casualties. The days fighting is described by Everard Wyrall as 'brilliant' – some 150 yards of German line captured with 'bomb and bayonet' – and many acts of bravery noted. Relieved and to Talus Boisé. To Citadel Camp (21/9), Méaulte (22/9), Citadel (25/9), The Quadrilateral (26/9), Carnoy Craters (28/9), trenches south of Gueudecourt (29/9). Advanced at 3.15 p.m. (1/10) and dug new forward line. Position held against counter attacks until relieved 11 a.m. (3/10). To Carnoy (4/10), front line (6/10). In support during attack on Rainbow and Cloudy Trenches (7/10) – moving forward later and consolidating gains. Relieved and to Méaulte (9/10). To Corbie (15/10), Allonville (19/10), Vaux (20/10), Riencourt (1/11), Warlus (18/11).

8th (Service) Battalion. 63rd Brigade, 21st and 37th Divisions: On left of 63rd Brigade's (21st Division) attack on Fricourt (1/7) – moved forward into No Man's Land just before zero hour – War Diary of 63rd Brigade noting that at this point almost all officers had become casualties. With some 50% losses – German lines entered and at midnight gains were being consolidated by just 100 men at the west end of Lozenge Wood – the sunken road and Lozenge Alley. Moved forward to Patch Alley (3/7). Relieved by 12th Manchester (4/7) and via Happy Valley and Méaulte to Dernancourt. Casualties since (1/7) – 443. Via Vaux, Bertangles and Talmas to Halloy where 63rd Brigade transferred to 37th Division (8/7). Took over trenches east of Hannescamps (11/7). To Hannescamps (14/7) and from there transferred to Vimy sector. Arrived Raincheval from Amplier (21/10). To Beauval (30/10), Léalvillers (12/11), Hédauville (14/11). From there assembled at Englebelmer and at midnight took over support positions at Beaucourt Trench. To Station Road (15/11) and from there worked on Engine Trench and provided carrying parties for forward areas. 'C' Company went forward to Ancre Trench and established post at Bois d'Hollande (16/11). German attack beaten off (17/11). Attack on Puisieux Trench (18/11) – advanced at 11 a.m. and immediately came under heavy machine gun fire – also high casualties from British barrage and attack halted. Later bombing parties from 'C' and 'D' Companies took Puisieux Trench south of Miraumont Road. Relieved by 4th Middlesex during evening and to support positions east of Beaucourt.

Prince of Wales's Own (West Yorkshire Regiment)

1st Battalion. 18th Brigade, 6th Division: Arrived Doullens from Ypres sector (2/8) and from there marched to Orville. To Acheux (4/8), Mailly-Maillet (6/8) and from there took over front line (Gordon Trench) from 3rd Worcestershire. Relieved and to Englebelmer (9/8). Working parties provided for front line. To front line (19/8), Bertrancourt (26/8), Amplier (27/8), Hem (28/8), Vignacourt (29/8), Rainneville (6/9), Vaux-sur-Somme (7/9), Sandpit Camp (11/9), Citadel Camp (12/9). Moved forward to Chimpanzee Trench in Brigade reserve (14/9). Relieved 2nd Durham Light Infantry north end of The Quadrilateral (16/9). Attacked The Quadrilateral (18/9) – 'D' Company bombers assaulted down Straight Trench just after zero hour – 'B' and 'C' attacked in the open and soon forced to retire to start line under heavy rifle and machine gun fire. Later 2 platoons of 'A' Company advanced and dug in at the quarry 250 yards in front of objective. War Diary records strong point captured by 'D' Company just after 6 a.m. – at 6.45 a.m. further strong points taken and consolidated. Relieved 2 p.m. to bivouacs near Talus Boisé. Casualties – 151. To Méaulte (19/9), reserve trenches between Trônes Wood and Guillemont (21/9), support line near Ginchy (23/9). Attack on Lesbœufs (25/9) – War Diary records 'A' and 'D' Companies advancing at 2.35 p.m. ('C' in close support) – moved through village into sunken road beyond with slight opposition – moved forward 50 yards and dug in at 3.5 p.m. Relieved and to assembly trenches during night (26/9). Casualties – 116. To Talus Boisé (28/9), Méaulte (29/9), Ville-sur-Ancre (30/9), Citadel Camp (7/10). Moved forward to Trônes Wood (8/10) and from there via Guillemont took over support line (Needle Trench). To front line (Cloudy and Rainbow Trenches) (10/10). Attack on Mild and Cloudy Trenches (12/10) – War Diary records assembly positions heavily bombarded by both British and German guns – 'D' Company advanced but under heavy machine gun fire immediately withdrew. Bombing attack on right by 'C' Company also failed. Relieved and to Trônes Wood (13/10). To front line (15/10), Trônes Wood (16/10). 'C' Company to support line (Needle Trench) (17/10). To Citadel Camp (19/10), Ville-sur-Ancre (21/10). Entrained at Méricourt for Allery (22/10). Entrained at Pont-Remy for Chocques (28/10).

2nd Battalion. 23rd Brigade, 8th Division: Assembled in Ryecroft Street during night (30/6) for attack towards Pozières. War Diary notes 21 officers and 702 other ranks breakfasted at 5.30 a.m. 'B' Company followed 2nd Middlesex into action 7.42 a.m. – 'A' at 7.52 a.m. Official History of The Great War records over 250 casualties while passing through German barrage on British front line and enfilade fire from La Boisselle. After heavy fighting around Ovillers Battalion withdrew to Millencourt just after midnight (2/7).

War Diary records just 5 officers and 212 men coming out of action. Sidney Rogerson in his book 'Twelve Days' recalls the attack and the dead hanging thick on the German wire. Entrained at Méricourt for Ailly-sur-Somme (2/7) and from there marched to La Chaussee. To Hangest-sur-Somme (4/7). Entrained at Longueau for Le Maisnil (6/7). Entrained at Chocques for Longpré (14/10) and from there marched to Fontaine. To Méaulte (17/10), Bernafay Wood in reserve (20/10), support positions (Windmill and Shin Trenches) facing Le Transloy (22/10). Attack on Zenith Trench (23/10) – 'B' and 'D' Companies moved forward to Spectrum Trench and captured Zenith After 8.15 p.m. (24/10). Relieved and to Bernafay Wood during night (30/10) – later to Mansell Camp. War Diary notes fighting strength upon going into action on (23/10) as 437. Casualties by (30/10) – 220, over 200 of these suffered by 'B' and 'D' Companies while holding line. The Bravery of stretcher bearers and orderlies working in the open under constant fire is also noted. To Citadel Camp (3/11), Bernafay Wood (7/11). Relieved 2nd Devonshire in front line between Lesbœufs and Le Transloy (10/11). Relieved and to La Briqueterie (13/11). To Citadel Camp (15/11).

1/5th Battalion (T.F.). 146th Brigade, 49th (West Riding) Division: From Aveluy Wood went to assembly positions in Thiepval Wood (1/7) – occupied British front line – later parties ordered up to assist 36th (Ulster) Division at the Schwaben Redoubt. Withdrew to Aveluy Wood (2/7). To Martinsart (3/7), Hédauville (5/7), Martinsart Wood (7/7) and in evening to Authuille. Took over front line (8/7), support line (16/7), front line Leipzig Salient (18/7), support line (19/7) – 'A' and 'B' Companies sent forward to assist 1/8th West Yorkshire in consolidating captured positions. To Hédauville (21/7), Bouzincourt (23/7), Forceville (25/7), front line trenches Quarry Post (27/7), Forceville (31/7), Hédauville (1/8), South Bluff, Authuille (3/8) – began front line duty Leipzig Salient. To South Bluff (10/8), front line (13/8), Acheux Wood (18/8), Forceville (26/8) and from there to Thiepval Wood – H.Q. at Belfast City trenches. To Gordon Castle trenches (28/8), Martinsart Wood (4/9), Forceville (5/9), Hédauville (18/9), Martinsart Wood (20/9), trenches between Leipzig Salient and Thiepval in close support (27/9). Attack on Schwaben Redoubt (28/9) – moved forward behind 7th Bedfordshire at 1 p.m. – War Diary records confused fighting in front and second line German trenches – 'hand to hand scraping' – gains held and consolidated. Withdrew to North Bluff, Authuille (29/9) and from there Martinsart Wood – later boarded buses for Arquèves. To Halloy (30/9), Warluzel (1/10), Humbercamps (10/10), front line Hannescamps sector (18/10), St. Amand (27/10), front line (2/11), Bienvillers (8/11), front line (14/11).

1/6th Battalion (T.F.). 146th Brigade, 49th (West Riding) Division: Advanced from Aveluy Wood to Thiepval Wood 9 a.m. (1/7) – moved forward for attack on Thiepval. Battalion historian Captain E.V. Tempest, D.S.O.,M.C. records – 'C' and 'D' Companies leading, 'B' in support, 'A' in reserve – vast majority of the men and many of the officers had only the vaguest idea of the direction in which Thiepval lay. Machine gun fire from village brought heavy casualties before British front line was reached. Attacked 4 p.m. – Captain Tempest notes no one advanced more than 100 yards and few men came back unwounded. Withdrew to Thiepval Wood. To Aveluy Wood (2/7), Martinsart (3/7), Hédauville (5/7). Moved forward to Martinsart Wood (7/7) and at 10 p.m to positions on Aveluy-Hamel Road, south of Aveluy Wood. To dug-outs near Crucifix Corner (8/7). Here Captain Tempest noted the exhausted 'remnants' of 3rd Worcestershire after its fighting at the Leipzig Salient. Relieved 1/7th West Yorkshire in Leipzig Salient (9/7). To South Bluff, Authuille (12/7), Leipzig Salient (13/7). In support of 1/7th West Yorkshire (14/7) – bombers drove back enemy counter attack. Enemy attacked using flamethrowers (15/7). Relieved and to Authuille Wood. To Forceville (27/7), Hédauville (1/8), trenches – Thiepval Avenue to Oban Avenue (3/8), Léalvillers (18/8), North Bluff via Hédauville (26/8), Aveluy Wood (2/9). Attack on trenches near St. Pierre Divion 5.10 a.m. (3/9) – heavy losses by machine gun fire from Pope's Nose – hand-to-hand fighting in German front line – strong counter attacks forced withdrawal. Casualties – 241. Relieved and to Forceville midnight. Captain Tempest notes (3/9) as 'the blackest day in the history of the Battalion.' To Hédauville (18/9), front line Thiepval sector (20/9). 'A' and 'B' Companies to Thiepval Wood, 'C' and 'D' to Englebelmer (25/9). To Macmahon's Post for attack on Thiepval (26/9) – 'A' Company helped consolidate gains – 'B' Company dug trench across No Man's Land to captured line. To Englebelmer (less 'B' Company) (27/9). 'B' Company joined Battalion (28/9). To Arquèves (29/9), Mondicourt (30/9), Sombrin (1/10), Pommier (10/10). Began duty in trenches Foncquevillers sector (18/10). To St. Amand (24/10), trenches Hannescamps sector (27/10), Bienvillers (2/11), front line (8/11), St. Amand (14/11).

1/7th Battalion (Leeds Rifles) (T.F.). 146th Brigade, 49th (West Riding) Division: Ordered forward from Aveluy Wood to Thiepval Wood 9.a.m. (1/7) – assembled in trenches around Belfast City – later took over British front line. 'C' and 'D' Companies moved forward to reinforce 36th (Ulster) Division in Schwaben Redoubt – withdrew during night. Cut off from his company, Corporal George Sanders with a party of 30 men held a position near Thiepval until relieved (3/7). Awarded the Victoria Cross. Withdrew to Aveluy Wood (2/7), Martinsart Wood (3/7). To Aveluy Wood (7/7), front line Leipzig Salient (8/7), South Bluff, Authuille (9/7), front line (12/7). Unsuccessful attack (14/7) – 2 companies moved forward 2.15 a.m. – later withdrew to South Bluff. To Campbell Post (16/7), Martinsart Wood (21/7), South Bluff and Forceville (24/7), front line (3/8), South Bluff (7/8), front line (10/8), South Bluff (13/8), Acheux Wood (18/8), front line Thiepval sector (26/8), Martinsart Wood (28/8), Aveluy Wood (2/9), Gordon Castle in reserve (3/9), Martinsart Wood (4/9), Forceville (7/9), Hédauville (18/9), front line (20/9), Mailly-Maillet Wood (27/9), Raincheval (29/9), Halloy (30/9), Coullemont (1/10), Sombrin (4/10), Humbercamps (10/10), front line Foncquevillers sector (18/10), Bienvillers (24/10), front line (2/11), St. Amand (8/11), front line (14/11), Bienvillers (20/11).

1/8th Battalion (Leeds Rifles) (T.F.). 146th Brigade, 49th (West Riding) Division: Moved forward from Aveluy Wood to Thiepval Wood in immediate support of 36th (Ulster) Division (1/7) – War Diary notes no advance made but heavy casualties. Withdrew to Aveluy Wood (2/7), Martinsart Wood (3/7). To Wood Post (7/7), front line Leipzig Salient (15/7), heavy German bombing attack repulsed (17/7). To South Bluff, Authuille (18/7), front line (19/7) – War Diary notes an attack – 'two trenches taken from Guards Fusilier Regiment'. To Forceville (20/7), Bouzincourt (23/7), Forceville (25/7), front line (31/7). Casualties for July – 16 officers, 369 other ranks. Attacked opposite The Nab (12/8) – War Diary notes objective almost taken but stopped short owing to unit on right held up – 'We however advanced our bombing block some thirty yards' (War Diary). To Martinsart Wood (15/8), Léalvillers (17/8), front line Gordon Castle (27/8), Hédauville (29/8). Casualties for August – 98. To Aveluy Wood (2/9), front line (3/9) – attacked 5.10 – 'unable to hold and consolidate.' Relieved and to Forceville. Casualties – 303. To Hédauville (18/9), front line (20/9), Mailly-Maillet (27/9), Raincheval (29/9), Halloy (30/9). Casualties for September – 393. To Humbercourt (1/10), Humbercamps (11/10), Bienvillers (18/10), front line Foncquevillers sector (24/10). Casualties for October given in War Diary as just 2 wounded and 1 man died of disease. To St. Amand (2/11), front line (8/11), Bienvillers (14/11).

9th (Service) Battalion. 32nd Brigade, 11th (Northern) Division: Entrained at Frévent for Beauval (3/9) and from there marched to Arquèves. To Senlis (6/9), front line Leipzig Salient (7/9). Withdrew to Crucifix Corner (10/9). To front line (14/9) and with 8th Duke of Wellington's made successful attack on Turk Street and the Wonder Work beyond. Relieved and to Crucifix Corner (15/9), casualties – 318. To Hédauville (16/9), Bouzincourt (18/9), Mailly-Maillet Wood (21/9), Ovillers (22/9), Bouzincourt (25/9), Crucifix Corner (26/9). Moved forward to support trenches around Mouquet Farm (27/9). Attack on Hessian Trench – advanced at 2.57 p.m. – War Diary records advance carried right through with great gallantry – a mass of barbed wire around the

Zollern Redoubt causing loss of direction and instead of arriving at Hessian Trench entered and captured Stuff Redoubt at about 3.15 p.m. Attacked eastern edge of Stuff Redoubt (still in German hands) (28/9) – unsupported and with no bombs forced to retire. Relieved after further action in Stuff Redoubt (1/10) – War Diary records that out of 4 companies (less 2 platoons) that took Stuff Redoubt on (27/9) only 1 officer and 24 other ranks answered roll call on morning of (1/10). Casualties – 268. To Varennes and from there marched to Acheux. Entrained at 6 p.m. for Candas and from there in buses to Beaumetz. To Pernois (14/11), Hérissart (15/11), Léalvillers (16/11).

10th (Service) Battalion. 50th Brigade, 17th (Northern) Division: Attack on Fricourt (1/7) – 2 companies moved forward at zero on left of assault – clearing enemy front lines with little loss. Supporting companies met heavy fire – machine guns having been brought from dug-outs. Regimental history by Everard Wyrall records that the latter were almost annihilated – survivors crawled back after dark. War Diary records the loss of Commanding Officer Lieutenant-Colonel Dickson with his second in command and adjutant (all killed), and casualties figures of 22 officers and approximately 750 other ranks. Withdrawn to Ville-sur-Ancre. 17th Division relieved (10/7) and began move to Amiens area. Moved to Bellancourt area (16/7). From Condé-Folie marched to Hangest-sur-Somme (23/7) and entrained for Méricourt. Here Max – Plowman (author of 'A Subaltern on the Somme') would be horrified by the 'cages' used for prisoners. From Méricourt to bivouacs on hill about a mile west of Dernancourt. To Belle Vue Farm (2/8), Pommiers Redoubt (4/8). Began tours in line at Longueval. In the trenches Max Plowman was repulsed by the 'sickly-sweet' odour of decaying bodies – 'literally we are the living among the dead' he said. At Pommiers Redoubt he saw one soldier collapse with fever (a legacy from his service at Gallipoli) and receive harsh treatment from the Medical Officer who was not familiar with such a complaint in France. The man was 'swinging the lead' said the doctor, and a 'bloody coward.' Relieved from forward area and to Belle View Farm (11/8). To Dernancourt (12/8). Entrained at Méricourt (14/8) for Candas and from there marched to Le Meillard. Later to Bonnières. To Halloy (17/8), Sailly-au-Bois (19/8) and from there front line duty Hébuterne sector. Rested between tours at Sailly and Bayencourt. To Halloy (17/9), later Barly, Maizicourt, Caours, Conteville, Frohen-le-Grand, Halloy (10/10), Talmas (20/10), Franvillers (21/10), Méaulte (22/10), Mansell Copse (28/10). Took over front line trenches north of Lesbœufs (29/10) – later in front of Le Transloy. Rested at Trônes Wood and Mansell Camp between tours. Entrained at Edgehill for Hangest (14/11).

11th (Service) Battalion. 69th Brigade, 23rd Division: Moved forward from

Coisy to Baizieux Wood area during night (1/7) – attached to 34th Division moved into line south-east of La Boisselle (3/7). Attack on Horseshoe Trench (4/7) – objective reached but withdrawal forced after counter attacks. Attacked 6.45 a.m. (5/7) Official History of The Great war records that fighting in Horseshoe Trench was continuous until 10 a.m. when most of the ground gained was lost to a strong counter attack. Renewed assault in afternoon – with 10th Duke of Wellington's cleared enemy from Horseshoe by 7 p.m. Relieved and to Bécourt Wood. To Albert (8/7), Scots Redoubt (10/7). Attack on Bailiff Wood – leading waves advanced 4.30 p.m. – wood and trenches to the north cleared and held against strong counter attacks. Later advanced to north-west corner of Contalmaison. Withdrawn to Bécourt Wood (11/7), via Albert to Franvillers (12/7), Millencourt (21/7). To Contalmaison (28/7), Albert (2/8), Contalmaison (5/8). Attack on Munster Alley (6/8) – relieved 8th Green Howards in captured line 9 p.m. – positions held against counter attacks throughout night. Relieved (7/8). To Bresle (8/8), later Bellancourt. Moved to Ypres sector (13/8). Arrived Longueau (11/9) and from there to Hénencourt Wood. To Millencourt (15/9), Martinpuich (18/9) – Posh Alley, Gunpit Road, Factory Line. To Willow Patch near Round Wood (22/9), Gourlay support trenches (26/9). To reserve line Le Sars sector (4/10), front line (5/10). Attack and capture of Le Sars (7/10) – on left of 69th Brigade's assaulted took and held second Flers Line north-west of Bapaume Road. Supporting companies caught by bombardment advancing from Destremont Farm to First Flers Line – Regimental history by Everard Wyrall recording that only 2 unwounded officers and 30 other ranks reached objective. Withdrew to Round Wood (8/10), Albert (9/10). Entrained for Ypres sector (12/10).

12th (Service) Battalion. 9th Brigade, 3rd Division: Arrived Doullens (1/7) and from there marched to Bernaville. To Vignacourt (3/7), Poulainville (4/7), Lahoussoye (5/7), Morlancourt (6/7), support line near Montauban – The Triangle (8/7), front line (10/7). Withdrew to the Loop and Montauban Alley (11/7). Assembled in Caterpillar Valley for attack on Bazentin-le-Grand (13/7). Moved forward at night and attacked 3.25 a.m. (14/7) – gain of objectives in front line and part of second reported by 4.30 a.m. Casualties – 253. Gains consolidated and held. Relieved and to bivouacs east of Talus Boisé (19/7). Moved forward and assembled in sunken road west of Longueval (22/7). Attack on Delville Wood (23/7) – advanced from Pont Street under heavy fire. Held up at Piccadilly and withdrew to Montauban Alley. Casualties – 163. To Sandpit Camp (24/7), Ville-sur-Ancre (27/7), Sandpit (12/8), Carnoy (14/8), trenches Maltz Horn sector (15/8). Attacks on Lonely Trench (17/8) and (18/8) unsuccessful. Withdrew to Silesia Trench north-east of Talus Boisé. Casualties – 205. To Ville-sur-Ancre (21/8). Entrained at Méricourt for Candas (23/8). Later transferred to Hulluch Sector. Entrained at St. Pol for Puchevillers (7/10) and from there took over front line west of Serre. To Colincamps (13/11).

15th (Service) Battalion (1st Leeds). 93rd Brigade, 31st Division: Moved forward from Bus-lès-Artois (30/6) for attack on Serre (1/7) – on right of assault Battalion was cut down in No Man's Land – all officers becoming casualties. Relieved from front line and to Louvencourt (5/7). To Beauval (6/7), Fienvillers (7/7). Entrained at Conteville for Berguette and Béthune sector (8/7). Arrived Doullens and marched to Famechon (7/10). To Courcelles (17/10). Began tours of duty Hébuterne sector (21/10). To Sailly-au-Bois (11/11), Coigneux Wood (12/11), Couin (14/11).

16th (Service) Battalion (1st Bradford). 93rd Brigade, 31st Division: Attack on Serre (1/7) – went forward behind 15th West Yorkshire at 7.35 a.m. – heavy casualties before reaching British front line. Regimental history by Everard Wyrall records no advanced past British wire and casualties totalling 537. Commanding Officer Major G.S. Guyon killed. Withdrew from front line (4/7). Entrained at Conteville for Béthune sector (9/7). Arrived Doullens (7/10) and from there marched to Famechon. Took over line Hébuterne sector (21/10). Regimental history notes raiding parties on (23/10) and (27/10). To Coigneux (30/10), front line (7/11), Coigneux (14/11).

17th (Service) Battalion (2nd Leeds). 106th Brigade, 35th Division: Entrained at Chocques for Frévent (2/7) and from there marched to Le Souich. To Bois de Warnimont (5/7), Varennes (10/7), Bresle (12/7). Arrived Talus Boisé (14/7) and ordered to stand by for duty in front line. Involved in various duties – provided carrying parties to forward areas, loaded trench mortar bombs at Carnoy. Also 2 attempts at burying a cable in Bernafay Wood. Constant shelling preventing work being carried out. To South Trench south of Montauban under orders of 26th Brigade, 9th Division ((18/7). 'Y' and 'Z' Companies attached to 9th Seaforth Highlanders at Montauban (19/7) and at night to Caftet Wood. Duties at South Street included burial of dead and salvage work. Relieved and to Caftet Wood (21/7). Moved forward to trenches south-west of Montauban (22/7). Attached to 9th Division for operations at Longueval and Delville Wood. From Montauban Alley 2 companies provided carrying parties (23/7). To positions north-east of Bernafay Wood (24/7) – burial duty, salvage work. To Caftet Wood (25/7). To Dublin Trench in reserve (29/7), Caftet Wood (31/7) and from there Sandpit Camp. War Diary records casualties since (13/7) as 10 officers and 304 other ranks. Not having been in action, these high figures indicate severity of shelling. To Morlancourt (1/8). Entrained at Méricourt for rest area near Foudrinoy

(5/8). Entrained for Méricourt (10/8) and from there marched to Morlancourt. To Sandpit Valley (16/8), Carnoy area and trenches south-east of Guillemont (20/8), Happy Valley (26/8). Entrained at Heilly for Candas (30/8) and from there marched to billets. Began move to Arras sector (31/8).

18th (Service) Battalion (2nd Bradford). 93rd Brigade, 31st Division: Moved forward from Bus-lès-Artois with 15th and 16th West Yorkshire during night (30/6). Attack on Serre (1/7) – followed 15th and 16th into action suffering over 400 casualties (including Commanding Officer Lieutenant-Colonel E.C. Kennard) during move towards British front line. Relieved (4/7). Entrained at Conteville for Béthune sector (8/7). Arrived Doullens from Lillers (7/10) and from there to Thièvres. To front line Hébuterne sector (21/10). Relieved (30/10), to front line (7/11), relieved (14/11).

21st (Service) Battalion (Wool Textile Pioneers). Pioneers, 4th Division: Headquarters at Bertrancourt (1/7) – 'A' Company could not carry out work digging communication trenches across No Man's Land due to heavy machine gun fire. Withdrew to British front and support trenches – returning to Bertrancourt after 2 days. War Diary records that 'D' Company and part of 'B' were engaged during 4th Division's attack between Serre and Beaumont-Hamel (2/7). 4th Division entrained at Doullens for Ypres sector (21/7). Arrived Longueau (18/9), located at Citadel Camp (30/9). Moved forward (8/10), took over camp near La Briqueterie (10/10). Work on roads. In front line throughout operations at Le Transloy Ridges (12/10)–(23/10). To Citadel Camp (23/10), later to Fresne.

22nd (Labour) Battalion. Arrived Heilly from Frévent (4/9) and from there marched to Sailly-le-Sec. Moved to forward area (6/9). Worked on road maintenance in Montauban, Guillemont, Bazentin and Longueval areas.

East Yorkshire Regiment

1st Battalion. 64th Brigade, 21st Division: In support of 9th and 10th K.O.Y.L.I. during attack towards Fricourt (1/7) – advanced under heavy machine gun fire – Crucifix Trench and sunken road taken – enemy counter attack from Shelter Wood at about 2 p.m repulsed – Commanding Officer Lieutenant-Colonel M.B. Stow mortally wounded. War Diary notes that due to heavy casualties, further advance was not possible – all efforts directed to consolidating and holding gains. Withdrew about 6.30 a.m. (2/7) to assembly trenches behind Sausage Support Trench. Bombers in action in trenches to left of position about mid-day. Relieved 8 p.m. (3/7) and to railway sidings near Dernancourt. Casualties – 460. Entrained for Ailly-sur-Somme (4/7) and from there marched to Yzeux. To Fourdrinoy (7/7), Ailly-sur-Somme (10/7). Entrained for Ville 1.40 a.m. (11/7) and from there to Corbie. Via Carcaillot Farm near Méaulte to Rose Cottage, Fricourt (13/7). At 12.25 a.m. (14/7) moved forward in reserve at south-east corner of Mametz Wood. Attached to 110th Brigade 'A' and 'B' Companies sent forward to reinforce 7th Leicestershire at north edge of Bazentin-le-Petit Wood – 'C' and 'D' followed later in afternoon. 'C' Company advanced into wood with little resistance and later held off counter attack – War diary records heavy casualties from own artillery. Further action in wood until relieved. Withdrew 8.30 a.m. (17/7). Rejoined 64th Brigade south-east corner of Mametz Wood – later to Carcaillot Farm. To bivouacs near Bécourt Wood (18/7). Casualties for operations (13/7)–(17/7) – 354. Entrained at Méricourt for Saleux (20/7). To Dreuil (21/7). Entrained at Longueau for St. Pol (23/7). Entrained at Frévent for Méricourt (13/9) and from there marched to Dernancourt. To Fricourt Camp (15/9) and from there to Pommiers Redoubt. Attack on Gueudecourt (16/9) – moved forward 2 a.m to Flers Trench just south of the village – later to Flea Trench – 'B' Company in action supporting 9th K.O.Y.L.I. Relieved and to Pommiers Redoubt. Casualties – 181. To Fricourt Camp (18/9). Pommiers Redoubt (22/9) and from there to positions just south of Longueval at 5 p.m. – assembly trenches dug during night near Gueudecourt. Assembled just north of Flers (24/9). Led attack with 10th K.O.Y.L.I. on Gueudecourt (25/9) – advancing at 12.35 p.m towards Gird Trench found enemy's wire to be intact and almost unaffected by the British bombardment. Took cover in shell-holes – at night withdrew to Switch Trench. War Diary notes strength as being just 5 officers and 118 other ranks. Moved forward to front line (26/9) and later to Gird Trench. New line consolidated and held. Relieved and to Longueval (27/9). Casualties – 260. To Buire (1/10). Entrained at Méricourt for Longpré (3/10) and from there marched to Yaucourt. Entrained at Abbeville for Chocques (8/10).

1/4th Battalion (T.F.). 150th Brigade, 50th (Northumbrian) Division: Arrived Doullens from Ypres sector (11/8) and from there to Vacquerie. To Molliens-au-Bois (16/8), Millencourt (17/8), Shelter Wood (9/9), north-west corner of Mametz Wood (10/9) and from there to forward trenches. Attack on Martinpuich (15/9) – from Swansea Trench advanced on right at 6.20 a.m. – Martin Trench taken and consolidated. Further action towards Starfish Line (16/9) – withdrawal ordered after 10 p.m. Relieved and to trenches near Bazentin-le-Petit Wood. Casualties – 250. To Quadrangle Trench (20/9), front line (23/9) – Prue Trench and Starfish Line. Regimental history by Everard Wyrall records 'small seizures of ground in front of Eaucourt l'Abbaye.' Withdrew to reserve line (28/9). In reserve during capture of Eaucourt l'Abbaye and enemy defences east and west of it. To front line (1/10), Mametz Wood (2/10), Albert (3/10), Baizieux (4/10), Contalmaison (23/10) – attached for work in line under 9th Division. To High Wood (24/10) – wood heavily shelled for 2 days. Moved to positions south-west of wood (26/10). Took turns in forward area – Everard Wyrall recording nearly a month of 'misery' in trenches about Flers. Entrained at Bazentin-le-Petit for Bécourt (18/11).

6th (Service) Battalion (Pioneers). Pioneers, 11th (Northern) Division: Arrived Bouquemaison from Arras sector (31/8). Moved by buses to Acheux (1/9) and from there marched to Aveluy ('A' and ''B' Companies), Usna Redoubt (HQ, 'C' and 'B'). Work began on trenches (Brimstone, Ration). 'B' Company dug two communication trenches from front line to recently captured Wonder Work (14/9) – H.Q at Crucifix Corner. H.Q. To Aveluy Château (15/9). Worked on clearing line for light railway to Pozières and digging communication trenches and dug outs. Began work on communication trench after capture of Zollern Redoubt (26/9). When work was held up by heavy fire from Mouquet Farm, Lieutenant T.B. Coultas (16 Platoon, D Company) ordered his men to put down their tools and take up rifles. He then lead an attack on the farm but almost at once was killed. A sergeant then took charge and was later successful in clearing the position. Only 13 out of the platoon's 33 men remained. Work continued in the area. Entrained at Acheux for Candas (1/10) and from there marched to Bernaville. To Domqueur (3/10), St. Ouen (4/10), Val de Maison (8/10), Martinsart Wood (9/10). Worked on light railways – Aveluy Siding, Authuille Wood, Pozières and on new camp at Dogs Leg. Moved into new camp (15/10). To Forceville (16/11). Worked on Varennes-Léalvillers Road.

7th (Service) Battalion. 50th Brigade, 17th (Northern) Division: In support at beginning of attack on Fricourt (1/7) – 'C' and 'D' Companies at Bécordel-Becort, 'A' and 'B' – Bonte Redoubt. 'C' and 'D' took over British front line shortly after zero – went forward for second phase of assault 2.33 p.m. Objective – Red Cottage could not be reached owing to heavy machine gun fire. 'B' Company having come forward could not get out of its front trenches. Relieved 5.30 a.m. (2/7) and to Ville. Casualties – 123. To Méaulte (3/7) – burying parties to Fricourt (5/7) – later took over front line. Bombing attack on Quadrangle Alley and Quadrangle Support failed (7/7). Withdrew to Railway Alley (8/7). Casualties 145. Renewed attack by 'C' and 'D' Companies (10/7) also failed. Casualties about 143. Relieved and to Grove Town Camp. Entrained for Saleux (11/7) and from there moved to Molliens-Vidames. To Vauchelles (15/7), Condé (22/7). Entrained for Méricourt (25/7) and from there marched to Dernancourt. To Belle Vue Farm (1/8), moved forward (2/8) took over Pommiers Redoubt (4/8), Montauban Alley (5/8), front line Longueval and Delville Wood (9/8). To Pommiers Redoubt (12/8), Dernancourt (13/8). Entrained at Méricourt for Candas and from there marched to Prouville (15/8). To Beauvoir-Rivière (16/8), Halloy (17/8), Bayencourt (21/8), front line Hébuterne (25/8), Sailly-au-Bois (31/8), front line (6/9), Bayencourt (12/9), Halloy (15/9), Frohen-le-Grand (20/9), Conteville (21/9), Le Plessiel (22/9), Neuilly-le-Dien and Acquet (6/10), Frohen-le-Grand and Frohen-le-Petit (7/10), Mondicourt (10/10), Souastre (11/10), front line Hébuterne (14/10) – War diary notes enemy observation balloon rose from behind Pigeon Wood and search-light from direction of Bucquoy. To Bayencourt (18/10), Halloy (19/10), Talmas (20/10), Lahoussoye (21/10), Méaulte (22/10), Mansell Camp (27/10). Moved through Guillemont and Ginchy to front line Lesbœufs sector (2/11). Unsuccessful attack on Orion Trench (5/11). Casualties – 193. Relieved (6/11). To front line (10/11) – War Diary notes that sand bags were wrapped round the legs in place of puttees. To Mansell Camp (13/11), Méaulte (14/11). Entrained at Edgehill for Hangest (15/11) and from there moved in lorries to Montagne.

8th (Service) Battalion. 8th Brigade, 3rd Division: Entrained at Wizernes for Candas (1/7) and from there marched to Franqueville. To Flesselles (3/7), Cardonnette (4/7), Corbie (5/7), Celestines Wood (6/7), Carnoy (7/7). Moved forward through Montauban (13/7) and assembled in Caterpillar Valley for attack towards enemy line between Longueval and Bazentin-le-Grand (14/7) – assault held up by uncut wire – heavy machine gun and rifle fire forced withdrawal to assemble positions. Commanding Officer Lieutenant-Colonel B.I. Way wounded at wire. Renewed attack with 2nd Royal Scots at 12.15 p.m. successful. Casualties – 459. Relieved and to trenches just north of Quarry during night (20/7). To Bernafay Wood (22/7). Two companies sent forward to hold north-east edge of Trônes Wood (23/7). To Happy Valley during night (25/7). To Méaulte (26/7), Happy Valley (13/8), 'A' and 'D' Companies to Citadel Camp (14/8). To Great Bear (15/8), Talus Boisé (16/8), front line south-east of Guillemont (17/8). Attacked south-east of Arrow Head Copse (18/8) – moved forward under fire from both flanks – bombers entered German line on right – part of 'B' Company gained hold on left. Unsupported on the flanks and forced to retire. Relieved and to Carnoy (20/8). Casualties – 170. To Méaulte (21/8) – War Diary notes 6 men and 2 horses badly wounded by bombs dropped from aeroplane (22/8). Entrained at Méricourt for Candas (23/8) and from there took over billets at Bernaville. Transferred to Hulluch sector (25/8). Entrained at St. Pol for Varennes (7/10) and from there marched to Mailly-Maillet Wood. To Bus-lès-Artois (17/10). 'A', 'B' and 'C' Companies to trenches Serre sector (29/10) and attached to battalions of 76th Brigade. H.Q. and 'D' Company to Courcelles (29/10), joined there by rest of battalion. To front line Serre sector (1/11), Louvencourt (4/11), front line (12/11). Attack on Serre (13/11) – in support moved forward behind 2nd Royal Scots at 5.45 a.m. – assault checked and withdrew to assembly positions by 10 a.m. Relieved and to Bus Wood (14/11). Casualties – 235. To Courcelles (15/11), front line (16/11), Courcelles (17/11).

10th (Service) Battalion (1st Hull). 92nd Brigade, 31st Division: In reserve during 31st Division's attack on Serre (1/7). Withdrew to Bus-lès-Artois (2/7), Beauval (5/7), Bernaville (6/7). Entrained at Auxi-le-Château for Robecq (8/7). Arrived Candas from Merville (8/10) and from there marched to Vauchelles. To bivouacs near Sailly-au-Bois (16/10), Rossignol Farm (17/10), Sailly (18/10), Hébuterne (20/10) – took over front line. To Coigneux and St. Léger (21/10). H.Q. 'B' and 'C' companies to Bois de Warnimont (30/10). To Bayencourt (10/11), front line (12/11). In reserve for attack north of Serre (13/11) – provided carrying parties. Withdrew to Bayencourt 7.30 p.m. To Bois de Warnimont (14/11).

11th (Service) Battalion (2nd Hull). 92nd Brigade, 31st Division: Remained in support trenches during attack on Serre (1/7). 'A' Company to Bus-lès-Artois, rest to Bois de Warnimont (2/7). To Beauval (5/7), Beaumetz (6/7). Entrained at Auxi-le-Château for Thiennes (8/7) and from there marched to Robecq. Entrained at Merville for Candas (8/10) and from there marched to Vauchelles. War Diary records training included practice attacks in conjunction with 'contact patrol' aeroplanes. Moved by bus to Sailly-au-Bois (16/10). Headquarters, 'C' and 'D' Companies to Bois de Warnimont (21/10). 'A' and 'B' to Bois de Warnimont (22/10). 'A' and 'B' Companies moved by bus to Sailly-au-Bois (28/10) and took part in unsuccessful raid on German line. Returned to Bois de Warnimont (29/10). To Rossignol Farm and front line (10/11). Attacked north of Serre (13/11) – in close support to 12th and 13th East Yorkshire, 'A' and 'B' Companies moved forward to Caber Trench 9.30 a.m. – trench heavily bombarded and withdrew to Nairn Trench. Returned

6 p.m. Relieved by 13th York and Lancaster and to Sailly-au-Bois 9 p.m. To Bois de Warnimont (14/11). War Diary records parties sent forward to clear battlefield during next few days.

12th (Service) Battalion (3rd Hull). 92nd Brigade, 31st Division: In reserve during attack on Serre (1/7). To Bois de Warnimont (2/7), Beauval (5/7), Bernaville (6/7). Entrained at Auxi-le-Château for Robecq (8/7). Arrived Candas from Merville (9/10) and from there marched to Vauchelles. Took over front line Hébuterne (16/10). To Sailly-au-Bois (20/10), Rossignol Farm (21/10), Bois de Warnimont (29/10), Rossignol Farm (10/11), front line (12/11). Attack north of Serre (13/11) – War Diary notes all objectives taken in under 20 minutes with few casualties – 'the barrage being excellent' – over 300 prisoners sent back – enemy twice counter attacked in force 'but were annihilated by our Lewis Guns.' It is also noted that due to failed assault by 3rd Division on right a withdrawal was forced during evening. The days fighting is recorded as being of the fiercest kind – hand-to-hand much of the time with the bayonet and bomb doing much work. Private John Cunningham awarded Victoria Cross. Withdrew to Rossignol Farm (14/11). Casualties – 383. German casualties estimated in War Diary at more than 1,000. To Bois de Warnimont at 3 p.m.

13th (Service) Battalion (4th Hull). 92nd Brigade, 31st Division: In reserve during attack on Serre (1/7). To Bois de Warnimont (2/7), Beauval (5/7), Prouville (6/7), Auxi-le-Château (8/7). Entrained for Robecq (9/7). Arrived Candas from Merville (9/10). To Sailly-au-Bois (16/10), trenches Hébuterne sector (17/10), Couin (21/10), Bois de Warnimont (30/10), Coigneux (10/11), assembly trenches (12/11). Attack north of Serre (13/11) – advanced on right 5.45 a.m. – War Diary notes that first wave had no difficulty in taking German first line – second and third also went through with ease. Battalion on right (2nd Suffolk) having fell back left right flank exposed. Withdrew after counter attacks 7.30 p.m. To Rossignol Farm at 11 p.m., Bois de Warnimont (14/11).

Bedfordshire Regiment

1st Battalion. 15th Brigade, 5th Division: Arrived Hem-Hardinval (13/7). To Puchevillers via Candas (14/7), Lahoussoye via Montigny (15/7), Ville-sur-Ancre (17/7), Pommiers Redoubt (19/7). In reserve to 5th Division's operations at High Wood. Took over line between High Wood and Delville Wood (23/7). Relieved and to Pommiers (25/7). Attack on Longueval (27/7) – heavy casualties from gas shelling during advance to forward positions and at assembly line – objectives later taken. To Pommiers (28/7). In action at Longueval (30/7) – line held. To Pommiers (31/7), bivouacs north-west of Dernancourt (2/8). Entrained at Méricourt for Hangest-sur-Somme (3/8) and from there to billets at Quesnoy. To Tailly (5/8), Longpré (24/8). Entrained for Méricourt (25/8) and via billets north-east of Buire to Sandpit Camp. To bivouacs near Bronfay Farm (26/8). Relieved 12th Gloucestershire at Silesia Trench (31/8). Attack on Falfemont Farm (3/9) – moving just left of main objective cleared enemy from Wedge Wood – Ginchy Road reached. Further action (4/9) – withdrawal from forward trenches ordered due to heavy casualties from own barrage – later advanced at 3 p.m. – objectives and many prisoners taken after hand-to-hand fighting and high loss – line consolidated from northern corner of Falfemont Farm. To Billon Farm (6/9), Citadel Camp (7/9), Morlancourt (9/9), Citadel (15/9), positions near Waterlot Farm under orders of 20th Division (16/9). Moved forward to old German line between Guillemont and Wedge Wood (18/9), support trenches Ginchy sector (20/9). To Oxford Copse (22/9). Attack on Morval (25/9) – in support passed through 1st Norfolk and took sunken road within 10 minutes of zero hour. To Oxford Copse (26/9), Citadel Camp (27/9). Entrained at Méricourt for Longpré (29/9). Entrained for Béthune sector (1/10).

2nd Battalion. 89th Brigade, 30th Division: From assembly positions near Maricourt moved forward for attack on Montauban (1/7) – followed 100 yards in rear of attacking battalions (17th and 20th King's) and took over Faviere and Silesia Trenches. Gains consolidated. Dug new trench (Bedford Trench) running east from Germans Wood to La Briqueterie Road. Relieved and to Bois des Tailles (4/7). To Billon Wood (8/7), trenches near Machine Gun Wood (9/7). Assembled in sunken road opposite La Briqueterie (10/7). In action at Trônes Wood (11/7) – after high losses remnants of 'A' and 'B' Companies dug in on eastern side of wood – strong bombing attack later forced withdrawal to La Briqueterie. Remaining companies withdrew after heavy fighting early (12/7). Casualties – 244. From La Briqueterie to Bois des Tailles (13/7), Vaux-sur-Somme (14/7), Happy Valley (19/7), Citadel Camp (20/7). Moved forward to assembly positions in sunken road opposite La Briqueterie (30/7). 'A' Company in attack (with French) on

Maltz Horn Farm. Later in reserve during attack on Guillemont – 'B' and 'C' companies dug new trench (300 yards) connecting Arrow Head Copse to north end of Maltz Horn Trench. Relieved and to Citadel. Casualties – 192. Entrained at Dernancourt for Longpré (2/8) and from there to billets at Vaux-Marquenneville and Fresneville. To Pont-Remy (3/8). Entrained for Merville (4/8). Entrained at Lillers for Doullens (18/9) and from there marched to billets at Gézaincourt. To Vignacourt (21/9), Dernancourt (4/10), Bazentin-le-Grand (10/10) – later to trenches north-west of Flers. Attack on Gird and Bite Trenches (12/10) – advanced at 2.05 p.m. – leading wave held up by strong machine gun fire about 60 yards in front of Gird. On right – 'C' and 'D' Companies cleared southern end of Gird towards Bayonet Trench. With 'B' Company, latter went on to take 200 yards of Bite. Withdrew to reserve trenches (Switch Line) west of Flers (13/10). Casualties – 252. To bivouacs just west of Montauban (14/10), Flers Trench in reserve (16/10), Mametz Wood (22/10), Buire (24/10). Entrained for Doullens ('C' and 'D' Companies from Méricourt, 'A' and 'B' Companies from Dernancourt) (26/10). Arrived 6 a.m. (27/10) and marched to Mondicourt.

4th Battalion (Extra Reserve). 190th Brigade, 63rd (Royal Naval) Division: Arrived Acheux (3/10). To Léalvillers (4/10), Hédauville (6/10). Moved forward via Mailly-Maillet (White City) to front line Redan sector. To Mailly-Maillet Wood (11/10), Arquèves (16/10), Léalvillers (17/10), Puchevillers via Arquèves and Raincheval (18/10), Varennes via Harponville (21/10), Englebelmer (30/10). Took over front line trenches (Knightsbridge) Hamel sector. To Puchevillers via Hédauville (7/11), Varennes (11/11), assembly trenches off Bedford Street and Victoria Street (12/11). In rear of assault towards Beaucourt (13/11). Provided carrying parties up to Beaucourt (14/11) – retiring to Robert's Trench 4 p.m. To bivouacs on Englebelmer-Martinsart Road (16/11). Assisted in clearing battlefield and burying dead (17/11). By buses to Longuevillette (18/11).

6th (Service) Battalion. 112th Brigade, 37th Division: From Bienvillers moved forward (1/7) – on left of 46th Division during its attack at Gommecourt, formed defensive flank and fired smoke bombs along front. To Halloy (2/7), Millencourt (6/7), positions just outside Albert (Tara-Usna line) in reserve (7/7), Heligoland trenches in support (11/7), Tara-Usna line (13/7). Attack on Pozières (15/7) – assault soon held up by machine gun fire and leading waves forced to retire. Casualties – over 244. To Albert (16/7), Bresle (19/7), Lahoussoye (20/7), Béhencourt (22/7), Bresle (30/7), Bécourt Wood (31/7), Bottom Wood in reserve (3/8), Bazentin-le-Petit (6/8). Took part in operations around Intermediate Line. To trenches between Bazentin-le-Petit Wood and Mametz Wood (10/8), Bécourt Wood (15/8),

Béhencourt (16/8). Entrained at Fréchencourt for Longpré (18/8) and from there marched to Airaines. Entrained at Longpré for Bailleul (20/8) and marched to Estaires. Arrived Longuevillette from Rebreuve (21/10). To Sarton (22/10), Beaussart (23/10), Arquèves (25/10), Sarton (27/10), Louvencourt (12/11), Mailly-Maillet via Bertrancourt (13/11). Took part in attacks on Frankfort and Munich Trenches (14/11) and (15/11). Withdrew to Waggon Road (16/11), Englebelmer via Mailly-Maillet (17/11). To positions between Hamel and Beaucourt (18/11).

7th (Service) Battalion. 54th Brigade, 18th (Eastern) Division: Took part in successful assault on Pommiers Redoubt (1/7) – led assault with 11th Royal Fusiliers – heavy casualties among officers – leading waves led by N.C.Os. Relieved after consolidation of Redoubt, Beetle Alley and New Trench and to Carnoy (2/7). Casualties – 321. At about 7 p.m. moved forward to reserve positions in former German trenches, Battalion H.Q. at Piccadilly. Withdrawn to Caftet Wood (3/7). To forward trenches (Pommiers and Caterpillar) (6/7). Relieved by 14th King's and to dugouts near Bronfay Farm (9/7). To Bois des Tailles (10/7), Trigger Wood (13/7), Maricourt (14/7). In reserve during 54th Brigade's attack on Trônes Wood. To Bois des Tailles (18/7). Entrained at Edgehill for Longpré (21/7) and via Wiry to Citerne. Entrained at Longpré for St. Omer (23/7). Arrived Raincheval (11/9). To Varennes via Arquèves, Léalvillers and Acheux (23/9), North Bluff, Authuille via Hédauville, Bouzincourt and Martinsart (25/9). In reserve during attack on Thiepval (26/9) – moved forward during night and made successful assault on north-western corner of village – 'C' and 'D' Companies advancing at about 5.45 a.m. (27/9). Fierce hand-to-hand fighting at Schwaben Redoubt (28/9). Second-Lieutenant T.E. Adlam awarded Victoria Cross. Withdrawn to Thiepval (29/9), Mailly-Maillet Wood (30/9). Entrained at Acheux for Candas (2/10) and from there to billets at Vacquerie and Gorges. To Beauval (15/10), Vadencourt Wood (16/10), Bouzincourt (17/10), Albert (19/10), front line (Regina Trench) (23/10), Albert (26/10), Regina Trench (3/11), Tara Hill (6/11), Regina Trench (12/11), huts in Mash Valley near Ovillers (15/11). Employed in improving communication trenches in area until (19/11).

8th (Service) Battalion. 16th Brigade, 6th Division: Entrained at Poperinghe for Amplier (2/8). To Puchevillers via Orville, Sarton, Marieux (4/8), Acheux via Raincheval, Arquèves, Louvencourt (7/8), Englebelmer (11/8). To Auchonvillers and trenches opposite Beaumont-Hamel (15/8), Beaussart (20/8), Amplier (28/8), Naours (29/8). Training program included practising communication with aeroplanes. Flares and flashing periscopes being used to mark position. To Villers-Bocage (6/9), Corbie (7/9), Bois des Tailles (8/9), Germans Wood near Maricourt (11/9). Relieved 8th Middlesex in trenches north-east of Leuze Wood (12/9). Two attacks made on The Quadrilateral (13/9) – 'B' Company bombing its way about 100 yards along German trench at 6 a.m. but forced to retire. Later, in frontal attack, enemy driven in from his advance post but Quadrilateral not taken. Renewed attack (15/9) also failed. Withdrew to reserve trenches south-east of Guillemont. Casualties since (13/9) – about 400. To Maltz Horn Farm (16/9), trenches south-east of Guillemont in reserve (18/9). Later withdrew to La Briqueterie. To Morlancourt (19/9). Dug in at north-east corner of Guillemont in support of 1st East Kent in front line (21/9). Later moved forward and in reserve during operations between Morval and Lesbœufs. Relieved and to trenches between Trônes and Bernafay Woods (26/9). To Méaulte via Mametz (30/9), Citadel Camp (7/10), Trônes Wood (11/10), trenches (Tatler and Punch) north-east of Ginchy (11/10). Relieved 1st K.S.L.I. east of Gueudecourt (13/10). To Méaulte (20/10), Corbie (21/10). Entrained for Longpré (23/10) and from there marched to Huppy. Entrained at Pont-Remy for Béthune (28/10).

Leicestershire Regiment

1st Battalion. 71st Brigade, 6th Division: Entrained at Proven (2/8) arrived early next morning at Candas. During the journey a serious accident was averted while the train was passing Frévent. The rear carriages having broke away while climbing a steep incline soon gathered speed and began to roll back down the line. Another train due – a pointsman quickly switched the carriages into a siding where they ran into buffers. Only 7 men and 5 horses being hurt. Marched to billets at Beauval. To Léalvillers (4/8), Mailly-Maillet Wood (5/8). Relieved 2nd Grenadier Guards right sector in front of Beaumont-Hamel (14/8). Relieved and to Mailly-Maillet Wood (19/8). To Louvencourt (27/8), Beauval (28/8), Flesselles (29/8), Cardonnette (6/9), Méricourt (7/9), Sandpit Camp area (8/9). Moved forward to front line (11/9). Began work carrying bombs and ammunition up to Trônes Wood (12/9). With 9th Norfolk formed up during night (14/9) on sunken Ginchy-Leuze Wood Road – battalion's left close to the village. War Diary notes advance of tank about 5.50 a.m. (15/9) which fired into German trenches – enemy's machine guns had no effect. Attacked 6.20 a.m. – 'B' and 'D' Companies advanced followed by 'C' and 'A' – immediate machine gun fire from enemy line – held up by strong wire net in front of trench leading from north-west corner of The Quadrilateral. Withdrew to Maltz Horn Farm (17/9). To front line under orders of 16th Brigade (18/9). Returned to Maltz Horn early morning (19/9). Upon arrival found no accommodation and moved on to billets at Ville-sur-Ancre. To Citadel Camp (22/9), Carnoy craters (24/9), reserve line (25/9), front line trenches east of Morval (26/9). Held Thunder Trench which was also occupied by the enemy – War Diary recording 'Huns harassed all day by rifle grenades and bombs.' To billets near Guillemont (28/9), Carnoy craters (29/9), Sandpit Camp (30/9). Casualties since (14/9) – 456. To camp south of Mametz (7/10), Bernafay Wood (8/10). Relieved 9th Suffolk in Needle Trench (15/10). Carrying parties to front line. 'B' and 'D' Companies moved forward to Rainbow Trench (17/10). Relieved and via Bernafay Wood to Sandpit Camp (20/10). To Corbie (21/10). Entrained for Airaines (24/10) and from there to billets at Sorel-en-Vimeu and Wanel. Entrained at Pont-Remy for Béthune area (29/10).

1/4th Battalion (T.F.). 138th Brigade, 46th (North Midland) Division: In reserve during attack at Gommecourt (1/7). Moved up from St. Amand and by 10 p.m. located in Midland Trench behind Foncquevillers. To Hannescamps sector (2/7). From Halloy to Bouquemaison (31/10), Nœux (1/11), Oneux (2/11), Drucat (3/11), Domvast (8/11), Drucat (11/11).

1/5th Battalion (T.F.). 138th Brigade 46th (North Midland) Division: War

Diary records positions at midnight (30/6) – 'A' and 'D' Companies in dug-outs and cellars Foncquevillers, remainder in assembly position Midland Trench. Attack on Gommecourt (1/7) – ordered to dig communication trench across No Man's Land parallel to Foncquevillers-Gommecourt Road (1/7). Work soon stopped due to heavy shelling and then assisted in 137th Brigade's assault. Remained in front line clearing dead and wounded. Relieved and to Bienvillers (3/7). Arrived Conteville from Villers-l'Hôpital (2/11). To Millencourt (3/11)

6th (Service) Battalion. 110th Brigade, 21st Division: In reserve at Humber-camps with 37th Division (1/7). Transferred with 110th Brigade to 21st at Talmas (6/7). To Hangest-sur-Somme (7/7). Entrained at Ailly for Méricourt (10/7) and from there marched to Fricourt. To Fricourt Wood (11/7) – 'A' and 'B' Companies taking over support line Quadrangle Trench. To Mametz Wood (13/7). Attack on Bazentin-le-Petit (14/7) – from assemble positions 100 yards in front of Mametz Wood moved forward 3.25 a.m. – leading waves entered enemy's front trenches – second line taken by 4 a.m. – line advanced into village 6.05 a.m. Held positions northern end of village southwards to Bazentin-le-Petit Wood against counter attacks until relieved during night (16/7). To bivouacs just south of Fricourt Wood. Casualties – 527. To Ribemont (17/7). Entrained for Saleux (20/7) and from there marched to Hangest. To Longpré (21/7). Entrained at Longueau for St. Pol (22/7). Entrained at Frévent for Dernancourt (13/9). To Fricourt Camp via Méaulte and Bécordel (15/9), Bernafay Wood (17/9). Worked on communication and support trenches. Moved forward through Delville Wood to assembly trenches (25/9). Attack on Gueudecourt – 'D' and 'C' companies to support line 1 p.m. Later moved forward to assist 8th and 9th Leicestershire fighting in Gird Trench – positions held during night – Pioneer Trench, Bulls Road. Advanced 4.30 p.m. (26/9) – village entered 5.30 p.m. War Diary records heavy sniping and machine gun fire at Lesbœufs-Factory Corner Road. Later moved on to orchards on northern and eastern outskirts. Positions consolidated and held against counter attacks. Relieved and to Bernafay Wood (29/9). Casualties – 211. To Dernancourt (2/10). Entrained at Edgehill for Longpré (4/10) and from there marched to Cocquerel. Entrained at Pont-Remy for Béthune (7/10).

7th (Service) Battalion. 110th Brigade, 21st Division: In reserve with 37th Division at Souastre (1/7). To Warlincourt (3/7). Transferred with 110th Brigade to 21st Division at Talmas (6/7). To Hangest-sur-Somme (7/7). Entrained at Ailly for Méricourt (10/7) and from there by bus to Méaulte. To Bottom Wood and Quadrangle Trench (11/7). To Fricourt (13/7), Mametz

Wood (14/7). Attack on Bazentin-le-Petit – advanced at 3.25 a.m. with 6th Leicestershire – 'D' Company on left and 'B' and 'C' in centre held up by machine gun fire. Enemy's front and second lines taken by 4.a.m. War Diary notes by this time only 2 officers left in action. Village later cleared and line established in Bazentin-le-Petit Wood. Relieved and to Fricourt Wood (16/7). Casualties – 553. To Ribemont (17/7). Entrained at Méricourt for Saleux (20/7) and from there marched to Hangest. To Longpré (21/7). Entrained for St Pol Area (22/7). Entrained at Frévent for Dernancourt (13/9). To Bécordel (15/9), bivouacs near Bernafay Wood (16/9). Attack on Gueudecourt (25/9) – 2 companies moved forward to Brown Trench north of Delville Wood in reserve and 2 behind Switch Trench in support. Bombers in action 7.15 a.m. (26/9) – Gird Trench taken. Relieved 6th Leicestershire in captured line north and north-east of Gueudecourt (29/9). Commanding Officer Lieutenant-Colonel W. Drysdale, D.S.O. killed by sniper. Relieved by 9th East Surrey and to Bernafay Wood (1/10). To Dernancourt (2/10). Entrained for Longpré (4/10) and from there to Pont-Remy. Entrained for Béthune (7/10).

8th (Service) Battalion. 110th Brigade, 21st Division: Transferred with 110th Brigade from 37th Division at Humbercamps to 21st at Talmas (6/7). To – Soues (7/7). Entrained at Ailly-sur-Somme for Méricourt (10/7) and from there by lorries to Méaulte. Moved forward to Fricourt during night and from there took over support trenches – Railway Alley, Sunshine Alley, Willow Trench, Willow Avenue. Assembled north edge Mametz Wood for attack on Bazentin-le-Petit during night (13/7) – 'D' Company advanced with 6th and 7th Leicestershire 3.25 a.m. (14/7) – Villa Trench taken. War Diary records not a single officer left and assault led by N.C.Os. Rest of Battalion went forward 4.25 a.m. reaching northern edge Bazentin-le-Petit Wood. Commanding Officer Lieutenant-Colonel J.G. Mignon killed during enemy counter attack up Aston and Villa Trenches. Relieved and to Ribemont (17/7). Casualties 426. To Méricourt (18/7). Entrained for Saleux (20/7) and from there marched to Soues. To Longpré (21/7). Entrained at Longueau for St. Pol (22/7). Entrained at Frévent for Dernancourt (13/9). To bivouacs between Fricourt and Méaulte (15/9). Moved forward to position about half-mile east of Trônes Wood in reserve (17/9). Carrying parties to front line. To assembly positions for attack on Gueudecourt during night (24/9). Attacked (25/9) – War Diary records assault as being with 'splendid heroism' – entered village and throughout night engaged enemy in hand-to-hand fighting. Relieved by 7th Leicestershire and withdrew to second line. Moved back to Swiss Trench (28/9), Bernafay Wood (1/10). To Dernancourt (2/10). Entrained for Longpré (4/10) and from there marched to Pont Remy. Entrained for Béthune (7/10).

9th (Service) Battalion. 110th Brigade, 21st Division: In reserve at Souastre with 37th Division (1/7). To Humbercamps (3/7). 110th Brigade transferred to 21st Division at Talmas (6/7). To Crouy (7/7). Entrained at Ailly-sur-Somme for Méricourt (10/7) and from there moved by bus to Méaulte. During night to Fricourt and from there took over recently capture Quadrangle Trench and Support. Relieved and to Fricourt (12/7). Carrying parties to Mametz Wood. Moved forward to southern edge of Mametz Wood 12.15 a.m. (14/7). In reserve for attack on Bazentin-le-Petit – 'B' Company reinforced 6th Leicestershire north edge Bazentin-le-Petit Wood. Moved forward to assist 6th, 7th and 8th Leicestershire at Bazentin-le-Petit Wood – heavy fighting and high casualties around north-west edge. 'A' Company took over and consolidated captured German first line. 'D' and 'B' Companies to Bazentin-le-Petit (16/7). Relieved and to Fricourt (17/7). Casualties – 412. To Ribemont (18/7). Entrained at Méricourt for Saleux (20/7) and from there marched to Crouy. To Longpré (21/7). Entrained at Longueau for St. Pol (22/7). Entrained at Frévent for Dernancourt midnight (13/9). To Fricourt (16/9), Bernafay Wood (18/9), Carrying parties to front line. Assembled in front of Gueudecourt – New Trench, Gap Trench (24/9). War Diary notes night spent deepening trench – New Trench only 1 foot deep. Attacked (25/9) – 'C' and 'D' Companies led with 'A' and 'B' behind – ran into German barrage early in advance before taking Goat Trench – 'D' Company entered Gird Trench after loss of all officers – leading waves of 'D' Company all killed or wounded from enfilade machine gun fire on right. Defensive flank formed along Watling Street (sunken portion of Ginchy-Gueudecourt Road). War Diary records tank clearing Gird Trench on right of Pilgrim's Way 6 a.m. (26/9) – over 350 prisoners taken. By 8 a.m. 'A' and 'B' Companies in Gueudecourt, 'C' and 'D' in Gird Trench. Withdrew to Switch and Gap Trenches 11 p.m. Relieved and to Bernafay Wood (1/10). Casualties – 286. To Dernancourt (2/10). Entrained at Edgehill for Longpré (4/10) and from there marched to Francieres. Entrained at Pont-Remy for Béthune (7/10).

11th (Service) Battalion (Midland Pioneers). Pioneers, 6th Division: Entrained at Proven for Fienvillers (2/8) and from there moved to billets at Beauval. To Raincheval (4/8), Acheux (5/8), Mesnil (6/8). Work carried out on trenches in Mailly-Maillet Wood. To Englebelmer (7/8). Working on Sloan Street and Robert's Trenches. To Acheux (8/8), bivouacs south-west of Louvencourt (9/8), Bertrancourt (12/8), Amplier (26/8), Authieule (27/8), Havernas (29/8), Poulainville (6/9), Corbie (7/9), Bois des Tailles (8/9). Work carried out on Méaulte railhead. Moved forward to bivouacs in old German trenches at Guillemont (11/9). Working in Flers-Quadrilateral line, clearing battlefield around Guillemont. To Happy Valley (20/9). Working on roads Ginchy-Lesbœufs. To Citadel Camp (30/9), Waterlot Farm (8/10), Citadel Camp (20/10), Méricourt (21/10). Entrained at Ailly-sur-Somme for Oisemont (22/10) and from there marched to Fresneville. To Longpré (27/10). Entrained for Béthune area (29/10).

Royal Irish Regiment

2nd Battalion. 22nd Brigade, 7th Division: In reserve for attack at Mametz (1/7) – 'A' Company sent forward at 10 p.m. to consolidate position in village – 'D' later reinforced 22nd Manchester. Both companies rejoined Battalion at dawn. Moving forward through Mametz (4/7) – attacked Strip Trench in front of Mametz Wood – heavy machine gun fire from Quadrangle Trench forced withdrawal to Mametz. Reformed at Mansell Copse. Assault made on Wood Trench and south corner of Mametz Wood 10.15 p.m. (5/7) – leading waves went forward – company assaulting Wood Trench found wire thick and uncut and were soon shot down. At Mametz Wood enemy put up strong counter attacks forcing withdrawal. Relieved 3.30 a.m. and to Mansell Copse (6/7). Later to billets at Heilly. Casualties since (1/7) – 227. Assembly positions taken up in Mametz Wood (13/7). Attack on Bazentin-le-Petit (14/7) – passed through 2nd Royal Warwickshire and into village – gains held against heavy shelling and series of strong counter attacks. Relieved during evening and assembled on road south of village – marched to Mametz Wood. Casualties – 326. Entrained at Albert for La Chaussee (20/7). To Dernancourt (13/8), Pommiers Redoubt (26/8). In action at Ginchy (3/9)–(4/9). Casualties – 326. Relieved and via Pommiers Redoubt to Buire (5/9). Entrained at Albert for Airaines (8/9) and from there to billets at Neuville-au-Bois. Began move to Ploegsteert area (18/9).

6th (Service) Battalion. 47th Brigade, 16th (Irish) Division: Moved from Loos sector and located in reserve north-east of Carnoy by (30/8). Moved forward and attacked towards Guillemont (3/9). Records note advance made in good order and with Pipes playing. Final objective taken by 3 p.m. – line consolidated and held against strong counter attacks. Relieved about 2.30 a.m. (4/9) and to Carnoy. Casualties – 311. To front line (7/9). Attack on Ginchy (9/9) – led assault with 8th Royal Munster Fusiliers – enemy found to be well prepared and their trenches little effected by British bombardment. Five machine guns situated on parapet of first objective were sufficient to hold back attack and sustain high casualties. Relieved at dawn (11/9) and to Vaux-sur-Somme. To Huppy (18/9). Entrained for Bailleul (21/9) and from there to billets at Méteren.

Alexandra, Princess of Wales's Own (Yorkshire Regiment)

2nd Battalion. 21st Brigade, 30th Division: In support during attack towards Montauban (1/7) – moving forward soon halted by machine gun fire – 200 casualties in No Man's Land – German front line reached and positions consolidated. Withdrew to original British line (4/7) and from there to Bois des Tailles. Took up positions just west of Bernafay Wood (8/7) – advanced east through the wood towards Trônes Wood 7.15 a.m. The short journey across Bernafay was difficult – shelling and debris causing great loss and hardship. The path from its eastern edge and across the open ground to Trônes was an even costlier operation – machine gun and rifle fire along with two field guns firing over open sights causing many casualties. Relieved at 7 p.m. and to La Briqueterie. Casualties for first week of Somme fighting – 433. To Morlancourt (11/7), Vaux-sur-Somme (12/7). Entrained at Vecquemont for Ailly-sur-Somme (14/7) and from there marched to Fourdrinoy. To Morlancourt (19/7), bivouacs in a valley west of Caftet Wood (20/7). Moved forward via Glatz Redoubt to assemble positions north of Trônes Wood (22/7). Attacked towards Guillemont (23/7) – advance south of village driven back – to the north attacking company more successful. Withdrew in evening to Happy Valley. Casualties over 250. Began move to Givenchy area (2/8). Entrained for Doullens (18/9). To Naours (21/9), Ribemont (4/10), Pommiers Redoubt (6/10). Took over Brigade reserve positions at Switch Trench (13/10). Attack on western end of Bayonet Trench and Bite Trench (18/10). Relieved by 18th King's and to Flers support trench. Casualties – 214. To Pommiers Redoubt (21/10), Dernancourt (24/10), Bailleulmont south-west of Arras (30/10).

1/4th Battalion (T.F.). 150th Brigade, 50th (Northumbrian) Division: Moved from Ypres sector to training area near Millencourt during second week of August. To support positions at Shelter Wood (10/9). Assembled in Eye and Swansea Trenches for attack between High Wood and Martinpuich (14/9). Went into action alongside 1/5th Green Howards (15/9) – their third objective (Martin Alley) taken by 10 a.m. Bombed eastward along Prue Trench (16/9). Relieved (19/9). From old German trenches at Bazentin-le-Petit Wood moved forward (22/9). To Starfish Trench and attacked towards Eaucourt l'Abbaye (26/9) – enemy trenches taken but later driven back to Starfish by strong counter attack. Relieved and to support positions (28/9). In reserve and support during 50th Division's operations at Eaucourt l'Abbaye and 151st Brigade's assault on Flers Line (1/10)–(3/10). Withdrawn to Albert. Casualties since (15/9) – 399. In the War Diary we read – 'considering the ground won and the fact that the right flank was always in the air, and in the night attack of (26/9) both flanks, the casualties are not excessive.' To Baizieux Wood (4/10), forward area (23/10) taking over positions on Martinpuich-Warlencourt Road and facing the Butte de Warlencourt. In reserve during 151st Brigade's assault on the Butte (5/11) and close support for 149th Brigade's operations on Gird Trench and Hook Sap (13/11)–(17/11). Relieved and to Albert.

1/5th Battalion (T.F.). 150th Brigade, 50th (Northumbrian) Division: Entrained at Bailleul for Doullens (11/8) and from there marched to Bernaville. After 3 days to Flesselles, and then via Molliens-au-Bois to Millencourt. Moved forward to Lozenge Wood in reserve to 44th Brigade (9/9). To Shelter Wood, Pioneer Alley and Swansea Trench (10/9). Successful operations between High Wood and Martinpuich (15/9)–(19/9). Casualties – 252. From reserve positions around Bazentin-le-Petit Wood moved forward for operations at Eaucourt l'Abbaye (22/9). Relieved and to Mametz Wood (29/9). To Albert (3/10), Baizieux (4/10), Mametz Wood (11/10). Employed on road works – enemy shelling causing over 60 casualties. To forward zone (23/10). In reserve and close support during operations at the Butte de Warlencourt and Gird lines. Relieved and to Albert (17/11).

6th (Service) Battalion. 32nd Brigade, 11th (Northern) Division: Arrived Senlis from Arras sector (3/9). Moved forward into Brigade reserve dug-outs at Crucifix Corner Thiepval sector (8/9). To Front line trenches (9/9). Attack and capture of Turk Street and the Wonder Work (14/9) – on left of assault bombers played an important role in this operation – gains consolidated and held against series of counter attacks. Relieved and to Hédauville (16/9). Casualties – 135 (included Commanding Officer Lieutenant-Colonel. C.G. Forsyth, D.S.O.). From Bouzincourt via Mailly-Maillet and Englebelmer to Martinsart and from there spent 3 days in trenches north of Ovillers. Returned to Bouzincourt and to Crucifix Corner (26/9). Attack (with 9th West Yorkshire) on Hessian Trench and Stuff Redoubt (27/9) – in afternoon 'B' and 'C' Companies took Hessian Trench – remainder entered Stuff Redoubt and here found what was left of 9th West Yorkshire. Captain A.C.T. White (6th Green Howards) then formed a composite battalion which fought until relieved during night (30/9). Via Bouzincourt to Varennes. Casualties – 396. Captain White was later awarded the Victoria Cross for his gallantry and leadership. Entrained at Acheux for Candas (1/10) and from there to Beaumetz.

7th (Service) Battalion. 50th Brigade, 17th (Northern) Division: In front of Fricourt (1/7). 'A' Company attacked 7.45 a.m. This, according to The Official History of The Great War, was in error and the men were practically all destroyed in the first 20 yards by a single machine gun. Remaining companies moved forward 2.30 p.m. Relieved during evening and to Heilly.

Casualties – 351. To Ville (3/7), Méaulte (5/7), Fricourt (7/7) – in afternoon to Fricourt Wood and Railway Alley – during night relieved 6th Dorsetshire south-west of Mametz Wood. Attacks on Quadrangle Support failed (8/7) and (9/7). Assisted 38th Division (on right) during attack on Mametz Wood (10/7). Entrained at Grove Town, for Saleux (11/7) and from there to billets at Molliens-Vidames. To Bellancourt (15/7), Dernancourt (22/7), Pommiers Redoubt (3/8). From there duty in line at Longueval and Delville Wood. To Dernancourt (13/8). Entrained at Méricourt for Candas (15/8) – marched via Heuzecourt, Bonnières, Doullens and Bayencourt to Hébuterne arriving (19/8). Took over trenches overlooking Gommecourt Wood. Moved to Third Army Training Area at Drucat, via Occoches and Maizicourt (22/9). To Halloy (6/10). Began 5 day march to Méaulte arriving (22/10). To Mansell Copse (28/10), bivouacs between Bernafay and Trônes Woods (29/10), front line between Lesbœufs and Gueudecourt (2/11). Unsuccessful attack with 7th East Yorkshire (5/11). Casualties among both battalions almost 300. Relieved and to camp near Montauban (6/11). On the march back Lieutenant-Colonel R. D'A. Fife records in his diary that two men were almost lost when they sank deep into mud. Their comrades pulling them free with the aid of ropes, both men lost their boots and one – his trousers. It is also on record that one of the men completed the journey to the camp at Montauban wearing 2 left boots, while the other, in 'the most comfortable boots' he ever wore, went on with a pair that had been obtained from a dead German. No mention is made of replacement trousers. To Molliens-Vidames (14/11).

8th (Service) Battalion. 69th Brigade, 23rd Division: Moved up to Bazieux Wood during night (1/7). To Albert (2/7). Placed at disposal of 34th Division and to positions on Tara Hill (3/7). Communication trench dug from old British line to Sausage Redoubt during night (4/7). Assisted 9th Green Howards during successful attack on Horseshoe Trench (5/7). Relieved and to bivouacs south of Albert (6/7). To reserve positions Belle Vue Farm (7/7), trenches in front of Bécourt Wood (8/7), Belle Vue Farm (9/7). To Horseshoe Trench (10/7) and assembled for attack on Contalmaison. Advanced at 4.50 p.m. – at about 500 yards from the village heavy machine gun and rifle fire inflicted great casualties – wire found uncut in front of first objective – advanced on to second line – 50% casualties before reaching hedge and wire netting in front of village – advanced through ruins – fire from rear. War Diary notes no more than 4 officers and 150 men reached village. Over 250 prisoners taken. Gains consolidated and held against counter attacks. Relieved and to Belle Vue Farm during night (11/7). Casualties – 300. To Franvillers (12/7), forward area Contalmaison (25/7), Albert (26/7), trenches in front of Switch Line (5/8). Attack on Munster Alley (6/8). For his part in this action Private W.H.Short would be awarded the Victoria Cross. During the 5 hour attack by a party of bombers, Private Short was wounded in the foot. He refused to go back for treatment and later on his leg was shattered. Laying in a trench he continued to support his comrades by preparing bombs. He died of his wounds before he could be carried from the trench. William Short is buried at Contalmaison Château Cemetery. Relieved and to Scots Redoubt (7/8). To Bresle (8/8). Entrained for Pont-Remy (11/8). Entrained for Bailleul (16/8). Left St. Omer (10/9), arriving Longueau (11/9) and from there marching to Hénencourt Wood. To Millencourt (15/9), reserve trenches near Bazentin-le-Petit Wood (18/9). From this position 8th and 9th Green Howards shared duties in front line. Took over part of line to right of Le Sars Road (2/10). 'C' Company and Battalion bombers attacked in evening (4/10) – gains consolidated and held against counter attacks. Withdrew into support at Prue, Starfish, Martin Alley and Push Trenches (5/10). 'C' Company reinforced 9th Green Howards in Le Sars (7/10). Relieved by 7th Cameron Highlanders and to Scots Redoubt (8/10). To Albert (9/10). Entrained for Ypres sector (12/10).

9th (Service) Battalion. 69th Brigade, 23rd Division: Moved from Coisy to Baizieux Wood during night (1/7). To bivouacs just outside Albert (2/7). Marched through town and out to positions on Tara-Usna Ridge (3/7). During attack on Horseshoe Trench (5/7) Second-Lieutenant D.S. Bell (with 2 other men) rushed an enemy machine gun that was enfilading Battalion with fire. Having fired into the crew with his revolver, the officer and his party then eliminated the gun with bombs. For this great act of conspicuous bravery he received the Victoria Cross. After 4 days in reserve took part in attack on Contalmaison (10/7) – delivering with 8th Green Howards main assault. On the left reached enemy's main trench and bursting through the wire entered village. At Roll Call in Contalmaison Village only the Commanding Officer Lieutenant-Colonel H.G. Holmes, his Second in Command and 5 subalterns remained out of the officers. The men totalling just 128. Casualties (438) included Second-Lieutenant D.S. Bell who was buried at Gordon Dump Cemetery. To Belle Vue Farm (11/7), Franvillers (12/7), front line (25/7), Albert (26/7), front line (5/8). In support during attack on Munster Alley (6/8). To Scots Redoubt (7/8). Entrained at Méricourt for Pont-Remy (11/8). From St Omer to Longueau (11/9) and from there marched to Coisy. To Hénencourt Wood (12/9), Millencourt (15/9), front line (18/9). Enemy attacked 'C' Company in Prue Trench (19/9) – lost ground later regained. In reserve positions at Bazentin-le-Petit Wood between tours in front line. To trenches near Martinpuich (1/10). Attack on Le Sars (7/10) – hand-to-hand fighting during capture of village – moved on to clear trenches north-east of Bapaume Road. Relieved and to camp near Round Wood (9/10), Albert (10/10). Entrained for Ypres sector (12/10).

10th (Service) Battalion. 62nd Brigade, 21st Division: Went into action at Fricourt in support of the main attack (1/7) – following 4th Middlesex, 'B' Company were gallantly led by Temporary Major S.W. Loudoun-Shand, who seeing that his men were in difficulty leaving their trenches immediately leapt on to the parapet and assisted then over the top. Under fierce machine gun fire the officer helped and encouraged his men but soon fell mortally wounded. For his conspicuous bravery and leadership, Major Loudoun-Shand was awarded the Regiment's second Victoria Cross of the war and the first of 4 to be awarded during the 1916 Somme fighting. His company suffered heavily in its attack – some 5 officers and 117 other ranks going into action – just 1 and 27 men coming out. Remainder of Battalion covered ground towards Crucifix Trench where they were to relieve 15th Durham Light Infantry. On second day of the battle, enemy were putting up great resistance from strongpoint known as The Poodles and 'A' Company after 2 hours of heavy fighting eventually cleared this area. Attack launched on Shelter Wood (3/7). Relieved by 10th Lancashire Fusiliers and via Buire entrained at Dernancourt for Ailly-sur-Somme. To Molliens-Vidame (7/7). Entrained at Ailly-sur-Somme for Corbie (11/7) and from there marched at night to Méaulte. Moved forward to Mametz Wood (12/7). During subsequent fighting in the wood, Battalion runners and linesmen received special praise from their commanders. Practically all had become casualties – Regimental historian Colonel H.C. Wylly records 'the direct route from company to Battalion H.Q could be traced by the numbers of runners and linesmen lying where they had fallen in their efforts to pass through the shelling.' Attack on trench running west of Bazentin-le-Petit (16/7). Relieved and to Mametz Wood. To Buire (17/7). Entrained at Dernancourt for Saleux (20/7) and from there marched to Molliens-Vidames. Entrained at Longueau for Arras sector (23/7). Entrained at Frévent for Albert (13/9) and from there marched to Dernancourt. To Bécordel-Bécourt (15/9), Pommiers Redoubt (16/9) – from there to trenches in front of Gueudecourt. Colonel Wylly records that it was necessary to keep wounded in the trenches for 3 days, the shelling being so intense that it was impossible to get them away. Relieved and to Fricourt (22/9). To Bernafay Wood in reserve (25/9), relieved 10th K.O.Y.L.I. in line south-east of Gueudecourt (26/9). To Bernafay Wood (29/9), Buire (1/10). Entrained at Dernancourt for Longpré (3/10). Entrained for Loos sector (7/10).

12th (Service) Battalion (Tees-side Pioneers). Pioneers, 40th Division: Reached Outrebois (5/11), Montigny (9/11), Bayencourt, via Beauval, Doullens (14/11). Attached to 31st Division for duty in Hébuterne Sector.

13th (Service) Battalion. 121st Brigade, 40th Division: Moved towards Somme after service in Loos sector (2/11). Camped at Neuville and Doullens before moving to Villers-sous-Ailly near Abbeville towards end of month.

Lancashire Fusiliers

1st Battalion. 86th Brigade, 29th Division: Moved into sunken road between British front line and Beaumont-Hamel – position, which runs north from Auchonvillers-Beaumont Road, occupied by 'B' and 'D' Companies, brigade bombers and 8 Stokes mortars. At 7.30 a.m. (1/7) leading companies left the road for German lines – these and subsequent waves soon cut down by machine gun fire. Also heavy losses among 'A' and 'C' Companies during their move forward from front line up to sunken road. Relieved and to Auchonvillers (3/7). Casualties – 486. To Mailly-Maillet Wood (4/7), Acheux Wood (5/7), front line Hemel (8/7), Mailly-Maillet Wood (15/7), Bus-lès-Artois via Bois de Warnimont (23/7), Beauval (24/7). Entrained at Doullens for Ypres Sector. Arrived Longueau (8/10) and from there marched to Daours. To Dernancourt (10/10), Mametz Wood (13/10), front line (Switch Trench) Flers (19/10), Delville Wood (25/10), Bernafay Wood (27/10), Mametz Wood (29/10), Méricourt (30/10), Corbie (31/10), Méaulte (16/11), North Camp, Carnoy (18/11).

2nd Battalion. 12th Brigade, 4th Division: Moved from camp at Bertrancourt into assembly positions just north of Mailly-Maillet (30/6). Between 8 and 8.30 a.m. (1/7) advanced and later crossed German line south of The Quadrilateral. Enemy soon counter attacked and a withdrawal made during night. Casualties – 368. To assembly trenches near Mailly-Maillet (3/7). Moved forward again during afternoon. To Mailly-Maillet (4/7). Relieved 1st Royal Irish Fusiliers in line during evening. Relieved and to Bertrancourt (11/7). To Auchonvillers (17/7), Vauchelles (21/7), Authieule (22/7). Entrained for Cassel (23/7). Entrained at Poperinghe for Saleux (17/9). To Coisy (18/9), Allonville (25/9), Corbie (26/9), Citadel Camp (8/10), Trônes Wood (9/10) and from there trenches half-way between Gueudecourt and Lesbœufs. Unsuccessful attack towards Le Transloy (12/10). Casualties – 345. Relieved and to Bernafay Wood (14/10). To reserve trenches south-east of Flers (19/10), Thistle Trench near Lesbœufs (22/10). Attack on Dewdrop Trench (23/10) – advanced 2.30 p.m. – heavy losses within first few yards – what remained of attacking force (2 officers and 65 men) dug in in front of Rainy Trench. Casualties – 208. Relieved and to La Briqueterie (24/10), Citadel Camp (25/10), Ville-sur-Ancre (27/10). Entrained at Méricourt for Airaines (29/10) and from there to Dreuil-Hamel. To Morival and Wiammeville (3/11), Maigneville (6/11).

2/5th Battalion (T.F.). 164th Brigade, 55th (West Lancashire) Division. Arrived Autheux (21/7). To Fransu (22/7), Fienvillers (24/7). Entrained at Candas for Méricourt (25/7) and from there to Méaulte. To Happy Valley (26/7), Bernafay Wood (31/7), Trônes Woods (2/8), Bernafay Wood (5/8).

Moved forward to Arrow Head Copse and took part in attack on Guillemont (9/8). Relieved and to Carnoy (10/8). To reserve positions Maricourt-La Briqueterie Road (12/8), Bronfay Farm (14/8), Méricourt (15/8). Entrained for Franleu (19/8). Entrained at Abbeville for Méricourt (30/8) and from there to Dernancourt. To Bécordel- Bécourt (6/9), trenches between Delville Wood, Trônes Wood and Ginchy (7/9). Attached to 16th (Irish) Division for attack on Ginchy (Hop Alley, Ale Alley, Pint Trench) (9/9). Casualties – 350. Relieved and via Fricourt to Ribemont (14/9). To Buire (16/9), Fricourt (17/9), Mametz (18/9), reserve line Delville Wood (20/9), support line Flers (27/9), Dernancourt via Mametz (29/9). Entrained at Edgehill for Elverdinghe (1/10).

9th (Service) Battalion. 34th Brigade, 11th (Northern) Division: Reached Acheux from Arras area (2/9). To Puchevillers (3/9), Bouzincourt (8/9). Working parties provided at Authuille Wood (11/9) and (12/9). Relieved Canadians in line east of Mouquet Farm (17/9). To Bouzincourt (19/9), Ovillers (21/9), Mailly-Maillet (22/9), front line (Constance Trench) opposite Mouquet Farm (25/9). Attack on farm and surrounding positions (Zollern Redoubt and Trench, Stuff Redoubt and Hessian Trench) (26/9)–(28/9). Relieved and to dug-outs at Ovillers. Casualties almost 400. To Varennes (30/9). Entrained for Candas (1/10) and from there to Berneuil. To Franqueville (3/10), Ribeaucourt (11/11), Franqueville (14/11), Pernois (15/11), Vadencourt (16/11), Puchevillers (17/11).

10th (Service) Battalion. 52nd Brigade, 17th (Northern) Division: At Bois des Tailles (1/7). To Morlancourt (2/7). Took over former German positions north of Fricourt (3/7). In action at Shelter Alley, Quadrangle Trench (5/7). Attack on Quadrangle Support Trench, Pearl Alley (7/7) – enemy in the former being unaffected by the British bombardment quickly fought off its attackers. On left – Pearl Alley taken and Contalmaison entered. Assault later driven back. Relieved and to Méaulte. Casualties – 407. To Ville-sur-Ancre (8/7), Riencourt (10/7), Villers-sous-Ailly (15/7). Entrained at Hangest for Buire-sur-l'Ancre (23/7). To Montauban Alley in reserve (1/8), Pommiers Trench in support (4/8), Fricourt (8/8), trenches Delville Wood (10/8). Attacked (12/8) – German position at south-east corner of Delville Wood taken. Relieved and to Fricourt. To Buire-sur-l'Ancre (13/8). Entrained at Méricourt for Fienvillers (15/8). To Remaisnil (16/8), Lucheux (17/8), Souastre (18/8). Took over trenches Foncquevillers sector (20/8) – resting between tours in village and Château de la Hale. To St. Amand (12/9), Halloy (21/9), Agenvillers (24/9). Via Doullens, Remaisnil, Bernâtre to Maison-Ponthieu (9/10), Frohen-le-Grand (10/10), Grenas (11/10), Brévillers (19/10), Coisy (22/10), Daours (23/10), Sandpit Camp (27/10), 'H' Camp Carnoy (30/10).

Took over trenches Gueudecourt sector (2/11). Attacked (3/11) – advance recorded as being through waist-high mud. Relieved and to Bernafay Wood (5/11). To front line Gueudecourt (8/11), Carnoy (10/11), Citadel Camp (11/11), Hangest (14/11), Ailly-sur-Somme (15/11).

11th (Service) Battalion. 74th Brigade, 25th Division: Moved from Rubempré to Warloy (1/7). To Bouzincourt (4/7), and later forward to Usna Hill Redoubt. To La Boisselle (6/7). Attacks and counter attacks at Ovillers (7/7)–(10/7). Relieved and via Bouzincourt to Senlis (11/7). Casualties – 171. To Usna Hill and from there took part in attacks at Ovillers (14/7)–(16/7). Relieved and via Bouzincourt to Forceville (17/7). To Beauval (18/7), Bus-lès-Artois (21/7), front line Beaumont-Hamel sector (24/7), Mailly-Maillet Wood (30/7), Bertrancourt (5/8), front line (7/8), Bus-lès-Artois (10/8), Acheux (15/8), Hédauville (19/8), trenches Thiepval (20/8), Bouzincourt (27/8), trenches near Ovillers (28/8), Bouzincourt (6/9), Léalvillers (7/9), Beauval (10/9), Candas (11/9), Franqueville (12/9), Forceville via Beauval (25/9), Hédauville (26/9), Bouzincourt (27/9) and from there to trenches in Thiepval Wood. Patrols engaged enemy during fighting for Schwaben Redoubt (28/9). Relieved and to Englebelmer (30/9), Bouzincourt (1/10). Relieved 11th Cheshire in Hessian Trench (6/10). In support Mouquet Farm (10/10)–(13/10), Hessian Trench (13/10)–(17/10), reserve Ovillers Post (18/10)–(20/10). Attack on Regina Trench (21/10). Relieved and to Bouzincourt (22/10), Vadencourt Wood (23/10), Beauval (24/10). Battalion inspected and congratulated by General Sir H. Gough (25/10) and Field-Marshal Sir D.Haig (26/10). Entrained at Candas for Caéstre (29/10).

15th (Service) Battalion (1st Salford). 96th Brigade, 32nd Division: On left of 32nd Division's assault at Thiepval (1/7). Casualties – 470 out of an attacking force of 624. Withdrawn to The Bluff (2/7). Via Martinsart Wood to Warloy (3/7), Léalvillers (5/7), Hédauville (7/7), Senlis (8/7), Bouzincourt in reserve (9/7), Ovillers in support (11/7), Senlis (16/7), Halloy (17/7), Bouquemaison (18/7). Began move to Cambrin sector (19/7). Arrived Vadencourt Wood from Orville (21/10). To Bouzincourt (23/10), Warloy (26/10), Hérissart (31/10), Warloy (13/11). In support lines at Thiepval and forward trenches around Beaumont-Hamel (14/11)–(17/11). Relieved and to Mailly-Maillet.

16th (Service) Battalion (2nd Salford). 96th Brigade, 32nd Division: In support during attack at Thiepval (1/7). Hearing that 15th Lancashire Fusiliers were in difficulties ahead, 'B' and 'C' Companies moved forward but were themselves swept by machine gun fire. Withdrawn via Aveluy Wood to Warloy (3/7). Casualties – 231. To Varennes (5/7), Bouzincourt (8/7), trenches at Ovillers (11/7). In support at Donnet Post (14/7). To Senlis (15/7), Halloy

(17/7), Bouquemaison (18/7). Began move to Cambrin sector (19/7). Arrived Authieule from Berlencourt (18/10). To Vadencourt (21/10), brickfields at Bouzincourt (23/10), Warloy (26/10), Rubempré (31/10), Warloy (13/11). In support lines Thiepval (14/11)–(17/11). Relieved and to Mailly-Maillet.

17th (Service) Battalion (1st South-East Lancashire). 104th Brigade, 35th Division: Moved down from the Béthune area to Bouquemaison (2/7). To Bus-lès-Artois (6/7), Léalvillers (9/7), Aveluy Wood via Bouzincourt (10/7), Happy Valley via Morlancourt (13/7), Maricourt (14/7), Talus Boisé (19/7), Bernafay Wood (20/7), Talus Boisé (24/7), Montauban (Dublin Trench) (25/7), Minden Post (26/7). Provided carrying parties for 89th Brigade during attack on Guillemont (29/7)–(30/7). Relieved and to Happy Valley (31/7). To Vaux-sur-Somme (2/8). Entrained at Méricourt for Saleux (5/8) and from there marched to Montagne-Fayel. Entrained at Airaines for Corbie (10/8) and from there to Vaux-sur-Somme. To Happy Valley (15/8), Talus Boisé (18/8). In reserve at Dublin Trench (19/8)–(22/8). To Angle Wood (22/8). Took part in attack (24/8). Relieved and via Casement Trench (Montauban) to Citadel Camp (26/8). Entrained at Heilly for Candas (30/8). Began move to Arras sector (31/8).

18th (Service) Battalion (2nd South-East Lancashire). 104th Brigade, 35th Division: Arrived Bouquemaison from Béthune area (4/7). To Bus-lès-Artois (8/7), Harponville (9/7), via Bouzincourt to Aveluy Wood (10/7), via Morlancourt to Happy Valley (13/7), Talus Boisé (18/7), trenches at Trônes Wood and Maltz Horn Farm (20/7). German attack (21/7). Raid on enemy positions (22/7). To Montauban (Dublin Trench) (23/7), Bernafay Wood (24/7), Trônes Wood and Maltz Horn Farm (25/7), Minden Post (27/7), Happy Valley (31/7), Corbie (2/8). Entrained at Méricourt for Saleux and Molliens-Vidame (5/8). Entrained at Airaines for Corbie (10/8). To Happy Valley (15/8), Talus Boisé (18/8), Montauban (Casement Trench) (19/8), Arrow Head Copse (22/8), Angle Wood (23/8), Billon Copse (25/8), Citadel Camp (26/8). Entrained at Heilly for Candas (30/8). Began move to Arras sector (31/8).

19th (Service) Battalion (3rd Salford). 14th Brigade, 32nd Division and Pioneers, 49th (West Riding) Division: Moved forward from Senlis to dug-outs at Black Horse Bridge near Authuille during night (30/6). In reserve – passed through Authuille Wood and followed 1st Dorsetshire towards Leipzig Redoubt (1/7). Heavy machine gun fire swept both battalions – redoubt eventually reached but only 2 officers and some 40 men were able to join what was left of the Dorsetshire. Withdrew to Authuille at midnight. To front line during night (2/7). Withdrew to Senlis (4/7). To Forceville (5/7),

Bouzincourt (7/7), Donnet Post near Ovillers (8/7). Took over line south and west of Ovillers (11/7). Attacks made (12/7) and (13/7) with some success. Withdrawn and via Bouzincourt to Warloy (15/7). To Beauval (16/7). Began move to Béthune sector (17/7). Battalion was now to convert to pioneers and leaving 32nd Division ordered to G.H.Q Troops for training (29/7). Allotted to 49th (West Riding) Division – arrived Forceville (6/8). Carried out work in Hédauville, Martinsart and Thiepval areas (7/8)–(24/9) – taking part in an attack north of Thiepval Wood (3/9). Moved to Coullemont and Arras sector (25/9).

20th (Service) Battalion (4th Salford). 104th Brigade, 35th Division: Arrived Neuvillette via Bouquemaison (3/7). To Bus-lès-Artois (7/7), Léalvillers (9/7), reserve positions Aveluy Wood (10/7), Morlancourt (13/7), Happy Valley (14/7), Montauban (Dublin Trench) (18/7), Talus Boisé (19/7), Dublin Trench (20/7), Bernafay Wood (21/7), Minden Post (26/7), Casement Trench, Glatz Alley, Minden Post (30/7), Happy Valley (31/7), Corbie (3/8). Entrained at Méricourt for Saleux and Camps-en-Amiénois (5/8). Entrained at Airaines for Corbie (10/8). To Happy Valley (15/8), Talus Boisé (18/8), Arrow Head Copse (19/8), Casement Trench (22/8), Angle Wood (26/8), Citadel Camp (27/8). Entrained at Heilly for Candas and Neuvillette (30/8). Began move to Arras sector (31/8).

Royal Scots Fusiliers

1st Battalion. 8th Brigade, 3rd Division: Arrived Candas (1/7) and from there marched to billets. To Flesselles (3/7), Vaux-sur-Somme (5/7), Carnoy (7/7) and from there Bronfay Farm. Took up positions in quarry north of Montauban (13/7). Attack on Bazentin-le-Grand (14/7) – in support leading waves held up at uncut German wire and forced to retire to start positions. Renewed attack more successful – gains held and consolidated. Relieved and to Longueval (19/7), Méaulte (25/7). Casualties since (7/7) – 370. Later in forward areas around Guillemont and Maltz Horn Farm. Occupied bivouacs and billets at Happy Valley, Great Bear, Talus Boisé, Sandpit Camp, Méaulte. Entrained at Méricourt for Candas (23/8). Began move to Béthune area (25/8). Entrained at St. Pol (7/10) and via Acheux and Vauchelles began tours in line Serre sector. Rest areas Bus-lès-Artois, Vauchelles, Courcelles. Attack on Serre (13/11) – on left of assault found German wire intact – small parties fought through to support line, but later forced to withdraw.

2nd Battalion. 90th Brigade, 30th Division: Assembled near Cambridge Copse for attack on Montauban (1/7). In support, followed 17th and 16th Manchester forward at 8.30 a.m. – village entered at 10.05 a.m. and Montauban Alley beyond soon after. Casualties – 170. Relieved from forward area (3/7). Successful attack on Maltz Horn Farm (9/7) – on right of assault took Maltz Horn Trench via sunken road leading from La Briqueterie – Commanding Officer Lieutenant-Colonel P.W.T. Macgregor-Whitton killed. Relieved and to Maricourt (11/7). Attack on Guillemont (30/7) – from assemby area east of Trônes Wood moved forward along Guillemont Road – village entered from south-west with few casualties – later became cut off – 650 casualties out of attacking force of 750 before relieved – majority either dead or missing. Moved to Béthune area (11/8). Returned to Somme and Flers area during October. Attack on Bayonet Trench (12/10) – withdrawal under heavy machine gun fire forced after advance of 150 yards. Transferred to Arras sector.

6th/7th (Service) Battalion. 45th Brigade, 15th (Scottish) Division: Arrived Prouville area (28/7). To Vignacourt (31/7), Bresle (4/8). Moved forward to forward area around Contalmaison (9/8). Attack on Switch Line (12/8) – objective taken and consolidated south-eastward from Munster Alley. In reserve during attack on Martinpuich (15/9). Relieved (18/9) and to rest areas around Baizieux Wood, Millencourt, Bresle. Back in forward area Le Sars sector by second week October. Rested out of line at Martinpuich, Contalmaison, Albert, Scots Redoubt.

Cheshire Regiment

1st Battalion. 15th Brigade, 5th Division: Arrived Puchevillers from Wamin (14/7). To Lahoussoye (15/7), Ville-sur-Ancre (17/7). Moved forward to Pommiers Redoubt (19/7). In reserve during 5th Division's operations at High Wood. To support positions 1 mile south of High Wood (23/7). Two companies relieved 1st Devonshire in trenches between High Wood and Longueval (25/7). Attack on Longueval (27/7) – leading waves met with strong machine gun fire and forced to retire. Relieved and to Pommiers Redoubt (28/7). To support line Delville Wood (31/7), Pommiers Redoubt (1/8), Dernancourt (2/8). Entrained at Méricourt for Hangest (4/8) and from there marched to Le Quesnoy. To Laleu (5/8). Entrained at Longpré for Méricourt (24/8) and from there marched to Sandpit Camp. To bivouacs south-west of Carnoy (26/8), Chimpanzee Trench (31/8), Angle Wood 1 a.m. (3/9) – later in action during attack on Falfemont Farm – 'D' Company assaulting left of objective forced back by strong machine gun fire. 'A' Company attacked during afternoon (4/9) – objectives taken and consolidated. Withdrew to Chimpanzee Trench (5/9) and from there marched to Citadel Camp. War Diary estimates casualties as 460. To Morlancourt (9/9) – War Diary notes village full of cavalry preparing to go forward. To Citadel Camp (16/9) and from there moved forward to reserve positions at Waterlot Farm. To support line Ginchy sector (18/9). Withdrew to positions around Guillemont (20/9), Oxford Copse (22/9). Moved forward to The Quadrilateral (24/9). Attack on Morval (25/9) – followed 1st Bedfordshire and by 3 p.m. held northern section of village. Relieved and to Oxford Copse (26/9). Casualties – 144. To Citadel Camp (27/9). Entrained at Grove Town for Longpré (29/9). Entrained for Béthune sector (1/10).

1/5th (Earl of Chester's) Battalion (T.F.). Pioneers, 56th (1st London) Division: From Souastre took part in attack on Gommecourt (1/7) – Battalion in addition to its normal duties would on several occasions be called upon to fight. Casualties – 203. Remained working in area. To Doullens (20/8). Entrained for Hiermont (22/8). To St. Riquier (23/8), Corbie (4/9), Citadel Camp (6/9), Contour Wood (7/9). Dug communication trench across Death Valley to the recently captured Leuze Wood (8/9). To Favier Wood (14/9). New trench dug in front of enemy positions at Bouleaux Wood (19/9) – named 'Gropi' after code word taken from name of Commanding Officer (Groves) and word pioneer. New position later extended by digging of Ranger Trench. To Sandpit Camp (27/9), positions south of Montauban (30/9). Took part in operations at Le Transloy. Relieved and to Citadel Camp (10/10). Casualties since (7/9) – 175. To Condé-Folie (15/10), Hallencourt (21/10). Entrained at Pont-Remy for Le Cornet-Malo north of Béthune (24/10).

1/6th Battalion (T.F.). 118th Brigade. 39th Division: Arrived Grouches-Luchuel (24/8). To Bus-lès-Artois (25/8). Took over trenches from 2nd Durham Light Infantry north of Thiepval (26/8). Relieved by 4th/5th Black Watch and to Englebelmer (5/9). To left sector Beaumont-Hamel (12/9) – 'The rats are quite a pest here. We have to hang our rations on lines. Then they are not safe as the rats can do tight-rope walking. They are a very hungry lot, as one of them bit the nose of one of our men whilst he was asleep' (recalled by Sergeant James A. Boardman, M.M. and Bar in Battalion history). Relieved and to Martinsart Wood (5/10). Took over left sector Thiepval (10/10). Attack on Schwaben Redoubt (14/10) – all objectives taken. Enemy counter attacks repulsed. Relieved and to Pioneer Road (16/10), Martinsart Wood (25/10). To reserve trenches Thiepval sector (29/10), Pioneer Road (30/10), Right River Section Thiepval (1/11), Pioneer Road (3/11), Thiepval (8/11), Pioneer Road (11/11). Moved forward to assembly positions in readiness for attack on St. Pierre Divion (12/11). Attacked 5.45 a.m. (13/11) – all objectives taken. Casualties – 275. Relieved and to Senlis Camp (14/11), Warloy (15/11), Orville (16/11), Doullens (18/11). Entrained for Poperinghe (19/11).

9th (Service) Battalion. 58th Brigade, 19th (Western) Division: Moved forward from Bresle during night (30/6) and assembled on railway embankment near Albert. Took up position in Tara-Usna Line 10 a.m. (1/7). Later moved forward to Bécourt Wood and from there relieved 34th Division holding German line around Lochnagar Crater. In action around La Boisselle (2/7)–(4/7). Relieved and to Tara-Usna Line. Casualties since (1/7) – 307. To positions on hill near Bécourt Wood (6/7), Heligoland trenches (7/7). 'A' Company in support of the 9th Royal Welsh Fusiliers. Relieved and to Albert (8/7). To Baizieux (9/7), Bécourt Wood (20/7), Mametz Wood (21/7). War Diary notes Mametz Wood as consisting of gaunt trunks of trees – dead branches covering the ground – shell holes making movement other than on foot impossible. The smell of dead bodies is also mentioned and that the only sign of life other than troops was a fair amount of magpies. Moved forward under orders of 57th Brigade to northern edge of wood 4 a.m. (23/7). War Diary records 2 captured Russian 8-inch guns c1880 near position. Provided carrying parties to front line. Two companies moved forward to line just south of Bazentin-le-Petit Wood (30/7). Relieved and to Fricourt Farm (31/7). To Béhencourt (1/8). Entrained at Fréchencourt for Longpré (3/8) and from there marched to Francieres. Entrained at Pont-Remy for Bailleul (7/8). Entrained at Bailleul for Doullens (5/10) and from there marched to Bois de Warnimont. To Sailly-au-Bois (7/10). Relieved 9th Welsh in trenches east of Hébuterne (9/10). Relieved by 6th Wiltshire and to reserve at Rossignol Farm (13/10). To Vauchelles (16/10), Rubempré (17/10). War Diary notes delayed start to march – Divisional Artillery had moved on same route and heavily loaded ammunition wagons experienced difficulty getting up steep hill on Vauchelles-Puchevillers Road. To Bouzincourt (21/10), camp just north-east of village (22/10). Working parties to forward area Thiepval. To front line Thiepval sector (Stuff Trench) (26/10). Relieved and to Donnet Post (30/10). To front line (Lucky Way) (2/11), Donnet Post (5/11), camp near Aveluy (9/11), front line (13/11), Marlborough Huts (16/11). Moved forward to Zollern Trench 2 p.m. (18/11) and assembled for attack on Desire Trench. Advanced 4.25 p.m. – War Diary notes thick fog – direction lost after reaching Stuff Trench – mud was deep and men could not get free – attack swung to left and later abandoned.

10th (Service) Battalion. 7th Brigade, 25th Division: Arrived Varennes from Puchevillers 1 a.m. (1/7). To Forceville (2/7) – at night to reserve positions Aveluy Wood. To Authuille Wood (3/7) and from there relieved 19th Lancashire Fusiliers in front line extending from Mersey Street to Chequer Bent Street. Relieved and to Aveluy Wood (7/7). To trenches La Boisselle sector (8/7). Enemy pattack driven back (9/7). Attacked (12/7) – 3 strong-points taken and consolidated. 'B' Company attacked line left of Ovillers – held up by machine gun fire – later occupied part of trench evacuated by the enemy. Attacked south of Ovillers 11 p.m. (14/7) – line entered in places – later forced to retire under heavy machine gun fire. Renewed assault during early morning (15/7) also driven back. Relieved and to bivouacs just outside Albert. Casualties – 400. To Forceville (16/7), Beauval (18/7), Bois de Warnimont (20/7). To Englebelmer (23/7) and from there took over forward trenches from 1st Royal Dublin Fusiliers. Relieved and to Bus-lès-Artois (6/8). To Vauchelles (11/8), Puchevillers (15/8), Hédauville (17/8), dug-outs near Authuille (18/8). Relieved 3rd Worcestershire in Leipzig Salient (23/8). To Hédauville (26/8), Bouzincourt (28/8), front line under orders of 75th Brigade (31/8), Bouzincourt (2/9), front line (3/9), Bouzincourt (7/9), Arquèves (8/9), Gézaincourt (10/9), Heuzecourt (11/9), Mesnil-Domqueur (12/9), Gézaincourt (25/9), Arquèves (26/9), Hédauville (29/9). Moved forward to trenches south face Stuff Redoubt (30/9) – planned attack cancelled and withdrew to support trenches (2/10). To Stuff Redoubt (7/10) – attack cancelled and withdrew to reserve line (8/10). To Stuff Redoubt (9/10) – successful attack on German held north face of redoubt 12.35 p.m. – forward posts established and counter attacks repulsed during evening. Relieved and to reserve line (10/10). To Crucifix Corner (15/10), Bouzincourt (16/10). Moved forward to positions north of Mouquet Farm, Hessian Trench and Zollern Trench (17/10). War Diary records all companies working as hard as possible carrying up materials for forthcoming attack. Relieved and to reserve line (19/10). 'D' Company to Stuff Redoubt (21/10). To Bouzincourt (22/10), Hérissart (23/10), Hardinval (24/10). Entrained at Doullens for Bailleul (29/10).

11th (Service) Battalion. 75th Brigade, 25th Division: Moved from Toutencourt to Hédauville during night (30/6). To Martinsart Wood (2/7). Moved forward via Black Horse Bridge and assembled for attack south of Thiepval during night. Attacked on right (3/7) – leading waves noted in War Diary as passing over No Man's Land in perfect order – heavy machine gun fire later brought assault to a standstill about 50 yards from German first line – 'line after line of troops were mowed down.' Official History of The Great War records some 60 men drifted to the right and joined Highland Light Infantry in the Leipzig Salient. Commanding Officer killed while going forward with reserve company. Withdrew to start positions. War Diary records 20 officers and 657 other ranks going into trenches, just 6 and 350 coming out during night (4/7). Relieved by 1st Wiltshire and to Aveluy Wood. To Albert (6/7) and from there moved forward to Usna Redoubt during night. To front line Ovillers (7/7) – patrols sent out along Albert-Bapaume Road. Unsuccessful bombing attack on southern edge of village (10/7). War Diary records sniper claimed 15 victims close to Battalion Headquarters. Relieved by 8th Border and to Usna Redoubt during night (11/7). Moved forward to Brigade reserve positions during night (13/7). Moved forward to front line in preparation for attack north of Ovillers Church during night (14/7). War Diary notes strength as about 100. 'C' and 'D' Companies lay out over the parapet throughout night but did not advance. Relieved and to Senlis (15/7). To Hédauville (16/7), Amplier (17/7), Vauchelles (21/7), Acheux (22/7). Took over line opposite Beaumont-Hamel (24/7). Relieved by 8th Border and to bivouacs near Mailly-Maillet (30/7). Provided working parties to front line trenches. To front line (5/8), Bois de Warnimont (10/8), Raincheval (15/8), Forceville (17/8), Hédauville (19/8), Aveluy Wood (19/8). War Diary notes the fighting of early July being in the thoughts of all original members. Except for nightly working parties found for digging new trench in No Man's Land in front of Thiepval, and the stinging of the mosquitoes, the stay in Aveluy Wood is recorded in War Diary as a very happy one and a 'veritable holiday.' 'B' and 'C' Companies to Authuille Wood (22/8), 'A' and 'D' to The Bluff near Black Horse Bridge (23/8). War Diary records that until end of August work was carried out on trenches under difficult conditions. In support during attack on Thiepval (3/9)–(7/9). Relieved and to Bouzincourt. To Léalvillers (8/9), Amplier (9/9), Autheux (11/9), Agenville (12/9), Amplier (25/9), Léalvillers (26/9). War Diary notes 'experiments undertaken in intensive digging.' To Bouzincourt (29/9), Crucifix Corner (30/9). Relieved Canadians in Hessian and Zollern Trenches (4/10). Relieved and to Ovillers Post (6/10). Work parties dug Bainbridge Trench. Relieved 10th Cheshire in reserve line (15/10). To Hessian and Zollern Trenches (16/10), reserve line (17/10), Hessian Trench (19/10). Attack cancelled and withdrew to reserve line. 'A' Company attached to 8th Border for attack on Regina Trench (21/10) – objective taken and 400 yards beyond. Relieved and to Albert (22/10). To Warloy (23/10), Authieule (24/10). Entrained at Doullens for Bailleul (29/10).

13th (Service) Battalion. 74th Brigade, 25th Division: From Warloy to Bouzincourt (3/7), trenches at Boisselle (5/7). Positions consolidated and held. Attacked Ovillers 8.05 a.m. (7/7) – objectives reached and consolidated. Casualties – 261. Successful bombing attacks (8/7) – trench leading to Ovillers Church taken. War Diary later records Battalion very weak and unable to take part in fighting. Provided carrying parties for Brigade. Relieved by 3rd Worcestershire (10/7) and via Bouzincourt to Senlis. Moved forward to Albert in support of 7th Brigade (13/7) – not required and withdrew to Marmont Bridge. Moved forward to trenches near Ovillers (15/7). Attacked (16/7) – over 120 prisoners taken at south-east corner of Ovillers. Relieved at midnight and to Bouzincourt. To Forceville (17/7), Beauval (18/7), Bus-lès-Artois (21/7), Mailly-Maillet Wood (24/7). Took over trenches south-west of Beaumont-Hamel (Mary Redan) (30/7). War Diary notes British aeroplanes flying low over enemy lines and firing into trenches. Relieved by 2nd Notts and Derby and to Beaussart (5/8). To Mailly-Maillet (7/8), Bertrancourt (9/8), Bus-lès-Artois (11/8), Léalvillers (14/8), Hedauville (18/8). Took over trenches Thiepval Wood (19/8). Relieved and to Bouzincourt (26/8). To reserve positions at Ovillers Post and Donnet Post (28/8), front line (Skyline Trench) (1/9). Relieved and to Bouzincourt (6/9). To Léalvillers (7/9), Puchevillers (8/9), Beauval (10/9), Candas (11/9), St. Ouen (12/9), Beauval (25/9), Hédauville (27/9), Ovillers Post in support of 146th Brigade (29/9). Relieved and to Bouzincourt (5/10). Relieved 2nd South Lancashire in Hessian Trench (6/10). Withdrew to reserve line (13/10). To Hessian Trench (16/10), reserve line (19/10), Hessian Trench (20/10). Attack on Regina Trench (21/10) – War Diary records that whole Battalion went over the parapet at 12.06 p.m. – German trenches entered – 250 prisoners taken. Relieved 6 p.m. (22/10) and to bivouacs near Albert. Casualties – 210. To Vadencourt (23/10), Beauval (24/10). Entrained at Candas for Caéstre (29/10)

15th (Service) Battalion (1st Birkenhead). 105th Brigade, 35th Division: Arrived Beauval from Sus-St.Léger (7/7). To Bus-lès-Artois (10/7), Warloy (11/7), Heilly Wood (12/7), Grove Town Camp via Celestines Wood (13/7). Later via Billon Wood took over trenches in Bernafay Wood. Carrying parties provided for front line. High casualties during bombardment (18/7). Relieved and to Talus Boisé (21/7). Working party of 500 to front line (23/7) – took over new bivouacs north of Carnoy. Moved forward to trenches south of Montauban (24/7). Took over trenches Maltz Horn area, Arrow Head Copse (26/7). Relieved by 16th Cheshire and to Talus Boisé (28/7). To reserve positions north of Carnoy (30/7), Sandpit Valley (31/7), Boisé des Tailles (1/8). Entrained at Méricourt for Saleux (5/8) and from there marched to Oissy. Entrained at Hangest for Méricourt (10/8) and from there marched to Citadel Camp. To Silesia Trench in Brigade reserve (19/8). Working parties to Arrow Head Copse. Moved forward to support trenches (21/8). Relieved and to Bronfay Farm (22/8). To Sandpit Valley (26/8), Bois des Tailles (28/8). Entrained at Heilly for Fienvillers (30/8) and from there marched to Heuzecourt. To Milly and Bout des Pres (31/8). 15th Cheshire was a 'Bantam' battalion and War Diary records recent drafts as 'undesirable degenerates of poor physique.' Began move to Arras sector (1/9).

16th (Service) Battalion (2nd Birkenhead). 105th Brigade, 35th (Division): Arrived Beauval from Sus-St.Léger (7/7). To Bus-lès-Artois (10/7), Heilly via Warloy (11/7), Grove Town Camp via Celestines Wood (12/7), Billon Wood (13/7). To trenches at Trônes Wood attached to 54th Brigade (16/7). 'W' Company moved forward to Waterlot Farm (17/7) – drove off enemy attack (18/7). War Diary records heavy bombardment of positions – Lewis gun buried 3 times but recovered and remained in action. Withdrew to Bernafay Wood (19/7). Casualties since (16/7) – 244. To Talus Boisé during night. To Carnoy (23/7) and from there to trenches south of Montauban. To Dublin Trench (26/7), trenches at Maltz Horn Farm (28/7). Relieved and to bivouacs south of Carnoy (30/7). To Sandpit Valley (31/7), Bois des Tailles (2/8). Entrained at Grove Town for Saleux (5/8) and from here marched to Molliens-Vidame. Entrained at Hangest for Méricourt (10/8) and from there marched to Citadel Camp. To front line Arrow Head Copse (20/8), Silesia Trench in reserve (22/8) and from there Bronfay Farm. To Sandpit Valley (26/8), Bois des Tailles (28/8). Entrained at Heilly for Candas (30/8) and from there marched to Beaumetz. To Lucheux (31/8). Began move to Arras sector (1/9).

19th (Labour) Battalion. Entrained at Bailleul for Heilly (17/7) and from there marched to Méaulte. Work began on railway around Fricourt and Mametz areas and the stations at Bazentin-le-Grand and Longueval. Moved camp to Bazentin-le-Grand (22/10) and later Longueval.

Royal Welsh Fusiliers

1st Battalion. 22nd Brigade, 7th Division: Attack on Mametz (1/7) – bombers worked up Sunken Road Trench towards Fricourt and both sides of The Rectangle. Regimental historian Major C.H. Dudley Ward, D.S.O.,M.C. records 5 lines of strong trenches captured on a front of 800 yards. Moved forward to positions facing southern edge of Mametz Wood (3/7). Attacked 12.45 a.m. (5/7) - objectives gained. Relieved and to bivouacs about 2 miles east of Méaulte. To Heilly (6/7), Citadel Camp (10/7). Moved forward to White Trench in support (14/7) – later to Bazentin-le-Petit Wood – attacked and held line Windmill to Cemetery. Withdrew to Mametz Wood (16/7). To Bazentin-le-Grand (19/7). Attack on right of High Wood (20/7). To Dernancourt (21/7). Entrained at Méricourt for Hangest (22/7) and from there marched to La Chaussée. To Dernancourt (12/8), north end of Bernafay Wood (26/8). Attack on Ale Alley (28/8) – bombing commenced 5 a.m. – enemy cleared and block set up near west end of objective. Advanced further along Beer Trench – heavy casualties among 'B' and 'C' Companies. Relieved and to Bonte Redoubt (29/8), Montauban Alley (1/9). To trenches eastern edge Delville Wood (2/9). Attack (3/9) – unsuccessful. To Bécordel-Bécourt (4/9), Buire (5/9). Entrained at Albert for Airaines (8/9) and from there marched to Mérélessart. Entrained at Pont-Remy for Godewaersvelde (17/9).

2nd Battalion. 19th Brigade, 33rd Division: Arrived Longueau from Givenchy sector (10/7) and from there marched to Cardonnette. To Daours (11/7), Buire-sur-l'Ancre (12/7), Méaulte (14/7), Delville Wood (15/7), Mametz Wood (16/7), Bazentin-le-Petit (18/7), High Wood (20/7) – attacked from eastern edge – ground gained but withdrawal later forced. To Buire-sur-l'Ancre (21/7), Bécordel-Bécourt (6/8), Fricourt Wood (13/8), High Wood (18/8). In action (20/8)–(21/8) – failed attempt to clear western edge. To Bazentin-le-Grand (22/8), High Wood (26/8), Fricourt Wood (27/8), Montauban Alley (29/8), Bécordel-Bécourt (30/8), Ribemont (31/8), Rainneville (1/9), Bernaville (2/9). Began move to St. Pol area (4/9). Arrived Humbercamps from Ivergny (10/9), Bienvillers (11/9), Hannescamps (16/9). Tours in front line. To Bienvillers (21/9), front line (27/9), Souastre (29/9), Lucheux (30/9), Beaucourt (18/10), Méricourt (19/10), Citadel Camp (21/10), Trônes Wood (22/10), trenches between Ginchy and Lesbœufs (23/10), front line Lesbœufs (24/10), Guillemont (28/10), bivouacs between Trônes and Bernafay Woods (30/10), La Briqueterie (31/10), front line Lesbœufs sector (3/11). In action (5/11) – moving forward up Lesbœufs-Le Transloy Road – some ground gained. To La Briqueterie (7/11), Méaulte (8/11) – War Diary notes Prince of Wales's had tea with officers. Entrained at Dernancourt for Airaines (11/11) and from there marched to Forceville and Neuville (12/11).

1 Members of 5th Battalion, Gloucestershire Regiment at their billet in Chelmsford just prior to going to France in March, 1915. From Gloucester, these Territorials would be involved in the fierce fighting around Ovillers and the Pozières Ridge during July and August, 1916. (*Ray Westlake Unit Archives*)

2 A member of the 11th Battalion Hampshire Regiment, his collar badge — a crossed rifle and pick indicating the Battalion's Pioneer role with the 16th (Irish) Division, and the letters "LG" above the chevron that the wearer is a Lewis gunner. During the 9 September attack on Ginchy, the Pioneers, with four extra Lewis guns, went into action with the 47th Brigade. (*Mike Ingray Collection*)

3 Corporal W.G. Clive, 1/15th London Regiment (Civil Service Rifles). This photograph was taken on 5 October 1915, just after the fighting at Loos. Corporal Clive was later killed at High Wood, 15 September 1916. (*Paul Reed*).

4 No. 13 Section, A Company, 16th (Service) Battalion, Royal Scots (2nd Edinburgh), Perham Down Camp, Salisbury Plain, 5 September, 1915. This battalion would suffer high casualties on 1 July; in the photograph D.N. Smart (back 1st left), J. Liddell (back 4th left), J.B. Mackenzie (back 5th left), C.D. Nisbet (front 1st left) and J.S. Jolly (front 2nd left) were killed and R. Gordon (front 4th left) and C.O. Gill (back 6th left) wounded, the latter losing his life later on 21 August. F.H. Scott (back 3rd left) was killed in April, 1917. (*John Bodsworth Collection*).

5   Colours of the 7th Battalion, King's (Liverpool Regiment) (T.F)
being handed over for safe keeping at Bootle, 15 August 1914. As part
of the 55th (West Lancashire) Division, 1/7th King's suffered high
casualties during the September battles at Guillemont, Ginchy and
Morval. (*Ray Westlake Unit Archives*)

6 Drummer, 19th (Service) Battalion, Durham Light Infantry (2nd County) at Perham Down Camp, Salisbury Plain prior to leaving for France in February 1916. This "Bantam" battalion from Hartlepool served with the 35th Division, its casualties throughout the July and August operations around Longueval, Delville Wood and Falfemont Farm totalling 60 officers and 316 other ranks. (*Ray Westlake Unit Archives*)

7. Drummer Walter Ritchie, 2nd Battalion, Seaforth Highlanders who won the Victoria Cross on 1 July, 1916, on the Redan Ridge, north of Beaumont Hamel. On his own initiative he stood on the parapet of the enemy's trench and, under heavy machine-gun fire, repeatedly sounded the "Charge", thereby rallying the men. Then throughout the day Drummer Ritchie carried messages over fire-swept ground showing the greatest devotion to duty. (*Ray Westlake Unit Archives*)

8 Sunken road just outside of Ginchy (Flers Road). Here, on 15 September, German machine guns swept through the ranks of the 2nd and 3rd Coldstream Guards advancing from the left. The attack held up, Lieut-Colonel John Vaughan Campbell, D.S.O. (3rd Coldstream) rallied the Guardsmen and with a blast from his hunting horn led the men on into the sunken road. He was later awarded the Victoria Cross for his gallantry and leadership. (*Ray Westlake Unit Archives*)

9 Men of the 8th Battalion, Black Watch, receiving their rum ration after the fighting at Longueval 14-18 July. (*Ray Westlake Unit Archives*)

10 2nd Battalion, Green Howards at La Neuville, Corbie, April, 1916. This photograph includes Lieut-Col. Walter Herbert Young, DSO (front row, centre) who in the following July led his battalion into action at Trônes Wood and Guillemont. Left of Colonel Young is Lieut Basil Gill (Adjutant) who was wounded at Trônes Wood and later killed during the attack on Bayonet and Bite Trenches, 18 October. (*Paul Reed*)

DAILY SKETCH.

GUARANTEED DAILY NETT SALE MORE THAN 1,000,000 COPIES.

No. 2,300.   LONDON, SATURDAY, JULY; 22, 1916.   [Registered as a Newspaper.]   ONE HALFPENNY

EAST SURREYS' GLORIOUS FOOTBALL CHARGE

Private Draper (wounded), one of the men who kicked the ball along. He is seen holding the historic football, which he had the honour to inflate on the parade ground yesterday.

Captain Wilfred P. Nevill, who kicked off and led the charge. He fell early in the fight, cheering on his men.

The East Surreys cheering their comrades who took part in the charge, many of whom (wounded) were on parade.

Colonel Treeby holding up the ball, which was sent over from the front, to be kept as a regimental trophy, of the glorious day.

The football which the East Surreys kicked off from the parapet and dribbled to the German lines when they made their glorious charge on July 1 was blown up on the Square at Kingston Barracks, the Headquarters of the Regiment, yesterday. Colonel Treeby, addressing officers and men, said the East Surreys had nobly played the great game. Five hundred of their comrades were killed and wounded in the charge, but they had not died in vain—they had helped to bring us nearer to the goal of victory.

11   Front page—*Daily Sketch*, 22 July, 1916 commemorating the attack of the 8th East Surrey Regiment at Montauban on 1 July. (*John Woodroff*)

1/4th (Denbighshire) Battalion (T.F.). Pioneers, 47th (2nd London) Division: Arrived Frohen-le-Petit from Ecoivres (1/8). To Yvrencheux (5/8), Domvast (11/8), Yaucourt-Bassus (20/8), Vignacourt (21/8), Pierregot (22/8), Bresle (23/8). Two companies to Fricourt Wood (27/8) – work on roads Mametz area. Two Companies to Albert (1/9) and joined working parties at Mametz. War Diary records 'specialist' training at Albert. To Fricourt Wood (12/9) – dug communication trenches in readiness for forthcoming operations at High Wood. To Bazentin-le-Grand area (28/9). Consolidated captured line at Eaucourt l' Abbaye (2/10). To Albert (9/10). Entrained for Ailly-le-Haut-Clocher (13/10). Entrained at Pont-Remy for Godewaersvelde (17/10).

9th (Service) Battalion. 58th Brigade, 19th (Western) Division: Moved forward from Bresle to Tara-Usna Line (1/7). Attack on La Boisselle 4 p.m. (2/7) – clearing western end of village establishing line near church by nightfall. Bombing attacks continued 2.45 a.m. (3/7) – enemy counter attacked and forced withdrawal to edge of village. Casualties – 164. To Tara-Usna Line (4/7). Secured right flank of advance on Contalmaison (7/7). Via Albert to Baizieux Wood (9/7), Bécourt Wood (20/7), Mametz Wood (21/7), support line Bazentin-le-Petit (23/7), Bécourt Wood (29/7), Lahoussoye (30/7). Entrained at Fréchencourt for Longpré (3/8) and from there marched to Pont-Remy. Entrained for Bailleul (7/8). Entrained for Doullens (5/10) and from there marched to Bois de Warnimont. To Sailly-au-Bois (7/10) – began tours in line Hébuterne sector. To Vauchelles (16/10), Toutencourt (17/10), Ovillers Post (18/10), support line – Regina and Hessian Trenches (26/10), Ovillers Post (30/10), support line (2/11), Ovillers Post (5/11), support line (11/11), Marlborough Huts (13/11), positions north-east of Authie Wood (14/11), trenches west of Stuff Redoubt (15/11), Aveluy (17/11).

10th (Service) Battalion. 76th Brigade, 3rd Division: Entrained at St. Omer for Doullens (1/7) and from there marched to Gézaincourt. To Naours (3/7), Rainneville (4/7), Franvillers (5/7), Celestines Wood (6/7), Bronfay Farm (8/7), Montauban Alley (13/7). Attack on Delville Wood (20/7) – encountered heavy machine gun fire while moving up Buchanan Street. Corporal Joseph Davies ('D' Company) and Private Albert Hill ('C') awarded Victoria Cross for gallantry during subsequent close quarter fighting. Withdrew to Breslau Trench 3.30 a.m. (21/7). Casualties – 228. To Bois des Tailles (25/7), Méricourt (28/7), Sandpit Camp (11/8), Talus Boisé (14/8), Casement, Dublin and Chimpanzee Trenches (16/8). Attack on Lonely Trench (17/8) – 2 companies failed at 10.30 p.m. and again at 4 a.m. (18/8). Other 2 companies renewed attack 2.45 p.m. – objectives taken and consolidated. Casualties – 224. To Happy Valley (20/8), Morlancourt (21/8). Entrained at Méricourt for Candas (23/8) and from there began march to St. Pol area. Entrained at St. Pol for Acheux (7/10). To Bertrancourt (8/10), Louvencourt (17/10) – tours in line Serre sector. To Bus-lès-Artois (21/10). Attack on Serre (13/11) – advance through mud waist-deep in places against uncut German wire failed. Casualties – 289. To Courcelles (15/11), trenches in front of Serre (17/11).

13th (Service) Battalion (1st North Wales). 113th Brigade, 38th (Welsh) Division: To Léalvillers from Toutencourt (1/7), Treux (3/7), Mametz (5/7) – Fritz Trench and Danzig Alley. Attack on Mametz Wood (10/7) – Commanding Officer Lieutenant-Colonel O.S. Flower killed in action at Wood Support Trench. Later advanced on to northern edge. Entrained at Méaulte for Longpré (12/7) and from there marched to Eaucourt. To Brucamps (14/7), Authie (15/7), St. Léger (17/7), bivouacs near Coigneux (18/7), line Beaumont-Hamel sector (24/7), Bus-lès-Artois (28/7), Sarton (29/7). Entrained at Doullens for Ypres sector (31/7).

14th (Service) Battalion. 113th Brigade, 38th (Welsh) Division: To Ribemont from Arquèves (3/7), Mametz (5/7) – Quadrangle Trench, Shelter Wood. Two companies to Danzig Alley (6/7) – remainder bivouacs near Carnoy. To Pommiers Trench (7/7), Minden Post (8/7). Attack on Mametz Wood (10/7) – in support behind 16th R.W.F. Relieved and to Citadel Camp (12/7). From there marched to Edgehill station. War Diary records that train did not arrive – Battalion instead boarded buses for Longpré (13/7). To Ergnies (14/7), St. Léger (15/7), Couin (17/7), Sailly Dell (18/7), trenches Beaumont-Hamel sector (24/7), Bus Wood (27/7), Sarton (28/7). Entrained at Doullens for Ypres sector (30/7).

15th (Service) Battalion (1st London Welsh). 113th Brigade, 38th (Welsh) Division: To Puchevillers (1/7), Léalvillers (2/7), Ribemont (3/7), Mametz (5/7), Minden Post (8/7), Fritz and Danzig Trenches (9/7). Attack on Mametz Wood (10/7) – in close support behind 16th R.W.F. Relieved in wood and via Queen's Nullah to Ribemont (11/7). Entrained at Méricourt for Longpré (12/7) and from there marched to Ergnies. To Authie (15/7), bivouacs near Couin (17/7), near Coigneux (18/7), trenches Auchonvillers sector (24/7), Bus-lès-Artois (28/7), Thièvres (29/7). Entrained at Doullens for Ypres sector (31/7).

16th (Service) Battalion. 113th Brigade, 38th (Welsh) Division: To Léalvillers from Puchevillers (1/7), Ribemont (3/7), trenches between Mametz and Mametz Wood (5/7). War Diary records withdrawal from line to bivouacs near Carnoy (6/7) due to overcrowding. Took over front line (8/7). Attack on Mametz Wood (10/7) – Commanding Officer Colonel Ronald Carden killed at edge of wood. The history of the Royal Welsh Fusiliers (Major C.H. Dudley Ward, D.S.O, M.C.) records that he led the attack with a coloured handkerchief tied to his stick – 'this will show you where I am.' With support of 15th R.W.F. entered wood and fought on until halted by fire from Wood Support. The history of the 38th (Welsh) Division (Lieutenant-Colonel J.E. Munby) records the advance towards Mametz Wood – 'wave after wave of men were seen advancing without hesitation and without a break over a distance which in some places was nearly 500 yards.' Withdrew to Méricourt (12/7). Entrained at Grove Town for Longpré and from there marched to Ailly-le-Haut-Clocher. To Brucamps (14/7), St. Léger (15/7), Mailly-Maillet (17/7), Bus-lès-Artois (28/7), Thièvres (29/7). Entrained at Doullens for Ypres sector (31/7).

17th (Service) Battalion (2nd North Wales). 115th Brigade, 38th (Welsh) Division: To Acheux from Toutencourt (1/7), Buire (3/7), Fricourt (5/7), trenches Mametz (6/7). Attack on Mametz Wood (10/7) – entered wood during afternoon and by 6.30 p.m. within 40 yards of of northern edge. Relieved (12/7). Via Warloy to Couin (15/7), Coigneux (14/7), trenches Hébuterne sector (18/7), Courcelles (22/7), trenches (26/7), Bus-lès-Artois via Courcelles (29/7). Entrained at Candas for St. Omer (31/7).

19th (Service) Battalion. 119th Brigade, 40th Division: Arrived Heuzecourt from Buire-au-Bois (5/11). Returned to Buire-au-Bois (15/11). To Villers-l'Hôpital (17/11), Neuvillette (18/11).

South Wales Borderers

1st Battalion. 3rd Brigade, 1st Division: Entrained at Chocques for Doullens (6/7) and from there marched to Bonneville. To Coisy via Vignacourt (7/7), Franvillers (8/7), Albert via Heilly and Ribemont (10/7). Moved forward under heavy attack from gas shells to reserve at Lozenge Wood (14/7). To support positions in Mametz Wood (15/7). Attack on enemy positions near Bazentin-le-Petit Wood – successful operation gaining some 1,200 yards of frontage with few casualties. To Lozenge Wood (18/7), Bécourt Wood (19/7), Albert (20/7), Lozenge Wood (22/7), Peake Wood (23/7). Relieved 1st Northamptonshire in front line near Contalmaison Villa (24/7). Attack on Munster Alley (25/7). To Millencourt (26/7). War Diary records the Drums of 5th S.W.B. meeting the 1st outside Albert and playing the senior Battalion through the town. To Bécourt Wood (15/8), Fricourt (19/8), Bazentin-le-Petit Wood (20/8). Attack on Intermediate Line (25/8). To Albert (27/8), Mametz Wood (2/9), High Wood (5/9). Attack on High Wood (8/9). To Mametz Wood (9/9), Lozenge Wood (10/9), Hénencourt Wood (11/8), Franvillers (12/9), Hénencourt Wood via Baizieux (16/9), Black Wood (18/9). Moved through Bécourt Wood, Lozenge Wood and Mametz to trenches between High Alley and Bazentin-le-Grand (19/9). To High Wood (23/9), Albert (25/9), Millencourt (28/9), Hénencourt Wood (29/9), Aigneville (2/10). Moved to Mametz Wood via Baizieux (31/10). Carried out road repair duties in the area. To Millencourt (10/11), Mametz Wood (17/11).

2nd Battalion. 87th Brigade, 29th Division: Attack on Beaumont-Hamel (1/7). Objective Y Ravine – left start positions at zero – soon cut down by machine gun bullets, most in leading waves would not get much further than their own wire. Those that did reach German line were quickly killed. Casualties – 372. Remained in forward area resting between tours in front line around Acheux. To Mailly-Maillet Wood (22/7), Bus-lès-Artois via Bertrancourt (24/7), Amplier (25/7). Entrained at Doullens for Ypres sector (27/7). Arrived Longueau (7/10) and from there marched to Cardonnette. To Buire via Allonville and Querrieu (10/10), camp south-west of Fricourt (13/10), Bernafay Wood (19/10). Moved forward at night through Longueval to front line (Grease Trench) Gueudecourt sector. To Pommiers Redoubt (29/10), camp about mile west of Fricourt (30/10). Entrained at Albert for Airaines (3/11). To Citadel Camp (14/11), La Briqueterie (15/11). From there to support trenches (John Bull, Ox, Hogg's Back) behind Lesbœufs.

5th (Service) Battalion (Pioneers). Pioneers, 19th (Western) Division: Headquarters at Long Valley (1/7) moving to Albert (4/7). Took part in 19th

Division's operations around La Boisselle (2/7)–(7/7). Played active role throughout the fighting in addition to usual duties digging communication trenches and constructing strong-points. To Baizieux Wood (9/7), Bécourt Wood (19/7). Operations around High Wood, Mametz Wood (22/7). To Fricourt Wood (26/7) and from there assembly positions between Bazentin-le-Petit Wood and Mametz. Under 57th Brigade moved forward to consolidate and hold recently captured Intermediate Line. Entrained at Méricourt for Longpré (3/8) and from there marched to Long. Transferred to Bailleul area (10/8). Entrained for Doullens (6/10) and from there marched to Terramesnil. To Coigneux (9/10). Worked on Hébuterne-Sailly Road. To Vauchelles (17/10), Toutencourt (18/10), the brickworks north of Albert (21/10), Aveluy (22/10). Worked on Stuff Redoubt, Zollern Redoubt and tramway near Mouquet Farm. Operations south of the Ancre around Grandcourt.

6th (Service) Battalion (Pioneers). Pioneers, 25th Division: At Senlis (1/7). To Bouzincourt (4/7). Operations around Leipzig Salient. To Aveluy Wood (7/7), Albert (9/7). Working in Ovillers and La Boiselle sectors. To Aveluy Wood (21/7), Bus-lès-Artois (22/7), Mailly-Maillet Wood (24/7), Beaussart (25/7), Authie (10/8), Léalvillers (14/8), Martinsart Wood (18/8), Aveluy (28/8), Acheux (7/9), Amplier (10/9), Fienvillers (11/9), Longuevillette (12/9), Amplier (25/9), Acheux Wood (26/9), Aveluy (29/9). Took part in fighting at Stuff Redoubt (9/10) and Regina Trench (21/10). To the brickworks north of Albert (22/10), Contay (23/10), Candas (24/10). Moved to Ypres sector (30/10).

10th (Service) Battalion (1st Gwent). 115th Brigade, 38th (Welsh) Division: Moved from Toutencourt to Acheux (1/7), Buire-sur-l'Ancre (3/7), bivouacs between Carnoy and Mametz (5/7), Caterpillar Wood (6/7). Followed 11th South Wales Borderers into action at Mametz Wood (7/7) – both swept by machine gun fire and forced to retire. Further and more successful attacks (10/7) and (11/7). Relieved from wood and to bivouacs between Carnoy and Mametz (12/7). To Couin (13/7), Courcelles-au-Bois (14/7), trenches in front of Colincamps (18/7), Courcelles-au-Bois (22/7), trenches Bus-lès-Artois (29/7). Entrained at Candas for St. Omer (30/7).

11th (Service) Battalion (2nd Gwent). 115th Brigade, 38th (Welsh) Division: Arrived Acheux from Toutencourt (1/7). To Buire-sur-l'Ancre (3/7), Carnoy (5/7), Caterpillar Wood (6/7). Attack on Mametz Wood (7/7) – heavy casualties from machine gun fire and forced to retire. Successful attack (10/7). Relieved and to Warloy (13/7). Took over trenches in front of Colincamps (14/7). Relieved by 10th South Wales Borderers and to Courcelles-au-Bois

(18/7). To trenches (23/7), Courcelles (27/7), Vauchelles (28/7). Entrained at Candas for St. Omer (30/7).

12th (Service) Battalion (3rd Gwent). 119th Brigade, 40th Division: Arrived Autheux from Bonnières (5/11). 'A' Company to Mon Plaisir Farm (8/11). To Fortel (15/11), Bonnières (17/11), D Bouquemaison (18/11).

King's Own Scottish Borderers

1st Battalion. 87th Brigade, 29th Division: Moved up from Acheux Wood during night (30/6) and took over support trenches on extreme right of 29th Division's line in front of Beaumont-Hamel. Followed 1st Royal Inniskilling Fusiliers into attack (1/7) – Regimental historian Captain Stair Gillon records the same machine gun fire that swept the Irishmen cutting into the Borderers 'they did not succeed in even reaching the few Fusiliers who were lying out in No Man's Land.' In 1 company alone there would be some 202 casualties out of its strength of 219. Battalion losses (according to Official History of The Great War) – 552. Withdrew to Fort Jackson 4 p.m. Took over trenches in front of Hemel (2/7). Relieved and to Acheux (8/7). Further tours in front line carried out until (24/7). Entrained at Doullens for Ypres sector (27/7). Arrived Longueau (7/10) and from there marched to Cardonnette. To Buire-sur-l'Ancre (10/10), Fricourt (13/10), Bernafay Wood (19/10), support and front line positions Gueudecourt sector (20/10). Relieved and to Bernafay Wood (27/10), Fricourt (30/10). Entrained at Albert for Airaines (3/11). To Buire-sur-l'Ancre (14/11), Fricourt (15/11). From there began tours in line Lesbœufs sector.

2nd Battalion. 13th Brigade, 5th Division: Moved from Arras area (13/7) – passing through Heuzecourt and Hérissart before reaching Franvillers (16/7). To Méaulte (17/7). Took over trenches between Bazentin-le-Grand and Longueval (19/7). 'A' and 'D' Companies attacked enemy position in front of Wood Lane (20/7) – objective taken and held until relieved at night by 14th Royal Warwickshire. Attack on Wood Lane (22/7) – Machine gun fire from High Wood caused high casualties – just 1 platoon reached objective. Relieved by 1st Norfolk and to Pommiers Redoubt (23/7). To trenches at Longueval and Delville Wood (29/7). Attacked north-west of Delville Wood 6.12 p.m. (30/7). Relieved and to Pommiers Redoubt (1/8), Dernancourt (2/8). Entrained for Airaines (4/8) and from there marched to Métigny. To Heucourt (5/8). Entrained for Méricourt (24/8) and from there marched to Dernancourt. To Happy Valley (25/8), reserve positions at Maricourt (26/8), trenches opposite Falfemont Farm (29/8). In preparation for assault on Falfemont Farm (3/9), assembled on slopes of the Leuze Wood spur, some 400 yards from objective. Attack commenced 8.50 a.m. – Official History of The Great War recording the task as 'impossible.' Battalion swept by rifle and machine gun fire in front and flank. Casualties – almost 300. Relieved and to Citadel Camp. To front line facing Falfemont Farm (10/9), Carnoy area (13/9), support positions north of The Quadrilateral (18/9). Attached to 95th Brigade for Battle of Morval (25/9) – passed through 1st Devonshire and into southern half of village. War Diary notes that nearly every man secured a trophy. Regimental historian – Captain Stair Gillon records that in accordance with orders, Battalion did not continue the advance 'but lay on the outskirts of the captured village taking pot shots at the Germans retiring from Combles.' Relieved and to Citadel Camp (26/9). Entrained to Hallencourt area (27/9). Entrained at Abbeville for Lillers (1/10). Casualties for Somme operations given in War Diary as – 42 officers and 1,110 other ranks.

6th (Service) Battalion. 27th Brigade, 9th (Scottish) Division: From Pommiers Redoubt provided carrying parties for 18th Division during its operations at Montauban (1/7)–(2/7). Later moved forward to eastern perimeter of village. Attack and capture of Bernafay Wood (3/7) – Official History of The Great War recording that with only 6 casualties – 6th K.O.S.B. and 12th Royal Scots covered 500 yards of flat ground – entered the wood and took possession. Remained in position under continuous bombardment until relieved and to Billon Wood (9/7). Casualties – 316. Provided working parties during fighting for Longueval (14/7)–(16/7). In action (17/7) – heavy casualties from machine gun and rifle fire during advance in the dark. Withdrew to Talus Boisé. To front line – Clarges Street and Pall Mall (18/7). Heavily shelled until relieved during night (19/7). Casualties – 126. Regimental historian – Captain Stair Gillon notes strength at this time as about 3 officers and 100 men. Entrained at Méricourt for Hangest (23/7) and from there marched to Cocquerel. Entrained at Pont-Remy for Diéval (24/7). To Barly north-west of Doullens (5/10), Mirvaux (7/10), Laviéville (8/10), Mametz Wood (9/10). Moved forward via High Wood to take over line at Eaucourt-l'Abbaye (18/10). Almost all unit diaries and histories concerned with the 9th Division record this journey as being full of horrors, death and a fate more diabolical than could ever be imagined. The mud and filth doing as much damage as the shelling. Relief completed 6 a.m. (20/10). In action at 4 p.m. (20/10) – the Nose being taken, evacuated, and reoccupied. Occupied Snag Trench by nightfall. To support at Flers Line during night (21/10), Mametz Wood (24/10), Bécourt (25/10), Franvillers (26/10), Mirvaux (27/10), Talmas (28/10). Moved by buses to Croisette south-west of St. Pol (29/10).

7th/8th (Service) Battalion. 46th Brigade, 15th (Scottish) Division: Reached Candas from Béthune sector (28/7). To Flesselles (31/7), Molliens-au-Bois (4/8), Franvillers (5/8), Bécourt (7/8) and from there to forward positions near Martinpuich. German counter attack – (17/8). Casualties – 224. Relieved by 10th Scottish Rifles and to camp just outside Albert on Amiens Road (18/8). To support trenches (29/8), front line (31/8), Scots Redoubt (4/9). Moved forward (14/9) – attack and capture of Martinpuich (15/9). Relieved and to Béhencourt (18/9). War Diary gives casualties since arriving in Fourth Army area (28/7) as 34 officers and 886 other ranks. To Albert (30/9), Scots Redoubt (9/10). Took over trenches near Le Sars (15/10). To Lozenge Wood (18/10), front line (28/10), Millencourt (3/11), Baizieux (13/11). Later to Havernas and Wargnies.

Cameronians (Scottish Rifles)

1st Battalion. 19th Brigade, 33rd Division: Entrained at Fouquereuil for Amiens (8/7) and from there to Longueau. To Poulainville (9/7), Daours (11/7), Buire (12/7), Méaulte (14/7), support positions Mametz Wood (15/7), trenches between Bazentin-le-Petit and High Wood (16/7). Attack on Switch Trench (17/7). Relieved and to Mametz Wood (19/7). Attack (with 5th/6th Scottish Rifles) on High Wood (20/7). Casualties – 382. Relieved and via Mametz Wood to Buire (21/7). To Bécordel-Bécourt (6/8), Mametz Wood (18/8), trenches near High Wood (19/8), Bazentin-le-Grand (20/8), High Wood (22/8), Crucifix Corner (26/8), Pommiers Redoubt (27/8), Fricourt Wood (29/8), Ribemont (31/8), Molliens-au-Bois (1/9), Vacquerie (2/9), Villers l'Hôpital (4/9). To St Pol area (5/9). Arrived Bienvillers and began duty in front line Foncquevillers sector (10/9). Via St. Amand to Lucheux (30/9), Doullens (8/10), Souastre and marched via Sailly-au-Bois to Hébuterne (11/10). To Bayencourt (15/10), via Souastre to Ivergny (17/10), Doullens (18/10), Buire-sur-l'Ancre (19/10), Citadel Camp (21/10), La Briqueterie (22/10), Guillemont (23/10). Took over trenches east of Lesbœufs (27/10). Attack on Hazy Trench (29/10). To La Briqueterie (30/10), Trônes Wood (3/11), Flers line (5/11), Carnoy (7/11), Méaulte (8/11), Hallencourt (9/11). Entrained at Buire for Citerne (11/11).

2nd Battalion. 23rd Brigade, 8th Division: In reserve at Ovillers Post during attack on Ovillers (1/7). Withdrew to Millencourt. Entrained at Méricourt for Ailly-sur-Somme (2/7) and from there marched to Yzeux. To Crouy-St Pierre (4/7). Entrained at Longueau for Béthune area (6/7). Entrained at Chocques for Pont-Remy (14/10). To Doudelainville (15/10). Moved by motor bus to Ville-sur-Ancre (17/10) and from there marched to Méaulte. To Trônes Wood (20/10), trenches south-east of Flers (21/10). Attack on Zenith Trench (23/10) – entered Orion Tench, but after heavy bombardment forced to pretire. Casualties – 240. To Trônes Wood (25/10), front line (27/10), Trônes Wood (29/10), Mansell Camp (30/10), Méaulte (31/10), Citadel Camp (3/11), Flers line (7/11), Carnoy (13/11), Citadel Camp (15/11).

5th/6th Battalion (T.F.). 19th Brigade, 33rd Division: Arrived Longueau (9/7). To Poulainville (10/7), Corbie (11/7), Buire-sur-l'Ancre (12/7), Bécordel-Bécourt (13/7). Moved forward to support positions at Mametz Wood (15/7) and from there front line between Bazentin-le-Petit and High Wood. Relieved and to Mametz Wood (18/7). Moved up Death Valley for attack on High Wood midnight (19/7) – rushed wood at 3.35 a.m. – Battalion historian records 'all opposition was wiped out by 3 p.m. and the wood was in full possession of the 19th Brigade.' Relieved during night after strong counter attacks and to

Mametz Wood. Casualties – 407. Battalion records give over half this number as missing – 'most never to be seen again.' Also noted are losses incurred since (14/7) – strength on that day – 40 officers and 1,067 other ranks. At Mametz Wood on (21/7), 5th/6th Scottish Rifles numbered just 199 all ranks. To Buire (22/7), Bécordel-Bécourt (6/8), support trenches near High Wood (18/8), front line between High Wood and Delville Wood (19/8). Battalion records note here the difficulty in moving troops around the battlefield under battle conditions. Apparently at one time during relief, no less than 5 commanding officers ('mostly angry') were undertaking to hand over or take over the same position. Took turns in line until relieved (27/8) – resting between tours at Mametz Wood, Fricourt Wood, Pommiers Redoubt. To Fricourt Wood (28/8), Bécordel-Bécourt(29/8), Ribemont (30/8), Pierregot (2/9), Autheux (3/9). To St Pol area (5/9). From Pommier and duty in line at Foncquevillers Battalion moved via Humbercamps to Doullens (1/10). To Bayencourt (11/10), Sailly-au-Bois (16/10) and from there front line duty Hébuterne sector. Relieved (19/10) and via Bayencourt to Doullens. Moved in French buses to positions between Buire and Ville-sous-Corbie (20/10). To Citadel Camp (21/10), Bernafay Wood (22/10), support line near Guillemont (24/10), Ox and Bovril support trenches (25/10), front line (27/10). Attack on Hazy and Boritska Trenches (29/10). Relieved and to Bernafay Wood (30/10), Carnoy (31/10). To Flers line (3/11). In reserve during 100th Brigade's attack on Hazy Trench (5/11). Took over captured positions at Lesbœufs after dark. Relieved and to Trônes Wood (6/11), Carnoy (7/11), Méaulte (8/11). Entrained at Edgehill for Airaines (11/11). To billets at Fresnes-Tilloloy and Vaux-Marquennville (12/11), Allery (17/11).

9th (Service) Battalion. 27th Brigade, 9th (Scottish) Division: Moved from Billon Wood into front line at Montauban (3/7). Relieved and to Billon Valley (8/7). Casualties 139. To Longueval (13/7). Attack on village (14/7). Relieved and to Cambridge Copse (15/7). To Caterpillar Valley (16/7). Took part in bombing attack north-west of Delville Wood (17/7). Relieved and to Talus Boisé. To support trenches Longueval (18/7), bivouacs east of Carnoy (19/7), Happy Valley (20/7). Entrained at Hangest for Vimy sector (23/7). Arrived Talmas (6/10). To Beaucourt (7/10), Laviéville (8/10). Moved via Albert, Fricourt, Mametz to bivouacs in Mametz Wood (10/10). To Flers line, Eaucourt-l'Abbaye sector (19/10), High Wood (23/10), Mametz Wood (24/10), Bécourt (25/10), Béhencourt (26/10), Pierregot (27/10), Talmas (28/10), Croisette south-west of St.Pol (29/10).

10th (Service) Battalion. 46th Brigade, 15th (Scottish) Division: Arrived Fienvillers (29/7). To Flesselles (31/7), Molliens-au-Bois (4/8), Franvillers (5/8). Moved forward through Albert into reserve trenches behind Contalmaison

(7/8) – Headquarters Shelter Wood, front companies outskirts of Mametz Wood. To front line facing Martinpuich (70th Avenue and Lancashire Trench) (11/8). Relieved and to Shelter Wood (14/8). Relieved 7th/8th K.O.S.B. in front line (18/8). To Bécourt Wood (19/8). Casualties from bombing by German aeroplanes. To trenches (Clark's and Brecon Sap) at High Wood (27/8) – two days in, two days out until relieved and to Bécourt (5/9). To Contalmaison (12/9). Moved forward during night (14/9) for attack towards Martinpuich – first objectives taken – village entered by 6.35 a.m. At 6.50 a.m., Battalion historian records – 'the telephone rang in Headquarters: is that you, Deans? said the signalling Sergeant. Yes! said Deans. Where are you? said the Sergeant. I am in Martinpuich, said Deans, smoking a fine Boche cigar. Can you smell it over the line?' Relieved and to Contalmaison (16/9). Casualties – 310. To Lahoussoye (18/9), Albert (30/9), Contalmaison (8/10). Work carried out on roads and trenches (Hook and Eye). To Le Sars sector (14/10), Scots Redoubt (18/10), Martin Trench (24/10), Le Sars sector (28/10). Relieved and to Bécourt Wood (1/11), Millencourt (2/11), Baizieux (5/11), Talmas (15/11).

Royal Inniskilling Fusiliers

1st Battalion. 87th Brigade, 29th Division: Attack at Beaumont-Hamel (1/7) – advancing on right of Brigade and south of the Y Ravine – soon cut down by machine gun fire from the front and both flanks. Those men that did get forward would be held up at uncut wire and the small parties that cleared this soon killed or taken prisoner. Withdrew to British line. Casualties (including Commanding Officer Lieutenant-Colonel R.C. Pierce who was killed) – 549. Remained in forward area – resting around Acheux and Mailly-Maillet. To Bus-lès-Artois (24/7), Amplier (25/7). Entrained at Doullens for the Ypres sector (27/7). Arrived Longueau and marched to Cardonnette (7/10). To Buire-sur-Ancre (10/10), Fricourt (13/10), Montauban (19/10). From there to front line Gueudecourt sector. To Fricourt (29/10). Entrained at Albert for Airaines (3/11). To Citadel Camp (14/11), Carnoy (15/11). Later began tours in front line Lesbœufs sector.

2nd Battalion. 96th Brigade, 32nd Division: In brigade reserve at beginning of 32nd Division's assault on Thiepval (1/7). Leading waves of 96th Brigade's attack (16th Northumberland Fusiliers and 15th Lancashire Fusiliers) had been cut down almost immediately after leaving their trenches. At 8.55 a.m. 1 company of the Inniskilling sent forward – later more of the Battalion went on, but all were to suffer the same fate as the leading units. Withdrawn to start lines. To Aveluy Wood (3/7), Warloy (4/7), front line Ovillers (9/7). Attacked west of village 9 a.m. – attached to 14th Brigade, objectives taken and held against strong counter attacks. Advanced during night (10/7) – after hand-to-hand fighting gained more ground. Another attack (13/7) – Regimental historian Sir Frank Fox recording that 2 companies co-operating with 17th Highland Light Infantry gained their objectives but later, and low in numbers, would be forced to retire. To Bouzincourt (14/7). Casualties during Ovillers operations – 267. Via Senlis, Halloy and Bouquemaison to Béthune sector (19/7). Returned to Somme area during third week of October – reaching Vadencourt Wood (21/10). To Bouzincourt (23/10), Warloy (26/10), Hérissart (31/10), Warloy (13/11), support positions Thiepval sector (14/11), Mailly-Maillet (17/11).

7th (Service) Battalion. 49th Brigade, 16th (Irish) Division: Arrived Longueau from Loos area (29/8) and from there marched to Vaux-sur-Somme. To Happy Valley (31/8), Citadel Camp (3/9). From there to Arrow Head Copse. To Guillemont-Leuze Wood Road (5/9) and there linked up with 5th Division at northern end of wood. Commanding Officer Lieutenant-Colonel H.N. Young wounded by sniper (6/9) – enemy attack during night beaten off. To support at Bernafay Wood (7/9). Ordered forward to Guillemont in support of 47th Brigade's attack on Ginchy (8/9). Moved on for attack (9/9) – suffering heavily on the way up from machine gun fire and shrapnel assault could not be carried out. Formed with 47th Brigade a defensive flank which was held against counter attacks. Relieved early morning (10/9). Casualties – 189. Regimental historian Sir Frank Fox recalls a grim but humorous remark during the move forward to Ginchy – 'everyone will receive a cross, whether wooden or military depends on your luck.' To Sailly-le-Sec (11/9), Bailleul near Abbeville (18/9). Entrained for Ypres sector (21/9).

8th (Service) Battalion. 49th Brigade, 16th (Irish) Division: Arrived Longueau from Loos area (29/8) and from there marched to Vaux-sur-Somme. To Happy Valley (31/8), Citadel Camp (3/9) and from there Arrow Head Copse. To front line Leuze Wood (5/9). Came under heavy bombardment and suffered high casualties while digging forward trench (6/9). To Bernafay Wood (7/9). Held support positions during attack on Ginchy (8/9). Commanding Officer Lieutenant-Colonel Dalziel Walton killed by a sniper (9/9). Moved forward in afternoon to support 47th Brigade's attack – later formed defensive flank with 7th Royal Inniskilling Fusiliers. Relieved early morning (10/9). To Sailly-le-Sec (11/9), Bailleul near Abbeville (18/9). Entrained for Ypres sector (21/9).

9th (Service) Battalion (Co. Tyrone). 109th Brigade, 36th (Ulster) Division: Assembled in Thiepval Wood for attack (1/7) – on right of Brigade's assault moved forward before zero hour into No Man's Land – leading waves advanced under machine gun fire from Thiepval – first objective taken. Moving on to second German line – attacked from rear by machine guns brought up from deep dug-outs. Enemy began counter attacks – low in numbers, without water and little ammunition, order given to withdraw to Crucifix. Later moved back to former German first line and by evening back in British line opposite. Casualties – 477. Victoria Cross awarded posthumously to Temp. Captain. Eric Bell who while attached to 109th Trench Mortar Battery went into the open and accounted for a number of the enemy with bomb and rifle. This officer, aged just 20, was never found and his name can now be seen on the Thiepval Memorial to the Missing. 36th Division relieved by 49th (2/7) – 109th Brigade moving back through Thiepval Wood to area around Martinsart and Hédauville. Transferred to Ypres sector (11/7).

10th (service) Battalion (Derry). 109th Brigade, 36th (Ulster) Division: Assembled in Thiepval Wood for attack (1/7) – advanced 7.30 a.m. – 'A' Company swept by machine gun fire from Thiepval upon leaving trenches – others sustained heavy casualties while crossing No Man's Land. Casualties estimated at almost 600. Withdrew to Thiepval Wood. To

Martinsart Wood (2/7), Hédauville (3/7). Transferred to Ypres sector (11/7).

11th (Service) Battalion (Donegal and Fermanagh). 109th Brigade, 36th (Ulster) Division: Moved forward from Thiepval Wood in support of attack (1/7) – high casualties from machine gun fire upon leaving wood and during attempt to cross No Man's Land. Withdrew during night. To Martinsart Wood (2/7), Hédauville (3/7). Transferred to Ypres sector (11/7).

Gloucestershire Regiment

1st Battalion. 3rd Brigade, 1st Division: Reached Doullens from Chocques (6/7) and from there bivouacked near Beauval. To Vignacourt (7/7), Rainneville (8/7), Franvillers (9/7), Albert (10/7), Contalmaison (The Cutting) (14/7). Attacked at midnight (16/7) – captured enemy positions north of village and both sides of Contalmaison-Martinpuich Road. To Scots Redoubt (18/7), Bécourt Wood (19/7), Albert (20/7), forward positions around Contalmaison (22/7), Scots Redoubt (25/7), Millencourt (26/7), Railway Copse (15/8), Black Wood (16/8), line west of High Wood (20/8), Bécourt Wood (28/8), Albert (30/8), The Quadrangle (2/9), positions north of Bazentin-le-Grand (5/9). Attack on south western face of High Wood (8/9) – leading waves gained objectives after high casualties from British barrage in assembly trenches. Later came under heavy fire and bombardment and withdrawal ordered to New Trench. Casualties – over 200. To The Quadrangle (9/9), Hénencourt Wood (11/9), Franvillers (12/9), Hénencourt Wood (15/9), Black Wood (18/9), Bazentin-le-Grand (19/9), east side of Mametz Wood (20/9), Black Wood (25/9), Millencourt (28/9), Hénencourt Wood (29/9), Feuquières (3/10), Baizieux (31/10), Millencourt (5/11), southern end Mametz Wood (10/11).

1/4th (City of Bristol) Battalion (T.F.). 144th Brigade, 48th (South Midland) Division: In reserve south of Sailly-au-Bois (1/7) – moving forward 8 a.m. to Mailly-Maillet. Withdrew to bivouacs near Sailly (3/7), Courcelles (4/7). To front line Serre sector (8/7), Courcelles (12/7), Bouzincourt (14/7), trenches in front of Ovillers (15/7). In action west and north-west of village (16/7)–(19/7). Withdrew to support lines at Donnet Post and Ribble Street. To front line (22/7) and in action around Pozières until (24/7). Withdrew to support. 'D' Company in front line (25/7)–(26/7). To Hédauville (27/7), Arquèves (28/7), Beauval (29/7), Franqueville (30/7), Autheux (8/8), Fienvillers (9/8), Puchevillers (10/8), Hédauville (12/8), support lines Ovillers sector (13/8), front line (15/8). 'A' and 'D' Companies attacked Skyline Trench 2 a.m. (16/8) – met with bombes, heavy rifle and machine gun fire. War Diary records that it was impossible to advance or withdraw. Relieved and to Bouzincourt. Moved forward to support at Ribble Street and Ovillers Post midnight (18/8). Attack on Leipzig Redoubt (21/8) – gains consolidated and held. Relieved and to Bouzincourt (23/8), Forceville (26/8). To trenches Auchonvillers sector (Mary Redan to Y Ravine) (27/8), Bois de Warnimont (6/9), Bus-lès-Artois (11/9), Orville (13/9), Autheux (18/9), Sus-St. Léger (30/9), Halloy (1/10), Souastre (3/10), trenches opposite Gommecourt (7/10), Souastre (12/10). Less 'B' and 'D' Companies to Warlincourt (13/10), 'B' and 'D' to La Haie (14/10), 'B' and 'D' to front line, 'A' and 'C' to La Haie (18/10). To Warlincourt and Grincourt (20/10), Sus-St. Léger (21/10), Bresle (25/10),

Albert (31/10), Bazentin-le-Petit (2/11), support trenches around Martinpuich (5/11), Le Sars (7/11), North Camp, Peake Wood, Contalmaison (9/11).

2/4th (City of Bristol) Battalion (T.F.). 183rd Brigade, 61st (2nd South Midland) Division: Arrived Heuzecourt and Grimont (15/11). To Franqueville (16/11), La Vicogne (17/11), Senlis (18/11).

1/5th Battalion (T.F.). 145th Brigade, 48th (South Midland) Division: Moved forward from Couin to reserve positions at Mailly-Maillet (1/7). To Couin (3/7), front line Hébuterne (4/7), Sailly Dell (8/7), front line (12/7), Couin (16/7), Bouzincourt (17/7), trenches north-east of Ovillers (19/7). In action around Pozières (21/7)–(23/7). Relieved and to bivouacs in Tara Valley. To front line (25/7), Léalvillers (26/7), Beauval (28/7), Cramont (29/7), Beauval (9/8), Varennes (10/8), Bouzincourt (11/8), reserve trenches near Albert brickworks (13/8). Attack by 'A' and 'D' Companies on Skyline Trench failed (16/8). 'B' and 'C' Companies in support of 1/4th Royal Berkshire north of Ovillers (18/8) – objectives taken and held. To front line – Skyline and Ration Trenches (19/8). Relieved 7. p.m. and to Bouzincourt. To support at Donnet Post (23/8), front line (25/8). In action (27/8). Relieved and to bivouacs north-west of Bouzincourt (28/8), Bus-lès-Artois (29/8). To trenches opposite Beaumont-Hamel (8/9), Bois de Warnimont (10/9), Beauval (11/9), Vacquerie and Gorges (18/9), Humbercourt (29/9), Warlincourt (1/10), Hénu (7/10), Warlincourt (8/10), Hénu (9/10), trenches Hébuterne sector (14/10), Hénu (16/10), Warlincourt (19/10), Humbercourt (20/10), Beauval (22/10), Talmas (23/10), Béhencourt (24/10), Millencourt (31/10), Dingle Camp (1/11), trenches north-west of Le Sars (2/11), Martinpuich (5/11), Dingle Camp (6/11), Shelter Wood (10/11), front line Le Sars (14/11), support line Martinpuich (16/11), front line (18/11).

2/5th Battalion (T.F.). 184th Brigade, 61st (2nd South Midland) Division: Arrived Neuvillette from Bouret-sur-Canche (6/11). To Bouquemaison (8/11), Bonneville (16/11), Vadencourt (17/11), Albert (18/11).

1/6th Battalion (T.F.). 144th Brigade, 48th (South Midland) Division: Moved forward from bivouacs west of Sailly-au-Bois to reserve line west of Mailly-Maillet (1/7). To Sailly (3/7), front line Serre sector (5/7), Courcelles (9/7), front line (12/7), Couin (14/7), Donnet Post (15/7), front line Ovillers sector (20/7). In action (21/7). To Donnet Post (22/7). Attacked on Pozières (23/7) – heavy casualties from machine gun fire – small party of bombers entered German line near railway but soon beaten back. Withdrew to Donnet Post. To Bouzincourt (26/7), Hédauville (27/7), Arquèves (28/7), Beauval (29/7), Fransu (30/7), Candas (9/8), Puchevillers (10/8), Bouzincourt (12/8), trenches north of Ovillers (13/8). Failed attack on south-western end of Skyline Trench (14/8)–(15/8). Withdrew to reserve at Ribble Street. To Bouzincourt (16/8), Usna Redoubt (19/8), front line (20/8), Bouzincourt (23/8), trenches east of Auchonvillers (26/8), Bus-lès-Artois (6/9), Sarton (13/9), Boisbergues (18/9), Sus-St. Léger (30/9), Halloy (1/10), St. Amand (3/10), Grenas and Halloy (4/10), Humbercourt (10/10), St. Amand (13/10), trenches Hébuterne sector (16/10), St. Amand (19/10), Sus-St. Léger (20/10), Bresle (25/10), Albert (31/10), Scots Redoubt (1/11), Flers Line (2/11), Le Sars (5/11), Scots Redoubt (7/11).

2/6th Battalion (T.F.). 183rd Brigade, 61st (2nd South Midland) Division: Arrived Fienvillers from Monchy-Breton (3/11). Moved out of Somme area and to Ternas (5/11). To Aveluy from St. Léger and attached to 19th Division (17/11).

8th (Service) Battalion. 57th Brigade, 19th (Western) Division: Moved forward to positions north of Albert 7.30 a.m. (1/7) and in Tara-Usna Line by 10 p.m. Attack on La Boisselle (3/7) – line running through ruins of church gained and consolidated. During action Commanding Officer Lieutenant-Colonel A. Carton de Wiart won the Victoria Cross. He had personally led the attack and after the other 3 battalion commanders of 57th Brigade had become casualties played an active role while holding positions against counter attacks. Withdrew to support line 9 a.m. (4/7) – returning to dug outs in La Boisselle at 5.p.m. Withdrew to Albert (5/7). Casualties – 302. To bivouacs north of Millencourt (9/7), south of Fricourt (19/7), old German line close to Bazentin-le-Petit (20/7). 'A' and 'C' Companies to village (21/7). To front line (22/7). Failed attack on Switch Line (23/7) – 200 casualties including Lieutenant-Colonel A. Carton de Wiart (wounded). Withdrew to support line. To Bécourt Wood (24/7), trenches in front of Bazentin-le-Petit (29/7). Attack on Intermediate Line 6.10 p.m. (30/7) – 'A' and 'B' Companies leading held up by machine gun fire and snipers from right. Withdrew at 9.30 p.m. Casualties – 169. To bivouacs near Bécourt Wood (31/7), Bresle (1/8). Entrained at Méricourt for Longpré (3/8) and from there marched to Bouchon. Entrained at Longpré for Bailleul (6/8). Entrained at Bailleul for Doullens (6/10) and from there marched to Amplier. To Bois de Warnimont (7/10), Warloy (17/10), brickfields on Bouzincourt-Albert Road (21/10), reserve line north of Ovillers and east of Authuille Wood (22/10), front line east of Thiepval – H.Q. Stuff Redoubt (24/10), Ovillers Post (26/10), reserve line north of Ovillers (30/10), Stuff and Regina Trenches (2/11), reserve line (3/11), Cromwell Huts near Crucifix Corner (5/11), front line near Schwaben Redoubt (8/11), Crucifix Corner (12/11), front line (17/11). Attacked south-western outskirts of Grandcourt 6.10 a.m. (18/11) – first objective reached and carried – heavy losses among supporting waves. Casualties – 295. Withdrew to Cromwell Huts (19/11).

10th (Service) Battalion. 1st Brigade, 1st Division: Entrained at Fouquereuil for Doullens (5/7) and from there marched to Naours. To Pierregot (6/7), Baizieux Wood (7/7), Albert (9/7), support line at The Dingle (10/7). War Diary records that between 400–500 bodies from the fighting around Fricourt were buried while in the area. To Albert (14/7), Bécourt Wood (17/7), Shelter Wood (19/7). New front line dug in front of Bazentin-le-Petit. To front line opposite Martinpuich (21/7). Dug new line 160 yards in advance of old. Failed attack on Switch Line (23/7) – Official History of The Great War noting – Battalion heavily punished by fire of machine guns concealed in long grass. Relieved 9.30 p.m. and to Shelter Wood. To Baizieux Wood (25/7), Bécourt Wood (14/8), front line Bazentin-le-Petit (15/8). Unsuccessful attack on Intermediate Line (17/8). Renewed attack also failed (19/8). To Mametz Wood (20/8), Bazentin-le-Grand (27/8), front line High Wood (29/8), Mametz Wood (31/8), Bazentin-le-Grand (2/9). 'C' and 'D' Companies attached to 1st Black Watch for attack on High Wood. To front line High Wood (4/9), Bécourt Wood (5/9). Attached to 3rd Brigade, attacked High Wood (9/9) – entered western face but forced out by bombing attacks and machine gun fire. Casualties – 122. To Millencourt (10/9), Béhencourt (11/9), Laviéville (16/9), Bécourt Wood (18/9), support line High Wood (19/9), front line (21/9), Bécourt Wood (25/9), Bresle (27/9), Quesnoy-le-Montant (3/10). War Diary records epidemic of German measles in 'A' Company which was sent to Franleu (29/10) where 8th Royal Berkshire were also infected. Rest of Battalion to Hénencourt Wood (31/10), Bécourt Camp (4/11), Bazentin-le-Grand (16/11), Flers Line in support (17/11).

12th (Service) Battalion (Bristol). 95th Brigade, 5th Division: Arrived Candas from Ivergny (14/7). To Puchevillers (15/7), Bresle (16/7), Bécordel-Bécourt (17/7), bivouacs east of Mametz (19/7), support line Caterpillar Valley (20/7). Moved up to Longueval (21/7), returned to Caterpillar Valley same evening. Took over front line at Longueval and south side of Delville Wood (23/7). Relieved and to Pommiers Redoubt (26/7). To front line (28/7). 'B' and 'C' Companies attacked 3.30 p.m. (29/7) – line north of Duke Street taken. Withdrew to Pommiers Redoubt. To camp west of Dernancourt (1/8). Entrained at Méricourt for Airaines (5/8) and from there marched to Vergies. Entrained at Longpré or Méricourt (24/8) and from there marched to camp west of Dernancourt. To Citadel Camp (25/8), reserve trenches near Talus Boisé (29/8), Bronfay Farm (31/8), trenches south of Guillemont (2/9). Attacked (3/9) – enemy's second position running from Wedge Wood to south eastern edge of Guillemont taken. Casualties – 328. Moved forward to Leuze Wood (5/9). Relieved and to Happy

Valley (6/9), Ville-sur-Ancre (9/9). Via Sandpit Camp to front line north of Bouleaux Wood (18/9). Relieved and to bivouacs south-east of Ginchy (20/9). To support line north-west of Wedge Wood (22/9), assembly trenches south-east of Ginchy (24/9). Attack on Morval (25/9) – with 2nd K.O.S.B. objectives taken – line of strong-points occupied south side of village. To Oxford Copse (26/9), Citadel Camp (27/9). Entrained at Grove Town for Longpré (29/9) and from there marched to Sorel. Entrained at Pont-Remy for Chocques and Béthune sector (1/10).

13th (Service) Battalion (Forest of Dean Pioneers). Pioneers, 39th Division: Arrived Bois de Warnimont from Beaudricourt (25/8). To Mailly-Maillet Wood (26/8). Began work in Thiepval area. Cleared trenches during attack (3/9). To reserve trenches attached to 118th Brigade (4/9). Returned to Mailly-Maillet Wood (5/9). To Mailly-Maillet (21/9), Englebelmer (3/10), Martinsart (4/10), Pioneer Road (7/10). 'A' Company helped consolidate gains after attack on north face of Schwaben Redoubt (14/10). Consolidated gains after attack on Stuff Redoubt (21/10). Assembled in Aveluy Wood for attack on Hansa Line (13/11) – began work repairing Hamel-St. Pierre Divion Road soon after objectives had been taken. To Warloy (15/11), Longuevillette (16/11), Autheux (17/11). Entrained at Doullens for Poperinghe (18/11).

14th (Service) Battalion (West of England). 105th Brigade, 35th Division: Entrained at Chocques for Bouquemaison (3/7) and from there marched to Lucheux. To Beauval (7/7), Bus-lès-Artois (10/7), Warloy (11/7), Heilly (13/7), Grove Town Camp (14/7), Billon Wood (15/7), support trenches La Briqueterie (17/7), northern end Trônes Wood (19/7). Relieved and to Talus Boisé (20/7). Casualties from shell fire – 107. To Casement Trench in reserve (24/7), Bernafay Wood in support (26/7), Talus Boisé (30/7), Sandpit Camp (31/7), Bois des Tailles (1/8). Entrained at Méricourt for Saleux (5/8) and from there marched to Riencourt. Entrained at Hangest for Méricourt (10/8) and from there marched to Citadel Camp. Working parties digging trenches in vicinity of Trônes Wood and Maltz Horn Farm (13/8)–(14/8). To Lancaster and Dawson Trenches (19/8), front line (Lamb Trench) near Arrow Head Copse (20/8). Relieved and to Bronfay Farm (23/8), Sandpit Camp (26/8), Bois des Tailles (28/8), Heilly (29/8). Entrained for Candas (30/8) and from there marched to Prouville. To Crouches (31/8), Lucheux (1/9) and from there by lorries to Agnez-lès-Duisans near Arras.

Worcestershire Regiment

1st Battalion. 24th Brigade, 8th and 23rd Divisions: At Molliens-au-Bois
(1/7) – moving in evening to Hénencourt Wood. 24th Brigade had in October 1915 been temporally placed into 23rd Division. To Dernancourt
(4/7), forward positions (Shelter Alley and Crucifix Trench), in front of
Contalmaison (6/7). Enemy attack beaten off (7/7) – later went forward
and at Contalmaison there would be fierce hand-to-hand fighting among
the ruins of the village – courageously – small parties hung on but these
were later forced to retire when ammunition and bombs ran out. Renewed
attack (8/7). Relived and to Lozenge Wood (9/7). Casualties – 348. To Bresle
(10/7), Molliens-au-Bois (11/7), Pierrepont (12/7), Poulainville (14/7). Later
entrained at Longueau for Béthune where Battalion rejoined 8th Division.
Arrived Longpré (14/10) and from there marched to billets at Citerne. To
Ville-sous-Corbie in French buses (16/10) and from there marched to Sandpit
Camp. To forward positions Lesbœufs-Gueudecourt line (19/10) – relieving
9th Norfolk in Rainbow and Shine Trenches and captured portion of Mild.
Relieved and to reserve positions in Needle Trench (22/10). One company
in support during attack on Mild Trench (23/10). To front line (25/10). Re-
lieved and to Trônes Wood (30/10), Sandpit (31/10), Carnoy (5/11). Relieved
2nd Worcestershire at Guillemont (6/11). Relieved 2nd East Lancashire in
Bennett Trench Lesbœufs sector (8/11). To La Briqueterie (9/11), front line
between Lesbœufs and Gueudecourt (13/11), support line at Flers (16/11),
Carnoy (17/11), Méaulte (18/11).

2nd Battalion. 100th Brigade, 33rd Division: Arrived Saleux from Béthune
area (9/7) and from there marched via St. Sauveur to Vecquemont. To
Morlancourt (11/7), Bécordel-Bécourt (12/7), via Mametz to Flatiron Copse
(14/7). Attack on High Wood (15/7) – parties soon fighting in the wood and
holding off strong counter attacks during general withdrawal. War diary of
100th Brigade records that 'the Worcesters are standing firm.' (Note: Regimental motto 'Firm') Withdrew to Mametz Wood (16/7). Battalion moved
forward through Bazentin-le-Petit and in reserve during 19th Brigade's attack
on High Wood (19/7). Relieved and to Bécordel-Bécourt (22/7). Casualties
since (15/7) – 205. To bivouacs between Albert and Dernancourt (23/7).
Relieved 6th Seaforth in trenches south-east edge of High Wood (7/8). By (9/8)
new line (Worcester Trench) constructed in advance of that held. Relieved by
16th K.R.R.C. and to reserve positions at Mametz Wood (10/8). To Bécordel-
Bécourt (13/8), trenches on edge of Delville Wood (19/8). Attack on Tea
Trench 6.45 p.m. (24/8). This German position had been so badly damaged
by shell fire that leading waves would pass right over it without knowing and
later report that they had not reached their objective. Relieved early morning

(25/8). Assembled at Fricourt and then marched 'with drums beating' (War Diary) triumphantly to bivouacs west of Bécordel-Bécourt. Casualties since (6/8) – 359. To Ribemont (29/8), Molliens (30/8), Talmas (1/9), Ribeaucourt via Naours, Havernas, Canaples, Bernaville (2/9). To St. Pol area (4/9). Reached Doullens (8/9) and from there to Halloy. To Humbercamps (10/9), reserve trenches at Foncquevillers (11/9), front line (20/9). Relieved and to Souastre (27/9). To Sombrin via Gaudiempré (28/9), Sus-St.Léger (29/9), Le Souich (30/9). Boarded French buses at Bouquemaison for La Neuville (19/10) and from there marched to Corbie. To Méaulte (21/10), Mansell Camp (22/10), La Briqueterie (25/10). Moved forward to line at Lesbœufs (Frosty Trench) (30/10). With 1/9th H.L.I. made assault on Boritska and Hazy Trenches (1/11) – advancing in thigh-deep mud leading waves would be cut down by heavy machine gun fire. Relieved by 16th K.R.R.C. and withdrew to positions near Lesbœufs (2/11). Renewed attack from French lines (5/11) more successful. Lieutenant. E.P. Bennett awarded Victoria Cross. Withdrew to Guillemont. Casualties – about 200. Relieved by 1st Worcestershire and to camp near Fricourt (6/11). Entrained at Buire for Airaines (10/11).

3rd Battalion. 7th Brigade, 25th Division: Moved forward from Puchevillers via Toutencourt and Harponville to reserve positions at Varennes (30/6). To Hédauville (2/7). By evening just inside south end of Aveluy Wood. Crossed the Ancre and into trenches at Authuille (4/7). Two companies moved forward in support of 1st Wiltshire then fighting at the Leipzig Salient (5/7). Relieved and to Crucifix Corner (7/7). Casualties – 188. To Aveluy Wood (8/7), Usna Hill (9/7). Relieved 9th Loyal North Lancashire in reserve trenches just beyond La Boisselle after dark. In action at Ovillers (10/7)–(17/7). Relieved and to Forceville. Casualties – 177. To Beauval via Acheux, Raincheval (18/7), Bois de Warnimont via Terramesnil, Sarton (20/7), Mailly-Maillet Wood (23/7). Relieved 10th Cheshire in line (31/7). To Bertrancourt (6/8), Sarton (11/8). Battalion inspected by H.M. The King (12/8). To Puchevillers (15/8), Hédauville (17/8). Took over line at Leipzig Salient (18/8). Attacked Hindenburg Trench (24/8) – going forward with 1st Wiltshire at 4.10 p.m. there would be hard fighting with bomb and bayonet – captured positions held under tremendous bombardment. Relieved and to Hédauville (26/8). Casualties – 234. To Bouzincourt (28/8). On loan to 75th Brigade moved forward to dug-outs by Black Horse Bridge near Authuille (2/9). In action at Leipzig Salient (3/9). Relieved and to Bouzincourt. Casualties included C.O. Lieutenant-Colonel. W.B. Gibbs (killed). Later to reserve positions at Acheux and Arquèves. To Maison-Rolland (8/9), Hédauville (24/9). Took over positions between Ovillers and Thiepval (30/9). In front line (2/10)–(12/10), support (13/10)–(15/10). To bivouacs near Bouzincourt

(15/10), Crucifix Corner (16/10). Provided carrying parties to front line. To Bouzincourt (20/10), Hérissart (23/10), Longuevillette (24/10). Entrained at Doullens for Flanders (29/10).

4th Battalion. 88th Brigade, 29th Division: From Louvencourt moved forward via Acheux Wood and Mailly-Maillet to reserve positions at Auchonvillers (30/6). What was left of the Newfoundlanders after the fighting at Beaumont-Hamel passed through (1/7). Moving forward for an attack at 11.30 a.m. some 100 men would be lost before reaching British front line. There is an interesting account in the Battalion's War Diary which illustrates the chivalry that often existed between each side. A member of the Battalion was out all night tending one of the wounded. At dawn the mist would lift to reveal that the two soldiers were only a few yards from the enemy. Immediately the Germans lifted their rifles but were soon ordered to stand down. Then an officer asked the Worcester in English if he would like to come in or return to his own lines. The man answered 'I'll go back to my own trenches sir' – he was then allowed to do so. Later 2 stretcher bearers would go out and bring in the wounded man. Relieved and to Mailly-Maillet Wood (14/7), Acheux Wood (17/7), Beauval (23/7). Entrained at Candas for Ypres sector (27/7). Arrived Longueau (8/10) and from there marched to Corbie. To Pommiers Redoubt (10/10), reserve trenches north of Delville Wood (the old German Switch Line) (11/10), front line on the outskirts of Gueudecourt (13/10). In action at Hilt and Grease Trenches (18/10). Withdrawn to Bernafay Wood (20/10). War Diary records a 'difficult' relief that resulted in some 60 casualties. Worked on road between Longueval and Flers. To front line (27/10), Pommiers Redoubt (29/10), Ville-sous-Corbie (31/10), Sandpit Camp (15/11), La Briqueterie (16/11). In line (Fall, Autumn, Winter Trenches) around Flers (18/11).

1/7th Battalion (T.F.). 144th Brigade, 48th (South Midland) Division: At 9.30 a.m. (1/7) moved forward through Bertrancourt and Beaussart to a position south-west of Mailly-Maillet. To Coigneux (3/7), Courcelles (4/7). Relieved 1/8th Worcestershire in line at Serre (8/7). Relieved (12/7). To Bouzincourt (14/7), trenches Ovillers sector (15/7). Battalion's line ran east and west through the ruined village, part being on the site of the destroyed church which according to the War Diary stood just four feet above ground level. The German deep dugouts below, however, were un damaged. In action (17/7)–(21/7). To Crucifix Corner (21/7), front line (27/7) – withdrew to Hédauville same evening. To Arquèves (28/7), Beauval (29/7), Surcamps (30/7), Candas (9/8), Puchevillers (10/8), Forceville (12/8), camp on cross-roads between Bouzincourt and Senlis (13/8). Took over line at Ovillers Spur (Skyline Trench) (19/8). In action until relieved (23/8) and to Bouzincourt/Senlis cross-roads. To Forceville (27/8), trenches facing

Beaumont-Hamel (28/8). Relieved and to Bus-lès-Artois (5/9). To Amplier (13/9). Arrived Foncquevillers and Souastre (7/10). In line Hébuterne sector (8/10)–(12/10). To St. Amand (12/10), Humbercourt (13/10), Ivergny (20/10), Bresle (25/10), Contalmaison (26/10). Provided carrying parties to front line. Later, and throughout November, began tours in trenches Le Sars sector.

2/7th Battalion (T.F.). 183rd Brigade, 61st (2nd South Midland) Division: Moved from training around Beuvoir-Wavans near Doullens to Autheux (15/11). To St. Ouen (16/11). Rushed forward in French buses to assist 19th Division at Hamel (17/11). Located in support trenches below Thiepval by the evening.

1/8th Battalion (T.F.). 144th Brigade, 48th (South Midland) Division: Moved forward with 1/7th Worcestershire to Mailly-Maillet (1/7). To Coigneux (3/7), Courcelles (4/7). Took over line at Serre. Relieved by 1/7th Worcestershire (8/7). To front line (12/7). Relieved by 16th Welsh and to bivouacs at cross-roads on south side of Sailly-St. Léger Road near Couin (14/7). To Bouzincourt (15/7). While working on a communication trench from La Boisselle forward towards Pozières (19/7) came under attack from a new type of gas shell. There would be just 18 men un affected by the gas and later the whole battalion had to be moved away for treatment. To Fransu (26/7), Houdencourt (30/7), Cayeux (10/8). returned to forward area (21/8) – joining 144th Brigade at Bouzincourt. Later almost 400 men would be pronounced unfit for duty – still suffering from the gas attack. To Forceville (26/8), trenches facing Beaumont-Hamel (27/8). Relieved and to Bus-lès-Artois (5/9). To Authuille (13/9), Warlincourt (10/10), Souastre (16/10). In line Hébuterne sector (16/10)–(20/10). Relieved and to Beaudricourt via Souastre. To Bresle (25/10), Albert (31/10), Contalmaison (1/11). Later, and throughout November took turns in trenches Le Sars sector.

2/8th Battalion (T.F.). 183rd Brigade, 61st (2nd South Midland) Division: Arrived Le Meillard (15/11), Surcamps (16/11).

10th (Service) Battalion. 57th Brigade, 19th (Western) Division: Moved up from camp near Dernancourt to Millencourt (30/6) and during night to assembly positions at Tyler's Redoubt. Ordered forward for attack on La Boisselle (1/7) communication trenches were found to be full of confusion – wounded being brought out, carrying parties going both ways. Rain had also rendered the route knee-deep in mud. Consequently, Battalion could not reach its start point in time and attack called off. Withdrawn to positions on Tara-Usna Ridge. Attacked (3/7) – hand-to-hand fighting in German trenches. There would be great acts of courage throughout the day – Lance-Corporal A.J. Gardner receive D.C.M. for gallantly leading his party – firing his Lewis Gun as he ran forward. The Victoria Cross was awarded to Private F.G. Turrall who courageously defended his wounded officer single handed all day and would later carry him back to safety on his back. Relieved and to Tara-Usna Line (5/7), Albert (6/7), Millencourt (8/7), Hénencourt (9/7), Laviéville (10/7), Millencourt (19/7). To assembly positions west of Fricourt (20/7). Moving up (21/7) – Battalion found itself next to 2nd Worcestershire at Bazentin-le-Petit. Several unsuccessful attacks made on enemy machine gun post. Withdrawn to valley just north of Flatiron Copse (23/7) and from there to Bécourt Wood. Relieved 9th Royal Welsh Fusiliers in front line Bazentin-le-Petit (29/7). Attack on Intermediate Trench (30/7). Relieved and to Bécourt Wood (31/7), Bresle (1/8). Entrained at Méricourt for Longpré (2/8) and from there to billets at Mouflers. Entrained at Longpré for Flanders (7/8). Arrived Doullens (6/10) and from there marched to Amplier. To Bois de Warnimont (7/10), Warloy (17/10), bivouacs near Albert (21/10), Regina Trench (22/10). Tours of duty in front and support line for next three weeks. Rested at Ovillers (3/11)–(4/11). To Aveluy (11/11). In reserve during 57th Brigade's attack (18/11). Withdrew to Aveluy (19/11).

14th (Service) Battalion (Severn Valley Pioneers). Pioneers, 63rd (Royal Naval) Division: Arrived Forceville (4/10). To camp midway between Beaussart and Mailly-Maillet (6/10). Carried out work on defences and roads. To new camp on outskirts of Englebelmer (17/10), valley between Englebelmer and Martinsart (21/10). Occupied temporary billets in Engle-belmer (1/11)–(4/11). Regimental historian Captain H. Fitz-M. Stacke records that these were rat infested – the men being glad to return to the valley and their tents. Played active role during 63rd Division's attack on Beaucourt (13/11)–(14/11) – moving forward with assaulting brigades and working under heavy shelling and counter attacks while consolidating gains. To Forceville (15/11).

East Lancashire Regiment

1st Battalion. 11th Brigade, 4th Division: In attack on Redan Ridge north of Beaumont-Hamel (1/7) – heavy losses soon after leaving assembly positions – War Diary notes line of shell holes in front of German wire held until ordered to retire during evening to Mailly-Maillet. To Bertrancourt (4/7), Mailly-Maillet (10/7), front line Beaumont-Hamel (15/7), Bus-lès-Artois (20/7), Beauval (21/7). Entrained at Doullens for Ypres sector (22/7). Arrived Longueau from Esquelbecq (18/9) and from there marched to Allonville. To Vaux-sur-Somme (25/9). To Corbie (30/9), Méaulte (1/10) – work carried out unloading trains. To Citadel Camp (8/10), bivouacs south of Montauban (9/10), trenches just east of Guillemont (16/10), front line Lesbœufs sector (17/10). Attack on Rainy and Dewdrop Trenches (18/10) – Regimental history notes advance as being over 'a vast lake of mud' – attackers being shot down, drowned in shell-holes or rounded up at daybreak. All officers in 2 leading companies lost. Casualties – 373. To Guillemont (20/10), front line in support (21/10), Bernafay Wood (22/10), Sandpit Camp (25/10), Méaulte (27/10). Entrained at Méricourt for Airaines (27/10) and from there marched to billets at Wanel and Sorel.

2nd Battalion. 24th Brigade, 23rd and 8th Divisions: Arrived Dernancourt (4/7). Moved forward to Patch Alley in preparation for attack on Contalmaison (6/7). Advancing from Shelter Wood at 10.15 a.m. (7/7) there would be stiff opposition from Peake and Bailiff Woods. Later 'B' and 'C' Companies worked around to the east of Peake Wood and entered southern end of village. Forced to withdraw after strong counter attacks on right and left. At Patch Alley by 4 p.m. To Birch Tree Trench and Shelter Alley at 10 p.m. (8/7). Relieved (10/7) and began march to Bresle – arriving (12/7). Casualties during Contalmaison operations – 277. Entrained for Fouquereuil and Béthune sector (16/7). There rejoined 8th Division. (24th Brigade had transferred from the 8th to the 23rd Division in October 1915). Entrained at Fouquereuil for Pont-Remy (14/10), from there via Méaulte to Montauban. To trenches Lesbœufs-Gueudecourt line (18/10). Attack on Mild Trench 2.30 p.m. (23/10) – 'A' and 'D' Companies carrying and holding objective. Communication trenches dug back to Shine Trench. Withdrew to Montauban (30/10). Casualties – 194. To Méaulte (31/10), Bernafay Wood (5/11) and from there moved into front line. Relieved in Bennett Trench and to Guillemont (8/11). Later moved to Carnoy. To reserve trenches Flers Line (15/11), Méaulte (17/11).

7th (Service) Battalion. 56th Brigade, 19th (Western) Division): Moved to small ridge overlooking Ovillers in readiness for attack (1/7). Orders did not arrive and withdrew to previous positions at Tara-Usna Line. That evening to railway line just south of Albert. 'C' and 'D' Companies and party of bombers loaned to 101st Brigade, 34th Division (2/7) – their task to clear Sausage and Heligoland Redoubts and if possible Scots Redoubt beyond. Battalion historian notes that the 2 companies were met at Bécourt Wood by the Brigade-Major (101st Brigade) who remarked upon the age of the officers – the oldest being 26. He openly stated that he did think the companies capable of carrying out their task. When relieved – all objectives had been taken and held against counter attacks. Some 800 yards of front and second line trench had been taken at a cost of just 19 casualties. To trenches in front of La Boisselle (4/7). Attacked through village (5/7) – heavy congestion in the trenches – enemy holding off attack with bombs. Renewed attack (6/7) more successful and enemy driven back. Withdrew to Albert (7/7) and from there to Millencourt and Hénencourt Wood (10/7). To Mametz Wood (19/7) and from there trenches in front of Bazentin-le-Petit. In support during attack on Switch Trench (23/7). Withdrew to south end of Mametz Wood and later Bécourt Wood (24/7). To Franvillers (1/8). Entrained at Fréchencourt for Longpré (3/8) and from there entrained for Bailleul (6/8). Arrived Doullens (5/10) and from there marched to Couin. To Sailly-au-Bois (11/10), front line Hébuterne sector (13/10), camp west of Albert (16/10), bivouacs just north of Albert (18/10), trenches in old German line east of Aveluy Wood (19/10), Stuff and Bainbridge Trenches, Schwaben Redoubt (24/10). Relieved after repulsing strong attack and to Donnet Post (26/10). From there took turns in line at Stuff Trench. Attacked (13/11) – moved forward through thick fog at 5.20 a.m. – all objectives taken by 7 a.m. Relieved in evening and to Aveluy. Moved forward to Hansa Trench (17/11). Attack on Baillescourt Farm beyond Grandcourt (18/11) – held up by machine gun fire and line established across front of village. Position held until relieved early (20/11) and to reserve dug-outs at St. Piere-Division.

8th (Service) Battalion. 112th Brigade, 37th Division: In line immediately to left of 46th Division during attack at Gommecourt (1/7). Battalion did not leave its trenches but fired smoke bombs and provided a defensive flank for attacking division. From Pommier to Halloy (3/7), Millencourt (4/7), marched through Albert and took up positions in the Tara-Usna Line (5/7). That evening to Bécourt Wood. To reserve trenches in Sausage Valley (7/7). Here Battalion historian noted – the dead of the Tyneside Scottish lay thick upon the ground from their attack of 1st July. Moved forward into support positions (11/7), front line (13/7). Attack on Pozières (15/7) – 'A' and 'B' Companies advanced at 9.20 a.m. – right flank on Contalmaison-Pozières Road – distance to objective 1,200 yards. Around Contalmaison Wood heavy machine gun fire swept leading waves who were forced to dig in near the chalk-pit. Another attempt during evening also brought to a standstill. Withdrew to support trenches at 2.30 a.m. (16/7) and from there Béhencourt. Casualties – 374. To Bécourt Wood (31/7), support in front of The Quadrangle (4/8), front line Bazentin-le-Petit (7/8) – bombing attack on Intermediate Trench. To Mametz Wood (11/8). Via Bruay, Béhencourt to Longpré and there entrained for Bailleul (20/8). Arrived at Bertrancourt (23/10). To Doullens (27/10), Mailly-Maillet (14/11), line between Beaumont-Hamel and Serre (15/11). Failed attack on Munich and Frankfort Trenches – 'D' and 'A' Companies advancing at 8.30 a.m. and finding wire uncut in front of Munich. Withdrew to Waggon Road. To Englebelmer (16/11).

11th (Service) Battalion (Accrington). 94th Brigade, 31st Division: Moved forward from Bois de Warnimont (30/6) and assembled (from Mark Copse to Matthew Copse) for attack towards Serre (1/7). From the moment advance commenced, great numbers fell from enemy's machine gun and rifle fire. One company, identified from the air by special markings on their backs, managed to get through German lines and into village. These men were never seen again. Withdrew to Louvencourt (4/7). Casualties – 584. Entrained for Steenbecque and bivouacs in the Foret de Nieppe (8/7). Arrived Doullens from Berguette (8/10) and from there marched to Sarton. To Bois de Warnimont (18/10), front line Serre sector (John Copse) (30/10), Sailly Dell (3/11), Coigneux and Courcelles (7/11), Bois de Warnimont (10/11). Further tours in front line throughout November, resting at Sailly-au-Bois.

East Surrey Regiment

1st Battalion. 95th Brigade, 5th Division: Arrived Longuevillette from Oppy (14/7). To Hérissart (15/7), Bresle (16/7), bivouacs just south of Bécordel-Bécourt (17/7). At Bécordel War Diary records that all officers were ordered to dress like the men and to carry rifles and bayonets which were obtained from members of the transport section. Moved forward to positions in and west of Longueval (19/7) – heavy casualties noted from shelling until (22/7). Attacked (23/7) – strong point captured west of northern end of Longueval but evacuated after counter attacks. Relieved during night and to trenches near Montauban. Casualties – 123. Moved forward to positions in Longueval and north-west corner of Delville Wood (27/7). Regimental history notes (29/7) as 'one of the most trying days experienced by the Battalion during the war' – shelling made communications from the rear almost impossible. As an example out of a 24 man water caring party from 14th Royal Warwickshire, just seven reached the front line. Attack at 3.30 p.m. on enemy posts north-west of Longueval – leading waves cut down by machine gun fire – survivors held out in shell holes until nightfall. Losses for period (27/7)–(29/7) – 320. Relieved midnight (30/7) and to Pommiers Redoubt. To Dernancourt (1/8). Entrained at Méricourt for Airaines (4/8) and from there marched to Epaumesnil. Entrained at Longpré for Méricourt (24/8) and from there marched to camp north of Buire. To Citadel Camp (25/8), Billon Farm (26/8). Dug assembly trench behind front line (28/8). War Diary notes 2 observation balloons hit by lightning (29/8) – occupants parachuted to safety. Took over positions south of Guillemont (Lonely Trench) (30/8). Withdrew to support line at Maltz Horn Farm (2/9). In support during attack between Guillemont and Wedge Wood (3/9). Took over sunken road south from Ginchy to Wedge Wood (4/9) – later 'A' and 'C' Companies took Valley Trench and Battalion moved into support at Leuze Wood. Relieved and to Happy Valley (6/9), Citadel Camp (9/9). To positions around Falfemont Farm and Angle Wood under orders of 13th Brigade (10/9). Rejoined 95th Brigade at Ville-sur-Ancre and Treux (14/9). To Sandpit Camp (18/9) and from there support trenches close to the Guillemont-Combles Road (just west of Leuze Wood). To Oxford Copse (22/9), north-west corner of Faviere Wood (24/9). From there to assembly trenches. Attack on Morval (25/9) – advanced at 12.35 p.m – 'B' company checked by enfilade fire, support companies pushed on and objectives gained. Relieved and to Oxford Copse (26/9). Casualties estimated at 203. To Citadel Camp (27/9). Entrained at Happy Valley for Longpré (29/9) and from there marched to Liercourt. To Béthune (2/10). Somme casualties given in Regimental history as 40 officers and 1,200 other ranks.

7th (Service) Battalion. 37th Brigade, 12th (Eastern) Division: Arrived Millencourt from Bresle (1/7) and from there took up reserve positions in front of Ovillers. Moved back to railway cutting behind Crucifix Corner (2/7) – returned to reserve line 11 p.m. To front line (3/7) – cleared dead from trenches after 37th Brigade's failed attack. To positions just north of Albert (6/7) – War Diary notes men's feet being very sore and swollen having stood in water for last 4 days. To front line (7/7). Attack south-west of Ovillers early morning (8/7) – objective taken and consolidated – advance continued along southern outskirts of village 9 a.m. – further ground taken and held. Relieved and to Warloy (10/7). To Vauchelles-les-Authie (12/7), Bertrancourt (21/7), Vauchelles (24/7), Martinsart Wood (25/7), front line just north of Ovillers (31/7), support line Ovillers Post (4/8), front line (10/8). Attack north of Ovillers (12/8) – 'B' and 'D' Companies advancing at 10.30 p.m. met strong fire and heavy bombing – support companies also lost heavily. Relieved and via Albert to Forceville (13/8). Casualties – 169. To Arquèves (14/8), Bus-lès-Artois (15/8), Halloy (16/8), Grand-Rullecourt west of Arras (17/8). Arrived Beaumetz (27/9), Lucheux (28/9), camp 2 miles south-west of Albert-Amiens Road (29/9). Via Montauban took over forward trenches at Gueudecourt (1/10). Relieved and to support line (Gird Trench and Bulls Road) during night (4/10), Longueval Valley (5/10). To reserve at Switch Trench south of Flers (6/10), Longueval Valley (9/10), Ribemont (19/10), Wanquetin west of Arras (21/10).

8th (Service) Battalion. 55th Brigade, 18th (Eastern) Division: Attacked from front line between Talus Boisé and Carnoy-Montauban Road towards Montauban Ridge (1/7). Symbolic of the first day of the Battle of the Somme and the way that men went forward in brave, confident and well disciplined order is the kicking of footballs into No Man's Land by men of the 8th East Surrey Regiment. 'B' Company on the left was led by Captain W.P.Nevill (East Yorks) who had provided each platoon with a football. Special permission to kick the footballs into action had been obtained – however, there would be a proviso that proper formation and distance had to be kept. The first ball was kicked by Captain Nevill and his 2 leading platoons moved forward towards the enemy's Breslau Trench some 400 yards ahead at 7.27 a.m. Soon machine gun fire from craters to the left would cut down the leading waves – Captain Nevill's body, along with two footballs, would later be found just outside the German wire. He is buried with others of the 8th East Surrey that fell on (1/7) at Carnoy Military Cemetery. Objective reached 12.22 p.m. – dug in on Mametz Road just west of Montauban. Relieved dawn (2/7) and to huts in Carnoy Valley. Casualties – 446. To Grove Town Camp (6/7), Celestines Wood (8/7), support trenches at

Maricourt (11/7), old German front line – (Silesia Trench) (12/7) – in support and reserve for operations at Trônes Wood. To Méricourt early morning (14/7) and in afternoon to Grove Town Camp. Entrained at Méricourt for Longpré (21/7) and from there marched to Doudelainville. Entrained at Pont-Remy for St. Omer (23/7). Arrived Lucheux from Arras sector (10/9). To Puchevillers (11/9), Aveluy (23/9). Dug assembly trenches in readiness for forthcoming attack on Thiepval. Took over south face of Schwaben Redoubt by midnight (29/9) – enemy bombing attack 6 a.m. (30/9) repulsed. Attacked 4 p.m. – east face of Schwaben Redoubt taken by 'C' Company – part of north side occupied and held until relieved dawn (1/10). Via dug-outs at Wood Post to Blighty Valley. Entrained at Acheux for Candas (5/10). To Gézaincourt (15/10), Rubempré (16/10), Albert (17/10), Fabeck and High Trenches between Monquet Farm and Courcelette (26/10), Albert (29/10), Warloy (31/10), Albert (4/11), trenches north of Mouquet Farm (8/11), Albert (10/11), Fabeck Trench (13/11). Attack and capture of Desire Trench (18/11) – 'B' and 'D' Companies going forward at 6.10 a.m. and consolidating line 150 yards beyond objective by 6.50. Relieved and to Ovillers (21/11).

9th (Service) Battalion. 72nd Brigade, 24th Division: Arrived Longueau from Bailleul (23/7) and from there marched to Saisseval. To Ailly (31/7). Entrained for Méricourt (1/8) and from there marched via Morlancourt to Sandpit Camp. To reserve trenches at Talus Boisé (10/8). Work on front line trenches – including digging of Lamb Trench across Guillemont-Trônes Wood sunken road (12/8). To front line near Arrow Head Copse (13/8). Attack on Guillemont (16/8) – 'C' and 'D' companies advanced from Lamb and New Trenches 5.42 p.m. – Regimental historians noting that leading waves had barely left their positions when they came under strong fire rifle from the front and machine gun fire from both flanks. As objective was reached there would be a tremendous volley of bombs. Casualties are given as 183 out of an attacking force of 249. Relieved by 8th Queen's early hours (17/8) – 'A' and 'B' Companies to Montauban and what remained of 'C' and 'D' to Talus Boisé. To La Briqueterie (18/8) in support of 73rd Brigade successful attack on Guillemont. Moved forward to new front line (21/8). To Citadel Camp (22/8), via bivouacs about one mile west of Dernancourt to Ribemont (25/8). To reserve trenches at Montauban (30/8), front line eastern edge of Delville Wood (1/9). Attack on Ale Alley and Beer Trench (3/9) – high casualties including Commanding Officer Lieutenant-Colonel de la Fontaine. Regimental history notes strength as 9 officers and between 100 to 150 other ranks commanded by the Adjutant, Lieutenant Clark. Relieved and to Fricourt (5/9), Dernancourt (6/9). Entrained at Edgehill for Longpré (7/9) and from there marched to Francieres. Entrained for Valhuon near St. Pol (19/9).

12th (Service) Battalion (Bermondsey). 122nd Brigade, 41st Division: Entrained at Bailleul for Longpré (23/8) and from there marched to Mouflers. Entrained at Longpré for Méricourt (6/9) – here Regimental history notes – 'A' Company rejoined Battalion from Fourth Army School having been on a 'special course of instruction.' To camp near Fricourt (11/9), trenches near Longueval and north-west of Delville Wood (14/9). Attack towards Flers (15/9) - following 18th K.R.R.C. passed through village and on to line some 300 yards beyond. Only one out of the 17 officers that went into attack would not become a casualty – losses including Commanding Officer Lieutenant-Colonel Walmisley-Dresser who would be fatally wounded. Among the men some 286 were killed, wounded or missing. Relieved 7.30 p.m. and to reserve line. To billets near Albert (18/9), Mametz Wood (3/10) and from there took over front line near Flers – Gird Support Trench north of Factory Corner. In action (7/10) – moving forward from Goose Alley at 2.10 p.m. reinforced 11th Royal West Kent in captured line. Withdrew to Switch Trench (9/10), Mametz Wood (11/10) and from there via Dernancourt to Ribemont. Entrained for Oisemont (17/10) and from there marched to Huppy. Entrained at Pont-Remy for – Ypres Sector (20/10).

13th (Service) Battalion (Wandsworth). 120th Brigade, 40th Division: Marched south from Averdoingt near St. Pol (2/11), reaching Mezerolles (4/11), Vacquerie (5/11), Doullens (12/11), Souastre (14/11). Relieved 4th K.O.Y.L.I. in left sector Hébuterne (15/11). To Couin (21/11).

Duke of Cornwall's Light Infantry

1st Battalion. 95th Brigade, 5th Division: Marched from Ivergny to Candas (14/7). To Toutencourt (15/7), Bresle (16/7). Bivouacked on a hill side south of Bécordel-Bécourt (17/7). Here – War Diary notes troops coming back from forward area – 'muddy and disreputable but all quite happy and cheerful, though obviously tired out.' Via Fricourt, Mametz and Montauban to forward positions near Longueval (19/7) – occupying sunken road leading to High Wood. Attacked (23/7) – made good headway but fierce counter attack forced assaulting waves to retire to Pont Street. Relieved by 1st Devonshire and to Happy Valley. To Longueval (28/7), Pommiers Redoubt (30/7), Méaulte (1/8). 500 casualties recorded since (19/7) – of these – 329 are given as missing believed killed. Number reflects severe shelling experienced throughout the whole time Battalion was in forward area. With 5th Division moved to Abbeville area, resting and training around Airaines and Belloy-St. Léonard. To positions on eastern slope of Maltz Horn Ridge (26/8), front line (Bodmin and Cornwall Trenches) (2/9). Took part in 95th Brigade's assault towards Leuze Wood – all objectives taken. To Happy Valley (6/9). Later to Ville-sur-Ancre. To Sandpit Camp (18/9) and from there via La Briqueterie into line at Morval. To support line at The Quadrilateral (21/9). Relieved and to Citadel Camp (27/9), Fontaine-sur-Somme (30/9). Entrained for Givenchy area (1/10).

1/5th Battalion (T.F.). Pioneers, 61st (2nd South Midland) Division: Left Laventie sector for the Somme (28/10). Reached Bonnières (6/11), Beaumetz (15/11) and from there to Martinsart Wood. To dug outs between Contalmaison and Pozières (17/11) .

6th (Service) Battalion. 43rd Brigade, 14th (Light) Division: Arrived Candas from Arras area (6/8) and from there entrained for Méricourt. To Albert (7/8), Montauban (12/8). Provided carrying parties for 6th Somerset Light Infantry then engaged at Delville Wood. To front line Delville Wood (15/8). Took part in attack on Hop Alley and Edge Trench opposite south-eastern corner of wood (18/8) – heavy casualties among 'B' and 'D' Companies while in assembly positions and after advancing 100 yards. Severe hand-to-hand fighting followed – 'D' Company reduced to 1 officer and about 20 men. Front line and captured positions held under heavy bombardment. Relieved and to camp west of Fricourt (20/8). Casualties – 366. Into support at Montauban Defences (25/8). To camp north-east of Dernancourt (30/8), Aumont (31/8). Arrived Albert (12/9). Moved forward to Pommiers Redoubt (14/9). Attack on Gird and Gird Support Trenches in front of Gueudecourt (16/9) – Battalion moved forward in a single wave 9.25 a.m. – heavy machine gun fire from right brought assault to a standstill. Renewed attack at 6.55 p.m. failed. Relieve and to Pommiers Redoubt (17/9). Casualties 309. Via Bécordel-Bécourt to Ribemont (18/9), Sus-St. Léger (22/9). Transferred to Arras sector (27/9).

7th (Service) Battalion. 61st Brigade, 20th (Light) Division: Arrived Halloy from Ypres sector (25/7). To Bois de Warnimont (26/7), Bus-lès-Artois (27/7), Mailly-Maillet (28/7), trenches Redan sector (3/8), Sailly Dell (7/8), Courcelles (13/8), Morlancourt via Méricourt (20/8), Happy Valley (21/8), front line trenches at Gillemont (22/8). Enemy attacks repulsed (23/8) and (24/8). To Carnoy (27/8). Relieved 10th Rifle Brigade between Trônes Wood and Guillemont (29/8). War Diary describes these positions as recently dug and having suffered from tremendous shelling. The trenches were knee-deep in mud and water and only one dug-out existed. Mention is also made of decaying bodies laying all around and the occasional cry for help from wounded lying out in No Man's Land. To Carnoy (2/9), eastern edge Bernafay Wood (3/9). Later ordered forward to western side of Trônes Wood and from there moved to La Briqueterie under orders of 59th Brigade. Sent forward in support of 10th K.R.R.C and 10th Rifle Brigade then fighting at Guillemont. From positions in sunken road just south of Guillemont moved back to La Briqueterie (5/9). Later to Carnoy. To Sandpit Camp (6/9), Citadel Camp (14/9), Talus Boisé (15/9) and from there via Waterlot Farm to positions east of Ginchy. Attached to Guards Division for operations at Lesbœufs. From position on right of road half-way between Ginchy and Lesbœufs attacked (16/9) – all 4 companies moving forward at 9.27 a.m. to within 70 yards of barrage and waited. Charged enemy's trenches 9.35 a.m. – first line quickly taken and held. Relieved and via Bernafay Wood to the craters at Carnoy (17/9). To Citadel (22/9), front line Gueudecourt (29/9) – left flank resting on village. Advance of between 250–500 yards made by 3 small groups during attack (1/10). Relieved and to Dummy Trench north of Bernafay Wood (3/10). In reserve at Needle Trench during 61st Brigade's attack on Rainbow, Cloudy and Misty Trenches (7/10). Later moved forward to establish strong-points in Rainbow. To Sandpit Camp (9/10) and later via Méaulte to Corbie. To Belloy-sur-Somme (31/10), Camps-en-Amiénois (2/11), Heucourt-Croquoison (14/11).

10th (Service) Battalion (Cornwall Pioneers). Pioneers, 2nd Division: Arrived Saleux from Arras area (21/7) and from there moved to billets at Vaux-sur-Somme. To Morlancourt (22/7). Took over from 20th K.R.R.C. (Pioneers) north of Caftet Wood (25/7). Work carried out around Delville Wood, Longueval, Guillemont, Bernafay and Trônes Woods – cutting communication trenches, constructing strong points and providing carrying parties throughout operations in the area. Assisted 2nd South Staffordshire during German attack in Delville Wood (28/7). To Sandpit Camp (10/8). Later to Coigneux. 2nd Division began to relieve Guards Division in Hébuterne sector (19/8). Battalion headquarters at Sailly Dell. Worked throughout Battle of the Ancre, including digging of Cat Tunnel. Moved to Louvencourt (18/11).

12th (Labour) Battalion. Went to France in May 1916 and served as Army Troops, Fourth Army. Worked close to the fighting throughout Somme offensive.

Duke of Wellington's (West Riding Regiment)

2nd Battalion. 12th Brigade, 4th Division: From assembly trenches east of the sugar factory on Mailly-Maillet-Serre Road moved forward 8.55 a.m. (1/7) in support of attack between Beaumont-Hamel and Serre. Advancing on Brigade's left fought through into The Quadrilateral – by nightfall holding Burrow, Wolf and Legend Trenches. Casualties – 323. Withdrew to Ellis Square in support (7/7). Two companies to Mailly-Maillet (8/7). Relieved by 1st Rifle Brigade and to bivouacs between Bertrancourt and Acheux (10/7). To front line east of Auchonvillers (17/7), Louvencourt (21/7), Authieule (22/7). Entrained at Doullens for Cassel (23/7). Arrived Bertangles (17/9). To Cardonnette (25/9), La Neuville (27/9), Corbie (1/10), Citadel Camp (8/10). Moved forward via Bernafay Wood to Flers Line (9/10). Attack near Lesbœufs (Spectrum Trench) (12/10) – forming with 2nd Lancashire Fusiliers part of assaulting force. Casualties – 342. After further action around Spectrum (23/10) withdrew to Bernafay Wood. To Citadel Camp (25/10), Méricourt (27/10). Entrained for Airaines (29/10) and from there to billets Forceville and Neuville. Left Somme area during first week of November.

1/4th Battalion (T.F.). 147th Brigade, 49th (West Riding) Division: Moved forward from Senlis midnight (30/6) into assembly trenches at Aveluy Wood. Later (around 11.30 a.m.) to Crucifix Corner. Relieved 1/5th West Yorkshire at Johnstone's Post (2/7). To Thiepval Wood (5/7), Aveluy Wood (7/7), Thiepval Wood (8/7). Took turns in line with 1/5th West Yorkshire. During this period in the front line Battalion's historian Captain P.G. Bales, M.C. noted the British dead still un cleared from the battlefield – 'the sunken Thiepval Road crowded as it was with the bodies of the Ulstermen who had fallen or crawled there to die on 1st July.' To Raincheval (19/8), Forceville (27/8), Martinsart Wood (2/9) – assembled in Thiepval Wood during night. From trenches along Hamel-Thiepval Road attacked just after 5 a.m. towards the Schwaben Redoubt – German line soon penetrated – strong machine gun fire from the Redoubt and Strasburg Line together with a determined counter attack forced withdrawal to Martinsart Wood. Casualties – 347. To Hédauville (7/9), Martinsart Wood (15/9), Crucifix Corner (16/9). In support Leipzig Redoubt (18/9), to front line, Leipzig Redoubt (21/9), Léalvillers (24/9), Halloy (25/9), Humbercamps (27/9), Bienvillers-au-Bois (28/9), left sub-sector, Hannescamps (29/9) – line crossing sunken Hannescamps-Essarts Road. To Souastre (3/10), left sub-sector, Hannescamps (9/10), Bienvillers-au-Bois (16/10), Humbercamps (18/10), St. Amand (19/10), Souastre (21/10), Foncquevillers (24/10) and duty in front line opposite Gommecourt Wood. To Souastre (30/10), front line (5/11). 'A' and 'B' Companies to Souastre (11/11) – 'C' and 'D' in Foncquevillers providing working parties to front line.

1/5th Battalion (T.F.). 147th Brigade, 49th (West Riding) Division: Marched from Warloy at night to assembly trenches in Aveluy Wood (30/6). Moved forward to South Bluff, Authuille (1/7). Tours of duty in front line Thiepval sector began (2/7) – Headquarters at Gordon Castle, support positions Belfast City, Johnson's Post, Harley Street, Paisley Avenue. Relieved and to Raincheval (19/8). To Forceville (27/8). Moved forward via Martinsart Wood to front line Thiepval (2/9). On left of 147th Brigade's attack on Schwaben Redoubt (3/9) – Official History of The Great War records that some loss of direction occurred during advance – heavy losses at German wire – failed to capture Pope's Nose. War Diary records assault as a failure 'the men fought splendidly and in many cases without N.C.O's or officers . . . As a proof of the hard fighting there were 350 casualties out of 450 who assaulted the German lines.' Relieved and to Aveluy Wood. To Hédauville (4/9). Via Martinsart Wood, Crucifix Corner to Leipzig Salient (15/9). 'C' Company in attack (16/9) – forced to retire after heavy shelling. Relieved by 1/4th West Riding and into Brigade support near Authuille (21/9). To Hédauville (24/9), Halloy (25/9), St. Amand (28/9), Pommier (1/10). Took over trenches in front of Gommecourt (9/10). To Pommier (18/10), St. Amand (21/10), Foncquevillers and Souastre (24/10), front line (30/10), Souastre (5/11), front line (11/11), Souastre and Foncquevillers (17/11).

1/6th Battalion (T.F.). 147th Brigade, 49th (West Riding) Division: Moved from Warloy into reserve positions in Aveluy Wood during night (30/6). Forward to Crucifix Corner (1/7), Belfast City in Thiepval Wood (2/7). Relieved 11 a.m. and withdrew to Aveluy Wood. To front line trenches just south of Thiepval Wood (4/7). Battalion began series of tours in front line – War Diary records section held as between Union Street and Thiepval Avenue – resting at North Bluff. To Forceville (19/8), Léalvillers (20/8), Forceville (27/8), trenches in Thiepval Wood (28/8). In support during attack on Schwaben Redoubt (3/9). Withdrew to North Bluff (4/9) and from there to Hédauville. Took over forward positions Leipzig Salient (15/9). Relieved and to Crucifix dug outs, Aveluy (23/9), Léalvillers (24/9), Mondicourt (25/9), St. Amand (27/9). Relieved 5th Scottish Rifles in trenches between Foncquevillers and Gommecourt (28/9). To Humbercamps (2/10), support positions Bienvillers (9/10), trenches Hannescamps sector (16/10), Humbercamps (18/10), Souastre (21/10), trenches Foncquevillers sector (24/10), Souastre (30/10), front line (5/11), Souastre (11/11), front line (17/11).

1/7th Battalion (T.F). 147th Brigade, 49th (West Riding) Division: Moved forward from Senlis to assembly trenches in Aveluy Wood (30/6). To South Bluff, Authuille (1/7). Relieved 1/5th West Yorkshire in trenches Thiepval sector (2/7). Tours of duty included work on new trench near Oblong Wood. Rested at North Bluff. Relieved and to Hédauville (19/8) – War Diary notes that Battalion had been in the line for 7 weeks without a break and with about 350 casualties. To Arquèves (20/8), Forceville (27/8), Aveluy Wood (28/8). Moved to assembly trenches at Thiepval Wood (3/9) and ordered to stand by. Withdrew to Hédauville 8.30 p.m. To Martinsart Wood (15/9) and moved forward by night to recently captured trenches south of Thiepval. Took part in successful attack (17/9). Casualties – 220. Relieved and into support at Leipzig and Lemberg Trenches (18/9). 'B' company to Authuille. To Crucifix Corner (19/9), front line (22/9). Relieved and to Hédauville (24/9), Halloy (25/9). To Souastre (28/9), Bienvillers (29/9), Humbercamps (3/10), front line Foncquevillers sector (9/10), Humbercamps (18/10), St. Amand (21/10), Souastre (24/10). Entry in War Diary (30/10) – 'Battalion paraded at 8.30 a.m. on clean fatigue. All ranks warned of the necessity for preventing waste in underclothing.' Moved to front line. To Foncquevillers (5/11), front line (11/11), Souastre (17/11).

8th (Service) Battalion. 32nd Brigade, 11th (Northern) Division: Arrived Senlis from Arras sector (6/9). Relieved 11th Cheshire in front line Thiepval sector (7/9). To Martinsart Wood (10/9). Attacked (14/9) – Official History of The Great War records advancing from Hindenburg Trench behind an excellent barrage at 6.30 p.m. – with 9th West Yorkshire 2 companies swept through German front line and then the Wonder Work. 250 yards of Hohenzollern Trench on the right – trench on left as far as the Thiepval Road also secured. War Diary notes – 'Objectives reached – attacking companies advanced 40 yards beyond and dug themselves in – communication trench to new position dug immediately.' Counter attacks repulsed (15/9). Relieved at 4 p.m. and to Hédauville. Casualties – 258. To Bouzincourt (18/9), Mailly-Maillet (21/9). Relieved 7th South Staffordshire in front line Ovillers (23/9). To Bouzincourt (26/9). Moved forward into support positions for attack on Hessian Trench and Stuff Redoubt (27/9). In action until relieved by 8th South Lancashire and to Bouzincourt (30/9). Casualties since (28/9) – 247. To Acheux (1/10). Entrained for Candas (4/10) and from there took buses to Maison-Roland. To Domléger (6/10), Berteaucourt (14/11), Rubempré (15/11), Acheux (16/11).

9th (Service) Battalion. 52nd Brigade, 17th (Northern) Division): At Bois des Tailles (1/7) awaiting orders to move forward. To Morlancourt (2/7), trenches around Fricourt (3/7). In action during operations at Contalmaison (4/7)–(7/7). Relieved and to Méaulte. Entrained at Méricourt for Ailly-sur-Somme (11/7) and from there marched to Molliens-Vidame. To Long (15/7). Entrained at Hangest for Méricourt (23/7) and from there marched through Ribemont to camp near Albert-Amiens Road. Moved forward via Fricourt to Longueval (1/8). In support during operations at Delville Wood. Relieved and to Pommiers Redoubt (5/8), Fricourt (8/8). To front line Delville Wood (10/8), Fricourt (12/8), bivouacs Albert-Amiens Road (13/8). Entrained at Méricourt for Candas (15/8) and from there to billets at Lucheux. To Souastre (27/8). Took over front line opposite Gommecourt Park (5/9). Relieved and to St Amand (11/9), Halloy (21/9), Barly (22/9), Montigny (23/9), Agenvillers (24/9), Hiermont (9/10), Barly (10/10), Halloy (11/10), Bouquemaison (19/10). Moved in buses to Poulainville (22/10) and from there marched to Cordonette. To Corbie (23/10), Sandpit Camp (27/10), Trônes Wood (29/10). Relieved 2nd Worcestershire in front line Gueudecourt sector (30/10). Relieved (2/11), back in line (5/11), relieved (8/11), line (10/11). To Carnoy (12/11), Mansell Camp (13/11), Méaulte (14/11). Entrained at Edgehill for Hangest (15/11) and from there to Picquigny. To Ailly-sur-Somme (17/11).

10th (Service) Battalion. 69th Brigade, 23rd Division: Moved from Coisy to Baizieux 8 p.m. (1/7). To bivouacs north-west of Albert (2/7), Bécourt Wood (3/7). Attack on Horseshoe Trench (5/7) – Official History of The Great War records advance over the open soon after 6 p.m. With 8th and 9th Green Howards cleared both Horseshoe Trench and Lincoln Redoubt at its western end. Withdrew to positions south of Albert (6/7). Moved forward to captured trenches on left of Lozenge Wood (7/7). Took over positions at Shelter Alley (9/7). Attack and capture of Contalmaison (10/7). Relieved and to positions north-west of Albert (11/7). To Franvillers (12/7), Molliens-au-Bois (13/7), Millencourt (21/7), Bécourt Wood (26/7). Moved through Contalmaison to front line (28/7). In action at Munster Alley (28/7)–(29/7). Casualties – 205. Relieved and to Scots Redoubt (30/7). Total casualties for July – 419. To Albert (1/8), Scots Redoubt (3/8). 'C' and 'D' Companies in front line Contalmaison (4/8)–(5/8). To Peake Wood (5/8), Bresle (8/8). Entrained at Méricourt for Pont-Remy (11/8) and from there marched to Buigny-l'Abbé. Entrained at Pont-Remy for Bailleul (16/8) and from there marched to Méteren. Arrived Longueau by train and marched to Coisy (11/9). To Hénencourt Wood (12/9), Millencourt (15/9). Moved forward to reserve trenches near Bazentin-le-Petit Wood (18/9). To Shelter Wood (22/9), Peake Wood (26/9), – Gourlay Trench (1/10). To front line Le Sars (2/10). Small party entered Flers support north off Bapaume Road (4/10) – held until bombs and ammunition ran out. In support during attack on Le Sars (7/10). Relieved and to Round Wood (8/10), Albert (9/10). Entrained for Longpré (12/10) and from there marched to Buigny-l'Abbé. Later transferred to Ypres sector.

12th (Labour) Battalion. Two companies ordered to the Somme from Ypres sector for work on Méaulte-Maricourt railway (8/7). Remainder followed (12/7). Camp near Contour Wood shelled (24/7). Worked on Méaulte-Trônes Wood, Méaulte-Fricourt, Fricourt-Longueval, Albert-Aveluy lines. Casualties from bombs dropped by enemy aircraft recorded in War Diary while 'X' Company were in camp near Bernafay Wood (23/10).

Border Regiment

1st Battalion. 87th Brigade, 29th Division: Followed 2nd South Wales Borderers into attack just south of Beaumont-Hamel (1/7) – War Diary notes that the Borderers were 'wiped out by machine gun fire in our own wire.' It is also recorded that Battalion suffered the same fate, just small groups of 6 or so being left and sheltering as best they could in shell holes. Advance brought to a standstill at 8 a.m. Withdrew to Acheux (2/7). Casualties – 619. To Mailly-Mallet (17/7), front line south of Beaumont-Hamel (22/7), Bus-lès-Artois (24/7), Amplier (25/7). Entrained at Doullens for Proven (27/7). Arrived Longueau (8/10) and marched to Allonville. To Buire (10/10), Fricourt (13/10), Bernafay Wood (19/10), Switch Trench (20/10), front line Gueudecourt sector (Grease and Gap Trenches) (21/10), Bernafay Wood (27/10), Albert (29/10). Entrained for Airaines (3/11) and from there marched to Allery. To Carnoy (15/11), front line Lesbœufs sector (16/11).

2nd Battalion. 20th Brigade, 7th Division: Moved forward from Morlancourt for attack on Mametz during night (30/6). Advanced in 4 lines 7.27 a.m. (1/7) – strong machine gun fire from both the village and Fricourt further to the left. All objectives – Danube Trench, Apple Alley, Shrine Alley, Hidden Lane taken by evening and gains consolidated. Casualties – 343. To Citadel Camp (3/7), Ribemont (5/7), Minden Post (11/7), trenches in front of Caterpillar Wood (13/7). Attack on Bazentin-le-Grand Wood (14/7) – first line moved forward to Flatiron Copse and from there crawled on to within 30 yards of enemy. Went into action at 3.25 a.m. taking all objectives and consolidating on a bank just beyond northern edge of wood by 4.40 a.m. Casualties – 220. To Pommiers Redoubt (15/7), Caterpillar Wood (19/7), Dernancourt (20/7). Entrained at Méricourt for Hangest (22/7) and from there marched to Breilly. Entrained at Hangest for Méricourt and marched to billets at Buire (12/8) – camp in field north of church. To Fricourt (3/9), via Montauban, Bernafay Wood to trenches around Ginchy (4/9). In support during operations at Ginchy and Guillemont. Via Montauban to bivouacs south of Fricourt (7/9), Buire (8/9). Entrained at Albert for Airaines (9/9). Entrained at Longpré for Bailleul (17/9).

1/5th (Cumberland) Battalion (T.F.). 151st Brigade, 50th (Northumbrian) Division: Arrived Candas from Godewaersvelde (11/8) and from there marched to Beaumetz. To Vignacourt (15/8), Rainneville (16/8), Baizieux Wood (17/8). 'B' and 'D' Companies to Baizieux (30/8). To Bécourt Wood (10/9). Work parties provided for burying of cables near Railway Wood. To Shelter Wood (14/9), Quadrangle Trench (15/9) and from there positions in the south-west corner of Mametz Wood. Later went on for attack on Starfish and Prue Trenches – War Diary records late arrival at assembly trenches and unable to advance with main waves. Moved forward at 11 p.m. to The Bow and dug in. Casualties – 6 officers and about 100 other ranks. Small parties reached Prue Trench (16/9) but driven back to The Bow. Renewed attack on Starfish Line (18/9) – leading waves went forward at 5.50 a.m. – driven back by heavy machine gun fire. 'A' Company to strong-point north-west corner of High Wood (19/9). Remainder withdrew to Swansea Trench. Battalion to south-west corner of Mametz Wood (20/9). To Swansea and Clark's Trenches (24/9), Prue Trench, Starfish Line and Crescent Alley (28/9). 'A' Company withdrawn from line and sent to isolation camp near Fricourt on account of outbreak of dysentery (29/9). Remainder sent forward to reinforce 1/8th D.L.I. during bombing attack on Flers Line. Attacked (1/10) – advanced with 1/8th D.L.I. – objectives taken and consolidated. Withdrew to Swansea Trench (2/10). To Bécourt Wood (3/10), Hénencourt Wood (4/10), Mametz Wood (17/10), Hénencourt Wood (22/10), bivouacs near Bécourt (23/10), Mametz Wood (25/10), Drop Alley and Flers Line (3/11). Took over front line (Snag Trench and Snag Support) during attack on Butte de Warlencourt (5/11). Relieved and to Mametz Wood (6/11). Working parties provided for road making.

6th (Service) Battalion. 33rd Brigade, 11th (Northern) Division: Arrived Léalvillers from Canettemont (2/9). To Bouzincourt (5/9), Donnet Post (6/9), front line facing Thiepval (12/9). Attacked and gained part of Danube Trench (16/9). To Ovillers (18/9), Englebelmer (20/9), Mailly-Mallet (21/9), Donnet Post (25/9), front line (26/9) – attacked Joseph and Schwaben Trenches 12.35 p.m. – objectives carried by 12.45 p.m. – 5 machine guns and 191 prisoners captured. Moved forward to reinforce 9th Notts and Derby in Zollern Trench (27/9) – 'C' Company attacked and took Hessian Trench 3 p.m. War Diary notes 'a bad night' in Hessian with heavy and very accurate shelling. Counter attack driven off about 7 p.m. Withdrew to support positions (First Street) (29/9). To Hédauville (30/9), Léalvillers (31/9), Montigny-les-Jongleurs (1/10), Cramont (2/10), Bonneville (14/11), Contay (15/11), Varennes (16/11).

7th (Service) Battalion. 51st Brigade, 17th (Northern) Division: Moved up from Morlancourt to old front line at Fricourt (2/7). To positions in front of Fricourt Wood for attack on Bottom Wood (3/7) – Railway Alley taken at 11.30 a.m. – 'D' Company going on up the slope encountered strong opposition at next trench before entering wood. Here for a time they would be surrounded by the enemy. Objectives later taken and consolidated. Relieved during night and to Fricourt Wood. To Méaulte (4/7), front line (Quadrangle Trench) (7/7). Bombing attack on Pearl Alley and Quadrangle

Support (8/7). To Fricourt Wood (9/7). Entrained at Dernancourt for Saleux (11/7) and from there marched to Saisseval. To Ailly-le-Haut-Clocher (14/7). Entrained at Hangest for Méricourt (23/7) and from there marched to bivouacs 1 mile north-west of Buire. To Pommiers Redoubt (1/8), front line Delville Wood (4/8). Attack at 4.30 p.m. (7/8) failed. To support positions at Montauban Alley (9/8), Bienvillers (15/8), front line Hannescamps sector (27/8), St. Amand (4/9), Halloy (11/9), Sailly-au-Bois (17/9), Humbercamps (19/9), Halloy (22/9), Barly (23/9), Hiermont (24/9), Barly (2/10), Halloy (3/10), Sailly-au-Bois (4/10), front line Hébuterne sector (5/10), Sailly-au-Bois (8/10), Souastre (14/10), Halloy (17/10), Doullens (19/10). Moved by buses to Méricourt (22/10) and from there marched to Ville-sur-Ancre. To Citadel Camp (27/10), Trônes Wood (29/10), support lines between Lesbœufs and Gueudecourt (Needle, Windmill and Mail Trenches) (30/10), front line (1/11). Successful attack on Zenith Trench (2/11) – gains held against counter attacks. To Montauban (3/11), support line (7/11), front line (8/11), support (10/11), Montauban (11/11), Sandpit Camp (12/11). Entrained at Edgehill for Hangest (15/11) – 'C' and 'D' Companies marching to billets at Le Mesge, rest to Le Mesge (16/11).

8th (Service) Battalion. 75th Brigade, 25th Division: From Forceville moved through Martinsart Wood to front line south of Thiepval (2/7). Attacked 6 a.m. (3/7) – about 180 yards of German line taken but later forced to retire. Casualties – 444. Withdrew to southern side of Aveluy Wood (4/7). Via Albert to reserve line trenches at Usna Redoubt (7/7), front line (11/7). Attack on southern side of Ovillers dawn (14/7) – all companies gained objectives with little resistance. To Senlis during night (17/7), Hédauville (18/7), Amplier (19/7), Acheux (23/7), Mailly-Maillet Wood (25/7), front line opposite Beaumont-Hamel (30/7), Auchonvillers (6/8), Bois de Warnimont (9/8), Raincheval (15/8), Forceville (17/8), Aveluy Wood (18/8), Hédauville (22/8), The Bluff and Aveluy Wood (25/8), front line (Hindenburg Trench) (26/8), Bouzincourt (1/9), front line (2/9), Bouzincourt (7/9), Léalvillers (8/9), Amplier (10/9), Domléger (12/9), Amplier (25/9), Léalvillers (26/9), Bouzincourt (29/9), Ovillers (30/9), trenches on right of Pozières (5/10), Crucifix Corner (6/10), front line (Stuff Redoubt) (15/10). Attack on Regina Trench (21/10) – objective taken – attack described in War Diary as 'sudden and swift.' To Bouzincourt (22/10), Warloy (23/10), Gézaincourt (24/10). Entrained at Doullens for Bailleul (29/10)

11th (Service) Battalion (Lonsdale). 97th Brigade, 32nd Division: Attack on Leipzig Salient (1/7) – advanced from assemble positions in Authuille Wood at 8 a.m. – War Diary records that Battalion came under very heavy Machine Gun Fire from The Nord Werk on right flank. Commanding Officer

Lieutenant-Colonel P.W. Machell killed along with almost all the officers. Casualties – almost 500. To Crucifix Corner (3/7), Contay Wood (4/7), Senlis (8/7), front line (9/7), Crucifix Corner (12/7), Bouzincourt (16/7). Began march to Béthune sector. Arrived Longuevillette from Moncheaux (18/10). To Hérissart (21/10), Bouzincourt (23/10), Hérissart (30/10), La Vicogne (31/10), Contay (13/11), Black Horse Bridge (15/11), Englebelmer (16/11), assembly positions Redan sector (17/11). Attack on Munich and Frankfort Trenches (18/11) – advanced at 6.10 a.m. – War Diary notes that leading waves got well over Munich Trench 'the spirit of the men being a fine sight to see in spite of the intense cold.' Later fell back to Waggon Road with high casualties. Relieved and to Mailly-Maillet (19/11).

Royal Sussex Regiment

2nd Battalion. 2nd Brigade, 1st Division: Entrained at Lillers for Candas (6/7) and from there marched to Flesselles. To Fréchencourt (8/7), Bresle (9/7), via Albert to Bécourt Wood (10/7), Fricourt (16/7), Contalmaison (18/7). Took over trenches opposite The Triangle (22/7). Attack (with 2nd K.R.R.C.) on Munster Alley (23/7) – Official History of the Great War records the 2 battalions coming under machine gun fire from the outset – their attempt to rush the trenches under cover of the barrage standing no chance of success. Withdrew to The Triangle. Casualties – 116. To Bécourt Wood (24/7), Franvillers (26/7), Hénencourt (30/7), Bécourt Wood (13/8). Moved via Mametz to front line High Wood (14/8). Attacked and captured part of new German trench running westwards across Bazentin-le-Petit Road from High Wood (16/8). German counter-attacks with flamethrowers (17/8). To Mametz Wood (18/8). Took over Clark's Trench (20/8) – failed assault towards ridge between High Wood and Martinpuich. German attacks repulsed. Relieved and via Mametz Wood to Albert. Casualties since (14/8) – 480. War Diary notes Albert bombed by aircraft (21/8). To Mametz Wood (27/8), trenches High Wood (31/8), Bécourt Wood (2/9). Working parties in Mametz Wood (4/9). To Lozenge Wood (5/9), High Wood (7/9). Attack on Wood Lane (9/9) – objectives taken – secured gains by digging defensive flank. To Bécourt Wood (10/9). Casualties – 262. Via Albert to Baizieux (12/9). Via Hénencourt and Albert to Bécourt Wood (19/9). To High Wood (Starfish Line) (25/9). Attack on Prue Trench (26/9)–(27/9). Casualties – 161. To Bécourt Wood (28/9), Millencourt (29/9), Tœufles (3/10), Bresle (31/10). Via Laviéville and Millencourt to Albert (5/11), High Wood (18/11).

1/5th (Cinque Ports) Battalion (T.F.). Pioneers, 48th (South Midland) Division: Located in and around Sailly-au-Bois (1/7). In the previous October war correspondent Philip Gibbs had visited the Battalion at Sailly and later feature them in an article published in The Daily Telegraph – 'I saw the courage of men who get no public credit for heroism, through day after day they live with immediate death lurking about them.' To Albert area (16/7) and from there worked around Ovillers and Pozières. To Aveluy (20/7). In action (21/7) – 2 companies came under attack while working. Counter attacked and went on to take and consolidate a strong point. To Acheux (28/9) and from there Souastre. Operating from camp near Bazentin-le-Grand by end October.

7th (Service) Battalion. 36th Brigade, 12th (Eastern) Division: Moved from billets at Fréchencourt to Baizieux Wood (1/7). Later into Albert-Bouzincourt reserve line. From these positions, Battalion historian records, 'we had a good view of the German and British trench systems extending from the

Albert-Bapaume Road up to Thiepval.' To railway cutting north of Albert station (3/7). Here Battalion witnessed a 12-inch howitzer working in collaboration with an aeroplane. The wireless direction used to plot the shots being subject to constant jamming by the Germans. To reserve line (4/7), trenches Ovillers sector (6/7). In attack with 8th and 9th Royal Fusiliers on village (7/7) – advancing at 8.30 a.m., War Diary recording heavy machine gun fire and bombardment by shrapnel shells. Withdrew via Crucifix Corner to Albert (8/7). Casualties – 461. To Senlis via Millencourt (9/7), Forceville (10/7), Bus-lès-Artois via Acheux (11/7), Sailly-au-Bois (14/7), Bus Wood (16/7), Mailly-Maillet (20/7), Bois de Warnimont (24/7), Hédauville (26/7). Took over support trenches between Ovillers and La Boisselle (27/7). Occupied trenches west of Pozières (30/7). Operations at Ration Trench, 6th Avenue accounting for some 224 casualties. To Albert-Bouzincourt reserve trenches (6/8), Bouzincourt (7/8), Varennes (11/8), Puchevillers (12/8). Began move to Arras sector (15/8). Arrived Bernaville from Agny (26/9). To Bouquemaison (27/9). Moved forward to Pommiers Redoubt (29/9). Took over trenches Gueudecourt sector (1/10). In support during attack on Bayonet Trench (7/10). Casualties since (1/10) – 182. Relieved and to Bernafay Wood (11/10). To front line (17/10). Attack on Bayonet Trench (18/10). To Mametz Wood (19/10), Fricourt (20/10), Buire (21/10). To Arras sector (22/10).

8th (Service) Battalion (Pioneers). Pioneers, 18th (Eastern) Division: From headquarters at Carnoy were involved in operations at Montauban (1/7). Consolidated strong-points and dug new communication trenches. War Diary records part of 'A' Company involved in fighting at Montauban Alley – 'D' Company bombers assisted in capture of The Loop. Relieved and to Grove Town Camp (7/7). Work began on Maricourt-La Briqueterie Road (10/7). To Copse Valley (12/7). Operations at Trônes Wood (13/7)–(14/7). Working in Guillemont area. Relieved and to Bois des Tailles (19/7). Entrained at Méricourt for Longpré (21/7) and from there marched to Hallencourt. Entrained at Pont-Remy for St. Omer (23/7). Arrived Doullens (31/8). To Forceville via Acheux (1/9), Aveluy Wood (3/9). Work commenced on tramway extension at Ovillers, light railways and roads. Thiepval operations (26/9)–(28/9). To bivouacs Pioneer Road (5/10). Relieved and to Acheux (7/10). Later entrained for Candas and from there marched to Bernaville. To dugouts in Usna Valley (12/10). Work on Sudbury and Cliff Trenches. Moved forward (21/10) and stood by until Regina Trench was captured. Communication trench then dug across No Man's Land. Work on Pozières Road, Mouquet Farm track, Courcelette Road. Ancre operations (13/11)–(18/11).

9th (Service) Battalion. 73rd Brigade, 24th Division: Arrived Saleux from Godewaersvelde (24/7) and from there marched to Montagne. To Corbie

(31/7), Happy Valley via Sailly-le-Sec (2/8), Citadel Camp (8/8). 'A' and 'B' Companies to Montauban (10/8), 'C' and 'D' to craters at Carnoy (11/8). Assembled at La Briqueterie (17/8). Attack on Guillemont (18/8) – 1 company reinforced 7th Northamptonshire in German line near The Quarry – position consolidated during night. Relieved and to Carnoy craters (20/8). Casualties – 186. To Sandpit Camp (22/8), bivouacs near Dernancourt (25/8), trenches Delville Wood (30/8). German attack 2 p.m. (31/8) – 'A' and 'D' Companies held line beyond Longueval-Flers Road. Withdrew to support line (3/9), reserve area (4/9). Casualties – 118. To Dernancourt (5/9). Entrained for Longpré (6/9) and from there marched to Brucamps. Entrained at Longpré for Béthune area (20/9).

11th (Service) Battalion (1st South Down). 116th Brigade, 39th Division: Entrained at Ligny-St-Flochel for La Souich (24/8). To Bois de Warnimont (25/8), Mailly-Maillet Wood (27/8). Took over trenches in front of Hamel (2/9). In attack 5.10 a.m. (3/9) – War Diary records first wave succeeding in entering enemy's front line – second and third, owing to enemy barrage across No Man's Land, suffered many casualties. Position between enemy's wire and front line held until withdrawn at 6.30 p.m. Relieved and to Englebelmer. Casualties – 299. To Beaussart (6/9) – 'a village containing sulky civilians' (Edmund Blunden). To Auchonvillers (14/9). Took over trenches Beaumont right sub section. War Diary records patrols finding enemy wire to be thick and no less than 5 distinct belts. For attack on Thiepval (26/9), and in cooperation with units on the right, dummies were made and put up over parapet to represent troops going over. Edmund Blunden notes in his book 'Undertones of War' that these were some 190 in number and produced by R.S.M. Daniels from sandbags and grass. Relieved and to Englebelmer (4/10). To Martinsart Wood (5/10), trenches at Hamel (7/10). Relieving 1/1st Hertfordshire and 4th/5th Black Watch in line from the Ancre to Piccadilly. Relieved by Hood Battalion and via Martinsart Wood to Authuille Wood (16/10). Moved forward (20/10) and in action (21/10). Stuff Trench captured. Casualties – 278. Relieved and to south side of Aveluy Wood (22/10). To River sector Thiepval (25/10), South Bluff (27/10), Thiepval Wood (29/10), Schwaben Redoubt (30/10), South and Central Bluff (1/11), Senlis (3/11), front line (5/11), Senlis (6/11). War Diary notes 'Zeppelins over at 11 p.m.' Relieved 1/1st Cambridgeshire in Schwaben Redoubt (10/11). To Warloy (14/11), Doullens (15/11). Entrained for Poperinghe (17/11).

12th (Service) Battalion (2nd South Down). 116th Brigade, 39th Division: Arrived Bois de Warnimont (25/8). To bivouacs near Englebelmer (27/8), Mesnil (2/9). Provided carrying and working parties during 116th Brigade's attack opposite Hamel (3/9). Relieved and to Fort Moulin. To Englebelmer bivouacs (4/9). Took over front line at Auchonvillers (10/9). Relieved by 11th Royal Sussex and to Beaussart (14/9). To trenches Redan left sub sector (19/9). Relieved and to Mailly-Maillet (30/9). To Auchonvillers in Brigade reserve (3/10). 'B' and 'D' Companies to bivouacs in Englebelmer Wood (6/10). Relieved 14th Hampshire in Auchonvillers North sector (7/10). Front extending from junction of Watling Street and Clive Trench to Beaumont-Hamel Road. To Englebelmer Wood (13/10). To Schwaben Redoubt (15/10). War Diary records 'D' Company on left coming under attack about 10 p.m. – enemy coming up Strasbourg Trench and using flamethrowers – 'attack beaten off with heavy loss to the enemy.' Relieved and to Aveluy (17/10). To Wood Post (21/10). 'C' Company marched to Schwaben Redoubt and took part in 116th Brigade's successful attack on Stuff Trench. Battalion moved forward 4.30 p.m. and took over captured positions. Relieved and to Martinsart (22/10). To River sector Thiepval (25/10). Relieved and to Pioneer Road (27/10), front line (30/10), North Bluff (1/11), Senlis (3/11). Moved forward to Brigade reserve at Thiepval (5/11). Occupied during early hours of the night in making a road through towards Crucifix Corner. Relieved and to Martinsart Wood (6/11). To front line (9/11), North Bluff (13/11), Warloy (14/11), Doullens (15/11). Entrained for Poperinghe (17/11).

13th (Service) Battalion (3rd South Down). 116th Brigade, 39th Division: Arrived Bois de Warnimont (25/8), Mailly-Mailly Wood (27/8). Took up assembly positions at Hamel (2/9). In support of 11th Royal Sussex during attack (3/9). Casualties – 135. Relieved and to Mailly-Mailly Wood (4/9), Bertrancourt (6/9). Relieved 1/5th Gloucestershire in Beaumont-Hamel sector (10/9). Relieved and to Mailly-Maillet (14/9). Took over trenches at Redan Ridge from 25th Royal Fusiliers (19/9). Relieved 1/1st Hertfordshire at Y Ravine (3/10). To Englebelmer Wood (10/10). Relieved 12th Royal Sussex in Redan sector (13/10). Relieved (16/10) and via Englebelmer Wood took over positions at Schwaben Redoubt sector. Carried out work in preparation for attack on Stuff Trench – communication trenches dug and dumps formed. To Wood Post (20/10). Moved forward for attack (21/10). Held captured positions until relieved (22/10) and to Martinsart Wood. War diary records the success being largely due to accuracy of artillery barrage – this enabling the infantry to get within 20 yards of objective before the barrage lifted. Relieved 4th/5th Black Watch at the Schwaben Redoubt (25/10). To North Bluff (27/10), left River Section Thiepval (30/10), Pioneer Road (1/11), Martinsart Wood (2/11), front line (5/11), Martinsart Wood (6/11), Thiepval (10/11), front line (12/11). Held line during attack (13/11). Relieved and to South Bluff 5 p.m. To Warloy (14/11), Authieule (15/11). Entrained at Doullens for Poperinghe (17/11).

Hampshire Regiment

1st Battalion. 11th Brigade, 4th Division: Advance at 7.40 a.m. during attack on the Redan Ridge (1/7) – swept by machine gun fire, hardly a man would reach the German wire, those that did being quickly killed. The Hampshire on this occasion was led by their Commanding Officer Lieutenant-Colonel Hon. L.C.W. Palk, who in front of his men calmly went forward carrying only his stick. He would be killed and number among the 500 or more (over 320 of these were killed) casualties. Relieved and to Mailly-Maillet. To Bertrancourt (4/7), front line Beaumont-Hamel (10/7), Mailly-Maillet (15/7). Entrained at Doullens for Ypres sector (23/7). Arrived Longueau from Esquelbecq (17/9) and from there marched to Cardonnette. To Corbie (25/9), Méaulte (7/10), Citadel Camp (8/10), Montauban (9/10), Brigade reserve east of Guillemont (17/10), support lines Lesbœufs (19/10), front line (Frosty Trench) (22/10). Attack on Boritska Trench (23/10) – 'C' and 'A' Companies led at 2.30 p.m. and immediately came under very heavy machine gun and rifle fire. The right eventually entered German front trench but after holding for a few hours were forced to retire. Casualties – 202. Via Trônes Wood to Mansell Camp (25/10), Méaulte (27/10). Entrained at Méricourt for Airaines (30/10) and from there marched to Mérélessart. To Ramburelles and Le Translay (2/11).

2nd Battalion. 88th Brigade, 29th Division: In reserve for attack at Beaumont-Hamel (1/7) – moving forward to St. John's Road during afternoon. To Mary Redan (3/7). Here, War Diary records – the enemy permitted parties to go out and bring in wounded. Trenches were repaired, arms and equipment recovered and the dead buried. To Mailly-Maillet Wood (10/7), Acheux Wood (17/7), Beauval (23/7). Entrained at Candas for Ypres sector (27/7). Arrived Longueau from Hupoutre (8/10) and from there marched to Corbie. To bivouacs between Pommiers Redoubt and Montauban (10/10), trenches south of Gueudecourt (Bulls Road) (11/10). In support during attack on Hilt Trench (12/10) – moving forward to captured positions during night. Withdrew to reserve positions (15/10). Assembled in Hilt Trench for attack on Grease Trench (18/10). – advanced at 3.40 a.m. – objective taken and held until relieved and to Bernafay Wood 8 p.m. (20/10). To front line north of Flers (27/10), Bernafay Wood (29/10), Mametz (30/10), Méricourt (31/10). Casualties for October – 331. To Sandpit Camp (15/11), Bernafay Wood (17/11) – 2 companies in Flers Support

11th (Service) Battalion (Pioneers). Pioneers, 16th (Irish) Division: Arrived Longueau from Auchel (28/8) and from there marched to Daours. To Sailly-le-Sec (31/8), Citadel Camp (1/9). Worked on communication trenches near front line, roads, carrying work at Chimpanzee Trench. To Bernafay

Wood (5/9) – improving and digging new trenches and erecting shelters. Took over defences at Guillemont (7/9). 'A' and 'B' Companies placed at disposal of 47th Brigade for operations at Ginchy, rest to Bernafay Wood (8/9). To Morlancourt (10/9), Corbie (11/9), 'C' and 'D' Companies to Méaulte (15/9). Battalion moved by bus to Airaines (18/9). Entrained at Longpré for Flanders front (21/9).

14th (Service) Battalion (1st Portsmouth). 116th Brigade, 39th Division: Entrained at Ligny-St-Flochel for Bouquemaison and from there to Le Souich (24/8). To Bois de Warnimont (25/8), Mailly-Maillet Wood (27/8), front line north-east of Hamel (2/9). Attacked (3/9) – 'A' Company took front line and held – 'B' occupying second. 'C' then advanced to wire and was repulsed by rifle and machine gun fire – retired with heavy casualties. Withdrew after strong counter attacks to Mailly-Maillet Wood. Casualties – 457. To Bertrancourt (6/9), Mailly-Maillet (10/9), front line Auchonvillers (14/9), Englebelmer (6/10), Y Ravine sector (10/10), Englebelmer Wood (16/10). Relieve 12th Royal Sussex at Schwaben Redoubt (17/10). Here conditions were of the worst kind – the wet, cold, mud and shortage of food, according to the history of the Hampshire Regiment, being more unbearable than the enemy's constant shelling and counter attacks. Cut off from their support, the Hampshire however would make good use of the enemy's belongings – rations and clothing being taken from the dead, positions improved with German spades and his bombs and ammunition turned against him. Relieved by 17th K.R.R.C. (20/10) and to Pioneer Road – 'D' Company remaining in line. 'D' Company in action against German attack (21/10). Rest of Battalion moved forward to Wood Post in support. To Senlis Camp (23/10), Thiepval (25/10), Pioneer Road (27/10), Thiepval River section (30/10), Pioneer Road (1/11), Martinsart Wood (3/11), Schwaben Redoubt (5/11), Senlis (6/11), Schwaben (10/11), Thiepval (12/11). Attack on Strasbourg Line (13/11) – relieved and moved back to Pioneer Road. To Warloy (14/11), Doullens (15/11). Entrained for Ypres sector (18/11).

15th (Service) Battalion (2nd Portsmouth). 122nd Brigade, 41st Division: Arrived Longpré from Bailleul (24/8) and from there marched to Villers-sous-Ailly. Entrained at Longpré for Méricourt (5/9) and from there marched to Dernancourt. To Fricourt (11/9), reserve trenches at Montauban 3 a.m. (12/9) – returned to Fricourt same evening. Relieved 20th Durham Light Infantry in trenches west of Delville Wood (13/9) – moving to assembly positions at 11 p.m. Attack towards Flers (15/9) – left trenches at 6.20 a.m. – War Diary notes left held up by machine gun fire for 10 minutes – many casualties. Later swept through village, holding gains until relieved at 7 p.m. To reserve positions at York Trench. Casualties – 292. To Dernancourt

(17/9), Mametz (2/10), front line north of Flers (3/10). German bombing attack repulsed (4/10). Some ground taken in Gird Lines (5/10). Counter attack driven off (6/10). Attack on Gird Lines (7/10) – enemy held ground inflicting high casualties. Withdrew to Brown Trench (9/10), York Trench (10/10), positions east of Mametz Wood (11/10), Méaulte (12/10). Entrained at Méricourt for Oisemont (17/10), arrived 11 a.m. (18/10) and marched to Huppy. Entrained at Pont-Remy for Ypres Sector (20/10).

South Staffordshire Regiment

1st Battalion. 91st Brigade, 7th Division: From Maricourt moved forward for attack on Mametz (1/7) – led assault with 22nd Manchester. Official History of The Great War records No Man's Land as between 100-200 yards wide – the German first line being crossed with little loss – heavy machine gun and rifle fire from Mametz and Danzig Alley inflicted high casualties during next advance. By 7.45 a.m. 700 yards had been covered – the line of Cemetery Trench immediately south of Mametz taken and consolidated – village entered later and western end of Danzig Alley (East) captured. To Buire (5/7), reserve line north of Bazentin-le-Grand (14/7) – attack on High Wood 7 p.m. – wood entered and held until withdrawal ordered 11.25 p.m. To positions behind Bazentin-le-Grand early morning (16/7). To Bécordel-Bécourt (19/7), Dernancourt (20/7). Entrained at Méricourt for Hangest (21/7) and from there to Vaux-en-Amiénois. Entrained at Vignacourt for Méricourt (12/8) and from there to Dernancourt. To Fricourt (26/8). Attack on Delville Wood (31/8) – bombed along Ale Alley and Hop Alley – heavy fighting in trenches east of wood – counter attack at 7 p.m. forced withdrawal into wood – Edge Trench held. Relieved and to Fricourt (5/9), Entrained at Albert for Oisemont (11/9) and from there to Doudelainville. Entrained at Abbeville for Ypres sector (18/9).

2nd Battalion. 6th Brigade, 2nd Division: Entrained at Bryas for Longueau (20/7). To Bois des Tailles (24/7), Carnoy (25/7), Delville Wood (27/7). Came under heavy bombardment followed by unsuccessful German attack 9.30 p.m. (28/7). To Carnoy (2/8), Bernafay Wood (5/8), Méaulte (12/8). Entrained at Méricourt-l'Abbé for Saleux (13/8). To Belloy-sur-Somme (15/8), Vignacourt (16/8), Fienvillers (17/8), Bois de Warnimont (18/8), front line Serre sector (20/8), Courcelles (24/8), front line (28/8), Courcelles (2/9), front line (5/9), Courcelles (9/9), front line (13/9), Couin (17/9), Bois de Warnimont (20/9), front line Hébuterne sector (1/10), Bertrancourt (5/10), Puchevillers (8/10), Bertrancourt (18/10), front line Serre sector (28/10), Bertrancourt (30/10), front line (12/11). Attack along the Redan Ridge (13/11) – uncut wire around The Quadrilateral held up advance – heavy casualties from machine gun fire. Withdrawal to British front line ordered. To Louvencourt (16/11).

1/5th Battalion (T.F.). 137th Brigade, 46th (North Midland) Brigade: Moved forward from Foncquevillers and in support for attack on Gommecourt (1/7). To Souastre (2/7), Berles-au-Bois (3/7). Arrived Yvrencheux from Bonnières (3/11). To Agenvillers (11/11).

1/6th Battalion (T.F.). 137th Brigade, 46th (North Midland) Division: Moved forward from Souastre to positions facing Gommecourt during evening (30/6). Attacked 7.30 a.m. (1/7) – on right of assault the smoke put down to cover attack was at first too thick and the men lost their way – later enemy sweep No Man's Land with machine gun fire – those that did manage to reach German wire would find it intact. Small party of 'D' Company gained hold in German front line, but were quickly overcome. Battalion history gives casualties as 239, most of which, it records, occurred within the space of a few minutes. Withdrew to St. Amand (2/7). Arrived Lucheux from Coullemont (31/10). To Yvrencheux (3/11), Agenvillers (11/11).

7th (Service) Battalion. 33rd Brigade, 11th (Northern) Division: Arrived Acheux from Liercourt (2/9). To Bouzincourt (5/9), front line Thiepval sector (6/9), Bouzincourt (12/9), Crucifix Corner (14/9), Bouzincourt (16/9), Ovillers sector (17/9), Mailly-Maillet (22/9), Martinsart Wood (25/9). In action (26/9) – clearing enemy from Midway Line and repelling bombing attack at Hessian Trench. Bombers advanced eastward along Zollern Trench (27/9). Relieved and to Acheux (1/10), Autheux (2/10), Domléger (3/10), Maison-Roland (5/10), Bonneville (14/11), Harponville (15/11), Varennes (16/11).

8th (Service) Battalion. 51st Brigade, 17th (Northern) Division: Moved forward from Morlancourt to front line at Fricourt (2/7) – in action at Bottom Wood (3/7). Relieved and to Ville (6/7). To Fricourt (7/7). Attack on Quadrangle Support (9/7) – advanced at 11.20 p.m. Official History of The Great War notes – part of trench occupied and all its garrison captured – but unsupported on flanks obliged to to fall back. Casualties – 219. Entrained at Dernancourt for Saleux (11/7) and from there marched to Fourdrinoy. To Bussus (15/7). Entrained at Hangest for Méricourt (23/7) and from there to Buire. To Pommiers Redoubt (1/8), front line Delville Wood (5/8). Unsuccessful attack 4.30 p.m. (7/8). To Fricourt (11/8), Buire (12/8), Gézaincourt (15/8), Bienvillers (16/8), Hannescamps (20/8), Bienvillers (27/8), Hannescamps (4/9), Halloy (12/9), front line Hébuterne sector (16/9), Mondicourt (22/9), Remaisnil (23/9), Yvrencheux (24/9), Frohen-le-Grand (2/10), Bayencourt (6/10), Hébuterne sector (9/10), Sailly-au-Bois (14/10), Doullens (19/10), Ville-sur-Ancre (22/10), Citadel Camp (27/10), Montauban (1/11). Entrained at Edgehill for Hangest (15/11) and from there to Riencourt.

9th (Service) Battalion (Pioneers). Pioneers, 23rd Division: Division moved to Baizieux area (1/7) and later Albert. Took part in operations at Contalmaison and Pozières Ridge. Engaged during fighting for Munster Alley (8/8). Division moved to Ypres sector. Returned to Somme beginning September – operations around Martinpuich and Le Sars. Withdrawn from forward area and later to Ypres sector beginning October.

12th (Labour) Battalion. Arrived Albert from Rouen (2/10). Worked Fricourt, Pozières, Contalmaison areas. War Diary notes documents of Contalmaison Church unearthed (22/10) and sent to Amiens Cathedral.

Dorsetshire Regiment

1st Battalion. 14th Brigade, 32nd Division: From Senlis Camp went forward through Aveluy Wood to Black Horse Bridge (30/6). Followed 11th Border towards Leipzig Redoubt in front of Thiepval Village (1/7) – advancing from Authuille Wood suffered high casualties before reaching British front line (about 100 yards). Company Sergeant Major R. Hodge recalls that during advance the sound of a flute was heard – Drum-Major Kerr was out in the open and encouraging the men forward with the Regimental March-Past. His arm was later shattered by a bullet. Relieved and to Authuille (2/7). Back in front line by night fall. Relieved and to Senlis (3/7). Casualties – 501. To Forceville (5/7), Bouzincourt (7/7). Relieved 9th Essex in front line near Ovillers (8/7) – bombing attacks – some ground gained. Relieved by 16th Lancashire Fusiliers and to Bouzincourt (11/7). To front line (14/7). One platoon in unsuccessful attack (15/7). Relieved and to Senlis. To Halloy (17/7), Brévillers (18/7). Began march to Béthune area (19/7). On the way history repeated itself when the Battalion reached Orlencourt. In 1817 the Dorsetshire (then 39th Regiment) was billeted in the village and 99 years later the Commanding Officer actually spent the night in the same house that his processor had. His host being the grandson of the original owner. Arrived Beauval (18/10). To Warloy (21/10), brickfields between Albert and Bouzincourt (23/10), Contay Wood (26/10), Harponville (9/11), Bouzincourt (13/11), Mailly-Maillet (15/11), front line (16/11). In support during 32nd Division's attack on Frankfort Trench and Ten Tree Alley between Serre and Beaumont-Hamel (18/11). Relieved and to Mailly-Maillet (23/11).

5th (Service) Battalion. 34th Brigade, 11th (Northern) Division: Arrived Acheux from Frévent (3/9) and from there marched to Puchevillers. To Bouzincourt (8/9), positions opposite Mouquet Farm (16/9) – the line (not more than shell-holes) running along Mouquet Road and through the farm. Battalion historian records how Mouquet Farm comprised 3 groups of building – 1 behind the British front line, another in No Man's Land and a third – still held by the Germans. The ruins were connected by tunnels and the enemy would often appear behind the Dorsetshire until men were posted at the exits. Several bombing raids carried out on fortified dug-outs under the farm – said to house at least 2 battalions of Germans. Relieved and to Albert (19/9). To Englebelmer (21/9), Ovillers (25/9). Attack on Mouquet Farm (26/9) – advanced from support trenches 12.35 p.m. – heavy casualties from enemy barrage before reaching first objective – all company commanders and company sergeant majors killed or wounded. Moved up to Zollern Redoubt 6.30 a.m. (27/9) and consolidated position. Advance on Stuff Redoubt driven back by machine gun and sniper fire. Improved communication trench back to Schwaben Trench (28/9). Relieved 5.10 p.m. and to Ovillers. Casualties estimated in War Diary as 423. To Varennes (30/9), Bernaville (1/10), Franqueville (3/10), Domqueur (7/10), St. Léger (14/11), Pernois (15/11), Harponville (16/11), Raincheval (17/11), Puchevillers (18/11).

6th (Service) Battalion. 50th Brigade, 17th (Northern) Division: Moved from Ville-sur-Ancre to Méaulte (1/7). Opposite the Fricourt Salient – went forward to – Bonte Redoubt by mid-day and in afternoon held reserve positions during 50th Brigade's attack. Relieved and to Méaulte (2/7). Engaged in carrying duties to new positions at Fricourt. To forward positions at Fricourt Wood, Railway Alley, Bottom Wood (6/7). Squad of bombers attacked Strip Trench (7/7) – heavy machine gun fire soon brought assault to a stand still. Battalion historian records that during this attack the clothing of wounded laying in the open was often set alight due to enemy's use of incendiary bombs. Renewed and more successful attack (8/7). Attack on Quadrangle Support between Mametz Wood and Contalmaison (9/7). Entrained at Grove Town for Saleux (11/7) and from there to Camps-en-Amiénois. To Buigny (15/7), Condé (22/7). Entrained at Hangest (23/7) – arrived Méricourt (24/7) and from there marched to bivouacs near Buire. To Belle Vue Farm (1/8), Pommiers Redoubt (4/8), forward trenches near Longueval (5/8). Dug new trench (Dorset Trench). Relieved and to Montauban Alley in reserve (9/8). To Belle View Farm (11/8), camp on hill above Dernancourt (12/8). Entrained at Méricourt for Fienvillers (14/8) and from there marched to Prouville. To Villers-l'Hôpital (16/8), Halloy (17/8), Sailly-au-Bois (20/8). Just before reaching Sailly, Battalion witnessed the death of musical artist Basil Hallam (Gilbert the Filbert) who fell from an observation balloon. Took turns in front line Hébuterne sector. A sample of trench humour is recorded by the Battalion's historian. Sent out to inspect and bring back a sample of the enemy's wire – also to report on gaps made by recent artillery bombardment; Lieutenant E.K.A. Boyce upon his return addressed 2 envelopes to Headquarters. One contained a small piece of wire, the other nothing. On the first he wrote: 'Herewith sample of wire,' on the other: 'Herewith sample of gap.' Relieved and to Bayencourt (31/8). To front line (6/9), Sailly-au-Bois (12/9), Halloy (16/9), Villers-l'Hôpital (20/9), Hiermont (21/9), Neuilly-l'Hôpital (22/9), Hiermont (5/10), Barly (6/10), Halloy (10/10), Sailly-au-Bois (17/10), Hénu (18/10), Halloy (19/10), Talmas (20/10), Franvillers (21/10), Méaulte (22/10), Mansell Camp (27/10), Trônes Wood (29/10) – relieved 2nd Scottish Rifles in line between Lesbœufs and Gueudecourt during evening. Took turns in and out of line resting at Trônes Wood. To Citadel Camp (11/11). Entrained at Edgehill for Hangest (15/11) and from there moved in buses to Molliens-Vidames.

Prince of Wales's Volunteers (South Lancashire Regiment)

2nd Battalion. 75th Brigade, 25th Division: Arrived Forceville (1/7). To Martinsart (2/7). Crossed the Ancre at Black Horse Bridge and attacked south of Thiepval (3/7) – 'D' Company led and entered enemy's front line but then checked by strong machine gun fire. Later all officers reported as missing. There would also be heavy casualties in supporting companies. Withdrew to Aveluy Wood. Casualties – over 300. To bivouacs below Usna Redoubt (7/7). 'A' Company attacked at Ovillers (12/7) – some ground gained and held against counter attacks. Advanced again (14/7) and took positions around Ovillers church. Withdrew to Senlis (17/7). Later to Hédauville, Amplier, Acheux, Mailly-Maillet. In front line opposite Beaumont-Hamel by end July. Later rested and trained in the neighbourhoods of Forceville, Varennes and Bus-lès-Artois. To reserve positions Aveluy Wood (20/8), front line Leipzig Salient (2/9). Attack on Thiepval (3/9) – leading waves enfiladed by machine gun fire and forced to withdraw. Casualties – 130 (included Commanding Officer Lieutenant-Colonel H.T. Cotton, D.S.O.) Withdrew to Bouzincourt. Later, via Léalvillers, Amplier and Acheux moved for rest and training to Abbeville area. Returned via Amplier, Léalvillers and Bouzincourt to Ovillers sector end September. Began duty in line Hessian Trench and Zollern Redoubt. From reserve line moved forward (19/10) to Stuff Redoubt. Attack on Regina Trench (21/10) – much ground gained and some 400 prisoners. Casualties – 188. Relieved (22/10). To Gézaincourt (24/10). Entrained at Doullens for Bailleul (28/10).

1/4th Battalion (T.F.). Pioneers, 55th (West Lancashire) Division: From Beaumetz-lès-Loges near Arras moved towards Somme (20/7). Arrived camp south of Fricourt (28/7). Worked La Briqueterie and Gillemont areas. Attack on Guillemont (8/8) – 'D' Company went forward with 164th Brigade – dug communication trenches back to British front line from captured positions until bombed out by counter attack. Second-Lieutenant G.G.Coutry awarded Victoria Cross for conspicuous bravery near Arrow Head Copse. Later constructed shelters around Chimpanzee Trench. Relieved during third week of August and to Aigneville. Returned to forward area and in bivouacs around Montauban by (3/9). Worked on Delville Lane, Crucifix Alley and Pommiers Redoubt. Active during September operations around Ginchy, Flers, Gueudecourt and Morval. 'D' Company dug out 2 tanks stuck in mud early in attack on Flers (15/9). Relieved beginning October and to Ypres sector.

1/5th Battalion (T.F.). 166th Brigade, 55th (West Lancashire) Division: Moved from Sombrin to Bouquemaison (20/7). Entrained at Candas for

Méricourt (25/7) and from there marched to Ville-sous-Corbie. To Sandpit Camp (27/7). Later in reserve around Citadel Camp. In reserve at Trônes Wood during 166th Brigade's attack on Guillemont (8/8). To Maltz Horn Farm area (12/8). 'D' Company in unsuccessful bombing raid (13/8). To Méaulte (15/8). Entrained Edgehill for Martainneville (19/8) and from there to Ercourt. Entrained Pont-Remy for Méricourt (30/8) and from there marched to bivouacs west of Albert. Moved forward to trenches in front of Delville Wood (5/9). With 1/10th Kings dug new forward line. Enemy attack on positions repulsed (9/9). Bombers attached to 164th Brigade gained some ground in Ale Alley during attack (10/9). Relieved and to Ribemont area (13/9). Back in line Flers sector by (17/9). 166th Brigade in support positions western edge of village. Relieved and to Pommiers Redoubt (23/9). To Ribemont (28/9). Entrained at Méricourt for Longpré (30/9) and from there marched to billets. Entrained at Abbeville for Proven (2/10).

7th (Service) Battalion. 56th Brigade, 19th (Western) Division: Went forward from Hénencourt Wood to trenches behind Tara-Usna line (1/7) – advanced in afternoon for attack on Ovillers. Orders later cancelled and by following morning withdrew to bivouacs at railway cutting south-west of Albert. Under orders of 57th Brigade to Tara-Usna line (3/7). 'A' and 'D' Companies attacked east of La Boisselle 9.30 a.m. – 'A' Company reached objective but soon driven back by strong counter attack. Later re took line and consolidated. On right, 'D' Company forced to retire after stiff opposition. Regimental historian Captain H. Whalley-Kelly records that 'D' Company lost its way and did not rejoin Battalion until (5/7). 'B' and 'C' Companies renewed attack 8.30 a.m. (4/7) – Captain Whalley-Kelly notes bitter fighting against stubbornly held positions in the ruins of La Boisselle – advanced step by step with bombs and Lewis guns – village cleared at point of the bayonet by 3 p.m. Relieved (6/7) and to Albert. To La Boisselle during night (7/7), bivouacs edge of Hénencourt Wood (10/7). Via Fricourt to Mametz Wood (19/7), front line Bazentin-le-Petit (21/7). Failed attack on Switch Line (23/7). Withdrew to Mametz Wood (24/7). To front line (27/7), Franvillers (31/7). Entrained at Fréchencourt for Longpré (3/8) and from there entrained for Bailleul (6/8). Arrived Doullens (5/10) and from there to Sailly-au-Bois. Began tours in line Hébuterne sector. To Albert and later from Aveluy Wood tours in line Thiepval sector. Attack on Lucky Way and Hansa Line (14/11) – checked by wire and forced to retire after heavy losses. Strength of each company reduced to average of 80 men. In action western outskirts of Grandcourt (18/11) – 2 companies advanced up St.Pierre Divion-Grandcourt Road. Village entered and strong-points taken.

8th (Service) Battalion. 75th Brigade, 25th Division: Moved forward from Hédauville to reserve positions in Aveluy Wood (1/7). In action south of Thiepval (3/7). To Tara-Usna Line (7/7). Attack towards Ovillers 4 a.m. (8/7) – German front line trench taken and consolidated. Attacked (9/7) – 'C' and 'D' companies suffered great losses from machine gun fire while attempting to take third line. Relieved and to Tara-Usna Line (10/7). In action during night (12/7) – assisting 8th Border and 2nd South Lancashire at Ovillers – 2 companies reached northern outskirts but later forced to withdraw to centre of village and dig-in. Positions held against strong counter attacks. Commanding Officer killed by sniper during attack on strong-point (16/7). Relieved and to Senlis (17/7). Later to Hédauville, Amplier, Acheux, Mailly-Maillet. To front line Beaumont-Hamel sector (31/7), Forceville (5/8). Later to Varennes. To reserve positions Aveluy Wood (20/8), front line Leipzig Salient (27/8). Attacked Hindenburg Trench 4 p.m. (28/8) – strong resistance quickly drove assaulting companies back with great loss. In support during attack on Turk Trench (3/9). Withdrew to Black Horse Bridge. Rested at Bouzincourt between tours in front line. To Cramont (7/9). Returned to Bouzincourt and from there Zollern Redoubt and Hessian Trench (30/9). Attack on Regina Trench (21/10) – bombers took positions in Stump Road. Objectives taken and consolidated. To Hem-Hardinval (24/10). Entrained at Doullens for Bailleul (28/10).

11th (Service) Battalion (St. Helens Pioneers). Pioneers, 30th Division: At Copse Ravine, Maricourt sector (1/7). During operations at Montauban consolidated strong-points and dug 4 communication trenches across No Man's Land. To Bois des Tailles (4/7). Began work in Bernafay Wood and Glatz Redoubt (5/7). To Grove Town Camp (12/7) – 1 company to 18th Division for work on La Briqueterie Road. Later to Happy Valley. To Festubert sector early in August. By end September under orders of 41st Division at Montauban. Carried out road works in area. Active during 30th Division operations at Le Transloy (10/10)–(18/10). To Arras sector end October.

Welsh Regiment

2nd Battalion. 3rd Brigade, 1st Division: Entrained at Chocques for Doullens (6/7) and from there marched to billets at Bonneville. To Rainneville via Vignacourt (7/7), Franvillers (8/7), Albert (10/7), Mametz Wood (15/7) – later advanced to south side of Bazentin-le-Petit Wood and in action north-westward. Attack on communication trench (later called Welsh Alley) running north-east to the Switch Line. (16/7)–(17/7). To Bécourt Wood (19/7), Albert (20/7), Bécourt Wood (22/7), Albert (23/7), Contalmaison in reserve (24/7). Relieved 1st Gloucestershire in front line south-east of Pozières (25/7). Attack on Munster Alley (26/7). Casualties – 132. To Millencourt (27/7), Bécourt Wood (15/8). Moved to Quadrangle Trench under orders of 2nd Brigade (19/8). To Bécourt Wood (20/8). Later to Mametz Wood and from there assisted 1st Northamptonshire in action at The Quarry. Took up positions in old German line between Bazentin-le-Petit and High Wood (21/8). War Diary records an incident here involving a single German soldier who was shot while attempting to get into the trenches. His papers later revealed that he was returning from leave and was trying to rejoin his unit at the position that he left it. Relieved and to Albert (27/8). Casualties – 267. To Lozenge Wood (2/9), north-east corner of Mametz Wood (5/9). Attacked High Wood with 1st Gloucestershire (8/9). Casualties – 208. To Mametz Wood (9/9), Hénencourt Wood (11/9), Franvillers (12/9), Hénencourt Wood (16/9), Black Wood (18/9), trenches north and north-west of Flers (21/9), Bécourt Wood (26/9), Millencourt (28/9), Hénencourt Wood (29/9), – Fressenneville (3/10). D Company to Bécourt (28/10), Baizieux (31/10). To Mametz Wood (1/11). Work carried out on roads and the clearing of the wood. 'D' Company rejoined (16/11).

1/6th (Glamorgan) Battalion (T.F.). Pioneers, 1st Division: Moved at midnight from Fouquereuil to Doullens (6/7). To Vignacourt (7/7), St. Gratien (8/7). 'A' and 'C' Companies to Dernancourt (working around Contalmaison) and 'B' and 'D' to Bell Vue Farm (clearing battlefield) (12/7). 'A' and 'C' to Contalmaison (13/7). 'B' and 'D' began work on roads and at Scots Redoubt (14/7). 'A' and 'C' to Albert (19/7). Battalion worked on new front line trench between Pozières and Bazentin-le-Petit Wood. To Baizieux Wood (26/7). Working around Hénencourt Wood and Albert. To Fricourt Wood (15/8). Working at Martinpuich, High Wood, Contalmaison. To Baizieux (14/9), Fricourt Wood (19/9), trenches off High Alley and Elgin Avenue (20/9). Dug communication trench (1,000 yards) from Switch Line to Starfish Redoubt. To Fricourt Wood (28/9). 'C' and 'D' Companies to Bazentin-le-Petit (17/11).

9th (Service) Battalion. 58th Brigade, 19th (Western) Division: Moved from position near the railway, 1/4 mile south-west of Albert, through town and into Tara-Usna Line (1/7). Party of bombers took part in assault on La Boisselle (2/7). Later moved into village and helped consolidate and extend position. Casualties – 124. To Heligoland Trenches (7/7) and took part in attack towards Bailiff Wood. Regimental historian Major-General Sir Thomas O. Marden records that companies during the advance lost direction and became mixed up with brigade on their right. Subsequently the Welsh got into Contalmaison and after a brave fight came out of action under a company sergeant major, all officers having become casualties. To reserve billets at Albert (9/7) and from there to Baizieux Wood. Casualties – 174. Via Hénencourt, Millencourt and Albert to Bécourt Wood (20/7), via Fricourt to trenches in southern half of Mametz Wood (21/7). To Bazentin-le-Petit in support (23/7), front line (27/7), Bécourt Wood (29/7), Béhencourt (30/7). Entrained at Fréchencourt for Longpré (3/8) and from there marched to Pont-Remy. To Bailleul (6/8). Entrained at Bailleul for Doullens (5/10). Arrived (6/10) and marched to billets at Bois de Warnimont. Via St Léger, Coigneux, Sailly-au-Bois to line Hébuterne sector (7/10). To Sailly (9/10), Vauchelles (16/10), Hérissart via Raincheval and Toutencourt (17/10), Bouzincourt (21/10), front line (Stuff Redoubt) (26/10), Donnet Post (30/10), Bulgar Trench (2/11), Leipzig Redoubt (5/11). In close support (11/11). Relieved 6th Wiltshire in line at Stuff Redoubt (13/11). 'A' Company carried out raid near Stump Road and Lucky Way due south of Grandcourt (14/11). To Wellington Huts (18/11).

10th (Service) Battalion (1st Rhondda). 114th Brigade, 38th (Welsh) Division: At Puchevillers (1/7). To Franvillers (3/7), Heilly (4/7), Citadel Camp (5/7), Pommiers Redoubt (9/7). In support during 114th Brigade's attack on Mametz Wood (10/7.) Casualties – 314. To Citadel Camp (12/7). At 4.30 p.m. marched to Méaulte and entrained for Longpré. To Vauchelles (13/7), Domqueur (14/7), Couin (15/7). Took over line G sector trenches near Hébuterne (16/7). To bivouacs near Sailly-au-Bois (19/7), front line (23/7), Bois de Warnimont (28/7). Entrained at Doullens for Arques near St. Omer (30/7).

13th (Service) Battalion (2nd Rhondda). 14th Brigade, 38th (Welsh) Division: Moved from La Vicogne to Puchevillers (1/7). To Franvillers (3/7), Heilly (4/7), Citadel Camp (5/7), Pommiers Redoubt via Minden Post (7/7). On right of 114th Brigade's attack at Mametz Wood (10/7). Relieved and via Minden Post to Citadel (11/7). Here the roll was called and 12 officers and 350 other ranks were unaccounted for (casualty figures given in regimental history as 290). Marched to Buire at 6 p.m. Entrained at Méricourt for Longpré (12/7) and from there marched to Vauchelles. To Domqueur (14/7), Couin (15/7), reserve positions at The Dell – Hébuterne sector (16/7). Working parties dug trench (320 yards) in No Man's Land (18/7). To Front line (20/7), Sailly-au-Bois (23/7), Authie (27/7). Entrained at Doullens for Arques (30/7).

14th (Service) Battalion (Swansea). 114th Brigade, 38th (Welsh) Division: Moved from Septenville to Hérissart (1/7). To Franvillers (3/7), Heilly (4/7), Citadel Camp (5/7), front line (White Trench) Mametz Wood (8/7). On left of 114th Brigade's attack at Mametz Wood (10/7). Casualties 388. Via Citadel to Buire (11/7). Entrained at Méricourt for Longpré (12/7) and from there marched to Mouflers. To Gorenflos (14/7), Couin (15/7), reserve bivouacs south-west of Sailly-au-Bois (16/7). Relieved 10th Welsh in right sub sector Hébuterne (19/7). To Sailly (23/7), Authie (27/7). Entrained at Doullens for Arques (30/7).

15th (Service) Battalion (Carmarthenshire). 114th Brigade, 38th (Welsh) Division. Moved: Moved from Septenville to Hérissart (1/7). To Franvillers (3/7), Heilly (4/7), Citadel Camp (5/7), Pommiers Redoubt (9/7). In reserve during 114th Brigade's attack on Mametz Wood (10/7). Casualties – 245. Relieved in wood (12/7) and via Citadel marched to Dernancourt. Entrained for Longpré and from there marched to Buigny-l'Abbé. To Domqueur (14/7), Couin (15/7). Relieved 1/5th Gloucestershire in front line between Serre and Puisieux Road (16/7). To Sailly-au-Bois (19/7), Bois de Warnimont Wood (28/7). Entrained at Doullens for Arques (30/7).

16th (Service) Battalion (Cardiff City). 115th Brigade, 38th (Welsh) Division: At Toutencourt (1/7). To Acheux (2/7), Buire (3/7), Carnoy via Méaulte and Bécordel-Bécourt (5/7). Moved forward to Caterpillar Wood (6/7). With 11th South Wales Borderers lead 15th Brigade's assault on Mametz Wood (7/7). Attacking towards the 'Hammerhead' the Welsh were soon swept by machine gun fire from the wood ahead and Flatiron and Sabot Copses to their right. Withdrew later with 283 casualties. In support of 113th and 114th Brigades in Mametz Wood (10/7). Took up positions along railway running through western side of wood (11/7). In attack at 3 p.m. Relieved (12/7). Casualties – 70. To Couin via Warloy, Méaulte, Buire, Ribemont (13/7). Via Courcelles and Colincamps relieved 8th Worcestershire in right sub sector Hébuterne (14/7). To Courcelles (18/7), front line (22/7), Courcelles (26/7), Vauchelles-lès-Authie via Bertrancourt, Bus-lès-Artois and Louvencourt (28/7), bivouacs between Beauval and Candas (30/7). Entrained for St. Omer (31/7).

17th (Service) Battalion (1st Glamorgan). 119th Brigade, 40th Division: Arrived Boisbergues from Bonnières (4/11). To Nœux (15/11).

18th (Service) Battalion (2nd Glamorgan). 119th Brigade, 40th Division: Arrived Le Meillard from Fortel (5/11). To Rougefay (15/11).

19th (Service) Battalion (Glamorgan Pioneers). Pioneers, 38th (Welsh) Division: Arrived Puchevillers (1/7). To Méricourt 3/7), Grove Town (5/7), Minden Post (6/7). Worked on road repairs. To Loop Trench (7/7), Minden Post (8/7) – worked on Queen's Nullah. To Mametz Wood (9/7) – took part in operations there until relieved and to Citadel Camp (11/7). Entrained at Grove Town for Longpré (12/7) and from there marched to Gorenflos. To Thièvres (15/7), The Dell (18/7). Worked on trench improvements. To Bois du Warnimont (28/7). Headquarters and 3 companies to Authieule, 'B' Company to Beauval (30/7). 'B' Company entrained at Candas for St. Omer, rest from Doullens (31/7).

Black Watch (Royal Highlanders)

1st Battalion. 1st Brigade, 1st Division: Arrived Doullens from Béthune (6/7) and from there marched to billets at Naours. To Molliens-au-Bois (7/7), Baizieux (8/7), Albert (9/7), Scots Redoubt (10/7), front line Contalmaison (11/7). Enemy counter attack driven off (12/7) – later advanced – Contalmaison Wood taken and posts established along Black Watch Trench. Attacked and captured Lower Wood (13/7) – Contalmaison Villa (14/7). Relieved and to Divisional reserve at Albert. Casualties – 138. To Bécourt (17/7). Moved forward to support line (19/7), front line Bazentin-le-Petit Wood (20/7). To Lozenge Wood (21/7), Shelter Wood (22/7), Bazentin-le-Petit Wood (23/7), Baizieux (25/7), Bécourt (14/8), support trenches at Bazentin-le-Petit (15/8). Unsuccessful attacks on Intermediate Trench (16/8)–(18/8). Casualties – 158. To Mametz Wood (19/8), Quadrangle Wood in support (20/8), High Wood (27/8), Bazentin-le-Grand (29/8), Quadrangle Wood (31/8). Attack on High Wood (3/9) – crater from mine blown under enemy's line at eastern edge of wood being scene of fierce fighting. Casualties – 201. To Bazentin-le-Grand (4/9), Black Wood (5/9), Millencourt (10/9), Lahoussoye (11/9), Bresle (16/9), Albert (18/9). Took over line opposite Flers (20/9) and with New Zealanders made attack on Drop Alley – 'B' Company making the assault and gaining back recently lost ground. To Mametz Wood (21/9), front line Flers (24/9). Attack down Flers trenches in support of New Zealand assault on Goose Alley (25/9). Casualties – 119. Relieved and to Mametz Wood. To Bresle (27/9), Miannay (3/10), Hénencourt (31/10), Bécourt (5/11), High Wood (16/11).

4th/5th Battalion (T.F.). 118th Brigade, 39th Division: Arrived Lucheux (24/8). To Bus-lès-Artois (25/8), Englebelmer (26/8). Took over line between River Ancre and Beaucourt Road and attacked enemy positions opposite Hamel (3/9) – 'A' and 'C' Companies advanced from Giant's Causeway at dawn – objective reached but later driven back by heavy machine gun fire. Renewed attack with 11th Royal Sussex – German support line reached and held until 4 p.m. Withdrew to Englebelmer. Casualties – 218. To front line Hamel sector (6/9), Mailly-Maillet Wood (12/9), front line (19/9) – holding trenches on high ground north-east side of the Ancre, ½ mile north from Beaumont-Hamel. To Senlis (6/10), front line Thiepval sector (10/10). Here Battalion held south face of Schwaben Redoubt, the higher northern side still in possession of the enemy. To Authuille Bluffs (12/10). Attack on north face of Schwaben Redoubt (14/10) – 'B', 'C' and 'D' Companies advanced at 2.46 p.m. with 'A' in close support – heavy casualties from British barrage among leading waves – objectives taken and held. Regimental history by Major-General A.G. Wauchope notes just 30 men of assaulting companies relieved shortly after 10.50 p.m. Enemy counter attacks driven off (15/10). Relieved and to Martinsart Wood (16/10). Casualties – 290. To the Bluffs (22/10), Schwaben Redoubt (23/10), Senlis (25/10). In his book 'Haunting Years' William Linton Andrews recalls that during the journey to Senlis – several men lost their boots in the mud and had to make the 6 or 7 mile march in stockinged feet. He was also told of one man who sank to his armpits in the mud, and was trampled to death. To front line Thiepval (29/10), Authuille Bluffs (3/11), front line Ancre sector (8/11), Senlis (10/11), Bluffs (11/11), Schwaben Redoubt (12/11). Attacked (13/11) – captured tunnels at St. Pierre Divion by 10 a.m. and that night dug in behind Hansa Line. Casualties – 152. To Martinsart Wood (15/11) and later Warloy. To Amplier (16/11), Candas (18/11).

1/6th (Perthshire) Battalion (T.F.). 153rd Brigade, 51st (Highland) Division: From Arras sector moved to Bray (12/7). To Morlancourt (13/7), Halloy (14/7), Fienvillers (16/7). Entrained at Candas for Méricourt (20/7). To Mametz Wood in reserve (21/7), support line (22/7), front into line Bazentin-le-Petit (26/7). Attacked eastern corner of High Wood (30/7) – advanced within 30 yards of enemy's front line – heavy casualties in leading companies – held down under heavy fire until ordered to withdraw at daybreak (31/7). Casualties – 260. To Méaulte (1/8), camp between Buire and Hénencourt (6/8). Entrained at Méricourt for Longpré (9/8). Later moved to Armentières sector. Entrained at Bailleul for Doullens (30/9) and from there marched to Beauval. To Vauchelles (2/10), Louvencourt (4/10), Courcelles-au-Bois (8/10), front line Hébuterne (12/10), Colincamps (14/10), Bus-lès-Artois (17/10), Forceville (18/10), front line Beaumont-Hamel (24/10), Mailly-Maillet Wood (26/10), Forceville (27/10), Raincheval (5/11), Mailly-Maillet Wood (11/11), front line (12/11). Attack on Beaumont-Hamel (13/11) – heavily losses at Y Ravine before moving around its northern side and pushing on into village. Casualties – 226. To Mailly-Maillet Wood (14/11), Raincheval (18/11).

1/7th (Fife) Battalion (T.F.). 153rd Brigade, 51st (Highland) Division: From Arras sector arrived Halloy (15/7). To Franvillers (16/7), Dernancourt (21/7). Moved forward via Fricourt and took up reserve positions at Mametz Wood (22/7). To front line High Wood (26/7). On left of 1/6th Black Watch during attack (30/7) – 'C' and 'B' Companies followed by 'A' and 'D' went forward at 6.10 p.m. – rifle and machine gun fire from wood soon brought assault to a standstill and withdrawal ordered. Relieved and to Fricourt Wood (31/7). Casualties – 155. To Méaulte (1/8), Méricourt (6/8). Entrained for Longpré (9/8) and later transferred to Armentières sector. Arrived Doullens (30/9) and from there marched to Beauval. To Vauchelles (2/10), Louvencourt (5/10), Bus-lès-Artois (8/10), Colincamps (12/10), front line Hébuterne (14/10), Bus-lès-Artois (17/10), Forceville (18/10), Mailly-Maillet (22/10), front line

Auchonvillers (30/10), Mailly-Maillet (3/11), Léalvillers (5/11), Mailly-Maillet Wood (12/11). In support during attack on Beaumont-Hamel (13/11) – 2 platoons going into action with 1/6th Black Watch, remainder providing carrying parties. To Mailly-Maillet Wood (15/11), Arquèves (18/11).

8th (Service) Battalion. 26th Brigade, 9th (Scottish) Division: At Grove Town in reserve (1/7). To Billon Copse (4/7), positions at Montauban and Bernafay Wood (8/7), Carnoy (11/7), Breslau Alley (13/7). Attack and capture of Longueval (14/7) – advanced with 10th Argyll and Sutherland 3.25 a.m. – main objectives taken by 10 a.m. after hard fighting and heavy casualties. Positions 400 yards south of village held. Enemy counter attack driven off (15/7). Further action in village and Delville Wood (18/7) – 'A' and 'D' Companies with 2nd Gordon Highlanders recaptured north end of Longueval during morning. Counter attack in evening drove companies back but enemy checked and driven back into Delville Wood. Outflanked – Battalion withdrew and held line at Clarges Street. To Carnoy (19/7). Casualties – 568. Strength 6 officers and 165 other ranks. To Sandpit Camp (20/7), Villers-sous-Ailly (23/7). Transferred to Vimy sector (25/7). Arrived Mezerolles (5/10). To Albert via Franvillers (7/10), High Wood in old German trenches north-east side of wood (9/10). To Flers Line in support of 9th Division's attack on Butte de Warlencourt (13/10). Strong German flamethrower attack held off (19/10). Casualties – 203. To High Wood (20/10), Albert (25/10), Franvillers (27/10), Molliens-an-Bois (28/10). Moved to Arras sector (29/10).

9th (Service) Battalion. 44th Brigade, 15th (Scottish) Division: Arrived Longuevillette (28/7). To Naours (31/7), Mirvaux (4/8), Lahoussoye (5/8), Baizieux (6/8), Albert (8/8), forward positions north of Contalmaison (14/8). Attack on The Elbow (17/8) – 2 companies with 7th Cameron Highlanders taking and consolidating objective. Casualties – 157. To Scots Redoubt (19/8), front line (24/8), Albert (30/8). Casualties since (14/8) – 249. To front line between High Wood and Bazentin-le-Petit (6/9). Attacked just outside north-west corner of High Wood (8/9) – 1 German trench carried and counter attack successfully held off. Battalion's historian Major-General A.G. Wauchope recalls that 1 of the prisoners captured at High Wood belonged to the Bavarian division that had been opposite 9th Black Watch at the Hohenzollern Redoubt back in September 1915. He had on him a German trench map showing the Battalion's positions. To Albert (9/9), Shelter Wood (11/9), front line Martinpuich sector (17/9), Laviéville (19/9), Franvillers (20/9). Casualties since (12/8) – 402. To Bécourt (6/10), front line Le Sars (8/10), Bresle (10/10). Further tours in the line began after (20/10), Battalion resting at Shelter Wood and Scots Redoubt. To Bresle (5/11).

12th (Labour) Battalion. After work in Belgium moved down to the Somme (17/7). Billets at first in Bois de Tailles and later Carcaillot Farm just by Méaulte. Work carried out on roads between Méaulte-Fricourt-Mametz and Maricourt. To Montauban (29/9). Duties here being on road from Carnoy to Montauban and at Trônes Wood. Moved back to Belgium and Poperinghe area. (5/11).

Oxfordshire and Buckinghamshire Light Infantry

2nd Battalion. 5th Brigade, 2nd Division: Left Pernes (Béthune area) (20/7) and after arriving at Saleux marched to Corbie. To Happy Valley (23/7), reserve trenches Montauban (25/7). Relieved 2nd H.L.I. at Waterlot Farm (28/7). Unsuccessful attack (30/7) – 'B' and 'C' Companies making repeated attempts on Guillemont Station. To Montauban in reserve (31/7). Casualties – over 200. To Waterlot Farm (1/8), Montauban (3/8). In support of 6th Brigade between Bernafay and Trônes Woods (8/8). To Sandpit Camp (10/8), Ville-sur- Ancre (11/8). Entrained at Méricourt-l'Abbé for Saleux (13/8) and from there marched to Ailly-sur-Somme. To Montonvillers (16/8), Candas (17/8), Bus-lès-Artois in reserve (18/8), trenches Beaumont section (23/8), Courcelles-au-Bois (29/8), front line Beaumont section (4/9), Coigneux Wood (10/9), front line (16/9), huts north of Bus-lès-Artois (19/9), Sarton (20/9), Bus-lès-Artois (2/10), Mailly-Maillet Wood via Bertrancourt and Beaussart (3/10). Took over trenches from 1st K.R.R.C. Serre left sub-sector (6/10). Relieved and to Léalvillers (8/10). To Arquèves (17/10), Mailly-Maillet (22/10), trenches Redan sector (25/10), Mailly-Maillet (27/10.) 200–300 men daily provided as working parties to forward area. Relieved and to Mailly-Maillet (11/11) – Hotel De Ville being given in records as Battalion's location. Moved up to assembly positions after dark (12/11) – in support of 24th Royal Fusiliers during operations along Redan Ridge and towards Beaumont Trench – small party driven back from Frankfort Trench. To Mailly-Maillet (17/11). Casualties – 248. To Bertrancourt (18/11).

1/4th Battalion (T.F.). 145th Brigade, 48th (South Midland) Division: Behind Coigneux (30/6). Moved forward to Mailly-Maillet in reserve (1/7). Marched via Englebelmer and Martinsart to Mesnil (2/7). Planned attack cancelled and returned to Mailly-Maillet. To Couin (3/7), trenches G sector Hébuterne (4/7). Relieved by 1/1st Buckinghamshire Battalion and to bivouacs between The Dell and Coigneux (8/7). 430 men supplied for carrying back gas cylinders from front line. Worked on new forward trenches during night (10/7). To G sector (12/7). An interesting report by 2nd Lieutenant Rawlinson tells of a patrol of four men led by him during night of (14/7). Being attacked by a German raiding party seeking unit identification, 2 men were taken prisoner and another that was killed had his shoulder straps cut off. The officer, lying wounded and pretending to be dead, had his revolver taken and his pockets searched. To bivouacs between Couin and St. Léger (16/7), Bouzincourt (huts in orchards on west side of village) via Authie, Bus-lès-Artois, Bertrancourt, Forceville and Hédauville (17/7). For operations between Pozières and Ovillers, moved forward through Albert (18/7) and took up assembly positions just outside of town. Attack (19/7) –

lost direction. Casualties – 100. Withdrawal to Bouzincourt. Moved forward early hours (21/7) – bivouacked in field about a quarter of a mile outside Albert just on south-east side Bapaume Road. Attacked just east of Pozières (23/7). Casualties given as 11 officers and 73 other ranks killed – many wounded. Withdrew to Bouzincourt crossing the Ancre between Albert and Aveluy. To Arquèves (26/7), Beauval (29/7), Agenville (30/7), Beauval (9/8), Varennes (10/8), Bouzincourt (11/8). Took over trenches east of Ovillers (13/8). Heavy shelling on Skyline and Ration trenches – enemy attacks driven off. Relieved and to positions between Albert and Bouzincourt (14/8). Casualties 153. To front line (16/8), Usna Redoubt (18/8), Bouzincourt (19/8), Ovillers Post, later Usna Redoubt (21/8), trenches north of Ovillers (23/8), dug-outs Ribble Street, near Ovillers Post (26/8), Bouzincourt (28/8), Bus Wood (29/8), trenches east of Auchonvillers (5/9), Bus-lès-Artois (8/9), Beauval (11/9), Fienvillers (18/9), Warluzel (29/9), Warlincourt (1/10), Warluzel (17/10), Beauval (22/10), Talmas (23/10), Lahoussoye (24/10), Millencourt (31/10). Moved forward via Albert and Fricourt (1/11) and took over support and reserve trenches between Martinpuich and Le Sars (2/11). To front line (5/11), support lines (6/11), reserve area near Martinpuich (7/11), Bazentin-le-Petit Wood (10/11), support trenches (15/11), front line (17/11).

2/4th Battalion (T.F.). 184th Brigade, 61st (2nd South Midland) Division: Arrived Neuvillette (6/11). To Bonneville (16/11), Albert (19/11).

1/1st Buckinghamshire Battalion (T.F.). 145th Brigade, 48th (South Midland) Division: Moved forward from Coigneux to Mailly-Maillet in reserve (1/7). To Couin (3/7), Sailly-au-Bois (5/7), trenches Hébuterne sector (8/7), Sailly-au-Bois (12/7), Senlis (14/7), Bouzincourt (17/7). Moved forward to gun-pits just outside of Albert (19/7). In action south-west of Pozières (21/7). Casualties – 154. Withdrew to gun-pits (22/7). In action east of Pozières (23/7) – all objectives taken. Withdrew to gun-pits. To Arquèves (26/7), Beauval (28/7), Domléger (29/7), Beauval (9/8), Varennes (10/8), Bouzincourt (11/8), gun-pits on Usna Hill (13/8). Relieved 1/4th Battalion in front line (14/8) and attacked west of Pozières during night. Moved forward up communication trenches from Ration Trench clearing enemy from most of Skyline Trench by 5 a.m. (15/8). Relieved and to positions between Albert and Bouzincourt (16/8). To Usna Hill via Aveluy (18/8), Bouzincourt (19/8), Donnet Post and Ovillers Post (21/8). Moved to trenches between Thiepval and Ovillers (23/8) and attacked at 3 p.m. Casualties – 112. To Usna Hill via Aveluy (25/8), Bouzincourt (28/8), Bus Wood (29/8), trenches Beaumont-Hamel sector (5/9), Mailly-Maillet (8/9), Bois de Warnimont (10/9), Beauval (11/9), Berneuil (18/9), Coullemont (29/9), St. Amand (1/10), trenches Y sector Hébuterne (5/10), Souastre (7/10), Hénu (8/10), Warlincourt (9/10), Warluzel (19/10),

Beauval (22/10), Talmas (23/10), Lahoussoye (24/10), Millencourt (31/10). To support and reserve trenches between Martinpuich and Le Sars (2/11), front line Le Sars (6/11), support line (8/11), Acid Drop Camp, Contalmaison (10/11), forward area around Le Sars (15/11).

2/1st Buckinghamshire Battalion (T.F.). 184th Brigade, 61st (2nd South Midland) Division: Arrived Barly (6/11), Fieffes-Montrelet (16/11), Harponville and Vadencourt (17/11), Albert (19/11).

5th (Service) Battalion. 42nd Brigade, 14th (Light) Division: Arrived Sus-St. Léger from Arras sector (27/7). To Mezerolles (29/7), Berneuil (31/7), Buire (7/8), Fricourt (12/8), Montauban (19/8). Attack on Delville Wood (24/8) – moved forward on left of 42nd Brigade making good progress through wood, left flank being on Flers Road. Relieved and to Fricourt (26/8). Casualties – 170. To Pommiers Redoubt (27/8), Fricourt (28/8), Dernancourt (30/8). Entrained at Albert for Airaines (31/8) and from there to Epaumesnil. Entrained at Airaines for Méricourt (11/9) and from there marched to high ground south-west of Albert. To Fricourt (13/9), Montauban (14/9). Attack on Gueudecourt (15/9) – on left of Brigade advanced at a good rate and subsequently placed left flank in the air. Casualties – 156. Attached to 43rd Brigade renewed attack (16/9). To Fricourt via Pommiers Redoubt (17/9), camp near Amiens-Albert Road (18/9), Grand-Rullecourt south-west of Arras (21/9).

6th (Service) Battalion. 60th Brigade, 20th (Light) Division: Arrived Lucheux from Ypres sector (25/7). To Vauchelles (26/7), Courcelles (28/7). Relieved 10th South Wales Borderers in trenches opposite Serre (29/7). To Courcelles (6/8), Sailly Dell (13/8), Amplier Camp (16/8), Candas (18/8), Ville-sous-Corbie (20/8). Moved forward to Trônes Wood (22/8). Provided working parties for support and front line positions. Attack on Guillemont (3/9) – attached to 59th Brigade advanced from Arrow and Sherwood Trenches behind 10th and 11th Rifle Brigade – almost all officers soon lost and some 278 casualties before first objective reached. Withdrew to the craters at Carnoy (6/9). To Bois des Tailles (7/9), Corbie (8/9), Méaulte (11/9), Citadel Camp (14/9), Carnoy Valley (15/9). Took over trenches around Waterlot Farm (16/9). To front line (18/9), Citadel Camp (21/9), Ville-sur-Ancre (22/9), Citadel Camp (25/9), trenches behind Morval (26/9), Carnoy Valley (28/9), Trônes Wood (29/9). Attacked (7/10) – with 12th Rifle Brigade cleared enemy from Rainbow Trench. To Bernafay Wood (8/10). Casualties – 243. To camp along Bray-Albert Road (9/10), Daours (15/10), Cardonnette (18/10), Vignacourt (19/10), Le Quesnoy-sur-Airaines (1/11), Corbie (16/11).

Essex Regiment

1st Battalion. 88th Brigade, 29th Division: Moved up from Louvencourt for attack on Beaumont-Hamel (1/7) – advancing at 11 a.m. would not get much further than British wire – machine gun fire soon inflicting over 200 casualties. Remained in forward trenches (Mary Redan, St. John's Road) until (6/7). Withdrew to Mailly-Maillet Wood. To Mary Redan (10/7), Acheux Wood (17/7), Beauval (23/7). Transferred to Ypres sector (27/7). Arrived Saleux (7/10) and from there marched to Corbie and later Longueau. Via Pommiers Redoubt to positions north of Delville Wood (Switch line) (10/10). Took over front line trenches on outskirts of Gueudecourt (11/10). Attacked north of village (12/10) – storming with Newfoundlanders a section of Hilt Trench. Some of the Essex reaching Grease Trench. Relieved and to Bernafay Wood (20/10). Into line north of Flers (26/10). To Bernafay Wood (29/10), Mametz (30/10), Méricourt-l'Abbé (31/10), Sandpit Camp (15/11), Trônes Wood (18/11).

2nd Battalion. 12th Brigade, 4th Division: Moved forward from Bertrancourt for attack between Beaumont-Hamel and Serre (1/7) advancing at 8.35 a.m. on left of Serre Road crossed German line and then moved to right of Pendant Copse. Later strong counter attacks would force Battalion back to the captured Quadrilateral. By evening strength stood at 2 officers and 192 other ranks. Total going into action – 24 officers and 606 men. Withdrew to Mailly-Maillet (5/7). To front line (7/7), Bertrancourt (11/7). 12th Brigade took over part of line in front of Auchonvillers (17/7) – 2nd Essex being in reserve positions. To Vauchelles (21/7), Authieule (22/7). Entrained at Doullens for Ypres sector (23/7). Arrived Saleux (18/9). To Bertangles (19/9), Vaux (21/9), Cardonnette (25/9), La Neuville (26/9), Citadel Camp (8/10). Moved forward via Trônes Wood to trenches between Gueudecourt and Lesbœufs (9/10). Took part in operations until relieved by 2nd Scottish Rifles (20/10). Withdrew to Trônes Wood. To assembly trenches (23/10) and took part in attack east of Lesbœufs and Gueudecourt. Casualties – 255. Relieved and to Trônes Wood (25/10), Citadel Camp (26/10), Méricourt (28/10), Frucourt (30/10), Bouillancourt (3/11).

9th (Service) Battalion. 35th Brigade, 12th (Eastern) Division: In reserve at Hénencourt Wood (1/7). To front line (2/7). Attack towards Ovillers (3/7). In this action The Official History of The Great War records how 1 company lost its way and drifted to the right towards La Boisselle where it took 220 prisoners. In action (8/7) – advance of 200 yards into village made with loss of Commanding Officer Major C.I. Ryan. Withdrew to Albert-Bouzincourt line (9/7). To Varennes (10/7), Bois de Warnimont (11/7), Bertrancourt (21/7), Mailly-Maillet (22/7), Bus-lès-Artois (25/7), Varennes (26/7), Bouzincourt

(30/7), Albert-Bouzincourt line (8/8), front line north-east of Ovillers (10/8). In attack on Skyline Trench (12/8) – strongpoints established and held. Relieved and to Bouzincourt (14/8), Bois de Warnimont (16/8). Transferred to Arras sector (17/8). Arrived Bécordel-Bécourt (1/10). Moved forward to divisional reserve at Montauban (2/10). To Gueudecourt sector (Gird Trench) (11/10), Flers (16/10). Attack on Bayonet Trench (18/10). Relieved and to Montauban. To Fricourt Camp (19/10), Mametz Wood (20/10), Dernancourt (21/10). Transferred to Arras sector (22/10).

10th (Service) Battalion. 53rd Brigade, 18th (Eastern) Division: Moved forward from Carnoy for attack south-west of Montauban 7.30 a.m. (1/7) – Battalion historians Lieutenant-Colonel T.M. Banks and Captain R.A. Chell noting the blowing of Casino Point mine which filled the air with debris injuring some of the men. Assaulted Pommiers Redoubt with 7th Bedfordshire and 11th Royal Fusiliers at 8.30 a.m. – bombing party clearing 400 yards as far as White Trench. 'B' and 'D' Companies moved forward into Caterpillar Wood (3/7) finding enemy had retreated. Relieved from Pommiers and to Bronfay Farm (7/7). To Grove Town Camp (9/7), Bernafay Wood (14/7), Billon Wood (17/7). In action at Delville Wood (19/7)–(21/7). To Grove Town (22/7) – later entrained for Longpré. Transferred to Armentières sector (24/7). Arrived Acheux from Halloy (11/9). To Forceville (18/9), Acheux (20/9), Aveluy (24/9). In action at Thiepval (26/9) – fighting eastern side of village and occupying Zollern Trench. Further gains into Bulgar Trench and Martin's Lane (27/9). Relieved and to Forceville (29/9). To Montigny-les-Jongleurs (5/10), Fieffes-Montrelet (13/10), Hérissart (14/10), front line Courcelette sector (17/10). In action at Regina and Stuff Trenches (21/10)–(23/10). Relieved and to Albert. To Front line (Fabeck Trench) (30/10), Regina Trench (31/10), Albert (3/11), Warloy (4/11), Albert (9/11). To forward trenches (Fabeck, Regina) (11/11), Albert (14/11).

11th (Service) Battalion. 18th Brigade, 6th Division: Arrived Acheux from Ypres sector (4/8). To Mailly-Maillet Wood (6/8), Acheux (9/8), Mailly-Maillet Wood (10/8), front line Hamel sector (12/8), Mailly-Maillet Wood (21/8), Bertrancourt (27/8), Amplier (28/8), Gézaincourt (29/8), Vignacourt (30/8), Rainneville (7/9), Sailly-le-Sec (8/9), Sandpit Camp (12/9), camp between Carnoy and Méaulte (13/9). Moved forward (15/9) and attacked from north-west of Leuze Wood towards The Quadrilateral – advance halted by heavy fire from Bouleaux Wood (right rear). Withdrew to trenches outside Guillemont (16/9). To Méaulte (20/9), trenches outside Ginchy (22/9), Bernafay Wood (23/9). Moved forward into assembly trenches (24/9). Attack on Lesbœufs (25/9). Remained in action (consolidation of sunken road) until (27/9). Relieved and to trenches north-east of Talus Boisé (28/9). To Méaulte

(29/9), Ville-sur-Ancre (30/9). To Citadel area (8/10) and from there moved to forward trenches at Gueudecourt. To Trônes Wood (11/10), Gueudecourt trenches (13/10). Attack on Mild and Cloudy Trenches (15/10). Relieved and to Trônes Wood (16/10), Citadel area (19/10), Ville-sur-Ancre (22/10), Wiry (23/10), Dreuil and Allery (25/10). Entrained at Pont-Remy for Béthune sector (29/10).

13th (Service) Battalion (West Ham). 6th Brigade, 2nd Division: Arrived Welcome Wood from Lens area (23/7). Moved forward to reserve positions north of Carnoy (25/7). To support (Breslau Trench) at Delville Wood (28/7). Relieved 17th Middlesex in Delville Wood (29/7). To Waterlot Farm (6/8). Withdrew to Carnoy (Mine Alley) (7/8). To Trônes Wood (8/8). In action at Guillemont (9/8) – attack south of the railway driven back. Relieved and to Happy Valley (10/8). Entrained for Saleux (13/8) and from there to billets at La Chaussee. To Vignacourt (16/8), Bernaville (17/8), Bois de Warnimont (18/8), Courcelles (19/8). Took turns in line Serre sector. To Bois de Warnimont (20/9). To trenches right sub section Sailly-au-Bois (1/10), Bertrancourt (3/10), Puchevillers (7/10), Bertrancourt (19/10), Mailly-Maillet Wood (21/10), front line (26/10), Bertrancourt (29/10), Mailly-Maillet (7/11), trenches Redan sector (11/11). Attack on The Quadrilateral (13/11). Withdrew to Mailly-Maillet (15/11).

Sherwood Foresters
(Nottinghamshire and Derbyshire Regiment)

1st Battalion. 24th Brigade, 8th and 23rd Divisions: With 23rd Division moved from Rainneville to Hénencourt Wood (1/7). Battalion had transferred with 24th Brigade from 8th Division in October 1915. To Dernancourt (4/7). Moved forward that night and took up positions in support near church at La Boisselle. Attacked (5/7) – Regimental historian Colonel H.C. Wylly records that fighting continued for some hours at close quarters – by 7 p.m. all companies except 'D' had been driven back, and though this company had captured and made good its objectives, it also had to be recalled about 9 p.m. Relieved and to Dernancourt (6/7). Took up positions along Fricourt Wood and Lonely Copse (7/7). Later to Shelter Wood. Withdrew to Patch Alley (8/7). Relieved and to Dernancourt (10/7), Bresle (11/7). Entrained at Longueau for Béthune sector (14/7). Casualties since (5/7) – 326. Rejoined 8th Division. Arrived Doullens (14/10). Via Pont-Remy, Ailly-sur-Somme, Amiens and Ville-sous-Corbie arrived at Sandpit Camp (16/10). Moved forward to Trônes Wood (19/10) and from there to forward positions Lesbœufs-Gueudecourt line. Colonel Wylly notes the journey from Trônes Wood as 'through a veritable sea of mud' – by the time trenches were reached hardly a rifle was in working order. Relieved and to Sandpit Camp (29/10). To forward area (1/11). Relieved (20/11).

2nd Battalion. 71st Brigade, 6th Division: Entrained at Proven for Candas (2/8). Arrived (3/8) and marched to billets at Beauval. To Mailly-Maillet Wood (5/8) and from there began tours of duty in trenches west of Beaumont-Hamel. Relieved and to Beauval (29/8). Later via Flesselles, Allonville, and Méricourt to Méaulte – arriving (7/9). Moved forward to trenches around Arrow Head Copse (11/9). In action at The Quadrilateral (13/9)–(17/9). Relieved and to Maltz Horn Farm. To Ville-sur-Ancre (19/9), front line (24/9) – trenches taken over north-west of Ginchy-Lesbœufs Road. Casualties for September – 654. From positions north of Lesbœufs carried out successful raid on German gun pits (15/10). Gains held and consolidated. Relieve by 2nd Northamptonshire and to Bernafay Wood (19/10). To Corbie (20/10). Entrained for Béthune sector (24/10).

1/5th Battalion (T.F.). 139th Brigade, 46th (North Midland) Division: Attack on Gommecourt (1/7) – moved forward from Foncquevillers during early morning – advanced 7.30 a.m. – machine gun fire swept leading waves as soon as they left parapet – small parties crossed German front line, then attacked from rear and cut off. Relieved 7 p.m. and to Bienvillers. Casualties – 494. Captain John Leslie Green (Medical Officer) awarded Victoria Cross – while wounded and under constant fire, Captain Green rescued an officer from the enemy's wire and was later killed while attempting to bring him in to safety. Arrived Third Army Training Area (St. Riquier) beginning of November.

1/6th Battalion (T.F.). 139th Brigade, 46th (North Midland) Division: Moved forward from Foncquevillers and in support for attack on Gommecourt (1/7). Withdrew to Bienvillers, Gaudiempré areas (2/7). Arrived Third Army Training Area (St. Riquier) beginning November.

1/7th (Robin Hood) Battalion (T.F.). 139th Brigade, 46th (North Midland) Division: Moved forward from Foncquevillers for attack on Gommecourt (1/7) – on left of Brigade's advance soon swept by heavy machine gun fire and leading waves driven back. Casualties given in Official History of The Great War as 409 out of an attacking force of 536. Withdrew to Bienvillers area. Arrived Third Army Training Area (St. Riquier) beginning November.

1/8th Battalion (T.F.). 139th Brigade, 46th (North Midland) Division: To assembly positions in front of Foncquevillers during night (30/6). Attack on Gommecourt (1/7) – from reserve line advanced about 8 a.m. – forward British trenches blown in and crowded with dead and wounded. Took over British front line during evening – 'A' Company searched No Man's Land for casualties. Relieved and to Gaudiempré (2/7). Arrived Neuvillette from Le Souich (1/11). To Maison Ponthieu and Third Army Training Area (3/11).

9th (Service) Battalion. 33rd Brigade, 11th (Northern) Division: Entrained at Frévent for Acheux (2/9). To Bouzincourt (5/9). Relieved 13th Cheshire in trenches at Ovillers (6/9). Withdrew to Ovillers Post and Donnet Post (12/9). To support positions (15/9), Constance Trench (16/9) – held against enemy counter attacks. To Mailly-Maillet (22/9). To Ovillers Post (25/9) and from there forward to Constance Trench. Attack on Schwaben, Zollern and Joseph Trenches 12.35 p.m. (26/9) – first objective taken by 12.48 p.m., second gained by 'B' and 'C' Companies by 1.45 p.m., third by 2.30 p.m. Advance continued – Official History of the Great War notes parts of all 4 companies later in Hessian Trench – more than half of 33rd Brigade's casualties (600) being sustained by the Foresters. Gains held until relieved by 1st Wiltshire and to Hédauville (30/9). Casualties for September – 492. To Acheux (1/10). Entrained for Candas (2/10) and from there marched to Boisbergues. To Agenville (3/10), Mesnil-Domqueur (5/10), Coulonvillers (11/11), Fieffes-Montrelet (14/11), Vadencourt (15/11), Hédauville (16/11), Camp near Martinsart (18/11).

10th (Service) Battalion. 51st Brigade, 17th (Northern) Division: Moved up from Morlancourt 11.50 p.m. (1/7) – 'A' and 'D' Companies to Bécourt, rest to Bonte Redoubt. 'A' Company in bombing attack along trench leading from Fricourt Farm eastwards during night (2/7) – 170 yards taken. Later during day (3/7) – 'D' Company moved forward up communication trench from Fricourt Wood to Railway Alley – 200 yards gained. Relieved and to Ville (4/7). Casualties – 141. To original front line near Fricourt (7/7) and from there via Lonely Copse to Quadrangle Trench. Attack on Quadrangle support. Relieved during evening and to Willow Trench and Red Cottage. Casualties – 252. 'A' and 'D' Companies to Quadrangle Trench (10/7). Entrained for Saleux (11/7) and from there marched to Crouy-St. Pierre. Total casualties since (1/7) – 381. To Ailly-le-Haut-Clocher (14/7). Entrained at Hangest for Méricourt (23/7) and from there marched to bivouacs north-west of Buire. To Pommiers Redoubt (1/8), relieved 22nd Royal Fusiliers in Mine trench (4/8). To Longueval (5/8). Unsuccessful attacks on Delville Wood (7/8). Withdrew to Montauban Alley (9/8). To Mine Trench (10/8), bivouacs near Buire (12/8). Casualties since (4/8) – 227. Entrained at Méricourt for Candas (15/8) and from there to Longuevillette. To Neuvillette (16/8), St. Amand (21/8). Relieved 7th Lincolnshire in trenches east of Foncquevillers (27/8). To Brigade Reserve at Bienvillers (4/9) – 1 company in dug-outs west of Foncquevillers. To Mondicourt (10/9), Halloy (11/9), Bayencourt (17/9), Humbercamps (19/9), Humbercourt (20/9), Doullens (22/9), Frohen-le-Petit (23/9), Conteville (24/9), Mezerolles (2/10), Halloy (3/10), Bayencourt (4/10), trenches east of Hébuterne (6/10), Bayencourt (9/10) – 1 company at Sailly-au-Bois until (11/10). To Lucheux (19/10), Méricourt (22/10), Citadel Camp (26/10), Camp, Montauban (29/10), front line Gueudecourt sector (30/10), Mansell Camp (1/11), support line (5/11), front line (6/11), Camp, Montauban (8/11), Sandpits Camp (11/11). Entrained at Edgehill for Hangest (15/11) and from there 'A' and 'B' Companies to Quesnoy. To Picquigny (16/11).

11th (Service) Battalion. 70th Brigade, 8th and 23rd Divisions: Attack on Ovillers (1/7) – heavy casualties moving forward to British front line from reserve at Authuille Wood – advanced to German first line – machine gun fire from front and both flanks holted attack in No Man's Land. Relieved at night and to Long Valley. Casualties – 518. To Dernancourt (2/7). Entrained for Ailly-sur-Somme (3/7) and from there marched to Agrœuves. Entrained at Saleux for Bryas (6/7) and from there to Bruay. Entrained at Pernes for Longueau (15/7) and from there marched to Poulainville. To Pierregot (17/7), Baizieux (20/7), bivouacs near Contalmaison (26/7), trenches north of Bazent-in-le-Petit (29/7). Withdrew to support trenches near Mametz Wood (2/8). To Franvillers (8/8). Entrained at Fréchencourt for Longpré (11/8) and from there marched to Pont-Remy. Entrained for Bailleul (13/8). Entrained at St. Omer for Longueau (10/9) and from there marched to Cardonnette. To Bresle (12/9), Black Wood (15/9), Contalmaison (18/9) – took over dug-outs in The Cutting. Carrying parties provided to front line. To Lozenge Wood (20/9). War Diary notes during following days the finding and burial in front of Authuille Wood of men from the Battalion killed on (1/7). Relieved 13th D.L.I. in front line (Push Alley – Prue Trench) (26/9). 'C' Company took 26th Avenue without loss (27/9). Attacks on Destremont Farm (28/9) – withdrew to support line. Attacked (1/10) – moved forward from The Tangle into assembly position in Destremont Trench 9.15 a.m. Attack on Flers Trench and Flers Support near Le Sars – 'A' Company on Right, 'D' on left – objective taken and consolidated. Relieved in evening (2/10) and to Lozenge Wood. Casualties – 169. Moved forward to Gourlay Trench in support of attack on Le Sars (7/10). Withdrew via Lozenge Wood and Fricourt to Bresle Wood Camp (8/10). Entrained at Albert for Longpré (12/10) and from there marched to Pont-Remy. To Gapennes (14/10). Entrained at St. Riquier for Proven (15/10).

12th (Service) Battalion (Pioneers). Pioneers, 24th Division: Arrived Saleux from Godewaersvelde (25/7). To Camps-en-Amiénois (26/7). Entrained at Picquigny for Méricourt (31/7) and from there marched to Morlancourt. To Citadel Camp (1/8), bivouacs south-east of Mametz and north-east of Carnoy (5/8). Worked in Bernafay Wood, Montauban, Trônes Wood and Guillemont areas. To Citadel Camp (23/8), billets near Heilly (27/8), Fricourt (30/8). Worked in Pommiers Redoubt, Crucifix Alley, Savoy Trench, Orchard Trench, Tea Trench, Montauban Alley. To Pont-Remy (17/9), Ferfay (19/9).

15th (Service) Battalion (Nottingham). 105th Brigade, 35th Division: Entrained at Chocques for Bouquemaison (3/7) and from there marched to Sus-St. Léger. To Beauval (7/7), Bus-lès-Artois (10/7), Warloy (11/7), Heilly (12/7), Grove Town Camp (13/7), Billon Wood (14/7). Relieved 6th Northamptonshire in trenches south-east of Trônes Wood (16/7). Attack on positions between Maltz Horn Farm and Arrow Head Copse (20/7). Withdrew at night and to Talus Boisé. To bivouacs near Minden Post (22/7), reserve line (Silesia Trench) (24/7). Consolidated position and 'Z' Company formed garrison at La Briqueterie (25/7). To Talus Boisé (26/7), Dublin Trench (28/7), bivouacs near Minden Post (29/7), Sandpit Valley (31/7), Bois des Tailles (1/8). Entrained at Méricourt for Saleux (5/8). To Molliens-Vidame (6/8). Entrained at Hangest for Méricourt (10/8) and from there marched to Citadel Camp. To Talus Boisé (20/8), Maltz Horn Trenches (22/8), Billon

Wood (23/8), Sandpit Valley (26/8), Bois des Tailles (28/8). Entrained at Heilly for Candas (30/8) and from there marched to Prouville. To Lucheux (1/9) and from there in buses to Wanquetin.

16th (Service) Battalion (Chatsworth Rifles). 117th Brigade, 39th Division: Arrived Neuvillette from Buneville (24/8). To Authie (25/8), Beaussart (28/8), front line Beaucourt sector (2/9). In reserve, provided carrying parties during attack (3/9). Relieved in evening and to Mailly-Maillet Wood. Casualties – 101. To Beaussart (4/9). front line (6/9), Beaussart (13/9), Bertrancourt (19/9), front line Hébuterne sector (20/9), Bertrancourt (1/10), Martinsart Wood (3/10), front line Schwaben Redoubt (5/10). Enemy attack with flamethrowers beaten off during night (7/10). Attacked 4.30 a.m. (9/10) forced to retire after 2 hours fighting. Relieved at 1 p.m. and to Authuille. Casualties – 238. To Senlis (10/10), front line left River section (15/10), Senlis (25/10), support line (27/10), Martinsart Wood (29/10), front line (Paisley Dump) (3/11),Senlis (5/11), Paisley Dump (6/11), South Bluff (8/11). Attack on St. Pierre Divion (13/11) – moved forward at 6.15 a.m. up the Ancre Valley from Mill Road – objectives taken. Relieved and to Paisley Avenue at 7.15 p.m. To Warloy (14/11).

17th (Service) Battalion. (Welbeck Rangers) – 117th Brigade, 39th Division: Entrained at Ligny-St. Flochel for Bouquemaison (24/8) and from there marched to Doullens. To Vauchelles-lès-Authie (25/8), Bertrancourt (28/8). Moved into trenches due south of Beaumont-Hamel (2/9). Attacked (3/9) – War Diary notes 20 officers and 650 other ranks going into action – advanced into No Man's Land 5.10 a.m. – German front line captured 6.00 a.m. – assault on second line held up by strong machine gun fire. Ordered to withdraw to Gordon Trench 1.50 p.m. To Mailly-Maillet Wood 7.30 p.m. Casualties – 454. To Bertrancourt (4/9), Mailly-Maillet Wood (6/9), front line (12/9), Beaussart (19/9), front line Serre sector (20/9), Bertrancourt (30/9), Hédauville (2/10), front line Thiepval sector (5/10). Enemy attack with flamethrowers driven back (8/10). To Martinsart Wood (10/10), front line Thiepval (River section) (16/10), North and South Bluffs (20/10). Carrying parties to front line – 'A' Company attacked south of River Ancre (21/10) – some ground gained near Pope's Nose. Took over former German front line in Thiepval (22/10). To North and South Bluffs (23/10), front line (24/10), South and Centre Bluffs (25/10), front line (27/10). Successful bombing attack 4.30 p.m. (29/10). Later relieved and to Senlis. To front line (3/11), Martinsart Wood (5/11), front line (6/11), Pioneer Road (8/11), Senlis (10/11). Moved forward to Paisley Avenue in reserve for attack (13/11) – 'A' and 'D' Companies sent forward to clear dugouts in captured trenches 9.15 a.m. Gains consolidated. Battalion H.Q. to Spey Side. Relieved and to Warloy (14/11). To Gézaincourt (15/11). Entrained at Candas for St. Omer (17/11).

20th (Labour) Battalion. Entrained at Bailleul for Acheux (4/8). Worked Albert, Contay, Senlis areas.

Loyal North Lancashire Regiment

1st Battalion. 2nd Brigade, 1st Division: Arrived Candas (7/7) and from there marched to Flesselles. To Fréchencourt (8/7), Bresle (9/7), Bécourt Wood (10/7), assembly positions western edge of Bazentin-le-Petit Wood (14/7). Attacked 9 a.m. (15/7) – 'A' and 'B' Companies took 300 yards of German front line and part of second from west edge of Bazentin-le-Petit Wood. Relieved and to Bazentin-le-Petit. To Bécourt Wood (16/7), reserve positions – Black Watch Alley, Quadrangle Trench, Peake Wood (18/7). Moved forward to trenches in front of Contalmaison (22/7). Attack on Munster Alley (23/7) – advanced at 2.30 a.m. – heavy machine gun fire forced withdrawal. To Bécourt Wood (24/7), Franvillers (26/7), Hénencourt Wood (30/7), Bécourt Wood (13/8), Mametz Wood (14/8). Relieved 2nd Royal Sussex in front line High Wood (17/8). In action (18/8) – 2 companies assaulted enemy line on north-western edge of wood at 2.45 p.m. – Official History of The Great War records that right company advanced too soon and was almost annihilated by the British barrage – left company reached objective without much opposition – confused fighting followed – gains consolidated. To Mametz Wood (19/8), Black Wood (20/8), Quadrangle Trench (27/8), Mametz Wood (31/8), Bécourt Wood (2/9), Mametz Wood (5/9). In reserve for attack on High Wood (9/9) – moved to Great North Road just south of Bazentin-le-Petit 6.30 p.m. and employed in digging communication trench. To Mametz Wood (10/9), Albert (11/9), Bazieux Wood (12/9), Bresle (13/9), bivouacs just south of Mametz Wood (19/9), Black Wood (20/9), front line Eaucourt l'Abbaye (25/9). Failed attack (26/9). Attacked (27/9) – 'B' Company under heavy machine gun and rifle fire – Flers Line taken. Block pushed forward 100 yards (28/9). Withdrew to Black Wood and from there to Millencourt (29/9). Casualties since (25/9) – 212. To Laviéville (3/10) and from there in buses to Chépy. To Bresle (31/10), Albert (5/11), support line near Bazentin-le-Grand (18/11).

1/4th Battalion (T.F.). 164th Brigade, 55th (West Lancashire) Division: Arrived Longuevillette (21/7). To Franqueville (22/7), Fienvillers (24/7). Entrained at Candas for Méricourt (25/7) and from there marched to Méaulte. To Happy Valley (26/7), Dublin and Casement Trenches near Guillemont (30/7). Took turns in line near Arrow Head Copse. Two platoons of 'D' Company attacked (5/8) – some ground gained (6/8). Relieved and to bivouacs south-west of Carnoy. To reserve positions Trônes Wood (7/8). Assembled east and west of Trônes Wood-Guillemont Road for attack on Guillemont (8/8) – War Diary notes confused fighting and loss of direction. Casualties – 221. Relieved and to Carnoy (9/8). To Méricourt (14/8). Entrained for Abbeville (19/8) and from there marched via Cambron and Gouy to billets at Saigneville. Entrained for Méricourt (30/8) and from there to Millencourt.

Casualties for August – 301. To camp near Fricourt (6/9). Took over trenches running from eastern side of Delville Wood towards Ginchy (7/9). Attacked (9/9) – Regimental historian records Battalion going forward at 5.25 a.m. – first objective – Hop Alley gained but second wave did not succeed in reaching Ale Alley. Hop Alley came under intense machine gun barrage and gunfire – survivors of 'B' and 'C' Companies withdrew to their original line. Casualties – 236. Relieved from forward area and to billets near Fricourt (12/9). To Ribemont (13/9), Buire (16/9), Fricourt (17/9), Mametz (19/9). Working parties provided to dig communication trench through Longueval. To front line near Flers (24/9). Relieved 1/7th King's in Gird Trench near Gueudecourt (26/9). In support during 164th Brigade's attack. Moved forward to captured positions (Gird Support) (27/9) – 1 company occupying sunken road running into Gueudecourt. Relieved by 10th Royal West Kent and via Mametz to Dernancourt (29/9). Casualties for September – 394. Entrained at Edgehill for L'Etoile (1/10). Entrained at Longpré for Poperinghe (3/10)

1/5th Battalion (T.F.). 166th Brigade, 55th (West Lancashire) Division: Arrived Neuvillette from Grand-Rullecourt (20/7). To Ribeaucourt (21/7). Entrained at Candas for Méricourt (25/7) and from there marched to Ville-sous-Corbie. To Sandpit Camp (27/7), Mansell Copse (30/7), Oxford Copse (1/8), bivouacs near Citadel Camp (6/8). In support during operations at Guillemont (8/8). Took part in failed attack (9/8). Consolidated line until relieved 8 p.m. (10/8). Casualties – 138. To Maltz Horn sector (12/8). Attacked (13/8) – leading waves soon driven back by strong machine gun fire. Relieved and to Méaulte (15/8). Entrained at Edgehill for Martainneville (19/8) and from there marched to Fresneville. To Ercourt (29/8). Entrained at Pont-Remy for Méricourt (30/8) and from there to bivouacs south-east of Albert. To front line Delville Wood (5/9). Relieved and to camp near Dernancourt (12/9). Casualties since (5/9) – 162. Moved forward to positions south of Albert (16/9), Pommiers Redoubt (17/9). Took over support line in Switch Trench (on right of Flers Road) at midnight. Worked on new communication trench (South Lancs Alley). To Pommiers Redoubt (23/9), Ribemont (28/9). Entrained at Edgehill for Longpré (30/9) and from there marched to Pont-Remy. Entrained at Abbeville for Proven (2/10).

7th (Service) Battalion. 56th Brigade, 19th (Western) Division: Moved forward to Tara-Usna Line in preserve (1/7) – planned attack on Ovillers cancelled. Relieved and to Railway cutting at Albert (2/7). To Tara-Usna Line in support (3/7). In action at La Boisselle (4/7)–(7/7). Relieved and to bivouacs to the rear of Tara-Usna Line. Via Albert to Hénencourt Wood (9/7), Bazentin-le-Petit via Fricourt (19/7). Attack on Intermediate Line (23/7) – withdrew to Mametz Wood after heavy casualties. Casualties since (19/7) – 301. To

Franvillers (29/7). Entrained at Fréchencourt for Longpré (1/8) and from there marched to Villers-sous-Ailly. Entrained at Longpré for Bailleul (7/8). Arrived Doullens (5/10) and from there to Coigneux. To front line Hébuterne sector (11/10), Sailly-au-Bois (13/10), Rossignol Farm (16/10), Vadencourt Wood (18/10), Bouzincourt (19/10), Aveluy (22/10), Donnet Post (27/10), Wood Post and Leipzig Redoubt (30/10), Donnet Post (1/11), Splutter Trench (5/11), Aveluy (8/11), forward positions around Stuff Trench (12/11). Attack on St. Pierre Divion and Hansa Line (13/11) – War Diary notes between 100–200 prisoners taken – casualties 86. Relieved and to Aveluy (14/11).

8th (Service) Battalion. 7th Brigade, 25th Division: Moved from Léalvillers to Forceville (1/7). To Aveluy Wood (2/7), reserve positions Crucifix Corner (3/7). Working parties to front line Leipzig Salient. To front line (7/7), Aveluy Wood (8/7) – at midnight to bivouacs near Albert-Pozières Road about 1 mile from Albert. Moved up into line south of Ovillers 8 p.m. (9/7). Attacked (10/7) – fighting along trench towards rear of Ovillers were counter attacked several times and made little progress. Casualties – 247. Relieved during evening (11/7) and to dug-outs in La Boisselle. Provided carrying parties during attack on Ovillers (14/7). To bivouacs near Albert (15/7), Forceville (16/7), Beauval (18/7), Bois de Warnimont (20/7), Englebelmer (23/7). Relieved 1st Wiltshire in front line (29/7). To Bertrancourt (6/8), Vauchelles (10/8), Puchevillers (15/8), Hédauville (17/8), South Bluff in support of forward line Leipzig Salient (23/8). Unsuccessful attack on Hindenburg Trench 7 p.m. (26/8). To Léalvillers (5/9), Raincheval (7/9), Longuevillette (10/9), Prouville (11/9), Coulonvillers (12/9), Longuevillette (25/9), Raincheval (26/9), Hédauville (29/9), Hessian Trench west of Stuff Redoubt (30/9), reserve line north of Ovillers (3/10), Stuff Redoubt (8/10), reserve line (9/10), Stuff Redoubt taking over captured northern face (10/10). Enemy counter attack driven off (12/10). 'B' Company attacked 2.46 p.m. (14/10) – objective (The Mounds) taken by 2.54 p.m. with slight loss. To Bouzincourt (15/10), Rubempré (22/10), Longuevillette (23/10). Entrained at Doullens for Bailleul (29/10).

9th (Service) Battalion. 74th Brigade, 25th Division: Moved forward from Warloy to Bouzincourt (3/7). Began tours in line La Boisselle sector. Took part in operations around Ovillers resting around Bouzincourt, Senlis, Forceville, Mailly-Maillet. Began duty in trenches Beaumont-Hamel sector end July. To Bertrancourt (7/8), Auchonvillers (9/8), Bus-lès-Artois (10/8), Acheux (15/8), Hédauville (18/8), Thiepval Wood (19/8), Bouzincourt (26/8), Ovillers (28/8), Bouzincourt (6/9), Léalvillers (7/9), Puchevillers (8/9), Beauval (10/9), Fienvillers (11/9), Fransu (12/9), Beauval (25/9), Forceville (26/9), Hédauville (27/9), Martinsart Wood (29/9), Aveluy (1/10), front line (5/10). Attack on Regina Trench (19/10). Withdrew to Hessian Trench (20/10). Attack on

Regina Trench (21/10). Relieved (22/10). To Toutencourt (23/10), Beauval (24/10). Entrained at Candas for Caéstre (29/10).

10th (Service) Battalion. 112th Brigade, 37th Division: From front line trenches fired smoke bombs along 46th and 56th Division's front and formed defensive flank during operations at Gommecourt (1/7). To Bienvillers (2/7), Halloy (3/7), Millencourt (6/7), Albert (7/7), Tara Hill (8/7), front line La Boisselle sector (11/7). Withdrew to close support at Heligoland trenches (13/7). To Chalk Pit (16/7) – later in failed attack on Pozières. Withdrew to Tara Hill (18/7). To Albert (21/7), Lahoussoye (22/7), Bresle (30/7), Bécourt Wood (31/7), Mametz Wood (6/8), trenches east of Bazentin-le-Petit (10/8). 'A' and 'C' Companies attacked Intermediate Line 2.a.m. (11/8) – objectives gained by 2.30 a.m. – 200 yards taken. Casualties – 101. To Bécourt Wood (13/8), Bresle (14/8), Lahoussoye (15/8). Entrained at Fréchencourt for Longpré (18/8). Entrained at Longpré for Bailleul (20/8). Arrived Hem-Hardinval from Séricourt (21/10). To Marieux (22/10), Beaussart (23/10), Vauchelles (25/10), Amplier (30/10), Doullens (31/10), Vauchelles (12/11), Bertrancourt (13/11), Mailly-Maillet (14/11), front line (15/11) and attack on Munich Trench – Official History of The Great War records Battalion arrived in start positions just 40 minutes before zero – troops lost direction in mist and sustained heavy casualties among officers. Fell back to Waggon Road. Relieved and to Mailly-Maillet (17/11) and from there to Englebelmer. To trenches east of Hamel (18/11) moving forward at noon to Station Road in support of 6th Bedfordshire.

1/12th Battalion (Pioneers) (T.F.). Pioneers 60th (2nd/2nd London) and 32nd Divisions: Arrived Boisbergues (29/10). To Ribeaucourt (3/11), Ailly-le-Haut-Clocher ('A' and 'B' Companies) and Famechon ('C' and 'D' Companies) (4/11). Left 60th Division and to Bernâtre (5/11), joined G.H.Q. Troops at Wamin (6/11). Entrained at Hesdin for Albert (16/11) and from there joined 32nd Division at Englebelmer. To Mailly-Maillet (18/11).

Northamptonshire Regiment

1st Battalion. 2nd Brigade, 1st Division: Entrained at Lillers for Candas (6/7) and from there marched to billets at Flesselles. To Fréchencourt (8/7), Bresle (9/7), via Albert to bivouacs in Bécourt Wood (10/7), forward positions at Contalmaison (15/7) – Battalion's right on north-west corner of Mametz Wood. To front line (18/7). Raiding parties attack Switch Line north-east of Pozières (20/7). Helped dig new advanced trench (Lancashire Trench) and from there renewed attack shortly after midnight (22/7) – part of Switch Line held – withdrawal forced after strong counter attacks. Relieved and to Albert (24/7). Casualties – 268. To Franvillers (26/7), Hénencourt Wood (29/7), Maxse's Redoubt just east of Albert (13/8), Bazentin-le-Petit (14/8), High Wood (15/8). 'C' and 'D' Companies attacked and captured part of new German trench running westwards across Bazentin-le-Petit Road from High Wood (16/8). New line held against counter attacks and subsequently named 'Clark's Trench' after officer in command of position. Further action towards Switch Line (17/8)–(20/8) – post established some 300 yards in front of Clark's Trench. Relieved and to Bécourt Wood (21/8). Casualties since (15/8) – 374. To front line High Wood (31/8), Albert (2/9), support trenches near Mametz Wood (5/9). Moved forward for attack on eastern corner of High Wood (9/9) – leading waves of 'B' Company advanced at 4.45 p.m. and occupied crater formed by mine blown just before zero – enemy soon counter-attacked and forced withdrawal. To left of crater – 'D' Company checked by machine gun fire as leading platoons left trenches. Relieved and to positions near Bécourt Wood (11/9). Via Albert to forward positions near Eaucourt l'Abbey (25/9). 'C' Company in attack on Flers Line (27/9). Relieved and to Albert (28/9). To Acheux-en-Vimeux (3/10), Bresle (31/10), Albert (5/11).

2nd Battalion. 24th Brigade, 8th and 23rd Divisions: Moved forward with 23rd Division from Molliens-au-Bois area to Hénencourt Wood in reserve (1/7). Battalion with 24th Brigade had transferred from 8th Division to 23rd in October 1915. To Dernancourt (4/7), Fricourt (6/7). Moved forward to positions at Lozenge Wood ('C' and 'D' Companies) and Crucifix Trench ('A' and 'B' Companies) in support of attack towards Contalmaison (7/7). Withdrew to Birch Alley. Renewed attack checked at Peake Wood (8/7) – withdrew to Lonely Copse by evening. To Bresle (taking over billets from 1st Battalion) (10/7), Molliens-au-Bois (11/7). Entrained at Longueau for Béthune sector (14/7). Rejoined 8th Division. Via Ville-sous-Corbie reached Sandpit Camp (16/10). Moved forward from reserve positions at Trônes Woods to Lesbœufs-Gueudecourt line (19/10). Lewis guns assisted 2nd East Lancashire during successful assault on Mild Trench (23/10). Relieved and to Sandpit Camp (29/10). Moved forward for tours of duty in front of Lesbœufs beginning November.

5th (Service) Battalion (Pioneers). Pioneers, 12th (Eastern) Division: Moved forward from Bazieux Wood (2/7) for work in support of 12th Division's operations at Ovillers – Aveluy Bridgehead defences, Ovillers Post, Rivington Tunnel. Via Albert to Vadencourt Wood (9/7), Bus-lès-Artois (11/7), Beaussart (21/7). Work in forward area near Pozières (22/7)–(24/7). To Bus-lès-Artois (25/7), Léalvillers (26/7), Aveluy Château (27/7). In forward area – Ration Trench, Second Avenue, Third Avenue (5/8)–(16/8). Via Authieule to Bouzincourt (17/8). Moved to Arras sector (18/8). Moved from Barly to Villers-Bocage (29/9), camp near Albert (30/9), Pommiers Redoubt (1/10), bivouacs between Bernafay Wood and Trônes Wood (2/10). Working near Flers, Cocoa Lane, Flers-Longueval Road, Rainbow Trench, Flare Alley, Hilt Trench, Grease Trench until to camp near Albert (30/10). To Arras sector (2/11).

6th (Service) Battalion. 54th Brigade, 18th (Eastern) Division: In attack (1/7) – reinforcing 11th Royal Fusiliers and 7th Bedfordshire in Pommiers Redoubt at 8.30 a.m. Casualties – 160. To The Loop (6/7), Bois-des-Tailles (9/7), via Billon Wood to Maricourt (13/7). Attack on Trônes Wood (14/7) – Sergeant William Boulter winning Victoria Cross for his action against hostile machine gun. Casualties – 285. In Maltz Horn Trench (15/7), Arrow Head Copse (16/7). To dugouts south of Maricourt (17/7), Bois des Tailles (18/7). Entrained at Edgehill for Bailleul area (21/7). Arrived at Arquèves (11/9), to Hédauville (23/9), South Bluff, Authuille (25/9). Attack on Thiepval (26/9). Casualties – 169. To South Bluff (27/9), Mailly-Maillet Wood (29/9). Entrained for Candas (3/10). To Berneuil (4/10), Beauval (15/10), Warloy (16/10), Bouzincourt (17/10), Albert (19/10), trenches north of Courcelette (Regina, Vancouver, Hessian) (25/10), Albert (29/10), Warloy (31/10), Albert (4/11), trenches Courcelette (6/11), Mash Valley (10/11), Warloy (11/11), Albert (13/11), Mash Valley (14/11), trenches near Mouquet Farm (18/11).

7th (Service) Battalion. 73rd Brigade, 24th Division: Arrived Amiens and marched to billets at Molliens-Vidames (24/7). Entrained at Hangest for Vecquemont (31/7) and from there marched via Corbie to Sailly-le-Sec. To Happy Valley (2/8), bivouacs near Citadel Camp (8/8), original British front line in front of Carnoy (14/8). Digging parties in Trônes Wood (15/8). Attack on Guillemont (18/8) – heavy fighting at The Quarry. Casualties –

372. To craters at Carnoy (19/8), Sandpit Camp (20/8), Dernancourt (25/8), trenches Delville Wood (30/8). Attached to 17th Brigade and took part of Tea Lane during night attack (3/9). To camp near Fricourt-Méaulte Road (4/9), Dernancourt (5/9). Entrained at Edgehill for Villers-sous-Ailly (6/9). To Vimy sector (20/9).

Princess Charlotte of Wales's (Royal Berkshire Regiment)

1st Battalion. 99th Brigade, 2nd Division: Entrained at Diéval for Longueau (20/7) and from there marched to billets at Morlancourt. To Sandpit Valley (23/7), front line at Longueval and Western portion of Delville Wood (24/7). Attack at Delville Wood (27/7) – advanced from South Street to captured Princes Street. Casualties – 252. Withdrew to Mine Support – strength just 280 – 4 companies organized into 2. To Bernafay Wood (30/7), Mine Support (1/8), Delville Wood (3/8), Mansell Copse (5/8), Sandpit Valley (8/8), Méricourt-l'Abbé (11/8). Entrained for Saleux (13/8) and from there marched to St. Sauveur. To Naours (16/8), Autheux (17/8), Vauchelles-lès-Authie (18/8), Bus-lès-Artois (20/8), front line Hébuterne (25/8). Relieved and to Sailly-au-Bois (29/8), front line (4/9), Couin (10/9), front line (16/9), Couin (20/9), trenches Serre sector – Flag Trench, South Avenue (30/9), Mailly-Maillet Wood (6/10), Arquèves (8/10), Mailly-Maillet Wood (17/10), Serre sector (20/10), Bertrancourt (22/10), Mailly-Maillet Wood (30/10), Serre sector (2/11), Mailly-Maillet Wood (5/11), Arquèves (7/11), Bertrancourt (11/11), Serre sector – Ellis Square East (12/11), front line (13/11). Attacked (14/11) – on right of assault there would be high casualties while crossing No Man's Land towards Munich Trench, some 10 men being left out of leading wave of 159. 'Hardly enough' – the Battalion diary states, to cope with the enemy when his line was eventually reached. On the left – assault on Serre Trench would meet with more success. Casualties – 157. Relieved and to Mailly-Maillet (16/11). Moved in lorries to Terramesnil (17/11).

2nd Battalion. 25th Brigade, 8th Division: Left Long Valley Camp (30/6) to take up Positions in readiness for attack on Ovillers (1/7). Very early in assault leading waves met tremendous machine gun and rifle fire and by 9 a.m. over half of Battalion had been lost. Withdrew to Long Valley. Casualties – 437. Entrained at Dernancourt for Ailly-sur-Somme (2/7). To Riencourt (4/7). Entrained at Longueau for Béthune sector (6/7). Entrained at Lillers for Longpré (14/10). Via Ville to Citadel Camp (16/10), moved forward via Trônes Wood into reserve and support positions (Punch, Serpentine Trenches) between Le Transloy and Gueudecourt (19/10). To Larkhill and Spider Trenches (22/10). Followed 2nd Lincolnshire and 2nd Rifle Brigade into attack on Zenith Trench (23/10). Led renewed attack with 1st Royal Irish Rifles 3.50 a.m. (24/10) – assault stopped by heavy fire after advancing 70 yards. Relieved and to Punch and Serpentine Trenches (27/10). Casualties – 212. To Trônes Wood (28/10), Citadel Camp (29/10), Méaulte (3/11), La Briqueterie (8/11). Relieved 1st Worcestershire in front line trenches

Lesbœufs sector (Snow, Frosty, Shamrock Trenches) (9/11). To Hogs Back
Trench (11/11), front line (14/11). Relieved from forward area and to Carnoy
(16/11), Sandpit Camp (17/11), Métigny (18/11).

1/4th Battalion (T.F.). 145th Brigade, 48th (South Midland) Division: From
Couin into reserve at Mailly-Mallet (1/7). Moved forward through Mesnil for
attack south of Beaumont-Hamel (2/7) – operation cancelled and returned via
Mailly-Mallet to Couin (3/7). To Sailly-au-Bois (5/7), front line Hébuterne
sector (8/7). Battalion historian Captain C.R.M.F. Cruttwell recalls these
trenches as being waist deep in water and covered in dead from the 31st
and 56th Divisions. Relieved and to Sailly-au-Bois (12/7). To Senlis (14/7),
bivouacs north of Bouzincourt (18/7), trenches west of Pozières (19/7). In
support of 1/4th Oxfordshire and Buckinghamshire during attack on Pozières
(23/7) – objectives taken. Attack on enemy strong point driven back (25/7).
Relieved and to bivouacs near Albert. To Bouzincourt (26/7), Arquèves
(27/7), Beauval (28/7), Cramont (29/7), Beauval (9/8), Varennes (10/8), bivouacs on Senlis Road just outside of Bouzincourt (11/8). Moved forward to line
east of Ovillers (13/8). Attack on Skyline Trench driven back (14/8). Bombing
attack by 'B' Company north of Ovillers (18/8)–(19/8) – objective held.
Relieved and to Senlis Mill (20/8). To Usna Redoubt (23/8), Ribble Street
Trench (25/8), front line (26/8). Trenches south-west of Pole Trench taken
(27/8). Relieved and to Bouzincourt (28/8). To Bus-lès-Artois (29/8), Mailly-
Maillet (6/9), trenches facing Beaumont-Hamel (8/9). Captain Cruttwell notes
that during this tour a number of small German balloons dropped propaganda
material behind the lines. The leaflets written in French referring to the
bombing by French airmen of German towns. Relieved and to Bois de
Warnimont (10/9). To Beauval (11/9), Candas (18/9). At Candas, Captain
Cruttwell records the locals seeing the Battalion's formation badge (a blue
heart) were disturbed and until things were explained, locked their doors and
refuse entry to any of the men. Thinking that the insignia was some symbol indicating a practice whereas the wearer tore out the hearts of his enemy, it was
decided that the Territorials were some kind of specialist storm troopers and
possible as aggressive to both friend and foe. To Sombrin (29/9), Warlincourt
(1/10), Souastre (5/10), trenches opposite Gommecourt (12/10). Relieved and
to Souastre (14/10). To Warlincourt (19/10), Coullemont (20/10), Beauval
(22/10), Talmas (23/10), Bellancourt (24/10), Millencourt (31/10). Moved
forward to Lozenge Wood (3/11), trenches south of Martinpuich (6/11),
support line Le Sars sector (7/11), front line (Flers Trench) (8/11). Relieved and to Lower Wood (10/11). To Prue Trench, Crescent Alley, 26th
Avenue (14/11), Flers Trench facing Butte de Warlencourt (16/11), Prue
Trench, 26th Avenue (18/11).

2/4th Battalion (T.F.). 184th Brigade, 61st (2nd South Midland) Division: Brigade began move towards Somme during first week November. Arrived Vadencourt (17/11) and from there to Albert.

5th (Service) Battalion. 35th Brigade, 12th (Eastern) Division: Moved up from Franvillers into reserve at Hénencourt Wood (1/7), front line facing Ovillers (2/7). Attack on western side of village (3/7) – hand-to-hand fighting in Shrapnel Trench. Withdrew to Albert. Casualties 332. To front line (6/7), Bouzincourt (8/7), Bois de Warnimont (11/7), in trenches Auchonvillers sector (21/7)–(26/7). To forward positions north-west of Pozières (7/8), enemy attacks (8/8) – part of Ration Trench lost. To Ovillers (10/8), Bouzincourt (13/8). Transferred to Arras sector (17/8). Returned to Somme and reached reserve positions at Bernafay Wood (2/10). To trenches near Flers (8/10), in support during attack on Bayonet Trench (12/10) and (18/10). To Mametz Wood (19/10), Arras sector (21/10).

6th (Service) Battalion. 53rd Brigade, 18th (Eastern) Division: In attack south-west of Montauban (1/7) – advancing under the falling debris of Casino Point mine. Mine, Bund and Pommiers Trenches taken – heavy losses at The Loop. Casualties – 351. To Carnoy (2/7), Grove Town Camp (7/7). From Trigger Wood to Talus Boisé (18/7), in action at Delville Wood (19/7)–(21/7) – heavy fighting around Princes Street. Casualties – 176. To Grove Town (22/7), Armentières sector (24/7). Returned to Somme and billets at Léalvillers (11/9). To Bouzincourt (16/9). From Forceville to Aveluy Wood (25/9), in reserve at Crucifix Corner during attack on Thiepval (26/9), took over front line (28/9), repulsed enemy counter attack (3/10). To Hédauville (5/10), from Acheux to Candas (6/10). To Albert and later trenches near Courcelette (14/10). In action during capture of Regina Trench (21/10). To Albert (22/10), Regina Trench (29/10), Brigade reserve positions (31/10). Battalion rested between tours in line around Regina Trench during November at Albert and Warloy.

8th (Service) Battalion. 1st Brigade, 1st Division: Entrained from Béthune sector for Doullens (6/7), to Molliens-au-Bois (8/7), Albert (9/7). trenches near Lozenge Wood (10/7), front line at Contalmaison Château (11/7). Patrol took The Cutting – sunken road running towards Mametz Wood occupied and enemy driven from Pearl Alley (12/7). Pearl and Lower Woods taken (13/7). Attack beyond Bazentin-le-Petit driven off (14/7). To Albert (15/7), Bécourt Wood (19/7), positions near Lozenge Wood (20/7), trenches west of Mametz (21/7), front line facing Martinpuich and in support of attack (23/7). To Baizieux Wood (25/7), Bécourt Wood (13/8), Brigade reserve trenches at northern edge of Mametz Wood (14/8), front line north of

Bazentin-le-Petit and attack on Intermediate Line (18/8) – assault driven back. Casualties – 167. To support trenches north of Mametz Wood (20/8), right sub-sector High Wood (29/8), Mametz Wood (30/8). Attack on Wood Lane (3/9). To Bécourt Wood (5/9), Millencourt (10/9), Lahoussoye (11/9), Bresle (16/9), Bécourt Wood (18/9), Bazentin-le-Grand (19/9), trenches east of High Wood (20/9) – 1 company in support of 1st Black Watch in attack on Drop Alley. 'D' Company in Flers Line (22/9). To Bazentin-le-Grand (24/9), Bresle (27/9). Moved to Abbeville area (3/10). 1st Brigade moved to Hénencourt (31/10) but Battalion remained in billets until (27/11) due to epidemic of German Measles.

Queen's Own (Royal West Kent Regiment)

1st Battalion. 13th Brigade, 5th Division: Arrived Hérissart from Outrebois (14/7). To Franvillers (15/7), Méaulte (17/7), trenches between Bazentin-le-Grand and Longueval (19/7), forward trenches High Wood (20/7) – 'A' and 'B' Companies in the track coming from south corner of wood towards Longueval. Attack on Wood Lane (22/7) – on left of 14th Royal Warwickshire advanced up eastern side of High Wood at 9.52 p.m. – machine gun fire from wood soon brought attack to a standstill – almost all officer casualties. Withdrew at dawn. Casualties – 421. To Pommiers Redoubt (23/7), Longueval (29/7). In support of 2nd K.O.S.B. during attack north-western edge of Delville Wood (30/7). Relieved and to Caterpillar Valley. To Pommiers Redoubt (31/7), Dernancourt (1/8). Entrained Méricourt (4/8) and to billets at Métigny (5/8). Battalion historian – Major C.V. Molony notes that on (19/7) the total strength of 1st Royal West Kent stood at over 1,100 all ranks. At the end of the month its fighting strength would be just 350. Entrained Longpré for Méricourt (24/8) and from there marched to bivouacs north of Buire. To Happy Valley (25/8), front line positions near Falfemont Farm (26/8). Withdrew to Dublin Trench in reserve (29/8). Assembled in trenches western edge of Angle Wood (2/9). In support during failed attack on Leuze Wood (3/9). Attack on Falfemont Farm (4/9) – advance between farm and Wedge Wood towards Leuze Wood more successful. Casualties – 201. To Citadel Camp (5/9), via Méricourt to front line trenches Leuze Wood (10/9), Dublin Trench (11/9), Billon Farm (13/9), Méricourt (14/9), Waterlot Farm (18/9), Maltz Horn Farm (20/9), front line facing Morval (22/9). Commenced construction of new advance assembly trenches. To craters at Carnoy (24/9), Wedge Wood (25/9), Citadel Camp (27/9). Entrained At Edgehill for Longpré (28/9) and from here to billets at Les Planches. Entrained at Abbeville for Béthune sector (1/10). Major Molony records Somme casualties as 31 officers and 900 other ranks.

6th (Service) Battalion. 37th Brigade, 12th (Eastern) Division: Moved from Bresle to Millencourt in reserve (1/7) – during night to trenches just west of Ovillers. In action (3/7) – 'A' and 'C' Companies went forward 3.15 a.m. on left flank and under heavy machine gun fire reach German front line in front of village. 'B' and 'D' following suffered high casualties and could not force attack through to second line. Withdrew 7.a.m. and in evening to Bouzincourt. Casualties – 394. To trenches Quarry Post area (5/7). Relieved and to Warloy (9/7). To Vauchelles (11/7), Bertrancourt (21/7), Vauchelles (24/7), Martinsart Wood (25/7), front line between Ovillers and Pozières (26/7). Local fighting and attacks on strong-points for next few days. To support line Ovillers Post (31/7). Relieved 6th East Kent in Ration Trench

(4/8) and in evening took strong-point on left of position. Relieved and to Bouzincourt (5/8). To front line (Ribble Street) (10/8). Failed attack at 10.30 p.m. (12/8). Relieved and to Forceville (13/8). To Acheux (14/8), Bus Wood (15/8), Halloy (16/8). Began move to Beaumetz area (17/8). Arrived Lucheux (28/9). Moved in French buses to camp west of Albert (29/9). To Longueval (1/10), Gueudecourt sector (4/10), front line northern side of village (6/10). Attack on Ration Trench (7/10) – suffered heavily from bombardment before moving forward at 1.45 p.m. – leading waves cut down in No Man's Land. 'C' Company advanced 150 yards but held up until withdrawn at nightfall. Relieved and to camp near Bernafay Wood (10/10). Casualties – 308. To Ribemont (20/10), Wanquetin (21/10).

7th (Service) Battalion. 55th Brigade, 18th (Eastern) Division: In reserve east of Carnoy for attack towards western end of Montauban (1/7) – 'A' and 'C' Companies moved forward 11 a.m. to assisted 8th East Surrey in Train Alley – 'A' held up at Pommiers Line with loss of almost all officers – 'C' took and consolidated Montauban Alley. To Bronfay Wood (4/7). Casualties – 183. To Mallard Wood (7/7), Trigger Wood (11/7), positions around Bernafay and Trônes Woods (12/7). Attack on Trônes Wood 7 p.m. (13/7) – assault reached railway line in centre of wood and line set up along eastern edge. Surrounded and cut off – isolated parties fought throughout night until relieved by 12th Middlesex and 6th Northamptonshire. Casualties – 250. To Grove Town Camp (15/7). Entrained at Méricourt for Longpré (20/7) and from there to St. Omer. Back at Puchevillers for three weeks training by beginning of September. To reserve positions around Hédauville (26/9) – moved forward in afternoon to Crucifix Corner. To Thiepval Château (28/9), captured positions at Schwaben Redoubt (29/9) – held against fierce counter attacks from the enemy. Relieved (5/10). Casualties – over 280. Only 1 officer that went into action on (29/9) remained, and he had been wounded 3 times. In reserve during attack and capture of Regina Trench (17/10) – taking over and holding captured positions until relieved (29/10). From Warloy in first week of November to camp near Albert and from there took turns in reserve and forward positions. Attack on Desire Trench (18/11) – on right 'B' Company reached objective against strong opposition – on left 'D' lost direction and surrounded would be almost totally lost.

8th (Service) Battalion. 72nd Brigade, 24th Division: Left Béthune area (24/7) and in neighbourhood of Sandpit Camp by (31/7). From Talus Boisé to trenches east of Trônes Wood (11/8) – occupied in digging new positions. Historian of the Regiment C.T. – Atkinson notes that although there would be no direct contact with the enemy, casualties from constant shelling amounted to 152 by (18/8). 'A' Company moved forward to recently captured positions at Guillemont (19/8) – dug new communication trenches – established strong-points while engaging enemy. To Citadel Camp (21/8), Ribemont (25/8), Delville Wood (30/8). In C.T. Atkinson's opinion the move into Delville Wood was perhaps the most trying experience in the Battalion's service. The last mile in pouring rain, under heavy shell-fire and through deep mud taking 11 hours to complete. Enemy attacked after 5 hour bombardment (31/8) – assault driven off by 'A' and 'B' Companies in front line. To Caterpillar Valley (2/9). Relieved and to Abbeville area for rest and training (5/9). Casualties during Somme operations – over 300. Later moved via St. Pol area to Vimy sector.

10th (Service) Battalion (Kent County). 123rd Brigade, 41st Division: Moved to Somme end August and went into training in neighbourhood of Gorenflos. Entrained Longpré for Méricourt (6/9) and from there marched to Bécordel-Bécourt. To Fricourt Camp (9/9), Support positions Montauban Alley (10/9). Two companies sent forward to construct new strong points just in front of line north of Delville Wood (11/9). To front line Delville Wood (12/9), reserve line (13/9), Pommiers Redoubt (14/9), reserve at York Trench (15/9). Later to Carlton Trench and stood by for attack on Flers. At about 10 a.m. received orders to move forward and by afternoon held Switch Trench. Withdrew during night (17/9) and via Pommiers Redoubt to Bécordel. To Pommiers Redoubt (27/9), trenches north-east of Flers (28/9), Pommiers Redoubt (1/10), bivouacs near Mametz Wood (3/10). Moved forward and provided working parties in front line during attack on Gird Trench (7/10). To Mametz Wood (10/10), Dernancourt (12/10). Entrained Edgehill for Oisemont (17/10). Later, via Pont-Rémy to Ypres sector.

11th (Service) Battalion (Lewisham). 122nd Brigade, 41st Division: From Bailleul reached Longpré (24/8) and from there marched to training area south-east of Abbeville. Entrained Longpré for Méricourt (6/9) and from there marched to Dernancourt. To bivouacs south-west of Fricourt (11/9), support positions north-east of Delville Wood (12/9). Attack towards Flers (15/9) – behind 15th Hampshire cleared Switch and Flers Trenches before entering Flers village and reaching final objectives – Box and Cox Trenches. Regimental Historian C.T. Atkinson makes special mention of the bravery and leadership of C.S.Ms – Halley and Judge who for best part of the fighting led the Battalion. Both later awarded the Military Cross. Withdrew 5.p.m. to positions south-west of Delville Wood. Casualties (including Commanding Officer Lieutenant-Colonel A.F. Townsend) – 343. To Dernancourt (18/9), Mametz Wood (2/10), trenches Eaucourt l'Abbaye sector (3/10). Attack on Gird Lines (7/10) – assault checked by machine gun fire from both flanks soon after advance at 1.45 p.m. C.T. Atkinson records that out of 16 officers and 465 other ranks that went into action, only 4 officers and less than 100 men survived. These held the line until relieved (8/10). To bivouacs near Mametz Wood (11/10), Dernancourt (12/10). Entrained Méricourt for Oisemont (17/10). To Forceville (18/10). Entrained Longpré for Ypres sector (20/10).

King's Own (Yorkshire Light Infantry)

2nd Battalion. 97th Brigade, 32nd Division: Moved forward from Kintyre and Caithness Trenches just east of Authuille in support of 17th and 16th H.L.I. 7.30 a.m. (1/7). Regimental historian Lieutenant-Colonel R.C. Bond, D.S.O. records heavy machine gun fire from direction of Thiepval – many casualties before reaching British front line. Further advance held up – 'A' Company with parts of 'C' and 'D' on right made better headway and followed 17th H.L.I. into front trench of Leipzig Salient. Passed through to positions opposite Fort Hindenburg – close quarter fighting followed throughout subsequent attacks and counter attacks. Withdrew to Crucifix Corner (2/7). Casualties over 340. To Contay Wood (3/7), Senlis (7/7), Authuille Wood (8/7), Bouzincourt (15/7). Began move to Béthune sector (16/7). Arrived Hem-Hardinal (18/10). To Hérissart (21/10), Bouzincourt (23/10), Hérissart (30/10), La Vicogne (31/10), Contay (13/11), Englebelmer (15/11). Took up positions at Beaumont-Hamel (17/11). In attack on Munich and Frankfort Trenches (18/11) – right of advance held up by fire from strong-point in Munich Trench – 'reluctant to accept defeat' records The Official History of The Great War, the men hung on in shell-holes until dusk. On the left – assault swept over Munich and continued down the hill to Ten Tree Alley. Regimental history records Ten Tree Alley attacked from south and south-west – the occupants (with 2nd Manchester) 'fought till they died.' Relieved and to Mailly-Maillet (19/11). Casualties 365.

1/4th Battalion (T.F.). 148th Brigade, 49th (West Riding) Division: In reserve at Aveluy Wood (1/7) – moving up to Thiepval Wood during evening and from there taking up positions for attack at midnight. Assault cancelled and back to Aveluy Wood. To Thiepval Wood (2/7), front line (4/7). Enemy attack driven off. Bombing attacks (5/7). Came under attack (7/7) – many casualties from new German 'Egg' bombs. To Martinsart Wood (8/7), Hédauville (11/7), front line Leipzig Salient (21/7). Attacked (23/7) – heavy casualties while crossing No Man's Land and forced to withdraw. To Authuille (25/7), Aveluy Wood (1/8), Hédauville (2/8), Aveluy Wood (7/8), Forceville (18/8), Puchevillers (19/8), Aveluy Wood (29/8), Martinsart Wood (2/9), Aveluy Wood (3/9), North Bluff (4/9), front line Thiepval sector (5/9), Hédauville (20/9), Arquèves (23/9), Humbercamps (24/9), Foncquevillers (26/9), Sombrin (10/10), Hébuterne (19/10), Souastre (6/11), Hébuterne (12/11), Souastre (15/11).

1/5th Battalion (T.F.). 148th Brigade, 49th (West Riding) Division. Moved up from Aveluy Wood 6 p.m. (1/7) and stood by in assembly trenches at Thiepval Wood for proposed (later cancelled) night attack on Thiepval.

To front line (4/7). 'A' Company attacked (5/7) – all officers became casualties. Enemy's subsequent counter attack driven off. Relieved and to Thiepval Wood (6/7). Casualties – 278. To Martinsart Wood (8/7), Authuille (21/7), front line Leipzig Salient sector (25/7). Unsuccessful attack by 'B' Company (28/7). To Authuille (30/7), Hédauville (9/8), Puchevillers (17/8), Forceville (25/8), Aveluy Wood (26/8), Authuille (28/8), Hédauville (20/9), Raincheval (23/9), Humbercamps (24/9), Souastre (28/9), Warluzel (10/10), Souastre (19/10), Hébuterne (25/10), Souastre (12/11), Humbercamps (13/11), Bienvillers (18/11).

6th (Service) Battalion. 43rd Brigade, 14th (Light) Division: Arrived Prouville (1/8). Entrained at Candas for Méricourt (7/8) and from there marched to Dermancourt. To Mametz (12/8), Longueval (15/8). In reserve and support during operations at Delville Wood. To Fricourt (20/8), Montauban (24/8). Carrying parties to front line. Took over trenches in Delville Wood during night (25/8). 'X' Company in action with 10th D.L.I. (28/8). Regimental historian Lieutenant-Colonel R.C. Bond, D.S.O. records all officers of 'Y' Company buried by a shell 4.45 p.m. Relieved and to Mametz at midnight. To Dernancourt (30/8), Dromesnil (31/8), Métigny (11/9), Méricourt (12/9), Dernancourt (13/9), Méaulte (14/9), Montauban (15/9). 'W' and 'X' Companies (attached to 41st Brigade) attacked east of Delville Wood 5.20 a.m. – came under fire from rear after crossing Ale Alley. All officers lost – what remained of the companies under their N.C.Os turned back and with bomb and bayonet dealt with their attackers. Later advanced and into Switch Trench. 'Y' and 'Z' Companies in attack on Gird lines in front of Gueudecourt (16/9). Relieved and to Fricourt (17/9). To Ribemont (18/9), Buire (19/9), Le Souich (22/9). Transferred to Arras sector (27/9).

7th (Service) Battalion. 61st Brigade, 20th (Light) Division: From Ypres sector reached Bois de Warnimont (25/7). To Bus-lès-Artois (26/7), Mailly-Maillet (28/7) – began tours of duty Redan sector. To Coigneux (7/8), Courcelles (14/8), Bois de Warnimont (16/8), Sarton (17/8), Longuevillette (18/8). Entrained at Candas for Méricourt (20/8) and from there marched to Morlancourt. To Happy Valley (21/8). In reserve and support positions during Guillemont operations. To Méaulte (6/9), Méricourt (8/9), Sandpit Camp (12/9), Citadel Camp (14/9), Trônes Wood (15/9). In action Lesbœufs operations (16/9) – all Headquarters officers and some 30 other ranks killed or wounded by 1 shell. In support of 59th Brigade (18/9). To Méaulte (22/9), Maltz Horn Valley (26/9), Morval (27/9), Gueudecourt (29/9), Trônes Wood (4/10). Attacked east of Gueudecourt 1.45 p.m. (7/10) – 'D' company took first objective (Rainbow Trench) by 1.48 p.m. Cloudy Trench taken later. Relieved midnight and via Montauban to Méaulte. Casualties – 190.

To Corbie (15/10), Cardonnette (19/10), St. Vaast (20/10), Montagne-Fayel (1/11), Riencourt (7/11), Montagne-Fayel (10/11), Métigny (14/11).

8th (Service) Battalion. 70th Brigade, 8th and 23rd Divisions: In action (with 8th Division) at the Ovillers spur (1/7) – attacking from in front of Authuille Wood good progress quickly made by leading waves and German first line entered. Following waves came under heavy machine gun fire from both flanks, losing 50% while crossing No Man's Land – close quarter fighting in German second and third lines. Withdrew to British front line during afternoon – all officers having become casualties. Regimental historian Lieutenant-Colonel R.C. Bond, D.S.O. records renewed attacks led by N.C.Os. Relieved and to Long Valley during night. Survivors – the medical officer and 110 other ranks, 25 officers and 659 other ranks having gone into action. Entrained at Dernancourt for Ailly-sur-Somme (2/7) and from there to Agrœuves. To Saisseval (4/7), Bruay near Béthune (6/7). To Poulainville (16/7) – Battalion with 70th Brigade had transferred to 23rd Division. To Mirvaux (17/7), Baizieux Wood (21/7), front line Bazentin-le-Petit Wood (26/7), Shelter Wood (1/8), Franvillers (7/8). Transferred to Armentières sector (17/8). Arrived Allonville (11/9). To Bresle (12/9), Black Wood (15/9), Peak Wood (19/9), Lozenge Wood (20/9), front line (27/9). To Martinpuich – assembled near Destremont Farm and in action at Flers Trench (1/10) – high casualties from shelling before attack commenced – 'A' and 'D' Companies gained and held objectives against strong counter attacks. Withdrew to The Dingle (2/10). Casualties – 259. To Contalmaison (4/10), Bresle (8/10), Francières (13/10), Agenvillers (14/10). Transferred to Ypres sector (16/10).

9th (Service) Battalion. 64th Brigade, 21st Division: Took part in operations at Fricourt (1/7). Attacked with 10th K.O.Y.L.I. at zero – 2 lines of enemy trenches taken within 10 minutes. Withdrew (2/7). Casualties – 455. To Dernancourt (3/7), Picquigny (4/7), Riencourt (7/7), Ville (10/7), Bottom Wood (13/7), Méaulte (17/7), Bécourt Valley (18/7), Ailly-sur-Somme (21/7). Began move to Arras sector (23/7). Arrived Dernancourt (13/9). To Pommiers Redoubt (15/9). In action during operations at Gueudecourt – advancing from south-eastern side of Flers towards Gird Trench (16/9) – took cover in shell holes 50 yards from objective. Withdrew during night to Lesbœufs-Flers Road. Casualties – 389. Relieved and to Fricourt (18/9). To Pommiers Redoubt (22/9). In support of 10th K.O.Y.L.I. during attack on Gird Trench (25/9). To front line and consolidated gains (26/9) – later advanced and occupied part of Gueudecourt-Le Transloy Road. Relieved during evening and to Trônes Wood. To Pommiers (29/9), Ribemont (30/9), Buigny (4/10). Began move to Béthune area (8/10). Regimental history gives killed and wounded during July-September fighting as 44 officers and 955 other ranks.

10th (Service) Battalion. 64th Brigade, 21st Division: In action at Fricourt (1/7). Attack at zero with 9th K.O.Y.L.I. on right – enemy front trenches taken and held. Withdrew (2/7). Casualties – 502. To Dernancourt (3/7), La Chaussée (4/7), Le Mesge (7/7), Ville (10/7), Bottom Wood (12/7). In action at Bazentin-le-Petit (15/7). To Méaulte (18/7), Dreuil (20/7). Began move to Arras sector (23/7). Arrived Dernancourt (13/9). Moved forward to Pommiers Redoubt (15/9). In close support during attack on Gird Trench (16/9). Withdrew to Flers Trench (17/9). Casualties – 185. To Fricourt (18/9), Bernafay Wood (22/9). Attack on Gird Trench (25/9) – on right of Brigade, held up in uncut wire and swept by machine gun fire from the front. Advanced and occupied part of Gueudecourt-Le Transloy Road (26/9). Relieved during evening and to Bernafay Wood. To Ribemont (30/9), Bellancourt (3/10). Began move to Béthune area (7/10). Regimental history gives killed and wounded during July-September fighting as 49 officers and 1,097 other ranks.

12th (Service) Battalion (Miners) (Pioneers). Pioneers, 31st Division: Attack at Serre (1/7) – 'A' and 'D' Companies advanced with 94th and 93rd Brigades 7.30 a.m. Casualties – 192. Held line for a period after withdrawal of assaulting battalions. After work on rear trenches moved back to Bus-lès-Artois (4/7). To Beauval (6/7), Prouville (7/7), Conteville (9/7). Transferred to Béthune sector (15/7). Arrived Doullens (8/10) and from to Terramesnil. To Sailly Dell (13/10). Worked in Hébuterne sector. Engaged during operations (13/11).

King's (Shropshire Light Infantry)

1st Battalion. 16th Brigade, 6th Division: Arrived Doullens from Ypres sector (3/8) and from there marched to Authieule. To Puchevillers (4/8), Acheux (7/8), Englebelmer (10/8), trenches opposite Beaumont-Hamel (15/8). Three companies to Mailly-Maillet (20/8). To Bertrancourt (27/8), Amplier (28/8), Naours (29/8), Villers-Bocage (6/9), Corbie (7/9), Bois des Tailles (8/9), Maricourt (12/9), positions just south-west of Guillemont (14/9). Stood by for attack on The Quadrilateral (15/9) but later cancelled due to heavy casualties among 16th Brigade. Renewed attack (18/9) – Regimental historian Major W. de B. Wood – assault commenced at 5.50 a.m. – 'C' and 'D' Companies took objective by 6.15 a.m. – 'A' and 'B' passed through and took more ground beyond The Quadrilateral. Withdrew to Morlancourt (19/9). Casualties – about 158. To trenches near La Briqueterie (21/9), assembly positions south-east of Ginchy (24/9). Attack on Morval (25/9) – advanced 12.35 p.m. with second wave – objective taken by 3 p.m. In trenches between Morval and Lesbœufs (26/9). Relieved and to La Briqueterie (27/9). To Méaulte via Montauban and Fricourt (30/9), Citadel Camp (7/10), Trônes Wood (8/10). From there to trenches south-east of Gueudecourt. In support of 2nd York and Lancaster during attack on Zenith Trench (12/10). Relieved and to trenches near Ginchy (13/10). To Mansell Camp (19/10), Méaulte (20/10), Bailleul (23/10). Began move to Béthune area (28/10).

5th (Service) Battalion. 42nd Brigade, 14th (Light) Division: Commenced move from positions east of Arras during last week of July. Reached Candas (31/7). Entrained for Méricourt (7/8) and from there marched to Buire-sur-l'Ancre. To Fricourt (12/8). Part of battalion on loan to 43rd Brigade as reserve and subsequently involved in attack on Delville Wood (18/8). To trenches at edge of Delville Wood (21/8). In centre of 42nd Brigade attack (24/8) – advancing at 5.45 a.m. clearing enemy from edge of wood – right flank un supported withdrew to second line. Casualties – 201. To Fricourt (26/8), Delville Wood (28/8), Fricourt (31/8) and from there moved by buses to Méricourt. Entrained there for Airaines and marched to Vergies – arriving 2.30 a.m. (1/9). To Méricourt (11/9). Moved forward to Montauban and via Delville Wood into action towards Gueudecourt (15/9) – 'C' and 'D' Companies capturing 3 field guns at Bull's Road. Relieved and to Montauban (16/9). Casualties – 264. Returned same day to front line – attack cancelled and withdrew. Moved to area around Albert and from there to Grand-Rullecourt.

6th (Service) Battalion. 60th Brigade, 20th (Light) Division: Arrived Lucheux from south of Armentières (25/7). To Vauchelles-lès-Authie (26/7),

Courcelles-au-Bois (28/7). Moving into line opposite Serre (29/7) it fell to the Battalion to clear what is described by its historian Major W. de B. Wood as trenches 'waist-deep with our dead.' Relieved and to Courcelles (6/8). To Coigneux (13/8), Amplier (16/8), Fienvillers (18/8), Ville-sur-Somme via Méricourt (20/8), Sandpit Camp via Méaulte (21/8), craters in old German line at Carnoy (22/8), front line Guillemont (27/8), Carnoy (2/9). In action at Guillemont (4/9)–(7/9). Relieved and to Bois des Tailles (7/9). To Corbie (8/9), Méaulte (11/9), Citadel Camp (14/9), reserve trenches in front of Waterlot Farm (16/9). Several enemy attacks successfully repulsed. Relieved and via Citadel to Ville (22/9). To Citadel (25/9), Maltz Horn Valley trenches (26/9), Carnoy (28/9), Trônes Wood (29/9). Into line right sub-sector of Divisional front (3/10). In reserve for Battle of the Transloy Ridges. Some 200 men assisted front line troops to consolidate positions (7/10). Relieved and to Carnoy (8/10). To Corbie via Daours (15/10), Cardonnette (18/10), Vignacourt (19/10), Crouy-St. Pierre (1/11), Corbie (16/11), Mansell Camp (18/11).

7th (Service) Battalion. 8th Brigade, 3rd Division: Arrived Fienvillers (1/7). To Flesselles (3/7), Cardonnette (4/7), Corbie (5/7), Carnoy (7/7). In action (14/7) – attacking enemy's front and support line running between Longueval and Bazentin-le-Grand Wood – gains held and consolidated. Casualties – about 400. Relieved and to Montauban (20/7). To Waterlot Farm and in action at Delville Wood (23/7). Relieved and to Méaulte (27/7). To Happy Valley (12/8), Great Bear Wood (14/8), Talus Boisé (16/8). In support during attack near Maltz Horn Farm (18/8). Lonely Trench (later renamed Shropshire) taken (19/8). Relieved and to Sandpit Camp (20/8). To Méaulte (21/8), Beaumetz (23/8). To Béthune sector (25/8). Via Acheux reached Mailly-Maillet (5/10). To Bus-lès-Artois (17/10), Courcelles (1/11), Louvencourt (4/11). In action at Serre (13/11). To Bus-lès-Artois (14/11), Courcelles (15/11).

Duke of Cambridge's Own (Middlesex Regiment)

1st Battalion. 98th Brigade, 33rd Division: Entrained at Chocques for Longueau (8/7), arrived (9/7) and marched to Coisy. To Corbie (11/7), Méaulte (13/7). Moved forward via Bécordel-Bécourt for attack (14/7) – operation cancelled and bivouacked just north of Fricourt. To Bazentin-le-Petit (15/7) and commenced attack on Switch Line – heavy machine gun fire from both flanks brought assault to a standstill after advancing through village. Relieved by 4th King's Liverpool and to bivouacs north-east of Mametz Wood. Casualties – 321. To Bazentin-le-Petit Wood (17/7), Mametz Wood (19/7), positions south of Bazentin-le-Petit (20/7) – returned to Mametz Wood same night. To Dernancourt (21/7), bivouacs on high ground west of Bécordel (6/8), Mametz Wood (13/8), High Wood (14/8), reserve trenches just south of Bazentin-le-Grand (17/8). 'B' and 'C' Companies moved forward to assist 2nd Argyll and Sutherland at High Wood (18/8). To trenches west of Longueval (24/8), bivouacs north-west of Dernancourt (30/8), St. Gratien (1/9), Fienvillers (2/9), Barly (4/9), Conchy-sur-Canche (5/9), Flamermont (6/9), Beaudricourt (8/9), Warluzel (10/9), Humbercamps (11/9), Sailly-au-Bois (19/9). Took over trenches Hébuterne sector (20/9). To Sailly-au-Bois (26/9), Guadiempre (30/9), Ivergny (1/10), Wanquetin (17/10), Ivergny (18/10), Daours (19/10), Méaulte (21/10). Trônes Wood (23/10), trenches Lesbœufs sector (24/10). Attack and capture of Rainy and Dewdrop Trenches (28/10). To Flers Line (29/10), front line (Stormy Trench) (1/11), Carnoy (4/11). Entrained at Edgehill for Longpré (9/11) and from there marched to Huppy.

2nd Battalion. 23rd Brigade, 8th Division: On right of 23rd Brigade's attack up Mash Valley towards Ovillers (1/7). Only 1 of the 23 officers that moved forward at zero hour returned un wounded and among the 650 N.C.Os and men that went over the top, just 50 were ably to answered roll call. Withdrew to bivouacs near Millencourt (2/7) and later entrained at Méricourt for Ailly-sur-Somme. From there marched to billets at La Chaussee. To Crouy-St. Pierre (4/7). Entrained at Longueau for Diéval (6/7) and from there marched to Barlin – Béthune Sector. Entrained at Chocques for Pont-Remy (15/10) and from there marched to Huppy. To Méaulte (17/10), Trônes Wood (20/10), front line (Spectrum Trench) (22/10). Attack on Le Transloy (23/10) – hand-to-hand fighting while securing first objective – Zenith Trench. Casualies – 230. To camp near Montauban (27/10), Mansell Camp (29/10), Méaulte (30/10), Citadel Camp (3/11), La Briqueterie (6/11), trenches between Lesbœufs and Le Transloy (7/11), Bernafay Wood (10/11), Carnoy (13/11), Citadel Camp (18/11).

4th Battalion. 63rd Brigade, 21st and 37th Divisions: On right of 63rd Brigade's (21st Division) attack at Fricourt (1/7) – 'A' and 'B' Companies moved forward into No Man's Land 5 minutes before zero hour and immediately swept by machine gun fire and forced to retire. Went forward again 7.29 a.m. and with no officers about 40 men reached German line and sunken road beyond. Remaining 2 companies also suffered heavy casualties while crossing No Man's Land. Official History of The Great War notes that 6 machine guns (2 between German front and support trenches, 4 at northern end of Fricourt) covered assault. In reserve at Lozenge Alley (3/7). Entrained at Dernancourt (4/7) and from there marched to Vaux. Casualties since (1/7) – 540. To Talmas (7/7), Halloy (8/7). Transferred to 37th Division. Began move away from the Somme (11/7) and via Hannescamps sector was at Vimy by end of July. Arrived Raincheval from Amplier (21/10). To Beauval (30/10), Doullens (8/11), Lucheux (10/11), Léalvillers (12/11), Hédauville (14/11) – took up assembly positions 1 mile south-east of Englebelmer. To reserve positions at Station Road, east of Hamel 2 a.m. (15/11) – provided carrying and working parties for battalions in front line. Moved forward to Beaucourt (18/11) and there held part of Puisieux Trench between the Ancre and Miraumont Road.

1/7th Battalion (T.F.). 167th Brigade, 56th (1st London) Division: In reserve at The Keep, Hébuterne during attack at Gommecourt (1/7). Two raiding parties sent out during evening – 1 into Gommecourt Park, the other to German line south of it. Held line Hébuterne sector. To Souastre (12/7), front line Foncquevillers (16/7), Souastre (20/7), trenches between Hébuterne and Foncquevillers (28/7), Souastre (5/8), front line (13/8), Souastre (19/8), Le Souich (20/8), Béalcourt (22/8), Gapennes (23/8). Assisted in demonstration of infantry in co-operation with tanks (the first in France) laid on for General Sir Douglas Haig (26/8). Further exercises with tanks before Marshall Joffre and French Staff (3/9). Entrained at St. Riquier for Corbie and from there marched to Bois des Tailles (4/9). To Billon Farm (6/9), Maltz Horn Farm (9/9), positions north-west of Wedge Wood (10/9). 'B' and 'D' Companies in bombing attacks on The Quadrilateral (11/9). To Billon Copse (12/9), positions between Falfemont Farm and Wedge Wood (13/9), assembly positions in Leuze Wood close to Guillemont-Combles Road (14/9). In action at Bouleaux Wood (15/9) – 'A' and 'C' Companies moving forward at 8.20 a.m. – Battalion historian Colonel E.J. King noting that these were in a moment practically annihilated leaving just 25 men. There would be no hesitation when 'D' and 'B' Companies advanced but these also came under heavy fire. Colonel King records casualties as 300 out of an attacking strength of 500. Of these some 125 were killed. To Falfemont Farm (16/9), Maltz Horn

Farm (18/9), front line north-west side of Bouleaux Wood (22/9). Here the same trench was held by the enemy, being separated by a tank that had fallen into the trench on (15/9). Withdrew to reserve positions (24/9). To Sandpit Camp (27/9), Trônes Wood (29/9), front line north-west of Lesbœufs (30/9), Trônes Wood (3/10), front line (6/10). Attack on Spectrum Trench (7/10) – objective taken. Casualties – 193. To positions near Flers (8/10), Citadel Camp (10/10), Ville-sur-Ancre and by buses to Flesselles (11/10), Longpré (19/10). Entrained for Merville (24/10).

1/8th Battalion (T.F.). 167th Brigade, 56th (1st London) Division: Moved forward from Souastre to reserve positions east of Sailly-au-Bois for attack at Gommecourt (1/7). Later took over front line at Hébuterne. To Bayencourt (5/7), front line (8/7), St. Amand (10/7), front line (12/7), Souastre (16/7), front line Foncquevillers (20/7), Souastre (28/7), front line (5/8), Souastre (13/8), Bouquemaison (18/8), Barly (22/8), Maison-Ponthieu (23/8). Entrained at St. Riquier for Corbie and from there marched to Bois des Tallies (4/9). Via Citadel Camp to Billon Farm (6/9), Casement Trench (9/9), trenches in front of Leuze Wood (10/9). 'A' and 'B' Companies attacked German positions on Ginchy-Morval Road midnight (11/9) – objective reached – some ground gained and held after strong counter attacks. Withdrew to bivouacs near German Wood. Casualties – 165. To support positions between Wedge Wood and Leuze Wood (14/9). Attacked (15/9) – heavy casualties while moving forward to Leuze Wood and during attack down north-west side of Bouleaux Wood at 1.40 p.m. Withdrew to Leuze Wood. To German Wood (18/9). Casualties – 245. To Casement Trench (24/9), Angle Wood (26/9), German Wood (27/9), Morlancourt (28/9), reserve positions Flers Line (30/9), front line north-west of Lesbœufs (3/10), support line (7/10), Trônes Wood (9/10), Citadel Camp (10/10). Boarded buses at Ville-sur-Ancre for Flesselles (11/10). To Airaines (19/10). Entrained at Longpré for Merville (24/10).

11th (Service) Battalion. 36th Brigade, 12th (Eastern) Division: Moved into Divisional reserve at Baizieux Wood (1/7). To Intermediate Line (2/7), reserve trenches south-east of Authuille Wood (3/7). Later moved forward and in support during 37th Brigade's attack on Ovillers. Collected at Crucifix Corner and to reserve positions south side of Authuille Wood. To front line (Longridge to Mersey Trench) (4/7), Albert (5/7), reserve trenches (Ribble Street) Ovillers sector (6/7), front line (7/7) – in support of attack on Ovillers – moved forward in evening and held captured positions. To Albert (8/7), Senlis (9/7), Forceville (10/7), Bus-lès-Artois (11/7), Mailly-Maillet (20/7), Bois de Warnimont (24/7), Hédauville (25/7), via Martinsart Wood to trenches north-west of Pozières (27/7). Unsuccessful attacks on enemy positions (28/7), (29/7), (30/7) and (31/7). To Bouzincourt (7/8), Varennes

(11/8), Puchevillers (12/8), Vauchelles (15/8). Began move to Arras sector (16/8). From Wanquetin to Bouquemaison (27/9), Pommiers Redoubt (29/9), reserve trenches south of Flers (1/10), front line (3/10), reserve (5/10). In support during attack on Bayonet Trench (7/10) – later took over front line. To Bernafay Wood (10/10), Fricourt Camp (19/10), Buire (21/10), Beaumetz (22/10), Wanquetin (24/10).

12th (Service) Battalion. 54th Brigade, 18th (Eastern) Division: In reserve at Carnoy (1/7) – moving in afternoon to captured German trenches – Bund, Emden and Triangle. Moved forward to White Trench, Beetle Alley, Maple Trench (2/7). To positions west of Bronfay Wood (6/7). Two companies to Carnoy (7/7). To Bois des Tailles (8/7), Maricourt (13/7) and from there assembled in trenches near Trônes Wood. Attack and capture of Trônes Wood (14/7) – under command of Lieutenant-Colonel F. Maxwell, V.C. followed 6th Northamptonshire into the wood. After confused fighting Colonel Maxwell placed the men from both battalions into a line (east to west) across the wood and facing north. Going forward – each man was ordered to fire as he advanced. On western side of the wood a machine gun would hold up the attack – Colonel Maxwell with 70 men clearing the strong-point. Withdrew to Maricourt (17/7). Casualties since (14/7) – 283. To Bois des Tailles (18/7). Entrained at Grove Town for Longpré (21/7) and from there marched to Mérélessart. Entrained at Longpré for St. Omer (23/7). Arrived Arquèves from Halloy (11/9). To Hédauville (23/9), front line Leipzig Salient (Campbell Post) (24/9). Attack and capture of Thiepval (26/9) – forming up astride Thiepval-Authieule Wood Road 'C' and 'B' Companies went forward at 12.35 p.m. – Regimental historian Everard Wyrall noting that attack preceded slowly with practically every yard of ground being fought for. Advance held up for a time by machine gun fire from Thiepval Château (south-western end of village) – a tank coming forward and clearing the way. During the battle 2 privates – F.J. Edwards and R. Ryder gained the Victoria Cross. Both men showing great courage and leadership after their officers had become casualties. Lieutenant-Colonel Maxwell once again inspired his men – Battalion Operation Orders ending with a message from the Commander saying that the Regiment had been given a great chance that will be achieved 'on our heads.' He instructed the Battalion not to stop or retire a yard and to be out to kill and get Thiepval on its Colours. Withdrew via Aveluy Wood to Martinsart Wood (27/9). Casualties – 432. To Mailly-Maillet Wood (29/9), Prouville (2/10), Beauval (15/10), Vadencourt Wood (16/10), Bouzincourt (17/10), Albert (19/10), front line (Regina Trench) (25/10), Albert (billets in Rue de Boulan) (29/10), Warloy (31/10), Regina Trench (6/11), Warloy (11/11), Albert (13/11), huts in Mash Valley near Ovillers (14/11), Warloy (21/11).

13th (Service) Battalion. 73rd Brigade, 24th Division: Arrived Saleux by train (25/7) and marched to billets at Molliens-Vidames. Entrained at Hangest-sur-Somme for Vecquemont (31/7) and from there marched to Corbie. To Happy Valley (2/8), trenches at Arrow Head Copse (17/8). Attack towards Guillemont (18/8) – advance on right of Trônes Wood Road checked by cross fire. Withdrew to La Briqueterie. To the craters in front of Carnoy (19/8). Sandpit Camp (22/8), front line positions at Delville Wood (30/8). Official History of The Great War records that after almost 400 had become casualties from German bombardment, Battalion was attacked and forced out of Tea Trench (31/8). To Pommiers Redoubt (1/9), Dernancourt (6/9). Entrained at Edgehill for Longpré (6/9) and from there marched to Mouflers. Entrained at Longpré for Fouquereuil and Béthune sector (19/9).

16th (Service) Battalion (Public Schools). 86th Brigade, 29th Division: During early morning (1/7) moved up from Auchonvillers to assembly positions at Cripp's Cut and Cardiff Street. In support to 86th Brigade's attack on Beaumont-Hamel – crossing the parapet, moved forward – Official History of The Great War noting that as they advanced the men could see much of the wire entanglement still uncut, and the various gaps in it full of dead and wounded. War Diary mentions little of this tragic day – 'Battalion in action 7.30 from support trenches.' Casualties are then given as 524 all ranks. Brigade records do not mention 16th Middlesex or how far they advanced. One source, however (H.L. Smythe) records that when Beaumont-Hamel was later taken in November the remains, paybooks etc of some 180 Middlesex men were found at the sunken road in No Man's Land. Relieved and to Auchonvillers (3/7). To Englebelmer (4/7), Knightsbridge Trench (8/7). Relieved by 1st Royal Dublin Fusiliers and to Englebelmer (15/7). To Bois de Warnimont (23/7), Beauval (24/7). Entrained at Doullens for Esquelbecq and Ypres sector. Arrived Amiens (9/10) and from there marched to La Neuville. To Dernancourt (10/10), bivouacs south-east of Mametz Wood (13/10). In forward positions near Flers (Switch Line) (19/10)–(27/10). Seventy casualties recorded for night (20/10)–(21/10). To Albert (29/10), Corbie (31/10), Méaulte (16/11), Carnoy (18/11).

17th (Service) Battalion (1st Football). 6th Brigade, 2nd Division: Entrained at Bryas for Longueau (20/7) and from there marched to Ville-sous-Corbie. To Bois des Tailles (23/7), reserve renches across Carnoy-Montauban Road (25/7), front line Delville Wood (27/7). Strong German counter attack repulsed (28/7). To support line Montauban Alley (29/7). Casualties since (27/7) – 237. War Diary notes that all ranks behaved with great gallantry and that devotion to duty was magnificent. To Waterlot Farm (5/8). Attack on Guillemot (8/8) – heavy losses at ZZ Trench and Machine Gun House.

Withdrew to Breslau Trench (9/8). Casualties – 203. To Happy Valley (10/8), Méaulte (12/8). Entrained at Méricourt for Saleux (13/8) and from there moved in buses to La Chaussée. To Vignacourt (16/8), Vacquerie (17/8), Bois de Warnimont (18/8), Courcelles (20/8), trenches east of La Signy Farm (22/8), Couin (26/8), trenches Serre sector (30/8), Couin (3/9), Serre sector (7/9), Couin (11/9), Serre sector (15/9), Bus-lès-Artois (20/9), Couin (1/10), Mailly-Maillet (4/10), Puchevillers (7/10), Acheux Wood (18/10), front line Redan sector (22/10), Mailly-Maillet (24/10), North Camp Bertrancourt (30/10), Redan sector (7/11), North Camp (9/11), Redan sector (12/11). Attack on the Redan Ridge (13/11) – followed 2nd South Staffordshire towards Pendant Copse – Regimental historian Everard Wyrall noting that all ranks were cheerful, and mouth-organs were played as the men went over the top. The South Staffordshire would be held up at uncut German wire and the Middlesex withdrawn to Legend Trench. To Mailly-Maillet (15/11), Louvencourt (16/11).

18th (Service) Battalion (1st Public Works Pioneers). Pioneers, 33rd Division: Arrived La Chaussee from Fouquereuil (9/7) To Poulainville (11/7), Treux (12/7), Méaulte (14/7), Bécordel-Bécourt (15/7). Worked on roads around Mametz Wood area. To south-east corner of Fricourt Wood (17/7). Involved in operations at High Wood. Dug communication trench from High Wood back to Longueval-Bazentin-le-Grand Road (21/7) – during evening 'A' and 'C' Companies called upon to engage the enemy in High Wood. To Ribemont (22/7), Dernancourt (6/8), St. Gratien (31/8), Villers-Bocage (1/9), Berneuil (2/9), Frohen-le-Grand and Frohen-le-Petit (4/9), Flers (5/9), Penin (6/9). Mondicourt (9/9), Humbercamps (10/9), Souastre (20/9), Grouches-Luchuel (18/10), Treux (19/10), Citadel Camp (20/10), bivouacs south-west of Bernafay Wood (23/10). Worked in Mametz and Delville Wood areas. To Citadel Camp (7/11), Pommiers Redoubt (10/11).

19th (Service) Battalion (2nd Public Works Pioneers). Pioneers, 41st Division: Arrived Longpré from Armentières sector (23/8) and from there marched to Ailly-le-Haut-Clocher. To Fricourt Camp (3/9). Worked on roads in the area and later took part in operations around Flers and Le Transloy Ridges. Official History of The Great War records that Battalion made a horse track – Montauban-Longueval-Flers, and another that ran to Gueudecourt. To Montauban (11/10). Worked in neighbourhood of Delville Wood. Entrained at Buire for Oisemont (16/10). To Hallencourt (18/10). Entrained at Longpré for Caéstre near St. Omer (20/10).

20th (Service) Battalion (Shoreditch). 121st Brigade, 40th Division: Arrived Fienvillers from Ransart (5/11). To Bonnières (15/11).

21st (Service) Battalion (Islington). 121st Brigade, 40th Division: Arrived Neuvillette from Estrée-Wamin (3/11). To Candas (5/11), Bonnières (15/11).

23rd (Service) Battalion (2nd Football). 123rd Brigade, 41st Division: Arrived Longpré from Armentières sector (23/8) and from there marched to Gorenflos. Entrained at Longpré for Méricourt (6/9) and from there to Méaulte. To camp south of Fricourt (9/9), front line north of Delville Wood (10/9), Montauban (12/9), front line (14/9). In reserve at start of advance towards Flers (15/9) – later moved forward from Carlton and Savoy Trenches, up Flers Road and occupied Hog's Head north of Flers Wood. Withdrew to positions east of Flers at nightfall and held under heavy bombardment until ordered back to Switch Trench during evening (16/9). Casualties – 195. To Carlton Trench (17/9), Bécordel (18/9), positions between Pommiers Redoubt and Montauban (27/9), Flers Avenue Trench (28/9), trenches west of Gueudecourt (30/9). Assisted New Zealand Forces during attack towards Eaucourt l'Abbaye (1/10). Withdrew at night to Montauban. To Mametz Wood (3/10), reserve positions at Carlton Trench (8/10), front line north-east of Eaucourt l'Abbaye (9/10), Mametz Wood (11/10), Dernancourt (13/10). Entrained at Edgehill for Oisemont (17/10) – arrived (18/10) and marched to Mérélessart. Entrained at Pont-Remy for Godewaersvealde (19/10).

King's Royal Rifle Corps

1st Battalion. 99th Brigade, 2nd Division: Entrained at Diéval for Longueau (20/7) and from there marched to Morlancourt. To bivouacs south-west of Fricourt (23/7), front line Delville Wood (24/7). The trenches taken over are described in Battalion's records as 'extremely complicated' apparently facing in 4 different directions. With 23rd Royal Fusiliers attacked Delville Wood 7 a.m. (27/7) – Princes Street taken with little loss. High casualties during enemy's subsequent counter attack. Sergeant Albert Gill killed and subsequently awarded the Victoria Cross for his bravery and leadership. Withdrew to support trenches near Montauban (29/7). Casualties – 322. To Montauban Alley (2/8), Delville Wood (3/8), Montauban (5/8), Bronfay Farm (8/8), Sandpit Valley (9/8), Méricourt (11/8), Bertangles via Saleux (13/8), Naours (16/8), Gézaincourt (17/8), Vauchelles-les-Authie (18/8), Bus-lès-Artois (20/8). Took over forward positions Hébuterne sector (25/8). Rested at Couin between tours. During raid carried out (25/9) – new collapsible wire entanglement was discovered that the enemy operated from back in their trenches. The hidden device popping out of the ground in front of any attackers. Relieved and to Mailly-Maillet Wood (7/10). To Raincheval (8/10), Mailly-Maillet (17/10), trenches Serre left sector (18/10), Bertrancourt (22/10), trenches Redan sector (2/11), Mailly-Maillet (6/11), Arquèves (7/11), Bertrancourt (13/11). Attack on Munich Trench (14/11). Casualties – 142. Relieved and to Mailly-Maillet Wood (17/11)

2nd Battalion. 2nd Brigade, 1st Division: Arrived Candas from Lillers (8/7) and from there marched to Flesselles. To Fréchencourt (9/7), Bresle (10/7), Bécourt Wood (11/7). Provided carrying parties for forward area around Contalmaison. To Scots Redoubt during afternoon (17/7). Relieved 2nd Welsh in positions west of Bazentin-le-Petit Wood (18/7). To Scots Redoubt (21/7), front line (22/7). Attack on Switch Line, north-east of Pozières (23/7) – advanced 12.30 a.m. – Battalion records (K.R.R.C. Chronicle, 1916) note that Germans had spotted assembly and at once opened up with violent machine gun fire from left flank. 'D' Company entered German line – other companies also successful. Unsupported on left and right – later forced to withdraw. Casualties included Commanding Officer Lieutenant-Colonel Bircham, D.S.O. who died of his wounds during night. Records note casualties since (30/6) as 591. Withdrew to Albert via Scots Redoubt. To Franvillers (26/7), Hénencourt Wood (29/7), Bécourt Wood (13/8), Mametz Wood (14/8). Moved forward to recently gained positions west and north-west of High Wood (18/8). Several enemy counter attacks repulsed (20/8). Relieved by 1st Gloucestershire and to Bécourt Wood. Casualties – 138. To Mametz Wood (26/8). Five days spent under constant howitzer fire. To front line High Wood

(31/8). Enemy attack driven off (2/9). To Black Wood in support (5/9), front line opposite Wood Lane (7/9). Attack on Wood Lane (9/9). To Bécourt Wood (10/9), Baizieux (12/9), via Millencourt and Albert to Lozenge Wood (19/9), Black Wood (20/9). When Battalion moved up to trenches near Eaucourt l'Abbaye (25/9) – P.D. Ravenscroft noted a panoramic view of German held country with green trees and ground free of shell holes. He records in his diary ('Unversed in Arms') that during the whole time his battalion had been on the Somme it had always fought uphill and had never seen more than 200 yards of the enemy's territory to its front. Attack on Flers Line (26/9) – 130 yards of trenches taken – chiefly, according to Battalion records by No. 8 – (Rhodesian) Platoon. Further attacks made (27/9) and (28/9). To Millencourt via Black Wood (29/9). Boarded French buses at Lavièville for Valines (3/10). To Bresle (31/10), Albert (6/11), Bazentin-le-Petit (19/11).

7th (Service) Battalion. 41st Brigade, 14th (Light) Division: Left Arras area for the Somme (29/7). Arrived Dernancourt (8/8). To Pommiers Redoubt (11/8), front line opposite Orchard Trench (12/8). Relieved by 8th K.R.R.C. (15/8) and to Pommiers Redoubt. To front line (17/8). Attack on Orchard Trench (18/8) – 'C' and 'D' Companies advanced 2.45 p.m – leading waves found German front trench almost totally destroyed from barrage. Further advance of 100 yards made – dug in under heavy machine gun and rifle fire – enemy counter attacks driven off. Relieved at night and to Pommiers Redoubt. Casualties – 272. Relieved 8th K.R.R.C. in Hop Alley (24/8). To Dernancourt (26/8). Entrained at Albert for Airaines (30/8) and from there marched to Métigny. To Dernancourt (10/9), camp near Fricourt (11/9), Montauban Alley (12/9), Delville Wood (14/9). In support of 8th K.R.R.C. during attack on Switch Trench (15/9) – later moved through 8th and took Gap Trench. Relieved during night and to camp at Fricourt. Casualties – 342. To Dernancourt (17/9), Lucheux (22/9). Transferred to Arras sector (26/9).

8th (Service) Battalion. 41st Brigade, 14th (Light) Division: Arrived Barly from Arras area (31/7). To Dernancourt (8/8), Pommiers Redoubt (11/8), trenches north-west of Delville Wood (15/8). Relieved (17/8). To Delville Wood (20/8). In action (21/8) – advance soon checked with a loss of almost 200 men. Withdrew to support line. To front line – Hop Alley (23/8). 'A' and 'D' Companies attacked (24/8) – small parties reached enemy line – forced to withdraw after dark with high casualties. Relieved by 7th K.R.R.C. and to Pommiers. To Dernancourt (26/8). Entrained at Albert for Airaines (30/8) and from there marched to Heucourt. To Dernancourt (10/9), Fricourt (11/9), Pommiers Redoubt (12/9). Moved up into Delville Wood during evening. Attack towards Flers 6.30 a.m (15/9) – heavy casualties before taking Tea Support and Pint Trench – part of Switch Line taken. Relieved during evening and to Fricourt (16/9). Casualties – 331. To Dernancourt (17/9), Lucheux (22/9). To Arras sector (26/9).

9th (Service) Battalion. 42nd Brigade, 14th (Light) Division: Arrived Fienvillers from Arras sector (1/8). Entrained for Méricourt (7/8) and from there marched to Buire (8/8). Via Dernancourt and Méaulte to bivouacs near Fricourt (12/8), Montauban Alley via Mametz (19/8). Battalion records (K.R.R.C. Chronicle 1916) record 32 aeroplanes overhead (mostly British) at 6.30 p.m. (20/8). There would be much fighting in the air 'without decisive result' and an enemy observation balloon shot down. Relieved 8th Rifle Brigade in Delville Wood (21/8). Attacked (24/8) – 'C' and 'D' Companies moved forward at 5.45 p.m. Enemy shelling increased – rifle and machine gun fire opened – all officers either killed or wounded. Records note that men were rallied and led by N.C.O's. In support – 'A' Company advanced at 5.45 p.m. – attack held up by wire and machine gun fire from strong-point in Edge Trench. Cleared by bombing attacks 2 a.m. (25/8). Casualties – 289. Relieved and by beginning of September resting at St. Maulvis. Entrained at Airaines for Méricourt (11/9) and from there marched through Buire and Dernancourt to camp in a field north of railway. To positions south of Bécordel-Bécourt (12/9), Pommiers Redoubt (14/9). Attack and capture of Gueudecourt (15/9). Commanding Officer Lieutenant-Colonel E.W. Benson killed during advance. Passed through Switch and Gap Trenches (held by the 7th and 8th K.R.R.C.) and dug-in at Gas Alley. Relieved 4.30 a.m. (16/9) and withdrew to Montauban Alley. To Bécordel-Bécourt (17/9), camp a mile north of Buire (18/9). To Arras sector and billets at Beaudricourt (22/9).

10th (Service) Battalion. 59th Brigade, 20th (Light) Division: Arrived Frévent from Ypres sector (25/7) and from there marched to Bouquemaison. To Bois de Warnimont (26/7), Sailly-au-Bois (27/7), trenches Hébuterne sector (29/7), Bois de Warnimont (7/8), Beauval (18/8). Entrained at Candas for Méricourt (20/8) and from there marched to Méaulte. To Citadel Camp (21/8), brigade reserve just south of Carnoy (22/8). Moved forward to trenches near Guillemont (2/9). Attack on Guillemont noon (3/9). Battalion records note – 'C' Company storming enemy front line prior to commencement of British barrage – enemy taken completely by surprise and with little resistance. Heavy casualties from own barrage – new line consolidated 100 yards forward of objective by 12.34 p.m. Gains held until relieved during morning (5/9) and to Minden Post. Casualties – 273. To Bois des Tailles (6/9), Corbie (8/9), Bois des Tailles (11/9), Happy Valley (14/9), Bronfay Farm (15/9). Moved forward via Talus Boisé and relieved 2nd Grenadier Guards in support lines before Lesbœufs (16/9). Relieved and via Sandpit Camp to Morlancourt (20/9). To Happy Valley (24/9), trenches south-east of Guillemont (25/9), Carnoy (27/9),

Bernafay Wood (2/10), front line south of Gueudecourt (3/10), Méaulte (8/10), Méricourt (9/10), Ville-sur-Ancre (11/10), Franvillers (18/10), Cardonnette (19/10), Picquigny (20/10). Via Saisseval and Ailly-sur-Somme returned to forward area during second week November. Billeted at Mansell Camp and Méricourt while carrying out road repair work.

11th (Service) Battalion. 59th Brigade, 20th (Light) Division: Arrived Frévent from Ypres sector (25/7) and from there marched to Bouquemaison. To Bois de Warnimont (26/7), Sailly-au-Bois (27/7), trenches Hébuterne sector (29/7), Bois de Warnimont (7/8), Beauval (18/8). Entrained at Candas for Méricourt (20/8) and from there marched to Méaulte. To Citadel Camp (21/8), trenches opposite Guillemont (22/8). Enemy attacks repulsed (23/8) and (24/8). Relieved and to old German front line. In reserve during attack on Guillemont (3/9) – carrying parties to front line – 'D' Company attacked to 10th K.R.R.C. Relieved from the front line and via Minden Post to Bois des Tailles (6/9). To Corbie (8/9), Bois des Tailles (11/9), Happy Valley (14/9), Bronfay Farm (15/9). Via Talus Boisé relieved 2nd Grenadier Guards in support lines before Lesbœufs (16/9). Failed attack (17/9). Dug assembly trenches. Relieved (23/9). To trenches near Arrow Head Copse (26/9), camp near Carnoy (27/9). Working parties provided for forward area. Withdrew with 20th Division second week October and later to training area at Ailly-sur-Somme. To Mansell Camp (14/11) and began road repair work.

12th (Service) Battalion. 60th Brigade, 20th (Light) Division: Moved to the Somme during last week of July – detraining at Frévent and marching to Courcelles-au-Bois. Took over trenches opposite Serre (6/8). Relieved and to Couin (14/8). Later to Amplier, Fienvillers, Ville and Méaulte before taking over old British line in front of Carnoy. To trenches opposite Guillemont (27/8). Enemy attacks beaten off (29/8) and (30/8). Relieved and to Bernafay Wood. To Carnoy (1/9), Bernafay Wood (3/9). Moved west of Trônes Wood during night and later fought off enemy attack. Via La Briqueterie to Corbie (5/9), Méaulte (11/9), Citadel Camp (14/9), Carnoy (15/9), Waterlot Farm (16/9). That night moved forward to the line opposite Morval (just south of the Ginchy-Lesbœufs Road). Repulsed enemy attacks (17/9) and (18/9). Relieved and to Citadel Camp (22/9). Later to Ville-sur-Ancre. To Ginchy (26/9), Carnoy (27/9), Trônes Wood (29/9), trenches between Gueudecourt and Lesbœufs (3/10). Successful assault on Rainbow Trench (7/10). To Sandpit Camp (8/10). Later to Corbie, Allonville and Flesselles. To Le Mesge (1/11), Corbie (16/11).

13th (Service) Battalion. 111th Brigade, 37th Division; Arrived Bresle from Arras sector (5/7). Provided carrying parties for 19th Division at Bécourt

Wood (7/7) and (8/7). To support and front line positions around La Boisselle (9/7). Relieved and to Albert (19/7). Casualties – 176. To Bresle (20/7), Albert (30/7), reserve line Mametz Wood (31/7), front line west of High Wood (2/8), Mametz Wood (6/8), divisional reserve at Quadrangle Trench (14/8), Bresle (15/8). Entrained at Fréchencourt for Citerne (18/8). Moved to Béthune area (20/8). Arrived Puchevillers (22/10). To Gézaincourt (30/10), Puchevillers (11/11), Hédauville (12/11), Englebelmer (13/11) – attached to 63rd Division, played important role during capture of Beaucourt. Further operations taking place at Munich, Muck and Railway Trenches. Relieved by 11th Royal Warwickshire (20/11) and to Englebelmer.

16th (Service) Battalion (Church Lads Brigade). 100th Brigade, 33rd Division: Arrived Saleux (9/7). Via St. Sauveur, Vecquemont and Morlancourt to reserve positions at Bécordel-Bécourt (12/7). To Flatiron Copse (14/7). In attack at High Wood (15/7). Later withdrew to Mametz Wood. In support at High Wood (19/7). To Bécordel-Bécourt and later billets at Albert. In reserve Mametz Wood (7/8). Relieved 2nd Worcestershire in front line High Wood (10/8). 100th Brigade into divisional reserve at Bécordel-Bécourt (13/8). To trenches edge of Delville Wood (19/8). In support (21/8). Attack on Tea Trench (24/8) – objectives taken. Relieved (25/8) and via Mametz Wood to Bécordel-Bécourt. To Ribemont (30/8), Molliens-au-Bois (31/8). From there began move towards Arras sector. Moved into reserve billets at Souastre during second week of September. To Hébuterne sector north of Gommecourt (19/9). Relieved and via Coullemont and Lucheux to Bouquemaison. To Corbie (19/10). Later to Méaulte, Mansell Camp and La Briqueterie. Took over line between Morval and Le Transloy (Frosty Trench) from 2nd Worcestershire (2/11). Successful assault on Hazy Trench (5/11). To Carnoy (6/11), Citadel Camp (7/11). Entrained at Buire for Airaines (10/11) and from there marched to Condé-Folie.

17th (Service) Battalion (British Empire League). 117th Brigade, 39th Division: Arrived Bouquemaison (24/8). To Authie (25/8), camp at Bertrancourt (28/8), front line trenches Hamel sector (2/9). Attacked (3/9) – with all officers killed or wounded, heroic leadership shown by N.C.Os and men. One small party entered enemy's second line led by a rifleman. Relieved and to Mailly-Maillet Wood. Casualties – over 300. To Bertrancourt (4/9), trenches Auchonvillers sector (6/9), Mailly-Maillet (12/9), Bertrancourt (19/9), front line Hébuterne sector (20/9), Bertrancourt (30/9), Martinsart (3/10), reserve line Authuille Wood (5/10). In support of 16th Sherwood Foresters at Schwaben Redoubt (9/10). To North Bluff (10/10), front line under orders of 118th Brigade (12/10). Successful attack with 4th/5th Black Watch and 1/1st Cambridgeshire on north face Schwaben Redoubt (14/10).

Relieved and to Pioneer Road (16/10). To front line attached to 116th Brigade (20/10). Strong enemy counter attack at the Schwaben repulsed. To Pioneer Road (23/10), North Bluff (24/10). Held Schwaben Redoubt (27/10)–(29/10). Relieved and to Senlis. To support line Thiepval (2/11). In Divisional reserve during assault on Hansa Line and St. Pierre Divion. To North Bluff (13/11). Moved north to Merckeghem (14/11).

18th (Service) Battalion (Arts and Crafts). 122nd Brigade, 41st Division: Left Bailleul for Longpré (24/8) and from there marched to Brucamps. Entrained at Longpré for Méricourt (6/9) and from there to Dernancourt. To Fricourt (12/9), Longueval (Savoy Trench) (13/9), Tea Trench in front of Delville Wood (14/9). Attack towards Flers (15/9). In Para 1 of Operation Orders regarding 18th K.R.R.C., Battalion is instructed to 'push home their attack with the utmost vigour . . . the enemy's moral is known to be very shaken.' Just before zero, one shell would hit the Rifles killing its Commanding Officer Colonel C.P. Marten, his Adjutant and 2 other officers. The attack went on – 18th K.R.R.C. doing all that had been asked of it. Casualties – over 350. To Dernancourt (19/9), Mametz Wood (2/10). Relieved New Zealand Rifle Brigade in line at Turk Lane (3/10). In attack on Gird Trench (7/10). Withdrew to Flers Trench (9/10). To Carlton Trench (10/10), Mametz Wood (12/10), Dernancourt (13/10), Doudelainville (17/10). Entrained at Longpré for the Ypres sector (20/10).

20th (Service) Battalion (British Empire League Pioneers). Pioneers, 3rd Division: Moved from Poperinghe (4/7) and via Candas and Morlancourt went into billets near Carnoy. Worked on bridging and road making in area. High casualties from shelling while working in Montauban Alley and Longueval areas. Took part in Bazentin Ridge operations (14/7)–(25/7). One company attached to 8th Brigade for its assault between Bazentin-le-Grand and Longueval (14/7) and during the fighting at Delville Wood (14/8)–(19/8). Moved to Béthune area (20/8). By (9/10) via Acheux working under orders of 5th Corps around Mailly-Maillet. To Courcelles (29/10).

21st (Service) Battalion (Yeoman Rifles). 124th Brigade, 41st Division: Left Ploegsteert area towards end of August, arriving Pont-Remy and moving for training Abbeville area. Via Longpré travelled to Fricourt area after first week of September – moving up to assault positions just north-east of Delville Wood (14/9). Attack on Flers (15/9) – lead assault with 10th Queen's – Tea Support cleared and Switch Line taken by 7 a.m. Later – Battalion's founder and Commanding officer the Earl of Faversham would be killed at western end of Bulls Road. When his body was found its burial would be supervised by a young officer with 21st K.R.R.C. – Anthony Eden. Relieved to support line and from there Dernancourt. Attack on Bayonet Trench (7/10) – in support relieved leading waves at objective. Casualties are recorded as high – strength of 124th Brigade holding Bayonet Trench being around that of a single battalion. Withdrew to Mametz and later Bécordel-Bécourt. Entrained for Airaines and later from Longpré to Méteren.

Duke of Edinburgh's (Wiltshire Regiment)

1st Battalion. 7th Brigade, 25th Division: In reserve at Varennes (1/7). Moved forward via Hédauville and Aveluy Wood into trenches at Authuille (2/7). Entered Leipzig Salient (3/7) and fought side-by-side with 3rd Worcestershire until relieved (7/7). To Crucifix Corner and later in reserve during operations at Ovillers. To Forceville and via Acheux and Raincheval to Beauval (18/7). To Bois de Warnimont via Terramesnil and Sarton (20/7), Mailly-Maillet Wood (29/7). Tours of duty in front line. Relieved and to Bus-lès-Artois (6/8). To Sarton (11/8), Puchevillers (15/8), Hédauville (17/8). Took over line at Leipzig Salient (19/8). Capture of Lemberg Trench (21/8). With 3rd Worcestershire, attacked and captured Hindenburg Trench (24/8) – gains held after hand-to-hand fighting and under tremendous bombardment. Relieved and to Hédauville (26/8). To Bouzincourt (28/8), Leipzig Salient (3/9). From Hindenburg Trench attacked German line south of the Wonder Work. Relieved and to Bouzincourt. To Léalvillers (5/9). To Raincheval (7/9), Hardinval (9/9), Beaumetz (11/9), Coulonvillers (13/9), Hardinval (24/9), Raincheval (27/9), Hédauville (29/9). Took over trenches between Ovillers and Thiepval (1/10). To Stuff Redoubt (3/10), support trenches at Thiepval (7/10), Stuff Redoubt (13/10) Donnet Post (17/10), trenches north of Mouquet Farm (18/10), Bouzincourt (22/10). Entrained for Flanders (30/10).

2nd Battalion. 21st Brigade, 30th Division: Carried supplies to forward area (1/7). In action at Montauban – assisted 90th Brigade in holding gains in village. Heavy casualties during enemy's bombardment and counter attacks (2/7). Relieved and to Bois des Tailles (3/7). Assembled in Bernafay Wood and La Briqueterie for assault on Trônes Wood and Maltz Horn Farm (8/7) – 'A' Company took objective at head of Maltz Horn Valley. Remaining companies crossing the space between Bernafay Wood and Trônes swept through southern half of wood and later held off strong counter attacks from its northern end. There would be great acts of bravery and leadership throughout the day. Commanding Officer Lieutenant-Colonel. R.M.T. Gillson having been wounded early in the assault, lay out in the open and refusing to be moved carried on directing his battalion. Private F. Matthews was severely wounded while attempting to deliver a message – the signal would be found still on him later in hospital in England. In total – 2 D.S.Os, 6 M.Cs, 4 D.C.Ms, 8 M.Ms and several Russian and Italian medals were awarded. Relieved and to Copse Valley. Casualties – 235. To Morlancourt (9/7), Vaux-sur-Somme (13/7). Entrained at Daours for Ailly-sur-Somme (14/7) and from there marched to St. Pierre-a-Guoy. To Morlancourt (18/7), Mansell Copse (20/7). Assembled just north of Trônes Wood (22/7). In reserve for attack on Guillemont (23/7). Relieved at night and to Happy

Valley. Moved forward to reserve position between Mametz and Carnoy (30/7). To Happy Valley (31/7). Entrained at Méricourt for Longpré (2/8). Began move to Givenchy area (3/8). Entrained at Fouquereuil for Doullens (18/9) and from there marched to Amplier. To Naours (21/9), Ribemont (4/10), Pommiers Redoubt (6/10). To Switch Trench (11/10), Flers Trench (12/10), front line (13/10), Flers Trench (15/10). Battalion historian Major W.S. Shepherd notes heavy and continuous shelling in Flers Trench – 'the Huns had got the exact range.' He records that the Battalion was worse off than in the front line and was glad when orders came on (17/10) for it to return to the front line. Attacked Gird Lines (18/10). Casualties – 364. To Pommiers Redoubt (21/10), Dernancourt (24/10), Bouquemaison (26/10), Humbercourt (29/10), Berles-au-Bois and Arras sector (30/10).

6th (Service) Battalion. 58th Brigade, 19th (Western) Division: From Albert moved forward (1/7) and took part in operations around La Boisselle (2/7) – assaulting western end of village and clearing by 9 p.m. Attack on Bailiff Wood (7/7) – objectives taken. To Baizieux Wood (9/7), Bécourt Wood (21/7), Mametz (22/7), trenches around Bazentin-le-Petit (24/7), Lahoussoye (31/7), Cocquerel (4/8), Kemmel sector (7/8). Arrived Vauchelles (17/10), to Hérissart (18/10), Bouzincourt (23/10), Crucifix Corner (24/10), front line Stuff Redoubt (26/10), positions near Aveluy (1/11), front line (3/11), Aveluy (6/11), front line (13/11) – failed attack on Stump Road. To positions near Authuille Wood (14/11), front line (16/11), positions near Aveluy (17/11).

Manchester Regiment

2nd Battalion. 14th Brigade, 32nd Division: Moved forward from Senlis Camp into positions at Black Horse Shelters and Crucifix Corner during night (30/6). Assembled in Authuille Wood for attack on Leipzig Salient (1/7) – objective taken and held against counter attacks. Withdrew to Senlis (3/7). To Forceville (5/7), Bouzincourt (7/7). Moved forward to Ovillers Post and in action western side of village (8/7)–(10/7) – some ground gained. To Bouzincourt (11/7), Ovillers Post (14/7). Transferred to Béthune sector (15/7). Arrived Beauval (18/10). To Warloy (21/10), brickfields near Albert (23/10), Contay (26/10), Bouzincourt (13/11), Mailly-Maillet (15/11) – relieved 1st Royal Berkshire in Serre Trench 11 p.m. Enemy bombing attack driven off (17/11). Attack on Munich Trench (18/11) – advanced eastwards along Lager Alley towards Serre – one company continued to Ten Tree Alley and there would be cut off. A report by a survivor recorded in Colonel H.C. Wylly's history of the Manchester Regiment notes that having halted on a small rise they refused to surrender and fought it out to the last. The bodies were found later all grouped together. Relieved and to Mailly-Maillet (20/11).

11th (Service) Battalion. 34th Brigade, 11th (Northern) Division: Entrained at Frévent for Acheux (3/9) and from there marched to Puchevillers. To Bouzincourt (8/9), Chalk Pit south-east of Pozières (17/9), front line Mouquet Farm sector (19/9). Relieved and to Aveluy (22/9). Moved from reserve line Crucifix Corner to Ovillers (26/9) – bombing parties and 1 platoon sent forward to Mouquet Farm. Battalion moved forward 3.28 p.m. – in action towards farm and surrounding positions – Zollern Redoubt, Stuff Redoubt, Hessian Trench until relieved to Kay Dump (29/9) – 'Q' Company remaining in Stuff Redoubt. Later into support at Mouquet Farm. Relieved and to Aveluy (30/9). Casualties since (26/9) – 309. Entrained at Varennes for Candas (1/10). To Prouville (2/10), Fransu (3/10), Contay (16/11), Puchevillers (17/11).

12th (Service) Battalion. 52nd Brigade, 17th (Northern) Division: Moved forward from Bois des Tailles to reserve line at Morlancourt (2/7). Took over support trenches north of Fricourt (4/7). Dug jumping-off trench east side of Pearl Alley during night (5/7). To Fricourt Wood (6/7). Attack on Quadrangle Support (7/7) – advancing in bright sunlight, one report notes that the enemy were alert and seeing a perfect target 'mowed down the ranks right and left.' Casualties – 555. Relieved and to Méaulte. To Ville-sous-Corbie (8/7). Entrained at Méricourt for Ailly-sur-Somme (10/7) and from there marched to Oissy. To Long (15/7). Entrained at Hangest for Méricourt (23/7) and from there marched to bivouacs near Dernancourt. To support trenches between Longueval and Bazentin-le-Petit (1/8). Attack on Orchard Trench 12.50 a.m. (4/8) – assault checked by heavy bombardment of shells and gas. Casualties – 171. Relieved and to Montauban Alley. To reserve line near Carnoy (5/8), Montauban Alley (10/8), reserve line west of Albert (11/8). Entrained at Méricourt for Candas (15/8). To Mezerolles (16/8), Grouches (17/8), Souastre (21/8), front line Foncquevillers sector (27/8). Withdrew to Brigade reserve (5/9). To St. Amand (10/9), Warlencourt (11/9), Grouches (21/9), Frohen-le-Grand (22/9), Maizicourt (23/9), Gapennes (24/9), Acquet (9/10), Frohen-le-Grand (10/10), Halloy (11/10), Bouquemaison (18/10), Corbie (23/10), Méaulte (27/10), camp north of Carnoy (29/10), trenches west of Le Transloy (30/10). Relieved by 9th Northumberland Fusiliers and to Trônes Wood (1/11). To trenches near Ginchy (4/11), camp near Carnoy (7/11), front line (10/11), Méaulte (15/11). Entrained at Edgehill for Hangest (16/11) and from there moved by bus to Saisseval.

16th (Service) Battalion (1st City). 90th Brigade, 30th Division: Assembled in Cambridge Copse for attack on Montauban (1/7). On left of 90th Brigade's assault (17th Manchester on right), advanced along east side of Talus Boisé at 8.30 a.m. – soon heavy casualties from machine gun situated in old German line near Breslau Alley – Train Alley reached – Lewis gun team cleared machine gun from strong-point. Continued advance – all company commanders casualties. Montauban entered at 10.05 a.m. Official History of The Great War records men of 16th Manchester drove German artillerymen from their guns in Caterpillar Valley. To Happy Valley (2/7), Cambridge Copse (8/7). Attack on Trônes Wood (9/7) – advanced from sunken road east of La Briqueterie 6.40 p.m. – took southern part of wood with little loss and dug in 60 yards from south-western edge. To Cambridge Copse (11/7), Daours (13/7), Celestines Wood (19/7), Happy Valley (20/7), Mansell Copse (22/7), Cambridge Copse (23/7). Attack on Guillemont (30/7) – moved forward from assembly trenches east of Trônes Wood – held up by uncut wire south of Guillemont Station and there sustained heavy casualties from enfilade machine gun fire. Withdrawal ordered. To Mansell Copse (31/7). Entrained at Méricourt for Longpré (2/8). Entrained for Béthune sector (4/8). Arrived Buire (10/10) and from there moved forward to positions west of Delville Wood. In reserve during attack on Bayonet Trench (12/10). To Montauban (20/10), Ribemont (22/10). Transferred to Arras sector.

17th (Service) Battalion (2nd City). 90th Brigade, 30th Division: Assembled in Cambridge Copse for attack on Montauban (1/7). Moved forward with 16th Manchester along east side of Talus Boisé 8.30 a.m. Official History of The Great War notes advance of both battalions being with remarkable steadiness and enthusiasm. Reached Train Alley and awaited orders to move on – advance continued – all company commanders casualties. Montauban entered 10.05 a.m. Relieved and to Happy Valley (3/7). To Oxford Copse (8/7). Attack on Trônes Wood (9/7) – advanced from Bernafay Wood 6 a.m. Official History records that due to gas shelling, respirators were worn – eye-pieces misting up from rain caused loss of direction. Eastern edge of wood reached 8 a.m – later suffered high casualties from German bombardment and forced to withdraw (less party of 40 men) to Bernafay Wood at 3 p.m. Party later resisted counter attack until overwhelmed. To Daours and Vecquemont (13/7), Celestines Wood (19/7), Happy Valley (20/7), Mansell Copse (22/7), Cambridge Copse (23/7). Worked on assembly trenches. Attack on Guillemont (30/7) – 2 companies advancing from Trônes Wood suffered high casualties before ordered to withdraw. To Mansell Copse (31/7). Entrained at Méricourt for Longpré (2/8). Entrained for Béthune area (4/8). Arrived Buire (10/10) and from there moved forward to Delville Wood. Attack on Bayonet Trench (12/10) – small parties entered objective but later forced to retire. Relieved from forward area and to Montauban (20/10), Ribemont (22/10). Transferred to Arras sector.

18th (Service) Battalion (3rd City). 90th Brigade, 30th Division: Assembled at Cambridge Copse for attack on Montauban (1/7). Withdrew to Train Alley (2/7), Happy Valley (3/7). Attack on Trônes Wood (7/7) – reinforced 18th King's and 19th Manchester in wood after dark. Commanding Officer Lieutenant-Colonel W.A. Smith killed. Withdrew (less one company) to La Briqueterie (9/7). Enemy counter attack repulsed. To Cambridge Copse (11/7), Bray (12/7), Celestins Wood (19/7), Mansell Copse (22/7), trenches Maricourt (Gibson Street) (23/7), Brick Lane (24/7), Mansell Copse (26/7), Trônes Wood (29/7). Attack on Guillemont (30/7) – advanced with left on Trônes Wood-Guillemont Railway – German front line taken – later forced to withdraw under heavy machine gun fire from The Quarry. Company Sergeant Major W.J.G. Evans awarded Victoria Cross. Relieved and to Citadel Camp (31/7), Mansell Copse (1/8). Entrained at Méricourt for Longpré (2/8). Entrained for Béthune area (4/8). Arrived Fricourt Camp (4/10). To Marlborough Wood (10/10), Factory Trench (11/10). Attack on Bayonet Trench (12/10). Withdrew to Marlborough Wood (16/10), Ribemont (22/10). Entrained for Doullens (25/10) and from there transferred to Arras area.

19th (Service) Battalion (4th City). 21st Brigade, 30th Division: Attack on Glatz Redoubt (1/7) – with 18th King's advanced up eastern slope of Railway Valley – held up by British barrage before taking Alt Trench. Relieved and to Oxford Copse (2/7). To Bois des Tailles (3/7). Attack on Trônes Wood (8/7) – 1 company reinforced 2nd Wiltshire in wood. Withdrew to Billon Valley (9/7). To Morlancourt (11/7), Corbie (13/7), Saisseval (14/7),

Morlancourt (18/7), Wellington Redoubt (19/7). Moved forward to Silesia Trench in support (22/7). Attack on Guillemont (23/7) – 3 companies moved forward from eastern side of Trônes Wood. Heavy casualties at uncut wire before entering village. Strong counter attack later forced withdrawal. Relieved during afternoon and to Happy Valley. Entrained at Méricourt for Longpré (2/8) and from there marched to Citerne. Entrained at Longpré for Berguette (3/8) and from there to Robecq. Arrived Doullens (18/9). To Naours (21/9), Ribemont (4/10), Pommiers Redoubt (6/10). Later to forward area around Flers. Attacked (18/10). Withdrew to Pommiers Redoubt (21/10), Dernancourt (25/10). To Bailleulmont area (30/10).

20th (Service) Battalion (5th City). 22nd Brigade, 7th Division: Attacked right of Fricourt 2.30 p.m. (1/7) – high casualties during advance on Sunken Road Trench – Commanding Officer Lieutenant-Colonel H. Lewis killed – heavy fighting in Bois Français Support, Orchard Alley, Zinc Trench. Relieved from Bois Français Support and to Caftet Wood (3/7) – later to bivouacs north-west of Carnoy. Casualties – 326. To Plum Lane and Danzig Trench in support of attack at Mametz Wood (4/7). To Heilly (5/7), Citadel Camp (10/7). Moved into reserve lines near Mametz Wood (14/7) – 'C' and 'D' Companies going forward to Bazentin-le-Petit in support of 2nd Royal Irish and 1st Royal Welsh Fusiliers. Moved forward to The Snout and support line along south-western edge of Bazentin-le-Petit Wood during night. Casualties during advance – 169. Relieved and to Dernancourt (21/7). Entrained at Méricourt for Hangest (22/7) and from there marched to Belloy-sur-Somme. Entrained at Hangest for Méricourt (12/8) and from there marched to Dernancourt. To Montauban (26/8) – relieving 12th King's in front line opposite Ginchy that night. During move forward 'B' Company and H.Q. lost 30 men (killed) when a shell hit store of Mills bombs. Further high casualties from shelling. Relieved and to camp near Fricourt (29/8). Casualties since (26/8) – 151. To front line (2/9). Attack on Ginchy (3/9) – village entered and line held south of church – strong counter-attack forced withdrawal to start lines near Guillemont. To camp near Fricourt at midnight. Casualties – 249. To Buire (5/9). Entrained at Albert for Airaines (8/9) and from there marched to Citerne. Entrained at Pont-Remy for Méteren (18/9).

21st (Service) Battalion (6th City). 91st Brigade, 7th Division: Moved forward from Bois des Tailles midnight (30/6) for attack on Mametz. From reserve 'A' Company followed advance into German front line – 'B' and 'C' moved forward 9.40 a.m. to assist 1st South Staffordshire on outskirts of Mametz. Later occupied western end of Danzig Alley. 'D' Company in action in afternoon at Queen's Nullah. Moved forward and occupied Bottom Wood (2/7). Relieved and to Buire (4/7). To Citadel Camp (11/7), Mametz

(13/7), valley near Sabot Copse (14/7). In reserve and support during attack on Bazentin-le-Grand Wood and High Wood. To Mametz (16/7) – providing rear guard on withdrawal of 91st Brigade from High Wood. To bivouacs between Bécordel and Méaulte (19/7), between Dernancourt and Buire (20/7). Entrained at Méricourt for Hangest (22/7) and from there marched to Bertangles. Entrained at Vignacourt for Méricourt (12/8). Relieved 20th Manchester in line south of Delville Wood (29/8). Relieved by 22nd Manchester and to Pommiers Trench (1/9). Moved forward to Montauban Alley (3/9), front line Delville Wood – Bitter Trench and South Street (4/9) – unsuccessful bombing attack at 2 p.m on Ale Alley. Relieved and via Montauban Alley to Bécordel-Bécourt (5/9). Casualties since (29/8) – 237. Entrained at Albert for Oisemont (11/9) and from there marched to Frucourt. Entrained at Abbeville for Ypres sector (18/9).

22nd (Service) Battalion (7th City). 91st Brigade, 7th Division: Attack on Mametz (1/7) – 'B' and 'D' Companies led assault at 7.30 a.m. reaching Bucket Trench and Danzig Alley. With high losses 'C' and 'A' in support moved on to Fritz Trench but were held up. Bombers cleared Bright Alley. Casualties – 390. Gains held and consolidated until relieved (5/7). Withdrew to Buire. To Citadel Camp (12/7), bivouac near Minden Post (13/7). Moved forward to Mametz Wood (14/7) and from there reserve positions just north of Bazentin-le-Grand for attack on High Wood. Moved into High Wood (15/7). Casualties during days fighting – 236. Withdrew to bivouacs near Minden Post (16/7). To Méaulte (19/7), Dernancourt (20/7). Entrained at Méricourt for Hangest (22/7) and from there marched to Frémont. Entrained at Vignacourt for Méricourt (12/8) and from there marched to camp north of Dernancourt. To camp near Fricourt (26/8), reserve line and Pommiers Trench (31/8), front line Delville Wood – Porter and Stout Trenches, ZZ Alley (1/9). Relieved and to camp near Fricourt (2/9). To Montauban Alley in reserve (3/9), Crucifix Alley in support (6/9) – 'C' and 'D' Companies moving forward to Folly Trench under orders of 8th Devonshire at 8.30 a.m. Remainder to front line (7/9). Relieved (8/9). Entrained at Albert for Oisemont (11/9) and from there marched to Huppy. Entrained at Abbeville for Ypres sector (17/9).

23rd (Service) Battalion (8th City). 104th Brigade, 35th Division: Arrived Neuvillette from Béthune sector (2/7). From there moved forward – reaching Talus Boisé (19/7) via Bus-lès-Artois, Léalvillers, Bouzincourt, Aveluy Wood, Morlancourt, Happy Valley, Billon Wood. To positions in front of Maltz Horn Farm (20/7) – unsuccessful attack at 11.35 a.m. Withdrew to Talus Boisé. Casualties – 157. To front line (23/7), Talus Boisé (25/7). Provided carrying parties for 90th Brigade during attack on Guillemont (29/7). To Happy Valley (30/7), Sailly-le-Sec (2/8). Entrained at Méricourt for Saleux

(5/8). Entrained at Airaines for Corbie (10/8). Arrived Happy Valley (15/8). To Talus Boisé (18/8), front line (19/8). Dug new trench (Bantam Trench) in advance of line during night (20/8). Relieved and to Citadel Camp (22/8). To front line (24/8), Citadel Camp (26/8). Entrained at Heilly for Candas (30/8) and from there marched to Neuvillette. Began move to Arras sector (31/8).

24th (Service) Battalion (Oldham) (Pioneers). Pioneers, 7th Division. Took part in attack on Mametz (1/7). Worked on communications trenches and strong points. Wired whole of front during night. Later took part in 7th Division's operations on the Bazentin Ridge (14/7)–(17/7) and attack on High Wood (20/7). 7th Division relieved and moved to rest and training area north-west of Amiens (21/7). Arrived Dernancourt (12/8) and from there to camp Fricourt area. Worked on roads Delville Wood area. Took part in operations around Guillemont (3/9)–(7/9). Division relieved and to Abbeville area (11/9). Began move to Ypres sector (17/9).

Prince of Wales's (North Staffordshire Regiment)

1st Battalion. 72nd Brigade, 24th Division. Entrained at Bailleul for Longueau (24/7) and from there marched to Fourdrinoy. Entrained at Ailly for Méricourt (29/7) and from there marched to Morlancourt. To Sandpit Camp (1/8), La Briqueterie (9/8) – 'A' Company heavily shelled in Teale Trench – 'C' Company dug 120 yards of communication trench from Guillemont-Trônes Wood Road northwards. To front line at Guillemont (12/8), La Briqueterie (15/8), Carnoy craters (17/8), La Briqueterie (18/8) – under orders of 73rd Brigade in support during attack on Guillemont – later moving up to front line. To Carnoy craters (19/8), Quarry Line (21/8), billets between Dernancourt and Millencourt and from there Ribemont (25/8). To Delville Wood (30/8). The dreadful conditions in the wood are recorded by the Battalion's historian – he notes that rotting corpses filled the wood – the smell penetrating the atmosphere. 'C' and 'D' Company's positions attacked (31/8) – enemy taking part of Edge Trench. To Montauban (2/9), Delville Wood (3/9), camp near Fricourt (5/9), Dernancourt (6/9). Casualties (30/8)–(6/9) – 221. Entrained at Dernancourt for Longpré (7/9) and from there marched to Bellancourt. Entrained at Abbeville for Bryas near St. Pol. (19/9).

1/5th Battalion (T.F.). 137th Brigade, 46th (North Midland) Division: Moved forward to front line facing Gommecourt (30/6). Attacked behind 1/6th North Staffordshire (1/7) – Battalion historian Lieutenant Walter Meakin notes heavy casualties from shelling in communication trenches at rear of British front line – only a few men reaching German line. A letter from Lance-Corporal R. Tivey recalls how he and his party set of over the top – the whole line falling as a man after going no further than 20 paces. Relieved early morning (2/7) and to Ransart. Casualties given in Battalion history as 6 officers and about 300 other ranks. To Humbercourt (28/10), Lucheux (29/10), Fortel (1/11), Noyelles-en-Chaussée (3/11), Domvast (11/11).

1/6th Battalion (T.F.). 137th Brigade, 46th (North Midland) Division: Attack on Gommecourt (1/7) – Official History of The Great War notes leading waves reached enemy wire where most were shot or bombed – few men entered front trench, but soon killed or driven out. Casualties – 305. Relieved and to Bailleulval (3/7). Arrived Gapennes (3/11). To Canchy (10/11).

8th (Service) Battalion. 57th Brigade, 19th (Western) Division: From Tyler's Redoubt moved forward to trenches on Albert-Bouzincourt Road 7.30 a.m. (1/7). At 4 p.m. marched through Albert to reserve in Tara-Usna Line. Ordered forward for attack on La Boisselle (2/7) – communication trenches are on record as being crowded and full of confusion – assembly positions not reached in time. Attack called off – 'D' Company remaining in front line. Battalion history records morning of (2/7) as quiet – the men after sleep being occupied in burying the dead of the 34th Division who lay around in large numbers. Assembled for attack (3/7) – moved forward 3.15 a.m. – Battalion history noting the advance as being against great opposition through the village almost to its outer edge. During enemy counter attack – Commanding Officer Major C. Wedgwood, D.S.O. would be killed by sniper fire. Relieved 6 a.m. (4/7). Casualties – 284. From Tara-Usna Line to Albert (6/7). To front line Bazentin-le-Petit (8/7), Albert (10/7), Millencourt (11/7), Bécourt Wood (19/7), Bazentin-le-Petit (21/7) – taking over line from the Cemetery to the Windmill. Relieved and to Bécourt Wood (24/7). Casualties from shelling – 141. To front line (28/7), Bécourt Wood (31/7), Bresle (1/8). Entrained at Méricourt for Longpré (3/8) and from there marched to L'Etoile. Entrained at Longpré for Bailleul (6/8). Entrained for Doullens (6/10) and from there marched to Thièvres. To Bois de Warnimont (8/10), Albert (20/10). Moved forward to line east of Thiepval – Stuff Redoubt. To Aveluy (25/10), front line (Danube Trench) (1/11), Aveluy (4/11), front line (9/11), Aveluy (13/11), Regina Trench (17/11). Attack south of Grandcourt (18/11) – Official History of The Great War records – Battalion on right of 57th Brigade's assault disappeared in the blizzard and for a time its fate was unknown. German trenches entered west of Stump Road – hand-to-hand fighting – heavy casualties. Survivors later withdrew up Battery Valley.

9th (Service) Battalion (Pioneers). Pioneers, 37th Division; Moved from Pas-en-Artois to billets in Hénencourt Wood (5/7). To Albert (7/7). Headquarters given in War Diary as the French Civil Hospital. Work carried out included new trenches in Bécourt Wood and Pozières areas, at Gordon Dump, and on a new road up Sausage Valley leading to the front line. To Bresle (23/7), Fricourt Wood (30/7). Worked up the valley north-east of Mametz and on strong-points at Bazentin-le-Petit Wood. To Bresle (15/8). Entrained at Fréchencourt for Hallencourt (18/8). To Béthune area (19/8). Marched from Maizières west of Arras to Authieule (21/10). To Beauval (8/11), Gézaincourt (9/11), Hédauville (11/11). Worked in Beaumont-Hamel area. Involved in operations on the Ancre (13/11)–(18/11). Relieved and to Mesnil.

York And Lancaster Regiment

2nd Battalion. 16th Brigade, 6th Division: Arrived Doullens from Ypres sector (3/8) and from there to Authieule. To Puchevillers (4/8), Acheux (7/8), Mailly-Maillet Wood (9/8), front line trenches north of Hamel (12/8). Relieved and to Mailly-Maillet and Auchonvillers (15/8). To trenches Beaumont-Hamel sector (20/8), Bertrancourt (27/8), Amplier (28/8), Naours (29/8), Villers-Bocage (6/9), Corbie (7/9), Bois des Tallies (8/9), Maltz Horn Farm, Chimpanzee Trench (11/9). Attack on Leuze Wood and The Quadrilateral (15/9) – followed 8th Bedfordshire and 1st East Kent into assault – soon checked by heavy machine gun fire – advance held up and all 3 battalions pinned down in start position. Renewed attempt made early evening also failed. Withdrew to sunken road, north-west corner of Leuze Wood (16/9). In action at The Quadrilateral (18/9) – bombed from south-east – moving on right to Middle Copse and on to north-east corner of Bouleaux Wood. Relieved and to Morlancourt (19/9). To La Briqueterie (21/9), assembly positions northeast of Ginchy (24/9). Attack on Morval (25/9) – all objectives taken within 15 minutes of zero – move forward described in Official History of The Great War as being 'a parade-like steady advance' going on to east of the Morval-Lesbœufs Road. Posts established running from Morval Mill north-west to Lesbœufs. Relieved and to La Briqueterie (26/9), Méaulte (30/9). Casualties for September – 360. Also recorded are 129 admitted to hospital through sickness. To Citadel Camp (7/10), via Trônes Wood to trenches south-west of Gueudecourt (8/10). Unsuccessful attack on Zenith Trench (12/10) – War diary records casualties as 230 out of 350. Withdrew to Trônes Wood (13/10), Mansell Camp (19/10), Méaulte (20/10), Daours (21/10). Entrained at Corbie for Longpré (23/10) and from there moved to Béthune sector.

1/4th (Hallamshire) Battalion (T.F.). 148th Brigade, 49th (West Riding) Division: In reserve at Aveluy Wood (1/7) – later moving forward to Thiepval Wood. In forward trenches until relieved (9/7) and to Aveluy Wood. To Martinsart Wood (11/7), Forceville (14/7), front line Leipzig Salient (20/7), South Bluff Authuille (23/7), Leipzig Salient (24/7), Wood Post (26/7), Martinsart Wood (4/8), Hédauville (7/8), Puchevillers (18/8), Hédauville (25/8), Aveluy Wood (26/8), Martinsart Wood (2/9), front line Thiepval sector (3/9), North Bluff (11/9), Varennes (20/9), Raincheval (23/9), Souastre (24/9), trenches Foncquevillers (26/9). Casualties period (1/7)–(25/9) – 21 officers, 731 other ranks. To Bienvillers (3/10), Humbercamps (9/10), Sombrin (10/10), Souastre (19/10), Hébuterne (20/10), Souastre (31/10), front line (6/11), Hébuterne (12/11), St. Amand (14/11), Bienvillers (18/11).

1/5th Battalion (T.F.). 148th Brigade, 49th (West Riding) Division: Moved forward in reserve from Aveluy Wood to Thiepval Wood (1/7). Attack on St. Pierre Divion (3/7). Casualties – 350. To Aveluy Wood (4/7), Thiepval Wood (5/7), Gordon Castle (6/7), North Bluff Authuille (7/7), front line Leipzig Salient (15/7), Authuille Wood (16/7), Quarry Post sector (19/7), South Bluff Authuille (26/7), Leipzig Salient (30/7), Hédauville (3/8), Aveluy Wood (9/8), Forceville (18/8), Puchevillers (19/8), Hédauville (29/8), Martinsart Wood (31/8), Thiepval Wood (4/9), Hédauville (20/9), Arquèves (23/9), St. Amand (24/9), Foncquevillers (27/9), Souastre (9/10), Warluzel (10/10), Souastre (18/10), Hébuterne (19/10), front line (20/10), Souastre (25/10), front line (31/10), Hébuterne (6/11), front line (12/11), Souastre (14/11).

6th (Service) Battalion. 32nd Brigade, 11th (Northern) Division: Arrived Raincheval from Arras sector (3/9). To Senlis (7/9), Martinsart Wood (8/9), front line Thiepval sector (10/9), Hédauville (15/9), Bouzincourt (18/9), Mailly-Maillet (21/9), via Martinsart Wood to front line Mouquet Farm (22/9). Attacked (24/9) – took north-western corner of farm but later forced to withdraw after strong counter attack. Relieved and to Varennes (25/9). Via Bouzincourt to Crucifix Corner (26/9), trenches Ovillers sector (27/9). Attack on Hessian Trench (29/9) – objective gained. Relieved and to Acheux (1/10). Entrained for Candas (2/10) and from there to Maison-Roland. To Agenville (6/10), Beaumetz (6/10).

7th (Service) Battalion (Pioneers). Pioneers, 17th (Northern) Division: Moved forward from Ville-sur-Ancre to Sandpit Camp (2/7). To Bécordel-Bécourt (3/7). Operations around Contalmaison. To Montigny (11/7), Eaucourt-sur-Somme (15/7), Cardonnette (21/7), L'Etoile (22/7). Entrained at Hangest for Méricourt (23/7) and from there to Dernancourt. To bivouacs south of Mametz (26/7), north-west of Dernancourt (29/7), near Fricourt (1/8). Operations at Longueval and Delville Wood. To bivouacs north-west of Dernancourt (12/8). Entrained at Méricourt for Candas (15/8) and from there to Béalcourt. To Halloy (17/8), Souastre (20/8), Doullens (21/9), Ribeaucourt (22/9), St. Riquier (23/9), Bayencourt (1/10). Communication trenches dug Hébuterne sector. To Mondicourt (19/10), Méricourt (22/10), Citadel Camp (27/10), Waterlot Farm (1/11), Montauban (15/11).

8th (Service) Battalion. 70th Brigade, 8th and 23rd Divisions: Attacked Ovillers (1/7) – with 8th K.O.Y.L.I. leading waves cleared German first line and entered second – here due to heavy losses assault checked and withdrawal forced. Casualties – 635. Relieved and via Long Valley to Dernancourt (2/7). Entrained for Ailly-sur-Somme (3/7) and from there to Argœuvres. To Saisseval (4/7), Bruay near Béthune (6/7). Entrained for Longpré (16/7) and from there to Poulainville. Battalion (with 70th Brigade) transferred to 23rd Division having been temporarily attached to 8th Division since October 1915. To Mirvaux (17/7), Baizieux Wood (21/7), trenches Contalmaison sector (25/7), Shelter Wood and The Cutting (28/7), Black Wood (2/8), Franvillers (7/8). Entrained at Fréchencourt for Armentières sector (11/8). Entrained at St. Omer for Longueau (10/9) and from there to Cardonnette. By bus to Bécourt Wood (12/9), forward trenches (14/9). In support for successful attack on Martinpuich (15/9). Relieved and to Black Wood (16/9), Scots Redoubt (18/9), trenches north of Peak Wood, Quadrangle Trench (22/9), front line Le Sars sector (28/9). Successful attack on Destremont Farm (29/9). To Scots Redoubt (2/10), Contalmaison (3/10), trenches south-west of Martinpuich (7/10). Attacked 4.50 a.m. (8/10) – 2 companies sweeping through Flers lines and establishing post 750 yards north-west of Le Sars at the Pys Road quarry. Relieved and to Lozenge Wood (9/10), Bresle (10/10). Entrained at Albert for Ypres sector (12/10).

9th (Service) Battalion. 70th Brigade, 8th and 23rd Divisions: Attack on Ovillers (1/7) – followed 8th K.O.Y.L.I. and 8th York and Lancaster – almost half of attacking force lost in No Man's Land by machine gun fire from Thiepval Spur. War Diary records out of 25 officers and 736 other ranks, just 180 returned. Via Long Valley entrained at Dernancourt for Ailly-sur-Somme (2/7) and from there to Argœuvres. To Poulainville (16/7). Battalion (with 70th Brigade) transferred to 23rd Division having been temporarily attached to 8th Division since October 1915. To Pierregot (17/7), Baizieux Wood (21/7), Shelter Wood (25/7), front line Contalmaison (27/7), Bécourt Wood (1/8), Franvillers (7/8). Entrained at Fréchencourt for Armentières sector (11/8). Entrained at St. Omer for Longpré (10/9) and from there to Cardonnette. By bus to Bécourt Wood (12/9), Gourlay Trench (14/9), front line (Push Alley) (15/9) in action at Martinpuich. To Black Wood (16/9), Shelter Wood (17/9), Bécourt Wood (22/9), support line (26/9), assembly positions in 26th Avenue (1/10) for attack on Le Sars. Relieved and to The Dingle (3/10). Casualties – 155. To Swansea and Clark's Trenches (7/10), Bécourt Wood (8/10), Bresle (9/10). Entrained at Albert for Ypres sector (12/10).

10th (Service) Battalion. 63rd Brigade, 21st and 37th Divisions: Attack on Fricourt (1/7) – in support moved forward at 8.40 a.m. Official History of The Great War records that Battalion suffered heavily in crossing No Man's Land – survivors reaching high ground and what remained of leading units. Advancing through German front trench and into sunken road – heavy machine gun fire from Fricourt and Fricourt Wood to the right – later held Lonely Trench against counter attack. Casualties – 306. Relieved (4/7). Entrained at Dernancourt for Ailly-sur-Somme and from there marched to

Vaux. To Talmas (7/7), Halloy (8/7). Transferred with 63rd Brigade from 21st Division to 37th. Transferred to Hannescamps and later Vimy sectors. Arrived Raincheval from Amplier (21/10). To Beauval (30/10). Via Léalvillers and Hédauville took up assembly positions near Englebelmer (14/11). Took part in operations around Beaucourt.

12th (Service) Battalion (Sheffield). 94th Brigade, 31st Division: Moved from Bois de Warnimont (30/6) and took up assembly positions for attack on Serre (1/7) – going forward on left of 94th Brigade's attack most of the Battalion would be pinned down in No Man's Land. A few men reached German line and some later entered Serre itself. Official History of The Great War notes that bodies of men from 12th York & Lancaster were found in the north-west corner of the village during attack of (13/11). Withdrew after dark to Roland Trench. To Louvencourt (4/7), Longuevillette (5/7). At Longuevillette the roll was called and over 500 casualties were recorded. Marched via Doullens to Frévent (8/7) and from there entrained for Steenbecque. Arrived Doullens from Berguette (8/10) and from there marched to Marieux. To Famechon (17/10), Bois de Warnimont (18/10). 'C' and 'D' Companies to Courcelles (21/10), returning to Bois de Warnimont (27/10) and replaced by 'A' and 'B.' Battalion to line at Hébuterne (31/10). To Sailly-au-Bois (3/11), Thièvres (7/11), Bois de Warnimont (12/11), front line at Hébuterne (14/11), Sailly Dell (18/11).

13th (Service) Battalion (1st Barnsley). 94th Brigade, 31st Division: Moved forward from Bois de Warnimont (30/6) and assembled for attack on Serre (1/7). Heavy casualties soon after leaving start positions. Withdrew to front line. Relieved and to Louvencourt (4/7). To Gézaincourt (5/7). Entrained at Frévent for Neuve Chapelle sector (8/7). Arrived Doullens from Berguette (8/10) and from there marched to Sarton. To Bois de Warnimont (18/10). Began tours in line between John Copse and Hébuterne. To Sailly-au-Bois (12/11). Moved forward to front line (13/11) – holding reserve positions during attack on Serre. Relieved and to Sailly-au-Bois (22/11).

14th (Service) Battalion (2nd Barnsley). 94th Brigade, 31st Division: Moved forward from Bois de Warnimont (30/6) and assembled for attack on Serre (1/7) – heavy casualties soon after leaving start positions. Withdrew to front line. Relieved and to Louvencourt (4/7), Gézaincourt (5/7). Entrained at Frévent for Neuve Chapelle sector (8/7). Arrived Doullens from Berguette (8/10) and from there marched to Gézaincourt. To Bois de Warnimont (18/10). Began tours in line between John Copse and Hébuterne. To Sailly-au-Bois (12/11). Moved forward to front line (13/11) – holding reserve positions during attack on Serre. Relieved and to Sailly-au-Bois (22/11).

Durham Light Infantry

2nd Battalion. 18th Brigade, 6th Division: Arrived Doullens from Ypres area (2/8) and from there to Amplier. To Acheux (4/8). Moved forward (6/8) – 2 companies in front line (Gordon Trench), 1 in support at Hamel, 1 at Mesnil in reserve. Relieved and to Beaussart (12/8). To Mailly-Maillet Wood (14/8). Working parties dug trench running south from Roberts Trench. Relieved 11th Essex in front line Hamel (20/8). Reserve company at Mesnil. Relieved by 1/6th Cheshire (26/8) and to camp just north of Acheux. To Amplier (27/8), Longuevillette (28/8), Vignacourt (29/8), Coisy (6/9), Sailly-le-Sec (7/9), Sandpit Camp (11/9), Citadel Camp (12/9). Moved forward to valley just south of Montauban (14/9). Assembled at The Triangle (15/9) and at 7.30 p.m. bombed down Straight Trench towards The Quadrilateral. Held up after advance of about 100 yards. Renewed attack made during morning (16/9) – held up by machine gun fire. Relieved by 1st West Yorkshire and withdrew to Trônes Wood. In reserve at Guillemont-Wedgwood Trench during attack on The Quadrilateral (18/9). Relieved and to Méaulte (19/9). To Trônes Wood (21/9) and from there took over trenches from 3rd Coldstream north-east of Ginchy. To Trônes Wood (24/9). Attacked and took sunken road west of Lesbœufs (25/9) – War Diary records few casualties and capture of 200 prisoners. Relieved and to Méaulte (29/9). To Méricourt (30/9), Citadel Camp (7/10). Moved forward via Trônes Wood to trenches near Gueudecourt (8/10). Withdrew to reserve bivouacs near Trônes Wood (9/10). To Needle Trench near Gueudecourt (11/10), Rainbow Trench (13/10). Took part in attack (15/10) – returning to Needle Trench. Casualties – 142. Withdrew to camp near Montauban (16/10). To Citadel Camp (19/10), Méricourt (21/10). Entrained for Oisemont (22/10) and from there to Forceville. To Longpré (27/10). Entrained for Chocques (28/10).

1/5th Battalion (T.F.). 150th Brigade, 50th (Northumbrian) Division: Arrived Doullens (11/8) and from there marched to Autheux. To Villers-Bocage (15/8), Molliens-au-Bois (16/8), Millencourt (17/8), via Albert to Bécourt Wood (9/9). Moved forward through Contalmaison and past Mametz Wood to trenches just south of Bazentin-le-Grand (14/9). Attack on Martinpuich (15/9) – in support moved forward at 6.20 a.m. – in captured positions (Martin and Hook Trenches) by 9 a.m. In his history of the Battalion Major A.L. Raimes recalls an interesting incident. During the night a German appeared and advised the Commanding Officer that if he moved to the trench on the left, he will find a much more comfortable dug-out. Attack on Prue and Starfish Trenches (16/9) – 'B', 'C' and 'D' Companies went forward at 9 a.m. in 3 waves and took western end of objective. Bombers attacked German held portion of Prue and Starfish 5.30 p.m. (17/9) – objective taken as far as The

Crescent. Relieved and to Bazentin-le-Grand (19/9). To Prue and Starfish (23/9), Clark's and Hook Trenches (25/9). Attack on Flers Line (26/9) – moved forward along Crescent Alley at 11 p.m. – part of Spence Trench taken. Patrol sent forward about noon (27/9) – took almost 400 yards of Flers Line. Relieved and to Bazentin-le-Grand (28/9). To Mametz Wood (29/9), Bazentin-le-Grand (1/10), Mametz Wood (2/10), Albert (4/10), Baizieux Wood (5/10), Millencourt (23/10), Bazentin-le-Grand (24/10), forward trenches Le Sars sector (28/10), Mametz Wood (3/11), forward trenches (6/11), support line (9/11), Bazentin-le-Grand (11/11), Bécourt (16/11). Casualties during Somme operations given in battalion history as approximately 500.

1/6th Battalion (T.F.). 151st Brigade, 50th (Northumbrian) Division: Arrived Candas from Godewaersvelde (10/8) and from there to billets Prouville area. To Vignacourt (15/8), Rainneville (16/8), Baizieux Wood (17/8), Bécourt Wood (10/9), Mametz Wood (14/9). Assembled in Hook Trench for attack (15/9) – advanced 9.40 p.m. – small parties entered Prue Trench. Official History of the Great War records that these were all killed or wounded. Others in Starfish Line driven out. Withdrew to Mametz Wood. Later in support line Bazentin-le-Petit and front line Eaucourt l'Abbaye. In action Flers Line (1/10) – right flank exposed – high casualties from machine gun fire. Objectives later taken and held against counter attacks. To Bécourt Wood (3/10), Hénencourt Wood (4/10). Later to Mametz Wood and worked on roads. Took over forward trenches facing Butte de Warlencourt. Attacked with 1/8th and 1/9th D.L.I. (5/11) – withdrew after fierce fighting to Mametz Wood (6/11).

1/7th Battalion (T.F.). Pioneers, 50th (Northumbrian) Division: Entrained at Godewaersvelde for Candas (11/8) and from there marched to Bernaville. To Vignacourt (15/8), Pierregot (16/8), Baizieux (17/8). 'A' and 'C' Companies to Bécourt (26/8). Worked on railway line from Bottom Wood to Contalmaison and roads Mametz Wood area. Remainder of Battalion to Bécourt (4/9). To Fricourt (14/9). Took part in operations around Starfish Line, Prue Trench. To Mametz (25/10). Work on communication trenches to front line. Took part in November operations around Butte de Warlencourt.

1/8th Battalion (T.F.). 151st Brigade, 50th (Northumbrian) Division: Arrived Candas from Godewaersvelde (10/8) and from there marched to Prouville. Battalion historian – Major E. Hardinge Veitch, M.C.,T.D. notes that this was the first time British troops had been billeted in the village. To Vignacourt (15/8), Villers-Bocage (16/8), Baizieux Wood (17/8), Bécourt Wood (10/9), The Quadrangle near Mametz Wood (14/9), trenches Bazentin-le-Petit (15/9). In reserve during operations between High Wood and Martinpuich. Bombing attacks on The Crescent repulsed (17/9). Moved forward into Clark's, Swansea and Eye Trenches for attack on Prue Trench 2 a.m. (18/9) – 'B' Company advanced but un supported was driven back with high casualties. To Mill Road, Bazentin-le-Petit (20/9), Quadrangle (22/9), support line Bazentin-le-Petit (24/9). Moved forward to Intermediate Line and 6th Avenue (27/9) – later took over trenches left sub-sector Eaucourt l'Abbaye. Attack on Flers Line near Le Sars (29/9) – at 5.55 p.m. 'A' Company began to bomb up 26th Avenue and into German front trench. Line cleared and communication trenches to second trench line entered. Counter attacks beaten off – later overwhelming numbers forced withdrawal. Battalion records make mention of bravery shown throughout, especially that of 2 brothers – Second Lieutenants G.R. and W.G. Russell who fought side by side. Renewed attack (1/10) – advanced with 1/5th Border in centre of 151st Brigade's assault – first objectives taken with ease. To Bécourt Wood (3/10), Hénencourt Wood (4/10), Mametz Wood (14/10), Hénencourt Wood (17/10), Bécourt Wood (23/10), Mametz Wood (25/10), front line (Snag Trench and support) (3/11). Attack on Butte de Warlencourt and Gird Trench (5/11) – heavy losses soon after leaving start positions and withdrawal ordered. Official History of The Great War notes that men had to pull each other out of the mud before advance could be made. To Mametz Wood (6/11).

1/9th Battalion (T.F.). 151st Brigade, 50th (Northumbrian) Division: Entrained at Godewaersvelde for Candas (11/8) and from there marched to Prouville. To Vignacourt (15/8), Rainneville (16/8), Baizieux Wood (17/8), Bécourt Wood (10/9), Mametz Wood (14/9), Hook Trench (15/9). With 1/6th D.L.I. carried out attack on Starfish and Prue Trenches – advanced under heavy machine gun and rifle fire from both flanks 9.40 p.m. Parts of first and second waves entered Starfish and moved on to within 30 yards of Prue and dug in. War Diary notes few managed to crawl back, rest killed. With 1/5th Border renewed attack on Starfish (16/9) – assault driven back. Further action and heavy losses (17/9) and (18/9). Withdrew to Clark's Trench. Casualties since (14/9) – 316. To south-west corner of Mametz Wood (21/9), front line (28/9). Attack on Flers Line (1/10) – came forward from support – first and second objectives taken and held against counter attacks. Lieutenant-Colonel R.B. Bradford awarded Victoria Cross. Withdrew to Prue Trench (3/10) and from there Bécourt Wood. To Hénencourt Wood (4/10), south-west corner Mametz Wood (11/10). Worked on roads around Contalmaison. To Hénencourt Wood (14/10), Bécourt Wood (23/10), Mametz Wood (25/10). Work on road from High Wood to Bazentin-le-Petit. To front line (Maxwell Trench) (3/11). War Diary notes Butte de Warlencourt seen very clearly. Attacked (5/11) – 'A' and 'C' Companies moved forward 9.10 a.m. – Quarry taken and Gird Line occupied by 10.30 a.m. Post established on Bapaume

Road. War Diary records machine gun in dug-out north-east side of Butte de Warlencourt held up advance. Enemy counter attacked about 3 p.m. – War Diary records withdrawal from Gird Line and holding out in Butte Alley – artillery barrage requested on area north of Bapaume Road – Small party holding shell-hole north-west side of Butte – desperate hand-to-hand fighting all afternoon – driven out of Butte Alley during night – Battalion with 1/6th D.L.I. in Maxwell Trench. Relieved by 1/5th D.L.I. (6/11) and to camp north-east corner Mametz Wood. Casualties – 406. To Millencourt (16/11).

10th (Service) Battalion. 43rd Brigade, 14th (Light) Division: Arrived Heuzecourt from Arras area (1/8). Entrained at Candas for Méricourt (7/8) and from there marched to camp north of Dernancourt. To Pommiers Redoubt (12/8) and from there took over front line north of Longueval – right of Battalion in Delville Wood. Line consolidated and communication trenches dug. Relieved (15/8). In support during 43rd Brigade's attack (18/8) – 'C' Company sent forward to strengthen line. Relieved and to Fricourt. To Delville Wood (Inner Trench, Devil's Trench) (25/8). Attack on Edge Trench (27/8) – objective taken and block established up Ale Alley. Relieved at night and to Fricourt. Casualties – 209. To Hornoy for rest and training end of August. Arrived Dernancourt (12/9). To Fricourt (14/9), Bernafay Wood via Pommiers Redoubt (15/9). Moved forward during afternoon through Delville Wood to trenches east of Longueval-Flers Road. At midnight went forward to front line facing Gueudecourt. Attack on Gird Lines 9.25 a.m. – leading waves soon checked by strong machine gun fire. In his book 'The Durham Forces in the Field' Captain Wilfred Miles records just about 100 men only being available for renewed attack at 6.55 p.m. Commanding Officer Colonel Morant having just 2 officers. Withdrew to Bulls Road. Captain Miles records an interesting story. Sergeant J. Donnelly being wounded while taking a message, was awarded the Distinguished Conduct Medal. Having been sent home and later placed with the 16th (Reserve) Battalion, Donnelly went missing and was subsequently posted as a deserter. Obvious anxious to rejoin his battalion he had made his way back to France and found the 10th. He went on to gain a bar to his D.C.M., the Military Medal and as an officer won the Military Cross. Relieved and to Pommiers Redoubt (17/9). Casualties – 397. To Ribemont (18/9), Brévillers and Le Souich (22/9). In Arras sector by (27/9).

11th (Service) Battalion. Pioneers, 20th (Light) Division: Arrived Doullens from Ypres area (25/7). To Couin (26/7), The Dell (28/7). Began work Colincamps-Hébuterne sector. Entrained at Candas for Morlancourt (20/8). To Citadel Camp (21/8), line in front of Trônes Wood (23/8). Worked on assembly trenches north of railway and in front of Arrow Head Copse under heavy shell fire. Attack on Guillemont (3/9) – consolidation work in village and at German strong-point in front of Arrow Head Copse. Relieved and to Carnoy dawn (4/9). Returned to forward area during afternoon. Later to Méricourt. To Citadel Camp (12/9), Talus Boisé (15/9), Bernafay Wood (17/9). Worked on roads and tracks through Trônes Wood and assembly trenches west of Lesbœufs. To Sandpit Valley (20/9). Later worked in Maltz Horn Valley and on track between Ginchy and Morval. To Talus Boisé (27/9), Trônes Wood (29/9). Two companies to Waterlot Farm, rest to third line trenches Gueudecourt sector (30/9). Took part in operations at Rainbow, Misty and Cloudy Trenches (7/10). Withdrew to Waterlot Farm (8/10), Méaulte (9/10) and from there Ville-sur-Ancre. To Citadel Camp (18/10). Worked on roads and unloading ammunition and stores. Entrained at Dernancourt for Saleux (1/11) and from here to Bourdon. To Picquigny (8/11). Moved by bus to Corbie (16/11).

12th (Service) Battalion. 68th Brigade, 23rd Division: Moved forward from reserve positions along railway embankment south of Albert to Bécourt Wood (4/7). Carrying parties for 69th Brigade in action at Horseshoe Trench. To front line (Birch Tree Avenue, Horseshoe Trench, The Triangle) (6/7). Attack on Contalmaison (7/7) – objectives taken and consolidated. Relieved and to Bécourt Wood (8/7). In action (9/7) – trench along Contalmaison Road taken – eastern side of Bailiff Wood reached. Counter attacks driven off (10/7). Withdrew to Albert. Casualties – over 240. Moved forward to reserve lines (15/7), trenches in front of Pozières (16/7). Attack on trenches south of Pozières (17/7) – uncut wire and heavy machine gun fire forced withdrawal. Casualties – 135. Relieved by 13th D.L.I. and to Albert. Later to Franvillers. Moved forward to trenches around Contalmaison (26/7). One company with 13th D.L.I. dug new trench (Butterworth Trench). To Bécourt Wood (28/7), front line (2/8), support trenches (4/8), Albert (7/8). Entrained for Armentières sector (11/8). Arrived Longueau (10/9) and from there marched to Molliens-au-Bois and later Millencourt. To Bécourt Wood (15/9), Gourlay Trench near Contalmaison Villa (18/9), front line (Prue Trench) (22/9). Unsuccessful attack on 26th Avenue 8 a.m. (24/9). Relieved (27/9). Worked on roads near Contalmaison and dug assembly trenches east of Martinpuich. To reserve positions Le Sars sector (3/10), front line (6/10). Attacked 1.45 p.m. (7/10) – 'A' and 'C' Companies took The Tangle and sunken Eaucourt l'Abbaye Road beyond. 'B' later moved through and gained ground at Le Sars. Relieved and to Bécourt Wood (8/10). Entrained for Ypres sector (15/10).

13th (Service) Battalion. 68th Brigade, 23rd Division: Moved forward from reserve trenches along railway embankment south of Albert to Bécourt Wood (4/7). Returned to former positions same day. To Bécourt Wood (6/7), front line (Birch Tree Avenue) (7/7). In action at Bailiff Wood (9/7). Relieved and to Albert (11/7). Moved forward to reserve lines (15/7), trenches near Contalmaison Wood (16/7). Relieved 12th D.L.I. in front line after attack near Pozières (17/7). Withdrew to Albert (19/7). Later to Franvillers. Moved forward to support trenches at Contalmaison by (26/7), front line south-east of Pozières (27/7). New trench (Butterworth Trench) dug. Ground gained in Munster Alley (28/7). Relieved and to Albert during night. To Peake Wood (1/8), front line (Butterworth Trench, Munster Alley) (2/8). Relieved and to positions near Contalmaison (3/8). Moved forward (4/8). Attack on Torr Trench 9.16 p.m. – 'D' Company suffered heavy casualties from close range machine gun fire while crossing Munster Alley. Second wave gained some ground and held against counter attacks. Relieved during evening (5/8) and to Albert. Entrained for Armentières sector (11/8). Arrived Longueau (10/9) and from there to billets. To Millencourt (12/9), Bécourt Wood (15/9) and from there marched forward to trenches near Bazentin-le-Grand. Provided carrying parties to 47th Division fighting at High Wood. 'B' Company in action at Drop Alley and Flers Trench (19/9). Relieved and rejoined Battalion at Bécourt Wood (20/9). To support line Martinpuich sector (22/9), front line (26/9). Withdrew during night to Bécourt Wood. To support positions Le Sars sector (3/10), front line (6/10). Attack on Le Sars (7/10) – 'C' Company held up by machine gun fire on outskirts of village – later 'B' Company in close support went forward and with 'C' passed through village. Relieved and to Bécourt Wood (8/10). Entrained for Ypres sector (15/10).

14th (Service) Battalion. 18th Brigade, 6th Division: Arrived Doullens from Ypres sector (2/8) and from there marched to Acheux Wood. To Englebelmer (11/8). Took over line north-east of Hamel (14/8). Relieved (26/8) and via Acheux, Amplier, Longuevillette arrived Vignacourt (30/8). To Coisy (6/9), Vaux-sur-Somme (7/9), Sandpit Valley (11/9), Citadel Camp in reserve (12/9). Went forward to Guillemont and stood by during attack (15/9). At night consolidated position on Ginchy-Leuze Wood Road. Dug assembly trench forward of position. Attack on The Quadrilateral (18/9) – objectives taken. Relieved at night and to Méaulte. To reserve line between Bernafay and Trônes Woods (21/9), trenches in front of Lesbœufs (just south of Ginchy-Lesbœufs Road) (23/9), reserve line (24/9), front line east of Lesbœufs (26/9), Méaulte (29/9), Ville-sur-Ancre (30/9), Trônes Wood (7/10). Moved forward to support line (10/10), assembly positions for attack (11/10). Attack on ainbow and Shine Trenches 2.05 p.m. (12/10) – 'D' and

'C' Companies entering Rainbow under heavy bombardment – 'B' later took Shine. Relieved by 11th Essex and to positions south of Gueudecourt during night (13/10). To Rainbow and Shine Trenches (15/10), Montauban (16/10). Casualties for October fighting – 189. To Citadel Camp (19/10), Ville-sur-Ancre (21/10). Entrained for Oisemont (23/10). Entrained for Chocques (29/10).

15th (Service) Battalion. 64th Brigade, 21st Division: Moved forward from Buire into assembly positions during night (30/6). Followed 9th K.O.Y.L.I. into attack (1/7) – 'A' and 'B' Companies leading crossed 200 yards of No Man's Land into German first line. Moved forward into sunken Fricourt-Contalmaison Road and Round Wood to the left. Crucifix Trench taken by 8.30 a.m. Attacks on Shelter Wood during afternoon. Relieved (2/7). Casualties – 388. Carrying parties to 62nd Brigade in Shelter Wood (3/7). To Lonely Copse (13/7), Mametz Wood in support (15/7). Withdrew same evening. Moved forward to front line Bazentin-le-Petit Wood (16/7). Relieved by 1st Middlesex and to bivouacs between Méaulte and Bécordel-Bécourt (18/7). Began move to Arras sector (20/7). Entrained at Frévent for Méricourt (13/9) and from there marched to Dernancourt. To Pommiers Redoubt (15/9), front line facing Gird Lines west of Gueudecourt (16/9). Unsuccessful attack 9.15 a.m. Withdrew to Flea Trench and from there to sunken section of Ginchy Road. To positions south of Flers (17/9) and later Pommiers Redoubt. Casualties – 438. To Bécordel-Bécourt (18/9), front line (22/9), reserve line (24/9). Advanced into captured Gird Lines east of Gueudecourt (26/9). Relieved during night and to positions on Gueudecourt-Lesbœufs Road. Later withdrew to Pommiers Redoubt. To Ribemont (1/10). Entrained for Longpré (3/10). To Béthune sector (8/10).

18th (Service) Battalion (1st County). 93rd Brigade, 31st Division: Moved up from Courcelles and (less 1 company) placed into reserve north of Colincamps for attack on Serre (30/6). 'D' Company attacked with 16th West Yorkshire (1/7) – a tremendous bombardment of their assembly positions would almost totally wipe out 'D' Company – few managed to reach German line and Pendant Copse, but these were never seen again. Only 10 men of the company would survive. Remainder of Battalion heavily shelled while moving forward towards British line. Casualties almost 300. To Louvencourt (4/7), Bernaville (5/7), Berneuil (7/7), Conteville (8/7). Entrained for Berguette and Béthune sector (9/7). Entrained at Lillers for Doullens (8/10) and from there marched to Orville Wood. To St. Léger (17/10), Sailly-au-Bois (21/10), front line Hébuterne sector (26/10), Rossignol Farm (30/10), front line (7/11), Sailly Dell (11/11). H.Q, 'A' and 'B' Companies to Courcelles, 'C' and 'D' to Rossignol Farm (14/11).

19th (Service) Battalion (2nd County). 106th Brigade, 35th Division: Entrained at Chocques for Frévent (2/7) and from there marched to billets. To Bois de Warnimont (5/7), Varennes (10/7), Bresle (12/7), Talus Boisé (14/7), trenches around Montauban (15/7), Longueval (18/7). Consolidated ground won by 9th Division and provided escorts for prisoners. Withdrew to Caftet Wood (20/7). Communication trench dug from Trônes Wood to Waterlot Farm and reserve lines south-west of Longueval. Moved forward from Caftet Wood to Silesia Trench. To sunken road south of Bernafay Wood in reserve (29/7). Returned to Caftet Wood same night. To Sandpit Valley (31/7). Casualties since (15/7) – 262. Later to training areas at Morlancourt and Foudrinoy. To Sandpit Valley (20/8), trenches Maltz Horn Ridge north of Hardecourt (22/8). Relieved and to Happy Valley (24/8). Casualties – 113. Entrained at Heilly for Candas (29/8). Began move to Arras sector (30/8).

20th (Service) Battalion (Wearside). 123rd Brigade, 41st Division: Entrained at Bailleul for Longpré (23/8) and from there marched to Yaucourt-Bussus. Entrained at Longpré for Méricourt (5/9) and from there to camp near Bécordel-Bécourt. To Fricourt (9/9), Carlton and Savoy Trenches (10/9). War Diary records congestion in trenches – 1 company moved to York Trench, another to Montauban Alley. Chain of 5 posts (100 yards apart) established 100–150 yards in advance of front line during night (11/9). Position noted as being 300–400 yards from German held Switch Line and isolated during day (12/9). Communication trench dug back to original line during night. Relieved and to trenches near Pommiers Redoubt (14/9). To Carlton and Savoy Trenches in reserve at midnight. Moved forward to Flers (16/9) and in action. War Diary notes 'a great battle' the men being perfect and behaving like veterans. Later followed in close support attack on Gueudecourt. Relieved during night (17/9) and via Montauban to Bécordel-Bécourt. To bivouacs east of Mametz (27/9), Smoke Trench and Fosse Way (28/9), Pommiers Redoubt (1/10), Mametz Wood (3/10), Switch Trench (7/10), front line north-west of Flers (8/10), Mametz Wood (10/10), Dernancourt (13/10). Entrained for Oisemont (17/10) and from there marched to Citerne. Entrained at Pont-Remy for Godewaersvelde (20/10).

22nd (Service) Battalion (3rd County Pioneers). Pioneers, 8th Division: Three companies moved forward from Millencourt (1/7). Marched through Albert for 8th Division's operations around Ovillers. Relieved by 5th South Wales Borderers (2/7). 8th Division relieved (3/7) and transferred to Cuinchy sector. Began move to Somme area (10/10). Arrived Citadel Camp (14/10). 'D' Company to work on roads around Montauban. To Waterlot Farm (20/10). Began work on communication trenches. Assembly trenches dug for attack on Zenith Trench (23/10). 'C' Company assembled in Spectrum Trench across Gueudecourt-Le Transloy Road. Followed assaulting troops forward into Zenith Trench and dug communication trenches back to front line. Relieved and to Montauban (30/10). To Citadel Camp (1/11). Casualties since (23/10) – almost 120. To La Briqueterie (7/11). Work around Ginchy, Lesbœufs, Le Transloy areas.

Highland Light Infantry

2nd Battalion. 5th Brigade, 2nd Division: Arrived Saleux from Pernes (20/7). To Vaux-sur-Somme (21/7), Happy Valley (23/7), Waterlot Farm (25/7), Montauban (28/7), Bernafay Wood (29/7), Montauban (5/8), Sandpit Camp (10/8), Ville-sur-Ancre (11/8). Entrained at Méricourt for Saleux (13/8) and from there to Breilly. To Flesselles (16/8), Candas (17/8), Bus-lès-Artois (18/8), Mailly-Maillet and front line (19/8), Colincamps and Courcelles (23/8), front line (29/8), Coigneux (4/9), front line Redan sector (10/9), Colincamps and Courcelles (17/9), Vauchelles (19/9), Bus-lès-Artois (2/10), Mailly-Maillet Wood (3/10), front line Redan sector (6/10), Léalvillers (8/10), Acheux Wood (17/10), front line (23/10), Mailly-Maillet (26/10), front line (29/10). Mailly-Maillet (30/10), front line (11/11). Attack on Beaumont-Hamel (13/11) heavy losses from sniper fire during advance – Beaumont Trench taken. Casualties – 236. Via Mailly-Maillet to Bertrancourt (15/11).

1/9th (Glasgow Highland) Battalion (T.F.). 100th Brigade, 33rd Division: Entrained at Lillers for Saleux (9/7) and from there marched through Amiens to Vecquemont. To Morlancourt (11/7), Bécordel-Bécourt (12/7), assembly positions between High Wood and Bazentin-le-Petit (14/7) – 3 platoons going into western side of wood to engage the enemy. Attack on Switch Line (15/7) – driven back by heavy machine gun fire to start positions. Casualties – 421. To Mametz Wood (16/7), Bazentin-le-Grand (19/7), Méaulte (22/7), bivouacs just south-west of Albert (23/7), High Wood sector (7/8), Bazentin-le-Grand (9/8), Bécordel-Bécourt (13/8), forward positions edge of Delville Wood (19/8). Two companies in failed attack midnight (21/8). To Pommiers Redoubt (22/8), Mametz (23/8), Longueval (24/8) – in support during 100th Brigade's successful assault on Tea Trench. Took over captured positions (25/8). To Fricourt Wood (26/8), Bécordel-Bécourt (28/8), Ribemont (30/8), St. Gratien (31/8), Talmas (1/9), Prouville (2/9), Fortel (4/9). Returned to Somme area – arriving Halloy (8/9). To trenches Foncquevillers sector (10/9), Souastre (19/9). Humbercourt (27/9), Lucheux (29/9), Bouquemaison (30/9). Arrived Corbie (19/10). To Méaulte (21/10), Mansell Camp (22/10), La Briqueterie (24/10), Carnoy (25/10), Trônes Woods (28/10), trenches Lesbœufs sector (30/10). Attack on Boritska and Hazy Trenches (1/11) – advancing thorough thick deep slime the Highlanders would soon be swept by machine gun fire and forced to retire – Commanding Officer Lieutenant-Colonel Stormonth-Darlin killed while leading battalion into action. Relieved and to Guillemont (2/11). To front line (5/11), Citadel Camp (6/11). Entrained at Buire for Airaines (10/11).

10th/11th (Service) Battalion. 46th Brigade, 15th (Scottish) Division: Arrived Candas (28/7). To Montonvillers (31/7), Molliens-au-Bois (4/8), Franvillers (5/8), camp on Fricourt-Contalmaison Road (7/8), front line Martinpuich sector (13/8). Attack on Switch Line (14/8). Attack on Switch Elbow (17/8). To Shelter Wood (18/8), bivouacs near Albert (20/8), support line Bazentin-le-Petit and High Wood (27/8), Swansea and Sanderson Trenches (29/8), support line (31/8), trenches High Wood left sub-sector (2/9), reserve line (4/9). Relieved and to Albert (5/9). To trenches Contalmaison sector (12/8). Attack and capture of Martinpuich (15/9). To Scots Redoubt (17/9), Laviéville (18/9), Béhencourt (19/9), Albert (30/9), Lozenge Wood (9/10). Via Contalmaison Villa to Martinpuich sector (14/10), front line Le Sars sector (17/10), Lozenge Wood (20/10), Le Sars sector (24/10), reserve line Martinpuich (26/10), Factory Lane (29/10), Scots Redoubt (31/10), Millencourt (1/11), Hénencourt Wood (5/11), Baizieux (6/11), Naours (15/11).

12th (Service) Battalion. 46th Brigade, 15th (Scottish) Division: Arrived Berneville (28/7). To Flesselles (31/7), Molliens-au-Bois (4/8), Franvillers (5/8), trenches south of Martinpuich (7/8). Attack on Switch Line (12/8) – checked by heavy machine gun fire on right of assault. Casualties – 252. Relieved and to The Dingle. To Fricourt (13/8), front line (18/8), bivouacs east of Albert (19/8), support trenches Bazentin-le-Petit-High Wood (27/8), Swansea Trench (28/8). War Diary notes 'A' and 'B' Companies surrounded and 4 officers and 130 other ranks taken prisoner (30/8). To The Dingle (5/9), trenches Martinpuich sector (12/9). In support for attack and capture of Martinpuich (15/9). To trenches north of Contalmaison (17/9), Laviéville (18/9), Lahoussoye (19/9), Albert (30/9). War Diary notes shell hit billets (7/10) – Commanding Officer and 7 officers casualties. To Lozenge Wood (9/10), trenches Le Sars sector (17/10), The Cutting, Contalmaison (20/10), Le Sars sector (28/10), Lozenge Wood (31/10), Millencourt (1/11), Hénencourt (5/11), Millencourt (6/11), Baizieux (13/11), Naours (15/11).

14th (Service) Battalion. 120th Brigade, 40th Division: Arrived Bernaville from Villers-l'Hôpital (5/11). To Doullens (12/11), Souastre (13/11), Hébuterne (14/11) – relieved 1/4th York and Lancaster in support trenches.

15th (Service) Battalion (1st Glasgow). 14th Brigade, 32nd Division: Moved up from Crucifix Corner to take up reserve positions in Authuille Wood (1/7) – remainder of 14th Brigade being ahead and attacking towards the Leipzig Salient. Two companies into action 6.15 a.m. (3/7). Casualties – 285. Relieved by 1st Wiltshire and to Senlis Camp (4/7). To Forceville (5/7), Bouzincourt (7/7). Relieved 7th East Surrey in trenches near Ovillers (8/7) – successful attack made on enemy strong-point 5.15 p.m. Another assault around western side of village (10/7) would also gain some ground. Relieved by 19th Lancashire Fusiliers and to Donnet Post (11/7). To Bouzincourt (14/7). Began move to La Bassée area (15/7). Arrived Beauval (18/10). To Warloy (21/10), Bouzincourt (Albert Road Camp) (23/10), Vadencourt (27/10). Moved into tents east of Aveluy (13/11). Providing working parties for forward zone. To Mailly-Maillet (15/11), front line Redan sector (16/11). Assault on German position near Ten Tree Alley (18/11). Relieved by 16th Northumberland Fusiliers and to Mailly-Maillet (20/11).

16th (Service) Battalion (2nd Glasgow). 97th Brigade, 32nd Division: In attack at Leipzig Salient (1/7) – on left of 97th Brigade – first objective the Wonder Work and the last, Mouquet Quarry some 2,300 yards from the British front line. Within moments of the men going forward they would be swept by machine gun fire and forced to fall back. Relieved at 3.30 a.m. (3/7). What was left of the Battalion withdrew to Crucifix Corner. Casualties – 554. To Contay Wood (4/7), Senlis Camp (7/7), Aveluy (8/7), Quarry Post, Nab sub-sector (10/7). Relieved by 6th K.O.Y.L.I. and to Bouzincourt (15/7). Began march to Béthune sector (16/7). Arrived Longuevillette (18/10). To Rubempré (20/10), Bouzincourt(22/10), Rubempré (30/10), Val des Maisons (31/10), Harponville (13/11), Pioneer Road near Aveluy (14/11), Englebelmer (15/11), Waggon Road, Beaumont-Hamel (17/11). During attack on Munich and Frankfort Trenches (18/11) all objectives were taken but later lost (except for part of Frankfort) during strong counter attacks. Withdrew to Mailly-Maillet (19/11). Casualties 403.

17th (Service) Battalion (3rd Glasgow). 97th Brigade, 32nd Division: Attack on Leipzig Salient (1/7) – led assault with 16th H.L.I. Official History of The Great War records leading companies moved out from front line at 7.23 a.m. – creeping forward to within 30 or 40 yards of German front line. At 7.30 rushed forward – overran German front line and obtained possession of Leipzig Redoubt – quickly moved on towards Hindenburg Trench but heavy fire from The Wonder Work brought assault to a standstill. Withdrew to Crucifix Corner (2/7). Casualties – 469. To Contay Wood (4/7), via Senlis Camp to Quarry Post (8/7), front line (10/7). Bombing attack north of Ovillers (13/7). To Bouzincourt (15/7). Commenced march to Béthune sector (16/7). Arrived Longuevillette from Mincheaux (18/10). To Bouzincourt (23/10), Rubempré (30/10), Val des Maisons (31/10), Vadencourt Wood (13/11), Martinsart Valley (14/11), Englebelmer (16/11), front line Beaumont-Hamel (17/11). Attack on Munich Trench 6.10 a.m. (18/11) – advanced checked by heavy rifle and machine gun fire. Casualties – 313. Relieved and to Mailly-Maillet (19/11).

18th (Service) Battalion (4th Glasgow). 106th Brigade, 35th Division: Arrived Frévent from Chocques (2/7) and from there marched to Brévillers. To Bois de Warnimont (5/7), Varennes (10/7), Billon Wood (14/7), Talus Boisé (15/7), Montauban Alley (16/7). Moved forward to trenches in front of Montauban (17/7) – 'Z' Company in front line Delville Wood in evening. In action (19/7). Relieved and to Carnoy. Casualties – 183. To reserve trenches Longueval (23/7), Carnoy (25/7), trenches north of Maricourt (26/7). Moved from Silesia Trench to Bernafay Trench (30/7) – later 2 companies to Maltz Horn Farm to reinforce 90th Brigade, others to Carnoy. To Sandpit Valley (31/7), Morlancourt (1/8). Entrained at Méricourt for rest area at Fourdrinoy (5/8). Entrained for Méricourt (10/8) and from there marched to Morlancourt. To Sandpit Valley (16/8), Carnoy (20/8), Happy Valley (26/8). Entrained at Heilly for Candas (30/8) and from there marched to Autheux. Began move to Arras sector (31/8).

Seaforth Highlanders
(Ross-Shire Buffs, The Duke of Albany's)

2nd Battalion. 10th Brigade, 4th Division: Moved forward 9 a.m. (1/7) – following 1st East Lancashire and 1st Hampshire into action on the Redan Ridge. War Diary records heavy machine gun fire from the front and the direction of Beaumont-Hamel – German front line passed then parties pushed forward and reached third line – withdrew after heavy casualties. Diary also notes the gallant action of Drummer W. Ritchie who was later awarded the Victoria Cross. Relieved by 1st Royal Irish Fusiliers at The Quadrilateral and withdrew to sunken Beaumont-Serre Road. Casualties – 394. To position on ridge just south of Mailly-Forceville Road (2/7). Relieved 1st Royal Irish Fusiliers in trenches west of Beaumont-Hamel (7/7). Relieved and to former position (14/7). To camp 1 mile south-west of Bertrancourt (17/7), Beauval (20/7). Entrained at Candas for Poperinghe (23/7). Entrained at Proven for Amiens (17/9) and from there marched via Camon and Allonville to Rainneville. To Corbie (24/9), Méaulte (25/9). War Diary notes Méaulte full of German prisoners employed in road mending. To Ville-sur-Ancre (28/9), Méaulte (30/9), La Neuville (1/10), Méaulte (7/10), Mansell Camp (8/10), camp eastern side of Guillemont (9/10). Moved forward through Ginchy to support trenches west of Lesbœufs (12/10). To front line (13/10). Attacked (14/10) – entered Rainy Trench and the gun-pits immediately south of Dewdrop Trench. Later counter-attack forced withdrawal. War Diary notes 'nothing was gained and our lines remained as before.' Relieved and to camp at cross roads south-west corner of Bernafay Wood (18/10). To assembly trenches on Ginchy-Lesbœufs Road (23/10). Moved forward through Lesbœufs to front line during afternoon. Withdrew and via Bernafay Wood to Sandpit Camp (24/10). To Corbie (27/10). Entrained for Airaines (30/10) and marched from there to Limeux. To Béhen, Trinquies and Bainast (2/11).

1/4th (Ross Highland) Battalion (T.F.). 154th Brigade, 51st (Highland) Division: Arrived Prouville (16/7) – War Diary notes village then mostly occupied by the Indian Cavalry Corps. Entrained at Candas for Méricourt (20/7) and from there marched to Méaulte. To reserve trenches Bazentin-le-Grand (21/7). Relieved 1/4th Gordon Highlanders at High Wood (23/7). In action until relieved by 9th Black Watch (26/7). Withdrew to Méaulte. Casualties since (21/7) – 186. To reserve positions at Fricourt Wood (1/8), Dernancourt (6/8). Entrained at Méricourt for Longpré (9/8) and from there marched to Liercourt. Entrained for Armentières sector (11/8). Entrained at Merville for Candas (30/9). To Sarton (3/10), Bus-lès-Artois (4/10), Courcelles (5/10), Colincamps (8/10), Louvencourt (12/10), Raincheval (17/10), Léalvillers (18/10). Relieved 1/6th Gordon Highlanders in reserve positions at Auchonvillers (2 companies) and in bivouacs at Mailly-Maillet Wood (22/10). Relieved 1/6th Black Watch in front line south of Beaumont-Hamel (26/10). To Léalvillers (30/10), Mailly-Maillet Wood (5/11), front line right sector Beaumont-Hamel (7/11). War Diary notes bad condition of trenches – a number of dug-outs collapsed and several men buried (2 killed). To Forceville (12/11). In reserve at Mailly-Maillet Wood during 51st Division's success at Beaumont-Hamel (13/11). Relieved 1/7th Argyll and Sutherland in front line (15/11).

1/5th (The Sutherland and Caithness Highland) Battalion (T.F.). 152nd Brigade, 51st (Highland) Division: Arrived Autheux from Beaudricourt (16/7). Entrained Candas for Méricourt (20/7) and from there marched to Buire – during evening moved forward to Fricourt Wood. To bivouacs west of Bécordel-Bécourt (24/7), Mametz Wood (26/7). Here heavy bombardment for 5 days resulted in 130 casualties. Moved forward to trenches at High Wood (1/8). Work carried out on positions – communication trenches dug and new line established 200 yards into wood. To support trenches near Bazentin-le-Grand (4/8). Relieved and to Edgehill (7/8). Entrained for Longpré (9/8). Entrained for Armentières sector (11/8). Arrived Doullens from Bailleul (30/9) and from there marched to Gézaincourt. To Bois de Warnimont (2/10). Relieved 1st King's in trenches near Hébuterne (4/10). Relieved and to Colincamps (6/10). To Louvencourt (8/10), Bus-lès-Artois (12/10). Two companies to Mailly-Maillet Wood, 'B' and 'D' to Auchonvillers (17/10). Mailly camp moved back to Forceville Road due to heavy shelling (20/10). Relieved 1/6th Seaforth in front line (21/10). To Léalvillers (22/10), bivouacs between Mailly-Maillet and Forceville (23/10), Arquèves (27/10), Mailly-Maillet Wood (30/10), Forceville (6/11). Attack on Beaumont-Hamel (13/11) – with 1/8th Argyll and Sutherland led 152nd Brigade's assault – left flank being on the Auchonvillers-Beaumont Road. War Diary records assault starting at 5.45 a.m. In the centre advance was delayed due to machine gun fire and uncut wire and the barrage lost – first German line easily carried (despite loss of direction in dense fog) followed by second. At third line enemy put up a stronger fight – 2 machine guns inflicting high casualties. With strength of just 90 men later went through Beaumont-Hamel and consolidated final objective. Relieved and to Mailly-Maillet Wood (14/11).

1/6th (Morayshire) Battalion (T.F.). 152nd Brigade, 51st (Highland) Division: Arrived Gézaincourt via Doullens (17/7). Entrained Candas for Méricourt (20/7) and from there marched via Buire to bivouacs near Fricourt Wood. To positions west of Fricourt (22/7), Bécordel-Bécourt (24/7), Mametz Wood in reserve (26/7). Moved forward into support trenches at Bazentin-le-Grand (1/8). Working parties supplied for completion of new line (Seaforth Trench) about 200 yards in advance of front at High Wood. To front line (4/8). Relieved and to position between Dernancourt and Buire (7/8). Entrained at Méricourt for Longpré (9/8). Entrained for Armentières sector (12/8). Entrained at Bailleul for Doullens (30/9) and from there marched to Gézaincourt. To Bois de Warnimont (2/10), Couin in Brigade reserve (4/10), Colincamps (5/10). Took over trenches Hébuterne sector (6/10). Relieved and to Colincamps (7/10). To Louvencourt (8/10), Courcelles (13/10), Bus-lès-Artois (16/10), Mailly-Maillet (17/10). Took over trenches Beaumont-Hamel sector (19/10). Relieved and to Forceville (21/10). To Léalvillers (22/10), Mailly-Maillet (23/10), Léalvillers (24/10), Forceville (30/10). Moved forward to Auchonvillers (12/11). In support during attack on Beaumont-Hamel (13/11) – 2 companies later carrying second objective. Held captured positions until withdrawn to Mailly-Maillet (15/11). Casualties – 273.

7th (Service) Battalion. 26th Brigade, 9th (Scottish) Division: From Celestines Wood moved to Grove Town Camp (1/7). To Billon Wood (4/7), trenches north-east of Carnoy (8/7), front line north-east corner of Bernafay Wood (11/7). Attack on Longueval (14/7) – in support at Montauban Alley and in action around Waterlot Farm. Positions held until relieved and to Carnoy (19/7). Casualties since (1/7) – 22 officers and 429 other ranks. To Sandpit Camp (20/7). Entrained at Méricourt for Hangest (23/7) and from there marched to Ailly-le-Haut-Clocher. Entrained at Longpré for Bryas (25/7) and from there to Bruay. Arrived Franvillers (7/10). To Albert (8/10). Entrained at Bécourt for Mametz (9/10) and from there marched to Bazentin-le-Grand. Moved forward into trenches north-east of Eaucourt l'Abbaye. Attack on Snag Trench (12/10) – advancing on right suffered heavily from machine gun fire upon entering No Man's Land. British barrage falling short also caused casualties. Relieved 3 a.m. (13/10) and to Bazentin-le-Grand. Casualties since (10/10) – 467. To reserve positions east of High Wood (18/10) – moved forward to Flers Line and Drop Alley at 5.30 p.m. Relieved and to Mametz Wood (19/10). To High Wood (23/10), Mametz Wood (24/10), Albert (25/10) – billets in Rue de Bécourt. To Franvillers (27/10), Pierregot (28/10), Dainville (29/10).

8th (Service) Battalion. 44th Brigade, 15th (Scottish) Division: Arrived Gézaincourt from Béthune area (28/7). To Naours (31/7), Mirvaux (4/8), Lahoussoye (5/8), bivouacs just east of Albert (8/8), Scots Redoubt (14/8), Peake Wood and Contalmaison (16/8). Moved forward to front line (17/8) – in action at Switch Elbow – detachment joining 7th Cameron Highlanders and driving enemy back. Relieved and to Scots Redoubt (20/8). Casualties since (17/8) – 210. To Peake Wood (22/8), Contalmaison (24/8), front line (26/8), Scots Redoubt (28/8), bivouacs east of Albert (30/8), Scots

Redoubt (4/9). Moved forward and in reserve during operations around High Wood (5/9)–(13/9). Relieved and to bivouacs east of Bécourt Wood. To Contalmaison and Peake Wood (14/9). Moved forward and in operations around Martinpuich (16/9)–(18/9). Withdrew to bivouacs east of Albert. To Laviéville (19/9), Franvillers (20/9), Bécourt Wood (6/10). Moved forward to trenches Le Sars sector (8/10). Relieved and to Martinpuich (15/10), Bazentin-le-Petit (18/10). To support trenches – Prue, Martin, Starfish (21/10), front line (24/10), support line (26/10), Contalmaison (28/10), Bécourt (1/11), Bresle (5/11).

9th (Service) Battalion (Pioneers). Pioneers, 9th (Scottish) Division: Head-quarters at Grove Town (1/7). Work carried out around Fricourt, Bernafay Wood, Trônes Wood. To Bray (6/7). Occupied during operations at Long-ueval and Delville Wood. To Bronfay Farm (17/7), Montauban (19/7), Bronfay Farm (20/7), Sandpit Valley (21/7). Entrained at Méricourt for Hangest-sur-Somme (23/7) and from there marched to Pont-Remy. Entrained for Diéval (26/7). Proceeded on motor buses from Villers l'Hôpital to Laviéville (7/10). To Albert (8/10), Bazentin-le-Grand Wood (9/10). Work in area included Cork Alley, Starfish, Rutherford Alley, Prue Trench, Bazentin-Eaucourt l'Abbaye light railway, Pioneer Alley. Entrained at Bottom Wood for Méaulte (27/10) and from there marched to Millencourt. To Rubempré (28/10). From Talmas by buses to Blangermont (29/10).

Gordon Highlanders

1st Battalion. 76th Brigade, 3rd Division: Entrained at St. Omer for Doullens (1/7) and from there marched to Gézaincourt and Bagneux. To Naours (3/7), Rainneville (4/7), Franvillers (5/7), Celestines Wood (6/7), Bronfay Farm (8/7), Montauban Alley (13/7), Caterpillar Valley (14/7). Attack on Longueval (18/7) – assaulted from west and occupied village up to Duke Street – line established north-western side of Delville Wood. Casualties – 333. Withdrew to Breslau Redoubt (19/7). To Delville Wood (21/7), Bois des Tailles (26/7), Méricourt (28/7), Sandpit Camp (11/8), bivouacs near Great Bear (14/8), Dublin and Chimpanzee Trenches (16/8), trenches in front of Maltz Horn Farm for attack (18/8) – sunken Hardecourt Road taken. Casualties – 261. To Happy Valley (19/8), Morlancourt (21/8). Entrained at Méricourt for Candas (23/8) and from there began march to St. Pol area. Entrained at St. Pol for Raincheval (7/10). To Acheux Wood (8/10), Vauchelles (17/10), Courcelles (19/10), trenches Serre sector (27/10), Bus Wood (29/10), assemble trenches (12/11). In rear of failed attack on Serre (13/11). Casualties – 141. Withdrew to Rob Roy Trench (14/11), Courcelles (17/11).

2nd Battalion. 20th Brigade, 7th Division: Attack on Mametz (1/7) – assaulted western side of village on right of railway – German first line reached then heavy machine gun fire from The Shrine – advanced on past Mametz Station (The Halt), Shrine Alley, Cemetery Trench and to objectives Bunny Alley and Orchard Alley. Withdrew to Citadel Camp (3/7). Casualties – 461. To Ribemont (6/7), Pommiers Redoubt (11/7), Mametz Wood (13/7), trenches Bazentin-le-Petit (14/7) – reinforced 2nd Royal Irish during counter attack. To The Halt (15/7). Attack on High Wood (20/7) – advanced at 3.25 a.m. taking first objective – Black Road. Moved on towards Wood Lane which could not be reached. Official History of The Great war records heavy fire from machine guns hidden in standing crops, and from High Wood which took Battalion in the rear. Withdrew to Black Road. To Dernancourt (21/7). Casualties since (14/7) – 262. Entrained at Méricourt for Hangest and from there marched to Picquigny (22/7). Entrained at Hangest for Méricourt (12/8) and from there to Buire. To Mametz (3/9). Attack on Ginchy (6/9) – after heavy losses from shelling during night advanced early hours of morning towards western side of village – held back by strong machine gun fire. Renewed attack in afternoon also repulsed. To camp south-west of Fricourt (7/9). Casualties – 240. To Buire (8/9). Entrained at Albert for Airaines (9/9). Entrained at Longpré for Bailleul (17/9).

1/4th Battalion (T.F.). 154th Brigade, 51st (Highland) Division: Entrained at Candas for Méricourt (20/7) and from there marched to Bécourt. Moved forward via Fricourt and Mametz to positions south-east edge of High Wood (21/7). Attacked 1.30 a.m. (23/7) – with 1/9th Royal Scots were swept by machine gun fire during advance – withdrawal forced by 3 a.m. To support trenches Bazentin-le-Grand. To Bécordel-Bécourt (26/7). Casualties since (21/7) – 328. Entrained at Méricourt for Longpré and from there marched to Bailleul (9/8). Entrained at Pont-Remy for Armentières sector (11/8). Arrived Candas (30/9) and from there to Autheux. To Sarton (2/10), Bus-lès-Artois (4/10), Courcelles (6/10), Colincamps (12/10), Louvencourt (16/10), Forceville (17/10), Léalvillers (18/10), Forceville (22/10), Raincheval (30/10), Mailly-Maillet (3/11), trenches Beaumont-Hamel sector (4/11), Mailly-Maillet Wood (7/11). Attack on Beaumont-Hamel (13/11) – moved forward to St. John's Road Trench for successful assault on Y Ravine. Withdrew to new Munich Trench and Waggon Road (18/11).

1/5th (Buchan and Formartin) Battalion (T.F.). 153rd Brigade, 51st (Highland) Division: Arrived Halloy (14/7). To Fransu (16/7). Entrained at Candas for Méricourt (20/7) and from there to Dernancourt. To Mametz Wood (21/7), trenches Bazentin-le-Grand (26/7). Attack on High Wood (30/7) – heavy losses during advance on Wood Lane. Casualties – 227. To support line Bazentin-le-Grand (31/7), Méaulte (1/8), camp between Buire and Hénencourt (6/8). Entrained at Méricourt for Longpré (9/8) and from there to Hocquincourt. Entrained at Longpré for Armentières sector (11/8). Entrained at Bailleul for Doullens (30/9) and from there to Beauval. To Authie (2/10), Bois de Warnimont (4/10), Bus-lès-Artois (Acheux Road Camp) (5/10), Courcelles (8/10), Acheux Road Camp (17/10), Forceville (18/10), trenches Beaumont-Hamel sector (20/10), Forceville (22/10), Mailly-Maillet Wood (27/10), Léalvillers (5/10), Mailly-Maillet Wood (11/11). Attack on Beaumont-Hamel (13/11). Casualties – 257. To Y Ravine (14/11), Mailly-Maillet Wood (15/11).

1/6th (Banff and Donside) Battalion (T.F.). 152nd Brigade, 51st (Highland) Division: Arrived Buire (20/7). To Bottom Copse (21/7), bivouacs west of Fricourt (22/7). Bécordel-Bécourt (23/7), Caterpillar Wood (25/7), Mametz Wood (26/7), trenches High Wood (1/8). Relieved and to bivouacs south of Fricourt (6/8), Buire (7/8). Entrained for Longpré (9/8). Entrained for Armentières sector (12/8). Arrived Doullens (30/9). To Longuevillette (1/10), Bois des Warnimont (2/10), trenches Hébuterne sector (4/10), Courcelles (7/10), Louvencourt (8/10), Bus-lès-Artois (12/10), trenches Beaumont-Hamel sector (17/10), Forceville (21/10), bivouacs south-west of Mailly-Maillet (22/10), Forceville (26/10), front line (31/10), Forceville (5/11). In reserve for attack on Beaumont-Hamel (13/11) – later moving forward to hold and consolidate captured positions. Casualties – 121. Withdrew to Mailly-Maillet Wood (16/11).

1/7th (Deeside Highland) Battalion (T.F.). 153rd Brigade, 51st (Highland) Division: Arrived Halloy (15/7). To Berneuil (16/7). Entrained at Candas for Méricourt (20/7) and from there marched to Dernancourt. To Caterpillar Wood (21/7), Mametz Wood (26/7), front line Bazentin-le-Grand (30/7), High Wood (31/7). Relieved and to bivouacs north-east of Méaulte (1/8). To Laviéville (6/8). Entrained at Méricourt for Longpré (9/8) and from there marched to Citerne. Entrained at Longpré for Armentières sector (11/8). Arrived Doullens from Bailleul (30/9). To Beauval (1/10), Authie (2/10), Bois de Warnimont (4/10), Louvencourt (5/10), Bus Wood (8/10), Colincamps (12/10), Bus Wood (17/10), Forceville (18/10), Mailly-Maillet (19/10), front line Beaumont-Hamel (22/10), Mailly-Maillet (24/10), Forceville (29/10), Raincheval (5/11), Mailly-Maillet Wood (11/11), front line (12/11). Attack on Beaumont-Hamel (13/11) – led assault with 1/6th Black Watch – 2 companies cleared German front line, passed eastern end of Y Ravine and consolidated gains. Casualties – 320. To Mailly-Maillet Wood (15/11), Raincheval (18/11).

8th/10th (Service) Battalion. 44th Brigade, 15th (Scottish) Division: Arrived Naours from Béthune sector (31/7). To Pierregot (4/8), Béhencourt (5/8), trenches east of Albert (8/8), via Scots Redoubt to Peake Wood (12/8), front line (14/8), Scots Redoubt (22/8), Contalmaison (24/8), front line (28/8), Albert (30/8), The Dingle (4/9), The Quadrangle (5/9), trenches Bazentin-le-Petit (8/9), bivouacs east of Albert (12/9), The Cutting, Contalmaison (14/9), Martinpuich (17/9), east of Albert (18/9), Laviéville (19/9), Franvillers (20/9), Bécourt Wood (6/10), trenches Le Sars sector (8/10), reserve line Bazentin-le-Petit (10/10), Crescent Alley (18/10), front line Le Sars (19/10), reserve line Bazentin-le-Petit (21/10), front line (31/10), Bécourt (2/11), Bresle (6/11).

9th (Service) Battalion (Pioneers). Pioneers, 15th (Scottish) Division: Arrived Pierregot from Béthune sector (4/8). To Béhencourt (5/8), Bécourt Wood (8/8) – working on Black Watch Alley, Yorkshire Alley. To The Cutting, Contalmaison (9/8) – work on communication trenches, strongpoints. To Black Wood (11/8), Bécourt Wood (12/8). Work included Fricourt area, Pearl Alley, Welsh Alley, trenches east of Contalmaison, Martinpuich sector. Attack on Martinpuich (15/9) – Gordon Alley, Gun Pit Road, Factory Lane. To Baizieux (19/9), Fricourt Farm (27/9), Bottom Valley (28/9). Work on Bapaume-Pozières Road, Caterpillar Valley. To Contalmaison Cemetery (9/10) – work Destremont Farm area (10/10), Crescent Alley (11/10), Le Sars sector, east of Martinpuich, Bazentin-Martinpuich Road, Scots Redoubt. To Pioneer Camp (17/11).

Queen's Own Cameron Highlanders

1st Battalion. 1st Brigade, 1st Division: Moved by train from Béthune area (6/7) and from Doullens marched through Beauval and Talmas to billets at Naours. To Mirvaux (7/7), Baizieux (8/7) – HQ at 19 York Street, rest in wood just west of the village. To Albert (9/7), Bécourt Wood (10/7), front line west of Contalmaison (11/7), trenches 500 yards south-west of Shelter Wood (12/7). 'C' Company moved forward to north-west corner of Mametz Wood (14/7). Battalion relieved and to Albert (15/7). To Bécourt Wood (17/7), Scots Redoubt (19/7). Men's packs stacked near sunken road south of Round Wood (21/7) and moved forward at 9.30 p.m. to front line north of Bazentin-le-Petit Wood. New trench dug 500 yards north of wood and facing German Switch Line. Attack launched from new trench (23/7) – soon driven back. Relieved during night and to sunken road south of Round Wood. Casualties – almost 200. Via Bécourt, Albert and Bresle to Baizieux (25/7), via Hénencourt and Millencourt to bivouacs near Bécourt Wood (14/8). Relieved 10th Lincolnshire in trenches at Bazentin-le-Petit (15/8). Moved back to old German line at southern edge of Bazentin-le-Petit Wood (17/8). To Mametz Wood (20/8), Lozenge Wood (21/8), trenches south-east of High Wood (27/8). Relieved by 8th Royal Berkshire and to Mametz Wood (29/8). To positions near Fricourt and Lozenge Woods (31/8), trenches south-east of High Wood (2/9). Attacked Wood Lane from Worcester Trench (3/9) – after early gains later forced to retire from strong counter attacks. Casualties – over 240. Relieved and to Albert (5/9). Working party to Mametz Wood (9/9). To Millencourt (10/9), Béhencourt (11/9), Bresle (16/9), Bécourt Wood (17/9) – at 5 p.m. to trenches at High Wood. Relieved by 10th Gloucestershire and to Bazentin-le-Grand (21/9). To Mametz Wood (25/9), Bresle (28/9), Saigneville (3/10), Hénencourt (31/10), camp east of Bécourt (5/11). Worked on road repairs. To huts near High Wood (16/11), front line east of Eaucourt l'Abbaye facing Butte De Warlencourt (17/11).

5th (Service) Battalion. 26th Brigade, 9th (Scottish) Division: Moved up to Celestines Wood (30/6) and remained in reserve until withdrawn to Grove Town during evening (1/7). To Billon Wood (4/7). In reserve south of Montauban at beginning of operations at Longueval and Delville Wood (13/7). Latter involved in heavy hand-to-hand fighting while clearing enemy from Longueval and Waterlot Farm. Relieved and to Carnoy (19/7). To Sandpit Camp (20/7), Ailly-le-Haut-Clocher (23/7), Bruay (26/7). Arrived Remaisnil (5/10). To Franvillers (7/10), Albert (8/10), reserve positions near Bazentin-le-Grand (9/10), support line (12/10), front line (Flers Line) just outside of Eaucourt l'Abbaye (13/10). Attack on Snag Trench (18/10) – section from Le Barque Road captured and held against counter attacks. Relieved and via Bazentin-le-Grand to Mametz Wood (19/10). To High Wood (21/10), Gird lines (23/10), Mametz Wood (24/10), Albert (25/10), Franvillers (27/10), Pierregot (28/10), Warlus (29/10). Transferred to Arras sector.

6th (Service) Battalion. 45th Brigade, 15th (Scottish) Division: Arrived Heuzecourt (28/7). To Vignacourt (31/7), Mirvaux (3/8), Bresle (4/8), Scots Redoubt (8/8), support positions at Contalmaison (10/8). Relieved 13th Royal Scots in front line (12/8). Attacked Switch Line during night. Withdrew to reserve positions near Shelter Wood (19/8). To front line Martinpuich (23/8). Co-operated with 1st Division during attack on Intermediate Line (24/8). Front line, support and reserve positions held until relieved (4/9). To reserve camp at Tara Valley. To Laviéville (5/9), Tara Valley (12/9), support lines (13/9). Attack on Martinpuich (15/9) – advancing through leading waves at 3 p.m. – drove enemy from north-eastern end of village. Casualties – 240. An interesting story regarding a wooden cross erected at the village is recorded in the Regimental history of the Cameron Highlanders. The names of the dead were stamped on metal strips and fixed to the cross. Later, 1 man that had been missing and believed killed would take his name down when passing through Martinpuich later in the war. Relieved in Tangle, Ham and Egg Trenches (16/9) and into reserve at The Cutting, Contalmaison and Pearl Alley (17/9). To Baizieux Wood via Millencourt (18/9), Bresle (4/10). Relieved 9th Green Howards west of Le Sars (8/10). To support positions at Destremont Farm (10/10), reserve line at Martinpuich (Ham Trench) (11/10), Contalmaison (Gourlay Trench) (17/10), Ham Trench (19/10), front line (Chalk Trench) (21/10), Prue and Starfish Trenches, The Cutting and Martinpuich (23/10), front line Le Sars (26/10), Martinpuich (28/10), Scots Redoubt (2/11), Albert (3/11), Franvillers (5/11).

7th (Service) Battalion. 44th Brigade, 15th (Scottish) Division): Arrived Occoches from Béthune area (27/7). To Autheux (28/7), Naours (31/7), Mirvaux (4/8), Lahoussoye (5/8), positions just outside Albert on Amiens Road (8/8), Divisional reserve at Black Wood (12/8), Peake Wood (14/8). Found working parties for digging of Highland Trench. To Contalmaison (16/8). Attack on Switch Elbow (17/8). Casualties – 241. Relieved by 8th Seaforth Highlanders and to Peake Wood (17/8). To support positions Contalmaison (20/8), front line (Gourlay, Cameron Trenches) (22/8). Relieved by 9th Black Watch and to Scots Redoubt (24/8). To reserve positions Contalmaison (26/8), support line (28/8), reserve positions between Bécourt and Fricourt (30/8), front line between High Wood and Bazentin-le-Petit (5/9), positions behind Bazentin-le-Petit Wood (7/9), Peake Wood (10/9), front line (Sanderson Trench) (11/9), bivouacs on Albert-Amiens Road (13/9), Shelter, Birch and Round Woods (14/9), support line (Ham, Egg,

Sanderson, Tangle Trenches) (18/9), Laviéville (19/9), Franvillers (20/9), Bécourt Wood (6/10), forward area Le Sars sector (Crescent Alley, Starfish, Prue Trenches) (8/10), The Cutting, Contalmaison (14/10), forward area (19/10), The Cutting (24/10), forward area (27/10), Bazentin-le-Petit (31/10), Bécourt Hill Camp (2/11), Bresle (5/11).

Royal Irish Rifles

1st Battalion. 25th Brigade, 8th Division: Moved up through Long Valley for attack at Ovillers (1/7). In support there would be heavy casualties – first from the German barrage, then from machine gun fire. Cyril Falls notes in his history of 1st Royal Irish Rifles that three companies attacked in line with one in support. So severe were the losses in moving up, he records, that 2 companies never got beyond the British front line. In the centre, what was left of 'C' Company just reached German line, but could not maintain its position – 'D' on the left fought through to the second but was also obliged to withdraw. Relieved at night and to Long Valley. Casualties – 446. Entrained at Dernancourt for Ailly-sur-Somme (2/7). Entrained at Longueau for Béthune area (6/7). Entrained at Lillers for Pont-Remy (14/10). By bus to Ville-sur-Somme (15/10). To Trônes Wood (19/10). Moved forward into line near Lesbœufs. Attack on Rainbow and Spider Trenches (23/10). Attack on Zenith Trench 3.50 a.m. (24/10) – Cyril Falls records that assault went forward well but within seconds was 'simply swept away.' Official History of The Great War notes the advance with 2nd Royal Berkshire as through mud and water – the barrage was lost and assault stopped by rifle and machine gun fire after 70 yards. Relieved and to Trônes Wood (26/10). Casualties since (23/10) – 215. To Needle Trench (27/10), Spider Trench in close support (28/10), Misty Trench (29/10). Relieved and to Trones Wood (30/10). To Citadel Camp (31/10), Méaulte (2/11), North Camp, Carnoy (8/11), Guillemont (9/11), line in front of Le Transloy (11/11). In Hoggs Back Trench (13/11). To Sandpit Camp (15/11).

2nd Battalion. 74th Brigade, 25th Division: At Harponville (1/7). To Senlis (2/7), Bouzincourt (3/7). Moved forward through Albert into assembly trenches at La Boisselle (6/7). Attacked (7/7) – In support moved forward to consolidate first gains. Cyril Falls records men's amazement at the German dug-outs in the chalk – there were kitchens, telephone exchanges and bunks. Bombers fought up communication trenches towards Ovillers (8/7). Enemy attacked from Contalmaison Wood (9/7). Relieved and to Senlis (10/7). Casualties – 334. Marched through Albert to reserve positions at Usna Hill (14/7). Took over line east of Ovillers (15/7). Attacked south-east of village at night with 13th Cheshire – heavy machine-gun fire from right flank forced withdrawal. Bombers in action (16/7) – fighting their way up enemy trench in order to relieved 1/5th Royal Warwickshire. Cyril Falls records the action as 'a strange affair' – the men were tired and those not fighting slept while fighting went on just 20 yards away. Relieved and to Bouzincourt (17/7). To Beauval (18/7), Bus-lès-Artois (21/7), Mailly-Maillet Wood (24/7). At night relieved 1st Royal Inniskilling Fusiliers right sub-sector Mary Redan. To

Mailly-Maillet Wood (30/7), Bertrancourt (5/8), front line Auchonvillers (7/8), Bus-lès-Artois (10/8), Acheux (15/8), Hédauville (18/8), North Bluff (19/8), Bouzincourt (26/8), trenches Ovillers sector (28/8), Donnet Post (2/9), Acheux Wood (7/9), Puchevillers (8/9), Beauval (10/9), Berneuil (11/9), Domqueur (12/9), Beauval (25/9), Forceville (26/9), Bouzincourt (27/9) – took over front line trenches Thiepval Wood. To Englebelmer (1/10), Ovillers Post (6/10), Mouquet Farm, Pozières Cemetery (8/10). Took over front line positions near Zollern Trench (13/10). In action from Hessian Trench (21/10) – carried bombs and ammunition forward during attack on Regina Trench. Relieved and to camp near Martinsart (22/10). To Harponville (23/10), Beauval (24/10). Entrained at Candas for Flanders (30/10).

7th (Service) Battalion. 48th Brigade, 16th (Irish) Division: Entrained at Chocques for Longueau (30/8) and from there marched to Corbie. To Sandpit Camp (31/8), Carnoy (3/9). Moved forward via Bernafay Wood into support at Guillemont (4/9). Three strong patrols into Ginchy (6/9). Took over front west of Ginchy line (7/9). Assembly trenches dug west of sunken road between Guillemont and Ginchy (some 200 yards in front of British line) during night (8/9). Attack on Ginchy (9/9) – new positions came under heavy bombardment from British artillery – news of their existence apparently having not reached the batteries. Moved forward 4.45 p.m. – 1st Royal Munster Fusiliers on right and 7th Royal Irish Fusiliers left – German front line on outskirts of Ginchy soon taken and consolidated. Relieved and to Carnoy (10/9) and from there in motor lorries to Happy Valley. Casualties – 307. To Corbie (11/9). Longpré (18/9). Entrained for Ypres sector (21/9).

8th (Service) Battalion (East Belfast). 107th Brigade, 36th (Ulster) Division: In reserve moved forward from Aveluy Wood and assembled in Thiepval Wood (1/7) – heavy casualties from shelling and machine gun fire from Thiepval. Advanced across No Man's Land under tremendous bombardment and fire – hand-to-hand fighting at Schwaben Redoubt. Relieved (2/7) – withdrew through Thiepval Wood and back to billets at Martinsart. To Harponville (4/7), Rubempré (5/7), Berneville (10/7). Entrained for Ypres sector (11/7).

9th (Service) Battalion (West Belfast). 107th Brigade, 36th (Ulster) Division: In reserve moved forward from Aveluy Wood and assembled in Thiepval Wood (1/7) – high casualties from shelling and machine gun fire from Thiepval while waiting order to advance. Crossed No Man's Land under heavy fire – close quarter fighting at Schwaben Redoubt. 36th Division relieved (2/7) – withdrew through Thiepval Wood and to billets around Martinsart. To Harponville (4/7), Rubempré and neighbouring villages (5/7), Berneville (10/7). Entrained for Ypres sector (11/7).

10th (Service) Battalion (South Belfast). 107th Brigade, 36th (Ulster) Division: In reserve moved forward from Aveluy Wood to assembly positions in Thiepval Wood (1/7) – Commanding Officer Colonel H.C. Bernard killed by shell. Crossed British front line and formed up in No Man's Land 7.45 a.m. under heavy machine gun fire from Thiepval – most officers and senior N.C.Os casualties – advanced 8 a.m. – German support line reached – heavy and confused fighting throughout day around Schwaben Redoubt. Remains of Battalion assembled at Crucifix corner 8.35 p.m. Withdrew to Thiepval Wood during night. Moved forward to German front line 1.30 p.m. (2/7). Relieved and withdrew to Martinsart. To Harponville (4/7), Rubempré (5/7), Berneville (10/7). Entrained for Ypres sector (11/7).

11th (Service) Battalion (South Antrim). 108th Brigade, 36th (Ulster) Division: Heavy casualties during moved forward from Thiepval Wood to assembly positions in No Man's Land 7.15 a.m. (1/7). Advanced 7.30 a.m. – leading waves of 'A' and 'B' companies crossed German front line by 7.35 a.m. – second line captured 7.50 a.m. – casualties from own barrage during advance to third line which was occupied 8.46 a.m. War Diary notes – little opposition so far – subsequently heavy machine gun and shell fire from both flanks – enemy counter attacks 3.30 p.m. – gradual retirement to second line forced – second line attacked from direction of Thiepval 8.30 p.m. – withdrew to first line. Withdrew to British front line 11.45 p.m. and from there Thiepval Wood. To Martinsart (2/7), Forceville (3/7), Puchevillers (5/7), Gézaincourt (10/7). Entrained for Ypres sector (11/7).

12th (Service) Battalion (Central Antrim). 108th Brigade, 36th (Ulster) Division: Attack made by 108th Brigade (1/7) split into two halves. North of the Ancre – 12th Rifles (less 'B' Company) on the left of 2 battalion front – 'B' Company divided and attached to 9th Royal Irish Fusiliers on right. Leading waves assembled in No Man's Land and moved forward towards objective – Beaucourt Station 7.30 a.m. – heavy machine gun fire immediately caused high casualties – 1 officer – Lieut. Sir Harry Macnaghten being one of the many that were killed. Back in the British line his servant – Private Robert Quigg finding that his officer was missing, made a number of attempts to fine the 22 year old Baronet. Although Quigg was unable to locate Sir Harry he did managed to bring back several wounded from No Man's Land. For his gallantry Private Quigg later receive the Victoria Cross. Relieved after days fighting and via Thiepval Wood moved to

Martinsart (2/7). To Forceville (3/7), Puchevillers (5/7), Gézaincourt (10/7). Entrained for Ypres sector (11/7).

13th (Service) Battalion (1st Co. Down). 108th Brigade, 36th (Ulster) Division: Assembled in Thiepval Wood for attack (1/7) – heavy casualties from shell fire. Moved out into No Man's Land just prior to zero hour – advanced 7.30 a.m. towards Schwaben Redoubt – many casualties from machine gun fire directed from St. Pierre Divion to the left – objectives later gained – withdrawal forced due to counter attacks, and little ammunition. War Diary notes – almost no information received during fighting due to most officers having become casualties and the difficulty of getting men across No Man's Land. Withdrew to Thiepval Wood. To Martinsart (2/7), Forceville (3/7), Puchevillers (5/7), Gézaincourt (10/7). Entrained for Ypres sector (11/7).

14th (Service) Battalion (Young Citizens). 109th Brigade, 36th (Ulster) Division: Moved forward from Forceville to assembly position (Elgin Avenue) in Thiepval Wood during night (30/6). War Diary records – heavy bombardment 'great trouble in keeping the candle alight.' The sound of a Water Hen calling to its mate and singing of a nightingale also noted. William Frederick McFadzean gave his life in order to save those of his pals. A box of Mills bombs having fell over and a pin dropped out, Private McFadzean immediately through himself upon the grenade and in doing so undoubtedly saved the lives of many that were in the crowded communication trench. He was awarded the Victoria Cross and his name is commemorated on the Thiepval memorial to the missing. Advanced behind 10th Royal Inniskilling Fusiliers 7.30 a.m. (1/7) – leading battalions reached German first line with few casualties – supporting lines cut down in waves as they emerged from Thiepval Wood – later fierce fighting at Schwaben Redoubt. War Diary records – messages received throughout day indicating hard and un supported fighting. Withdrew to Thiepval Wood. To Martinsart Wood (2/7), Hédauville (3/7). Transferred to Ypres sector (11/7).

15th (Service) Battalion (North Belfast). 107th Brigade, 36th (Ulster) Division: Moved forward into assembly positions in Thiepval Wood during night (30/6). Attacked in support of 108th Brigade 7.30 a.m. (1/7) – followed 11th and 13th Royal Irish Rifles forward – 'A' and 'B' Companies reached German first line by 7.45 a.m – 'C' and 'D' held up by machine gun fire from St. Pierre Divion and from German dug-outs to rear. Heavy fighting in German second and third lines – high casualties and reinforcements un available. Withdrew to British front line during night. Remains of Battalion went forward to assist fighting in German front line 2 p.m. (2/7) – held position until relieved 8 a.m. (3/7). Withdrew to Martinsart. Casualties – 318. To Harponville (4/7), Rubempré (5/7), Berneville (10/7). Entrained for Ypres sector (11/7).

16th (Service) Battalion (2nd Co. Down) (Pioneers). Pioneers, 36th (Ulster) Division: From bivouacs in Aveluy Wood operated on Divisional front in preparation for attack on Thiepval Ridge (1/7). Work included communication trenches from Thiepval Wood to front line, road across Authieule marches and 1,000 yards of trench tramway. Attempt to dig communication trench during attack abandoned – company instead held British front line. Employed bringing in wounded and carrying supplies forward. Worked on communication trenches, road and railway repairs until relieved (8/7). Rejoined Division and transferred to Ypres sector.

Princess Victoria's (Royal Irish Fusiliers)

1st Battalion. 10th Brigade, 4th Division: From Bertrancourt went to assembly positions in sunken Beaumont-Sere road north of Auchonvillers (30/6). Moved forward with 1st Royal Warwickshire on right 9.10 a.m. (1/7) – heavy fire soon brought advance to a standstill – both battalions holding out in British front line. Attempt by 'C' Company to relieved 2nd Seaforth Highlanders at The Quadrilateral driven back – 'D' Company reached Quadrilateral after dark and held until ordered to withdraw next morning. To front line Auchonvillers sector (4/7). Relieved and to bivouacs near Forceville (7/7). To front line (14/7), Bertrancourt (17/7), Beauval (20/7). Entrained at Candas for Ypres sector (23/7). Entrained at Proven for Longueau (17/9) and from there marched to Coisy. Via Allonville to Corbie (24/9). Brigade attack practised at Querrieu on way. To Méricourt-l'Abbé (25/9), Daours (30/9), Méaulte (7/10), Mansell Camp (8/10). Moved forward to south-east corner of Trônes Wood (9/10) and in afternoon via Guillemont and Ginchy took over trenches east of Lesbœufs. Attack on Rainy and Dewdrop Trenches (12/10). Relieved and to Trônes Wood (16/10). Casualties for period (9/10)–(14/10) – 385. To support positions on Ginchy-Lesbœufs Road (23/10). Via Bernafay Wood to Sandpit Camp (24/10), Corbie (27/10). Entrained for Airaines (30/10) and from there marched via Hallencourt to Bailleul south of Abbeville. To billets around Grébault-Mesnil (2/11).

7th (Service) Battalion. 49th Brigade, 16th (Irish) Division: Entrained at Fouquereuil for Longueau (29/8) and from there marched to Vaux-sur-Somme. To Happy Valley (31/8), Citadel Camp (3/9), via Billon Farm took over Dublin Trench (4/9). Moved forward to Angle Wood (5/9) – dug support trenches near Falfemont Farm. Later (attached to 15th Brigade, 5th Division) in attack south-west of Combles – attacking Combles Trench 4 p.m. – Official History of The Great War records – leading waves coming upon wire amongst the standing corn and tall weeds could not get forward due to machine gun fire. Another attempt made 7.30 p.m. also failed. Relieved and to Angle Wood (6/9). Casualties 273. To Bernafay Wood (7/9). Moved forward to Guillemont Station (8/9). Attack on Ginchy (9/9). Casualties – 143. Relieved and to Billon Farm (10/9), Sailly-le-Sec (11/9), Fontaine (18/9). Entrained for Ypres sector (21/9).

8th (Service) Battalion. 49th Brigade, 16th (Irish) Division: Entrained at Fouquereuil for Longueau (29/8) and from there marched to Vaux-sur-Somme. To Happy Valley (31/8), Citadel Camp (3/9). Via Billon Farm to Casement Trench (4/9). Moved forward from Chimpanzee Trench into Leuze Wood Trench (5/9) – advanced across Combles-Ginchy Road and entered Bouleaux Wood (6/9). Relieved and to Arrow Head Copse (7/9). Casualties – 182. To Guillemont (9/9), Billon Farm (10/9), Sailly-le-Sec (11/9), Hallencourt (18/9). Entrained for Ypres sector (21/9).

9th (Service) Battalion (Co. Armagh). 108th Brigade, 36th (Ulster) Division: On right of 108th Brigade front for attack on north bank of the Ancre (1/7) – main objective being the station at Beaucourt. Began advance across some 600 yards of No Man's Land 2 minutes before zero (7.28 a.m.) – high casualties before reaching gaps in British wire. Came under heavy fire from machine gun brought up through tunnel and placed at top of shaft – attack called to a holt and withdrew to start positions by 8.a.m. Temp. Lieutenant Geoffrey St. George Shillington Cather awarded Victoria Cross for his efforts in retrieving wounded throughout evening and until his own death next morning. At roll call there would be no officers and just 80 men unwounded. To Martinsart area (2/7), Rubempré (5/7). Later via Berneville to Ypres sector.

Connaught Rangers

6th (Service) Battalion. 47th Brigade, 16th (Irish) Division: Arrived Heilly from Loos area (29/8) and from there marched to Méaulte. Via Citadel Camp to front line positions at Guillemont (31/8). Attacked (3/9) – some 200 casualties (most from British bombardment falling short) before leaving start lines. One N.C.O. reported that at zero the enemy's position ahead was 'bristling with machine guns and sending us bullets in shovel falls.' He also noted the death of Commanding Officer Lieutenant-Colonel Lenox-Conyngham who springing forward at the head of his men pointed with his cane to the enemy position – 'that Connaught Rangers is what you have to take' were his last words. Attacking on northern side of Mount Street and from Rim Trench, passed through The Quarry and took all objectives. During the battle Private T. Hughes would win the Victoria Cross. Wounded, he returned to the fighting after having his wounds attended to, and single-handed put out of action a German machine gun. Relieved and to Carnoy (5/9). Strength just 124. Moved forward to Bernafay Wood (6/9) and from there into assembly trenches at Guillemont. Attack towards Ginchy (9/9) – leading waves immediately swept by machine gun fire. Relieved by 4th Grenadier Guards and to the craters at Carnoy (10/9). To Happy Valley (11/9), Vaux-sur-Somme (12/9), Huppy (18/9). Entrained at Abbeville for Bailleul (21/9).

Princess Louise's (Argyll and Sutherland Highlanders)

2nd Battalion. 98th Brigade, 33rd Division: Entrained at Chocques for Longueau (8/7) and from there marched to Coisy. To Corbie (11/7), Ville-sur-Corbie (12/7), Méaulte (13/7), southern edge of Fricourt Wood (14/7). Attack on High Wood (15/7) – in action around Windmill, Bazentin-le-Petit. Casualties – 117. To south end of Mametz Wood (16/7). Moved forward to support at Bazentin-le-Grand Wood (18/7) – returning to Mametz Wood same day. Moved forward to trenches north of Bazentin-le-Petit (20/7) – attacked along Bazentin-High Wood Road. Relieved and to Dernancourt (21/7). To reserve trenches Mametz Wood (6/8), High Wood (13/8), Mametz Wood (14/8), High Wood (17/8). Attack on High Wood (18/8). Casualties – 189. Via Mametz Wood to Fricourt Wood (19/8), via Pommiers Redoubt to front line (Wood Lane) (25/8). Withdrew to support line (29/8), Dernancourt (31/8). By bus to St. Gratien (1/9). Via Candas to Fienvillers (2/9), Mezerolles (4/9), Echovirus (5/9), Sus-St. Léger (8/9), Humbercourt (10/9), Bayencourt (21/9), trenches Hébuterne sector (25/9), Souastre (1/10), Sus-St. Léger (2/10). By bus to Corbie (19/10). To Sandpit Camp (21/10), Bernafay Wood (23/10), trenches Lesbœufs sector (24/10). Attacked (30/10) – occupied Stormy Trench and valley in front of Le Transloy. To Trônes Wood (1/11), La Briqueterie (3/11), Sandpit Camp (5/11). Entrained at Edgehill for Doudelainville (9/11).

1/6th (Renfrewshire) Battalion (T.F.). Pioneers, 5th Division: From Grand-Rullecourt to Bernaville (12/7), Fienvillers (14/7), Puchevillers (15/7), Toutencourt (16/7), Treux (17/7), bivouacs near Fricourt Wood (19/7). Operations at High Wood (20/7)–(25/7), Longueval (27/7)–(28/7). Entrained at Méricourt for Hangest (4/8) and from there to billets at Warlus. Entrained at Longpré for Méricourt (24/8) and from there to Fricourt. To bivouacs on Fricourt-Bray Road (25/8) – work near Trônes Wood, Angle Wood, roads near Guillemont. To Morlancourt (13/9), bivouacs west of Billon Wood (18/9), Ginchy-Wedge Wood Road (20/9), trenches Ginchy-Morval Road (24/9). Operations at Morval (25/9)–(26/9), casualties – 77. To Citadel Camp (27/9). Entrained at Edgehill for Béttencourt-Rivière (29/9). Later to Béthune sector.

1/7th Battalion (T.F.). 154th Brigade, 51st (Highland) Division: Arrived Bernaville from Ivergny (16/7). Entrained at Candas for Méricourt (20/7) and from there to Queen's Wood near Fricourt. Moved forward to positions near Flatiron Copse (21/7), trenches High Wood (24/7). Relieved and to bivouacs near Bécordel-Bécourt (26/7). To Mametz Wood (1/8), bivouacs near Dernancourt (6/8). Entrained at Edgehill for Longpré (9/8) and from there marched to Limeux. Entrained at Pont-Remy for Armentières sector (11/8). Entrained at Merville for Candas (30/9) and from there to Fienvillers.

To Thièvres (3/10), Bus-lès-Artois (4/10), Courcelles (8/10), Louvencourt (13/10), Raincheval (18/10), Léalvillers (19/10), Forceville (20/10), trenches east of Auchonvillers (22/10). Relieved by 1/9th Royal Scots and to Mailly-Maillet Wood (26/10), Raincheval (30/10). To front line (4/11), Mailly-Maillet Wood (8/11). In reserve for attack on Beaumont-Hamel (13/11). Attacked Munich and Frankfort Trenches 7.30 a.m. (14/11) – southern portion of Munich taken by 8. a.m. but withdrawal forced soon after 11 a.m. Renewed attack (15/11) – small parties reached Frankfort – unable to hold forced to retire to New Munich. To dug-outs in Beaumont-Hamel (16/11).

1/8th (The Argyllshire) Battalion (T.F.). 152nd Brigade, 51st (Highland) Division: Arrived Doullens (17/7) and from there marched to Gézaincourt. Entrained at Candas for Méricourt (20/7). To Fricourt Wood (21/7), Bécordel-Bécourt (24/7), Mametz Wood (26/7), Fricourt Wood (27/7), front line High Wood (5/8), bivouacs west of Fricourt (7/8). Entrained at Edgehill for Longpré (9/8). Entrained for Armentières sector (12/8). Entrained at Bailleul for Doullens (1/10) and from there marched to Gézaincourt. To Bois de Warnimont (2/10), Sailly-au-Bois (4/10), trenches Hébuterne sector (6/10), Bus-lès-Artois (8/10), trenches Beaumont-Hamel sector (17/10), Mailly-Maillet (20/10), Léalvillers (22/10), Mailly-Maillet Wood (1/11), Forceville (6/11). Assembled in Hunters Trench for attack on Beaumont-Hamel (12/11). Attacked (13/11) – with 1/5th Seaforth led 152nd Brigade's assault – advancing north of Auchonvillers-Beaumont Road sustained heavy casualties from machine gun fire before first objective was taken – deep mud then hindered advance on to second line – all objectives taken and held. Casualties – 266. Relieved and to Mailly-Maillet Wood (14/11).

10th (Service) Battalion. 26th Brigade, 9th (Scottish) Division: In reserve Celestins Wood (1/7). Later to Grove Town. Moved forward to Billon Wood (4/7), trenches at Montauban and west of Bernafay Wood (8/7), Talus Boisé (11/7). Moved forward to Valley Trench and support (13/7). Attack on Longueval (14/7) – assembling on northern slopes of Caterpillar Valley – took left of 26th Brigade's assault (8th Black Watch on right). Battalion historian Lieutenant-Colonel H.G. Sotheby records that attack was a complete surprise – German front line being penetrated while the Pipes played Regimental March and the 'Charge.' All companies held strong positions by nightfall. To Longueval (15/7). In action Delville Wood (18/7). To Carnoy (19/7). Casualties since (14/7) – 435. To Sandpit Camp (21/7). Entrained at Méricourt for Vimy sector (23/7). Arrived Mezerolles (5/10). To Franvillers (7/10). Moved forward through Albert (8/10) and to positions at Bottom Wood. Took over trenches Flers Line (9/10). With 7th Seaforth – 'C' and 'D' Companies attacked towards Butte de Warlencourt (12/10) – heavy machine gun fire from Snag Trench blocked attack – leading waves digging in 150 yards from their start points. Relieved before dawn and to trenches east of High Wood. Into support trenches Drop Alley, Flers Line (18/10). Ahead – 8th Black Watch were under attack – the enemy using flamethrowers and inflicting high casualties. Colonel Sotheby records 'all rifles, Vickers, Lewis and Stokes guns out of action owing to mud.' Supplies of bombs carried forward through mud 3 foot deep. To Bazentin-le-Grand during night. Colonel Sotheby records the 2½ mile journey as taking 6 hours through deep mud with the loss of many men. Later returned to front line – planned attack cancelled and moved back to Mametz Wood (24/10). To Albert (25/10), Franvillers (27/10), Simencourt near Arras (28/10).

11th (Service) Battalion. 45th Brigade, 15th (Scottish) Division: Arrived Prouville (28/7). To Vignacourt (31/7), Molliens-au-Bois, (3/8), Bresle (4/8), The Cutting, Contalmaison (8/8), front line – Butterworth Trench, Munster Alley (9/8), Scots Redoubt (10/8), support line Contalmaison (12/8), bivouacs east of Albert (14/8), front line Martinpuich – Welsh Sap (19/8), The Cutting (21/8), support line (24/8), front line – Pioneer Alley, Sanderson Trench (25/8), Shelter Wood (28/8), Welsh Sap, Swansea Trench (31/8), Middle Wood (3/9), bivouacs south-west of Albert on main Amiens Road (4/9), Laviéville (5/9), Amiens Road (12/9), Shelter Wood (13/9), Sanderson Trench, 6th Avenue, Welsh Alley (14/9). Attack on Martinpuich (15/9) – led assault with 13th Royal Scots. Official History of The Great War records – attack met little opposition – bombardment having been effective. Battalion bombed Tangle South and encountered some resistance in sunken Longueval-Martinpuich Road. Withdrew to Gourlay Trench (17/9), Morlancourt (18/9). To Baizieux Wood (19/9), Bresle (4/10), Martinpuich (8/10), Lozenge Wood (14/10), Martinpuich (18/10), front line Le Sars sector (19/10), Martinpuich (21/10), Lozenge Wood (24/10), Le Sars (31/10), Lozenge Wood ' (2/11), Albert (3/11), Baizieux (8/11), Lahoussoye (9/11).

14th (Service) Battalion. 120th Brigade, 40th Division: Arrived Ribeaucourt from Beauvoir-Wavans (5/11). To Bonneville (11/11), Doullens (12/11), Thièvres (14/11).

Prince of Wales's Leinster Regiment (Royal Canadians)

2nd Battalion. 73rd Brigade, 24th Division: Left Ypres area (25/7) – entraining for Amiens and from there marching to billets at Molliens-Vidame. To Vaux-sur-Somme (31/7), Happy Valley (2/8). Now 7 miles from the fighting it was possible for parties to go forward and gain actual front-line experience. Battalion historian Lieutenant-Colonel F.E. Whitton records that several 'excursions' were made to Fricourt and Mametz and it was noted how the enemy's highly developed defences and elaborate trench systems were so much different on the Somme to those in Belgium. To Citadel Camp (8/8) and later bivouacs at Carnoy. Carried out work on communication trench from Bernafay Wood across the open ground to Trônes, through the wood and out to its east side where War Diary records – the Buffs of 17th Brigade (8th Bn.) could be seen just ahead in the front line. Covering a distance of 1,500 yards work had to be done in semi-darkness but the task was soon completed and 'Leinster Avenue' as it became known was later put to good use during the attacks on Guillemont. In support for attack on Guillemont (18/8) – could advance no further than British front line which was held until relieved by 1st North Staffordshire at midnight. Withdrew with high casualties to the craters at Carnoy. Parties provided for work in Trônes Wood. Moved back beyond Carnoy (21/8). To front line (23/8) – position being in sunken road running between Trônes Wood and Guillemont. A vivid description of the conditions here is provided by a member of the 73rd Hanoverian Fusiliers, the German regiment then facing 2nd Leinster at the village end of the road. In his diary, the Fusilier notes the sunken road as appearing only as a series of huge shell holes, filled with uniforms, equipment and weapons – 'everywhere arms, legs and heads were sticking up, torn limbs and bodies were lying all about.' Relieved and to Dernancourt (26/8). To support line at Longueval (30/8), position in old German trench on high ground due west of Longueval. Enemy took part of Brigade line near Delville Wood (31/8). Engaged in recapture around Orchard Trench until relieved (2/9). To Fricourt. Casualties – 584. Entrained for Longpré and billets at Brucamps (7/9). Entrained at Longpré for Béthune (20/9) and from there marched to Bruay.

7th (Service) Battalion. 47th Brigade, 16th (Irish) Division: Arrived Heilly from Loos area (27/8) and from there, via Happy Valley, Carnoy and Montauban, took over line at Guillemont – south-east of Waterlot Farm (31/8). Attack on Guillemont (3/9) – Lieutenant-Colonel F.E. Whitton, historian of the Leinster Regiment records – 'the 7th Leinsters had bombed, captured, bayoneted or brained with the butts of their rifles all the Germans in the first trench . . . a short breathing space was allowed and then the Battalion pushed on to Green Street which was captured with similar success.' Lieutenant J.V. Holland awarded Victoria Cross for his gallantry while leading a party of bombers through the village. Relieved and to Carnoy (5/9). Casualties – 231. Here, Colonel Whitton recalls that it was difficult to tell whether the camp was German or Irish. Almost every man possessing a German helmet and greatcoat. To La Briqueterie (6/9), positions east of Guillemont (8/9). In support during attack on Ginchy (9/9). Relieved with heavy casualties and to Carnoy (10/9). Strength just 15 officers and 289 other ranks. On the journey, and while passing Trônes Wood, War Diary notes 'a new pattern armoured machine' moving into the wood. To Vaux-sur-Somme and billets 4 miles south of Abbeville (18/9). Entrained at Abbeville for Bailleul (21/9).

Royal Munster Fusiliers

1st Battalion. 48th Brigade, 16th (Irish) Division: Entrained at Chocques for Longueau (29/8) and from there marched via Villers-Bretonneux to Corbie. To Bernafay Wood via Méricourt, Ville-sous-Corbie, Montauban – arriving (4/9). Conditions in the wood are recorded as 'terrible' – there was no shelter of any kind and a continuous bombardment (mostly gas shells) over a 24-hour period accounted for some 212 casualties. To trenches across railway south of Ginchy (5/9). Attacked (9/9) – with 8th Royal Munster Fusiliers on right moved forward at 4.45 p.m. – relieved by 1st Welsh Guards at 10.30 p.m. after heavy fighting. To Carnoy (10/9). Strength before attack recorded as 18 officers, 515 other ranks. After – 5 officers, 305 other ranks. To Corbie (12/9), Longpré (18/9). Commenced journey to Messines Sector (21/9).

2nd Battalion. 3rd Brigade, 1st Division: Arrived Doullens from Loos area (7/7) and from there via Bonnyville, Canaples, Vignacourt, Bertangles and Franvillers reached Albert (10/7). When positions at Contalmaison were taken over (14/7) the village, which lay in a hollow, was found to be reeking of poison gas. Successful attack during night (16/7) – took objectives (first and second lines) and rapidly moved on to German third line of defence. Having halted his battalion the Comanding Officer Temp. Lieutenant-Colonel W.B. Lyons (Royal Irish) tried unsuccessful to gain permission to go on and take the stubbornly held Pozières – which according to reports 'lay at the Munster's mercy.' The fighting beyond Contalmaison was of the bloodiest hand-to-hand kind – 'the bayonet on this occasion' Battalion historian Lieutenant-Colonel H.S. Jervis records – 'playing a more important part than the bullet.' Relieved by 1st Northamptonshire having spent 100 hours under continuous bombardment (mostly gas) and to Albert (18/7). Casualties since (14/7) – 205 (including 50 gassed). In reserve and support positions during 3rd Brigade's operations around Contalmaison. To Millencourt (27/7), line north of Bazentin-le-Petit via Bécourt Wood (20/8). Failed attack on enemy section of Intermediate Line (24/8). Relieved by 1st South Wales Borderers and to Bécourt Wood (25/8). Casualties since (21/8) – 217. Moved into support trenches between Bazentin-le-Petit and Mametz Wood during first week of September. Involved in unsuccessful attempt to clear High Wood (9/9). Relieved and to Franvillers (12/9). To line between Martinpuich and Flers (17/9). Enemy attacks beaten off (22/9). Relieved (25/9) and via Albert, Millencourt and Hénencourt moved to Feuquières (3/10). To Mametz Wood area end of October. Work carried out on road repairs near High Wood.

8th (Service) Battalion. 47th Brigade, 16th (Irish) Division: Entrained at Chocques for Heilly (29/8) and from there moved to bivouacs south of

Méaulte. To Bernafay Wood (30/8). To assembly trenches 3 a.m. (3/9) in readiness for attack on Guillemont – many casualties from British barrage falling short. Advancing at 12.30 p.m. – cleared enemy from Guillemont – Battalion H.Q. established in village by 2.35 p.m. – later advance made to sunken road east of Guillemont. Three heavy counter attacks beaten off before relieved by 12th Rifle Brigade 2 a.m. (4/9). Moved to road north of Bernafay Wood and then to Carnoy. Casualties – 265. Relieved 8th Royal Dublin Fusiliers in sunken road east of Guillemont (7/9). Strength 200 all ranks. Moved forward to Ginchy (9/9). On left of 47th Brigade's attack (6th Royal Irish on right) launched in late afternoon – high casualties and little advance made. Artillery bombardment having had small effect on enemy's trenches resulted in great opposition – most of Battalion advanced no further than 100 yards from start point. Relieved by 4th Grenadier Guards and to Vaux-sur-Somme (11/9). Entrained for Bailleul (21/9).

Royal Dublin Fusiliers

1st Battalion. 86th Brigade, 29th Division: Attack on Beaumont-Hamel (1/7) – followed 2nd Royal Fusiliers towards Hawthorn Ridge – moving forward from Essex Street and 88th Trench, leading waves would get no further than their own front line. The few that did get on were soon swept by machine guns well sighted on the gaps in the British wire. Casualties – 305. Remained in forward area billeting at Mailly-Maillet Wood. To Bois de Warnimont (23/7), Beauval (24/7). Entrained at Doullens for Esquelbecq and Ypres sector (27/7). Arrived Dernancourt (10/10). To south-east corner of Mametz Wood (13/10). Later began tours in forward area around Flers. Withdrew to Delville Wood before moving for rest at Corbie by end October. To Méaulte (16/11).

2nd Battalion. 10th Brigade, 4th Division: Attack on the Redan Ridge (1/7) – leading waves soon came under fire and only a few reached German front line. Casualties – 325. To Mailly-Maillet (3/7), front line (7/7), camp on Forceville Road (15/7), Bertrancourt (17/7), Beauval (20/7). Entrained at Candas for Proven (23/7). Entrained from Ypres sector and reached area around Coisy (17/9). To Corbie (24/9), Méricourt (25/9), Daours (30/9), Méaulte (7/10), Mansell Camp (8/10), positions east of Trônes Wood (9/10), support line west of Morval (10/10). In action east of Lesbœufs (12/10) – failed assault on gun pits in front of Hazy Trench (14/10). To positions near Montauban (18/10), trenches in sunken Ginchy-Lesbœufs road (22/10). Attack on Gun Pits (23/10) – objective secured together with additional strong-point further on. Sergeant Robert Downie awarded Victoria Cross. Casualties – 182. To Mansell Camp via Trônes Wood (25/10). Entrained at Carnoy for Corbie (27/10). Entrained for Airaines (30/10).

8th (Service) Battalion. 48th Brigade, 16th (Irish) Division: Entrained at Chocques for Longueau and from there to billets at Corbie (29/8). To Sandpit Camp (31/8), Billon Farm (3/9), La Briqueterie (4/9), front line south of Ginchy (5/9). Attack on Ginchy (9/9) – followed 1st Royal Munster Fusiliers into assault and took attack through village at 5.25 p.m. Casualties – 227. Via Bernafay Wood cross-roads to Happy Valley (10/9), Corbie (11/9), Béttencourt (18/9). Entrained at Longpré for Ypres sector (21/9).

9th (Service) Battalion. 48th Brigade, 16th (Irish) Division: Entrained at Chocques for Longueau and from there to billets at Corbie (29/8). To Sandpit Camp (31/8), Billon Farm (3/9), Sherwood and Fagan Trenches in front of Trônes Wood (4/9). Advanced via Guillemont to western edge of Leuze Wood (6/9). To Sherwood and Fagan Trenches (7/9). Attack on Ginchy (9/9) – helped clear western part of village. Casualties – 209. To Carnoy (10/9), Corbie (11/9), Airaines (18/9). Entrained at Longpré for Ypres sector (21/9).

10th (Service) Battalion. 190th Brigade, 63rd (Royal Naval) Division: Arrived Acheux (3/10). To Léalvillers (4/10), Hédauville (7/10), Mailly-Maillet Wood (8/10), front line Redan sector (11/10), Léalvillers (17/10), Puchevillers (19/10), Hédauville (21/10), bivouacs near Englebelmer (30/10), billets in Englebelmer (31/10), front line Hamel left sub section (3/11), Varennes (7/11), Puchevillers (9/11), Hédauville (11/11). Moved forward via Englebelmer to assembly positions in Robert's Trench (12/11). Attack on Beaucourt (13/11) – strong-points cleared (14/11) – assisted in rounding up over 400 prisoners. Casualties – 242. To camp on Englebelmer-Martinsart Road (16/11). Clearing battlefield Gordon Trench (17/11). Via Englebelmer by buses to Authieule (18/11).

Rifle Brigade (The Prince Consort's Own)

1st Battalion. 11th Brigade, 4th Division: Attack on Redan Ridge (1/7) – held up by fire from Ridge Redoubt and The Quadrilateral soon after leaving trenches – entered German line by 10 a.m. – heavy close quarter fighting along trenches – driven back after counter attack. Relieved and to Mailly-Maillet (2/7). Casualties – 474. To Bertrancourt (4/7), Mailly-Maillet (10/7), front line south of Serre Road (15/7), Bus-lès-Artois (20/7), Beauval (21/7). Entrained at Doullens for Ypres sector (23/7). 11th Brigade began journey back to Somme (16/9) – resting and training around Allonville and Vaux-sur-Somme before moving up to Montauban at beginning of October. To front line west of Lesbœufs (16/10). In action east of Lesbœufs on northern slopes of Morval Spur towards Le Transloy (17/10) and (18/10). Casualties – 261. Relieved and to Guillemont (19/10). Moved forward (22/10). Attack on Boritska Trench (23/10). Relieved and to Trônes Wood in evening. Casualties – 122. Via Mansell Camp entrained at Méricourt for Airaines (30/10) and from there marched to Hocquincourt. To Rambures (5/11).

2nd Battalion. 25th Brigade, 8th Division: Attack on Ovillers (1/7). Relieved shortly after midnight and to Long Valley. Entrained at Dernancourt for Ailly-sur- Somme (3/7) and from there marched to St. Sauveur. To Fourdrinoy (4/7). Entrained at Longueau for Béthune area (6/7). Entrained at Lillers for Pont-Remy (15/10) and via Amiens and Ville went to Citadel Camp. Moved up into line near Lesbœufs via Trônes Wood (19/10). Attack on Zenith Trench (23/10). Casualties – 238. To Trônes Wood (25/10), front line (28/10), Citadel Camp (30/10), front line (9/11).

3rd Battalion. 17th Brigade, 24th Division: Left Kemmel for Somme (23/7) and after training at Riencourt moved to Camp at Méaulte. To Carnoy Valley (7/8), Bernafay Wood in reserve (12/8), Carnoy Valley (14/8). Attacked towards High Holborn between Guillemont and Delville Wood (18/8) – gained some ground including Guillemont Station. Casualties – 225. Renewed attack by 'D' Company (21/8) – all officers ¾ of assault lost. Remainder (23 men) under a sergeant held gains until relieved after dark. Via Montauban to Albert (22/8), Montauban in reserve (27/8). Attack on Orchard and Tea Trenches (1/9). Casualties – 211. To Albert (2/9). 24th Division began move away from Somme fighting (6/9). Via Dernancourt and camps in Abbeville area reached front line at Vimy Ridge (12/9).

7th (Service) Battalion. 41st Brigade, 14th (Light) Division: Began moved towards Somme early in August and via Doullens, Albert and Montauban took over trenches west of Delville Wood (12/8). Relieved by 8th Rifle Brigade and to Montauban (14/8). To front line (17/8). On left of 41st brigade during attack on Orchard and Wood Lane trenches (18/8). Casualties – 270. Relieved at midnight and to Montauban. To line south-east of Delville Wood (25/8), Dernancourt (27/8). Entrained for Airaines (28/8) and from there marched to Warlus Camp near Amiens (28/8). Entrained for Dernancourt (8/9). To Montauban (12/9), Delville Wood (14/9). Attacked 8 a.m. (15/9) – Gap Trench close to Flers taken and ground held. Relieved at midnight and into reserve at Delville. Casualties – 267. To Dernancourt (17/9), Lucheux (22/9), Gouy-en-Artois, south-west of Arras (26/9).

8th (Service) Battalion. 41st Brigade, 14th (Light) Division: Arrived Longue-villette (1/8). To Dernancourt (7/8). Went forward via Pommiers Redoubt to positions in north-east corner of Delville Wood (13/8). In support during attack on Orchard and Wood Lane Trenches (18/8). Took over trenches in Delville Wood (19/8). To Pommiers Redoubt (25/8), Dernancourt (26/8), Laleu (31/8). Entrained for Dernancourt (10/9). To Fricourt Camp (11/9), forward area east of Delville Wood (12/9). Attacked and captured Switch Trench (15/9). Casualties – over 400. To Fricourt Camp (16/9), Dernancourt (17/9). Later to sector south-west of Arras.

9th (Service) Battalion. 42nd Brigade, 14th (Light) Division: Left Grand-Rullecourt for Barly (29/7). To Candas (31/7), Buire-sur-l'Ancre (8/8). Via Dernancourt, Méaulte and Montauban took over trenches near Delville Wood (19/8). Assisted during attack on Delville Wood (24/8). To Le Fay (1/9). Entrained for Dernancourt (11/9). Moved to forward area and in line at Delville Wood by (15/9). Attack towards Flers – lost heavily from enfilade machine gun fire from right flank while approaching Bulls Road – Lieutenant-Colonel. T.H.P. Morris mortally wounded and every other officer hit except one junior subaltern. Casualties – 294. To Montauban Alley (16/9), camp near Albert (17/9), Grand-Rullecourt (25/9).

10th (Service) Battalion. 59th Brigade, 20th (Light) Division: Arrived Sailly-au-Bois from Ypres area (27/7). To trenches south of Hébuterne (28/7). Relieved and to Beauval (18/8). To Doullens (19/8), Méaulte (20/8), camp about 3½ miles north of Bray (21/8), Carnoy craters (22/8). Heavy casu-alties from enemy shell fire. Successful attack around Guillemont (3/9). Relived and to Minden Post by 8.30 (5/9). Casualties – almost 300. To Talus Boisé (6/9), Corbie (7/9), Talus Boisé (11/9), trenches north-east of Ginchy (16/9). At dawn (17/9) it was found that position held was in fact a German communication trench running at right angles to enemy's line. In the evening an attempt was made to adjust the situation, but this would fail. Relieved and to Méaulte (19/9). To Morlancourt (22/9), Carnoy (27/9), trenches near Gueudecourt (4/10), camp near Montauban (7/10), Méaulte

(8/10), Méricourt (9/10). Later to Breilly. To Saisseval (2/11), Méricourt (15/11).

11th (Service) Battalion. 59th Brigade, 20th (Light) Division: Moved from Locre to Authie (26/7) and from there took turns in line near Hébuterne. To Méaulte (20/8), Citadel Camp (21/8), La Briqueterie (22/8), trenches in front of Guillemont (24/8) – came under attack in evening and during next day. To Irish Alley in support (28/8). Successful attack at Guillemont (3/9). To Carnoy (5/9), Talus Boisé (6/9), Corbie (8/9). From Talus Boisé moved into trenches north-east of Ginchy (16/9). Attack towards Lesbœufs (17/9). To Montauban (19/9). Later to Sandpit Camp. To Morlancourt (22/9), Carnoy (27/9). Casualties for September – 292. To Méaulte (8/10), Ville-sur-Ancre (9/10), Franvillers (18/10), Picquigny (21/10), Ville-sur-Ancre (15/11).

12th (Service) Battalion. 60th Brigade, 20th (Light) Division: Left Bailleul (23/7) and via Sarton and Bus-lès-Artois went into camp at Courcelles-au-Bois (29/7). To trenches opposite Serre (6/8), Couin (14/8), Amplier (16/8), Méaulte via Fienvillers and Ville (21/8). To trenches on Carnoy-Montauban Road (22/8). Battalion records note that during evening 3rd Rifle Brigade passed down the road from front line and the 11th went by them in the opposite direction. At the same time the 7th, 8th, 9th and 10th Battalions were all close by. At 5 p.m (3/9) moved forward into trenches west of Trônes Wood and relieved 8th Royal Munster Fusiliers after that battalion's attack on Guillemont earlier in the day. To the craters in front of Carnoy (5/9), bivouacs 2 miles from Bray (7/9), Corbie (8/9), Méaulte (11/9), Citadel Camp (15/9), trenches south of Ginchy (16/9). In action at The Quadrilateral and in the fighting towards Morval. To Citadel Camp (20/9), Ville (22/9), Citadel Camp (25/9), forward trenches (27/9), Talus Boisé (28/9), positions west of Trônes Wood (29/9), Carnoy (4/10), Montauban (6/10). Attack (with 6th Ox. & Bucks and 7th King's Own Yorkshire Light Infantry) on Rainbow Trench (7/10). Casualties – 234. Only 2 company officers survived. To Sandpit Camp (8/10), Corbie (15/10), Flesselles via Allonville (19/10), Hangest-sur-Somme (1/11), Corbie (16/11).

13th (Service) Battalion. 111th Brigade, 37th Division: Arrived Humbercourt from Bailleulval (3/7). To Bresle (5/7), Albert in reserve to 56th Brigade (6/7), Tara-Usna Line (7/7). Relieved 8th North Staffordshire in front line La Boisselle during evening. Battalion historian D.H. Rowlands notes the dead of the Tyneside Scottish all around, many still with bolt-covers on their rifles. Withdrew to support line (10/7). Orders received to attack at 8.45 p.m. This assault was later cancelled but news of this came too late and Battalion went forward towards Ovillers as planned. A distance of 200 yards was covered and enemy's third line reached. Over 200 prisoners taken. Casualties – including Commanding Officer, Adjutant and all Company Commanders – over 400. Withdrew to original German second line (just beyond Lochnagar Crater) (11/7). To Tara-Usna Line (12/7), trenches south-east of La-Boisselle (15/7), Albert (19/7), Bresle (20/7), Albert (30/7), trenches south-west of Mametz Wood in reserve (31/7). Heavy casualties from shelling during night (6/8). Moved forward to support line south-east of Bazentin-le-Petit (8/8). To reserve line (11/8), Bresle (14/8). Entrained at Fréchencourt for Citerne (18/8). Moved to Béthune area (19/8). Arrived Gézaincourt (21/10). To Puchevillers (22/10), Longuevillette (30/10), Puchevillers (11/11), Hédauville (12/11). Moved south of Englebelmer and attached to 63rd (Royal Naval) Division (13/11). Later through Hemel to assembly positions. Attack on Beaucourt Trench from Railway Alley to a point 400 yards north-west (14/11) – with 1/1st Honourable Artillery Company on right and 13th Royal Fusiliers on left objectives taken. In action at Munich, Muck and Railway Trenches (15/11). Withdrew to reserve line during night. To Englebelmer (20/11).

16th (Service) Battalion (St. Pancras). 117th Brigade, 39th Division: Arrived Doullens from Béthune area (24/8). To Vauchelles-les-Authie (25/8), Bertrancourt (28/8). To forward zone (2/9). Attacked north of the Ancre (3/9). Relieved at night and to bivouacs near Mailly-Maillet. Casualties – over 400. To Bertrancourt (4/9), Mailly-Maillet (6/9), reserve trenches Hébuterne (11/9), front line (13/9), Courcelles-au-Bois (19/9), front line (20/9), Courcelles-au-Bois (31/9), Hédauville (2/10), trenches near Thiepval (5/10), dug-outs on Martinsart Road (10/10). In support during 118th Brigade's successful assault on the Schwaben Redoubt (14/10). Attack on Stuff Redoubt (21/10) – objective Pope's Nose. Casualties – 138. To Martinsart Road dug-outs (24/10), trenches River Ancre sector (27/10), Schwaben Redoubt (3/11), Senlis (5/11). Later to Thiepval. To Martinsart Wood (11/11), Thiepval (13/11). In support during 39th Division's attack on St. Pierre Divion. To Warloy (14/11), Bollezeele, north of St Omer via Beauval and Candas (15/11).

Honourable Artillery Company (Territorial Force)

1/1st Battalion. 190th Brigade, 63rd (Royal Naval) Division: Left Divisional training area at Marquay near St. Pol, entrained for Acheux (3/10). To Varennes (4/10), Mailly-Maillet Wood (8/10). Took over line Redan right sector (10/10)–(15/10). Here A.O. Pollard V.C. in his book 'Fire-Eater' noted that the neighbourhood was alive with artillery and that it was obvious that Staff were making preparation for a big attack. To Mailly-Maillet Wood (15/10), Léalvillers (17/10), Puchevillers (18/10), via Varennes to Hédauville (21/10). 500 men engaged in digging a buried cable trench from Mesnil to Hamel (23/10). Via Englebelmer to Mesnil (30/10). Once more A.O. Pollard observed preparations for the coming battle – noting 12-inch naval guns in the orchard between Martinsart and Mesnil, and lines of 6-inch howitzers. Relieve 7th Royal Fusiliers in right sub sector at Hamel (3/11). Relieved by Hood Battalion and to Englebelmer (6/11). To Hédauville (11/11), via Mesnil to assembly positions on the rising ground in front of Beaucourt (12/11). Successful attack on Beaucourt (13/11) – casualties reducing Battalion to strength of a single company. Relieved by 10th York and Lancaster just before dawn (15/11) and to start positions near Hemel. To Martinsart (16/11), via Hédauville to Authuille (17/11), via Doullens to Le Meillard (19/11).

Monmouthshire Regiment (Territorial Force)

1/1st Battalion. Pioneers, 46th (North Midland) Division: From Headquarters at Foncquevillers assembled (1/7) in positions facing Gommecourt. Moving forward with assaulting troops work began improving and digging communication trenches. Under constant fire throughout. Casualties just under 100. Via Pommier left for sector south-west of Arras and billets at Berles (2/7).

1/2nd Battalion. Pioneers, 29th Division: Attack on Beaumont-Hamel (1/7) - stood by under heavy bombardment. Planed consolidation work could not take place owing to failure of attack. In his history of the Battalion Captain G.A. Brett recalls that on (1/7) only 200 men could be issued with helmets. The remainder (wearing their soft caps) were instructed to replace these with helmets taken from the dead as soon as possible. Captain Brett notes that within hours every man had a steel helmet. Withdrew to Mailly-Maillet Wood by midnight. For next weeks worked on a series of front line and communications trenches from the Redan down to the Ancre. These improved positions were to be those used by the 51st (Highland) Division at the beginning of its successful assault at Beaumont Hamel the following November. Moved to Ypres sector (24/7). Back on the Somme and in camp at Montauban (6/10). Captain Brett recalls that on the march to Montauban one man fell out. He was later delivered in fine style by a staff car also occupied by the Prince of Wales. Worked principally on road improvements around Ginchy, Lesbœufs and Flers.

1/3rd Battalion. Pioneers, 49th (West Riding) Division: Moved forward from Bouzincourt to 36th (Ulster) Division's area in front of the Schwaben Redoubt during evening (1/7). Work included digging of communication trenches around the Thiepval and La Boisselle areas. To Hédauville (10/7), Forceville (5/8). Battalion had been low in numbers for some time and replacements were becoming difficult to find. Subsequently, and while at Forceville, orders were received to disband. Personnel to various other regiments, including sister battalions – 1/1st and 1/2nd Monmouthshire.

Cambridgeshire Regiment (Territorial Force)

1/1st Battalion. 118th Brigade, 39th Division: Arrived Grouches (24/8). To Bus-lès-Artois (25/8), front line just north of Hamel (26/8) – Battalion history notes Headquarters in Knightsbridge and a long journey down to front line by Gabion Avenue. In reserve during attack (3/9) – later held line against German counter attack. Withdrew to Mailly-Maillet Wood. To front line (12/9). Relieved by 1/1st Hertfordshire and to Aveluy Wood (3/10). In his contribution to the Regiment's war history Brigadier-General E. Riddell notes the particular long period of time spent by his battalion in the line at this time. He also mentions the intensity of the enemy's shelling and records an average of 74 shells a day landing in his lines. To dug-outs on North and South Bluffs, Authuille (4/10). Provided carrying and burial parties to Schwaben Redoubt. Brigadier-General Riddell notes the danger of using Martin's Lane as an approach to The Schwaben Redoubt. An alternative and safer route was discovered and in this the body of a runner was found still grasping a scrap of paper. The message suggested that stretcher-bearers should not use Martin's Lane. It also requested that the messenger might not be used again as he had already frequently risked his life that day. Attack on north face Schwaben Redoubt (14/10) – with 4th/5th Black Watch took objective – held and consolidated gains. Relieved and to Wood Post (15/10). Casualties – 213. To Senlis Camp (16/10), old German dug-outs at Thiepval (22/10). Battalion history notes that these were some 20 feet underground and 3 or 4 of them easily accommodated the whole battalion. Attack on St. Piere Divion (13/11) – objectives (part of Mill Trench and Beaucourt Mill) taken by 10 a.m. Relieved and via Warloy entrained at Doullens for Ypres sector (19/11).

London Regiment (Territorial Force)

1/1st Battalion (Royal Fusiliers). 167th Brigade, 56th (1st London) Division: In reserve at Hébuterne during attack on Gommecourt (1/7). To Sailly-au-Bois (3/7), Hébuterne (5/7), Souastre (10/7), Forceville (16/7), Souastre (20/7), Foncquevillers (28/7), Souastre (6/8), Le Souich (22/8), Mezerolles (23/8), Noyelles-en-Chaussée (24/8), Bois des Tailles (5/9), Billon Farm (6/9). Attack on Leuze Wood (9/9). To Maltz Horn area (11/9). Provided carrying parties to forward area around Guillemont. To Billon Farm (12/9), trenches in Leuze Wood (14/9). In action at Bouleaux Wood (15/9) – penetrating German front trenches through almost to Middle Copse. Withdrawn to Wedge Wood (18/9). To Billon Farm (19/9), Leuze Wood (22/9), Bully Beef Trench north-west of Bouleaux Wood (25/9), Angle Wood (26/9), Méaulte area (27/9). Via Trônes Wood to line at Lesbœufs (30/9). Attacked Spectrum Trench (7/10). Relieved and to Citadel Camp (9/10). Casualties – 347. To Bertangles (11/10), Longpré (24/10). Began move to Laventie sector (27/10).

1/2nd Battalion (Royal Fusiliers). 169th Brigade, 56th (1st London) Division: In reserve at beginning of attack on Gommecourt (1/7) – sent forward about 2 p.m. under heavy machine gun fire from Gommecourt Park. Withdrew in evening to line in front of Hébuterne. Casualties – 253. To Souastre (3/7), Foncquevillers (4/7), front line (6/7), Foncquevillers (8/7), St. Amand (12/7), front line east of Hannescamps (14/7), St. Amand (19/7), front line (21/7), resting between tours at Bienvillers. To Ivergny (18/8), Maizicourt (22/8), Canchy (23/8). Entrained at St. Riquier for Corbie (3/9), to Happy Valley (4/9), support positions at Falfemont Farm and Angle Wood (6/9). In support during 169th Brigade's attack around Leuze Wood (9/9) – heavy casualties at Loop Trench (10/9). Relieved and to Citadel Camp. To Billon Farm (12/9), Angle Wood (13/9). Attack on Loop Trench (15/9) – objective taken along with end of Combles Trench. To Falfemont Farm (17/9), Combles and Leuze Trenches (18/9), Combles entered (26/9) – 'A' and 'C' Companies moving through village and setting up positions in front of railway. Via Casement trench to Méaulte (27/9), in reserve near Carnoy (29/9), to trenches midway between Lesbœufs and Ginchy (30/9), front line east of Lesbœufs (2/10) – Rainy, Burnaby and Burnaby Support Trenches. Relieved by 1/4th London and to reserve positions between Trônes and Bernafay Woods (3/10), Flers Line (8/10), Citadel Camp (9/10), Ville-sur-Ancre and moved by French buses to Breilly (10/10). To Bailleul (21/10). Entrained at Pont-Remy for Berguette (23/10). Total Somme casualties (excluding those of 1st July) given in Battalion history (Major W.E. Grey) as 628.

1/3th Battalion (Royal Fusiliers). 167th Brigade, 56th (1st London) Division: On extreme left of 56th Division's attack at Gommecourt (1/7) – 2 companies remaining in trenches and providing carrying parties, 2 with 1/4th Lincolnshire filling in the gap between the 56th and 46th Divisions in front of Gommecourt Park. To Sailly-au-Bois (3/7), front line Hébuterne (5/7), Bayencourt (9/7), Souastre (10/7), Hébuterne (12/7), Souastre (16/7), front line Foncquevillers (20/7), Souastre (29/7), front line (6/8), Souastre (18/8), Bouquemaison (19/8), Barny (23/8), Conteville (24/8), Corbie (4/9), Bois de Tailles (5/9), Citadel Camp (6/9), Billon Farm (7/9), Casement and Dublin Trenches (9/9), Leuze Wood (10/9), Casement Trench (13/9). In support at Wedge Wood during operations around Bouleaux Wood (15/9)–(18/9). In action objectives Bouleaux Wood, Middle Copse (18/9)–(22/9). To Angle Wood Valley (22/9), Morlancourt (28/9), Trônes Wood (30/9), Flers Line (3/10). Attack on Spectrum Trench checked (8/10), withdrew via Trônes Wood to Citadel Camp (9/10), Montonvillers (10/10), Airaines (19/10), La Gorgue (24/10).

1/4th Battalion (Royal Fusiliers). 168th Brigade, 56th (1st London) Division: In support on left of 168th Brigade's attack at Gommecourt (1/7) – at 8.45 a.m. 'A' and 'C' Companies went forward to assist 1/12th London in German first line and would later fight their way into second and third. Withdrew to trenches west of Hébuterne during evening. Casualties – 324. To St. Amand (2/7), front line Hébuterne sector (3/7), St. Amand (6/7), Bayencourt (10/7), front line (17/7), Sailly-au-Bois (23/7) – 'B' Company remaining in the Keep at Hébuterne. To front line (31/7), Bayencourt (4/8), front line (10/8), Sailly (16/8) – 'C' Company remaining in the Keep. To Halloy (18/8). Entrained at Doullens for St. Riquier and from there marched to Le Plessiel (22/8). Entrained at St. Riquier for Corbie and marched to Vaux-sur-Somme (3/9). To Citadel Camp (4/9), Casement Trench (5/9), Chimpanzee Trench (6/9) – moved forward to support trenches at rear of Leuze Wood on Wedge Wood-Ginchy Road. Attack on Leuze Wood-Quadrilateral Line (9/9) – objective south-east of The Quadrilateral reached. Via Casement Trench to Billon Farm (10/9). Casualties since (5/9) – around 272. To Angle Wood Valley (14/9), support line at Leuze Wood (18/9), Falfemont Farm (20/9), Casement Trench (22/9), positions facing Bouleaux Wood (24/9). In action (25/9) – objectives taken northern end of Bouleaux Wood. To Casement Trench (27/9), Ville-sur-Ancre (28/9), positions between Trônes and Bernafay Woods (30/9), front line east of Lesbœufs (3/10). In action (7/10) – Hazy Trench held against strong counter attacks. Casualties – 300. Withdrew to Trônes Wood. To Citadel Camp (11/10), Ville-sur-Ancre and by buses to St. Vaast-en-Chaussée (12/10), Citerne (20/10). Entrained at Longpré for Merville (24/10).

1/5th Battalion (London Rifle Brigade). 169th Brigade, 56th (1st London)

Division: On left of Division's attack at Gommecourt (1/7) – driven out of enemy trenches with great loss. In his report of the battle, Lieutenant-Colonel A.S.Bates gives strength of his battalion at time of assembly for action as 23 officers and 803 other ranks. At 5 p.m. in the British line he would count just 89 unwounded men. Total casualties given in Regimental history as 588. To Bayencourt (2/7), St. Amand (3/7), Foncquevillers (6/7), Hannescamps (8/7), Bienvillers (16/7), Hannescamps (19/7), Bienvillers (23/7), Hannescamps (30/7), St. Amand (7/8), Hannescamps (15/8), St. Amand (20/8), Sus-St-Léger (21/8), Wavans (22/8), Cauchy (23/8), Corbie (3/9), Happy Valley (4/9), Chimpanzee Valley (6/9), trenches around Falfemont Farm (7/9), Leuze Wood (8/9). Bombers attacked and took 200 yards of Combles Trench – driven out by counter attack 5.15 a.m. next morning. Attack against Loop Trench repulsed (9/9). To Citadel Camp (11/9), Billon Farm (12/9), German's Wood (13/9). Bombers attacked up Loop Trench, Down Combles Trench and to Angle Wood (15/9). To Loop Trench (16/9). Bombers in action (18/9) – withdrew to Angle Wood. To trenches in front of Combles (24/9). Attack and capture of Combles (26/9). To Méaulte (27/9), Talus Boisé (29/9), Guillemont (30/9), front line Lesbœufs (2/10), bivouacs between Bernafay and Trônes Woods (4/10). Attack on Hazy and Dewdrop Trenches (8/10). To Trônes Wood (9/10), Mansell Copse (10/10), Picquigny (12/10), Huppy (21/10), Pont-Remy (23/10), Paradia (24/10).

1/6th Battalion (Rifles). 140th Brigade, 47th (2nd London) Division: Reached Millencourt after 11 day march from Vimy sector (5/8). Left Millencourt (20/8) and via L'Etoile, Naours, Mirvaux reached Franvillers (23/8). To Black Wood (12/9). Moved forward to Bazentin-le-Grand and from there assembled in Worcester Trench (14/9). Attack on High Wood (15/9) – heavy casualties during advance – Cough Drop captured and consolidated. Flers Line assaulted (16/9) – Drop Alley taken and held. Relieved from Cough Drop (20/9) and to Hénencourt. To Albert (29/9), Mametz Wood (2/10), front line around Eaucourt l'Abbaye (4/10). Took part in operations at the Butte de Warlencourt (6/10)–(9/10). To Mametz Wood (9/20), Albert (10/10). Moved to Ypres sector (14/10).

1/7th Battalion. 140th Brigade, 47th (2nd London) Division: Reached Yvrencheux after marching from Vimy sector (4/8), Le Plessiel (5/8), L'Etoile (20/8), Naours (21/8), Mirvaux (22/8), Franvillers (23/8), Albert (12/9), trenches in front of High Wood (14/9). Attack on High Wood (15/9) – Switch Line on eastern side of wood reached and held. Moved back to reserve line (17/9), took over Starfish line (18/9). To Bottom Wood (19/9), Albert (20/9), Hénencourt Wood (21/9), Bécourt Wood (29/9), Mametz Wood (1/10) – that night moving forward to positions near Bazentin-le-Petit –

Chester Street and Mill Street. To trenches near Eaucourt l'Abbaye (5/10), Flers Line (6/10). Attack on the Butte de Warlencourt (7/10) – leading waves wiped out by machine gun fire. To Albert (10/10). Total casualties for High Wood and the Butte de Warlencourt – 30 officers and 600 other ranks. Entrained for Longpré (13/10), arrived (14/10) and marched to Brucamps. Entrained at Longpré for Caéstre (16/10).

1/8th Battalion (Post Office Rifles). 140th Brigade, 47th (2nd London) Division: Began march from Vimy sector (21/7), reaching Conteville (4/8), Caours (5/8). Via Vauchelles, Naours, Beaucourt reached Franvillers (23/8). From here the forthcoming attack on High Wood was practised at Round Wood. To Bécourt Wood (13/9). Assembled at High Wood (14/9). Attacked (15/9) – advanced at 7.20 a.m. and entered Flag Lane (140th Brigade's second objective) on right of assault. Successful attack on Flers Line (18/9). Relieved and to Hénencourt. Casualties – over 300. To Albert (29/9), via Mametz Wood to forward area at Eaucourt l'Abbaye (4/10). Attack on Snag Trench in front of Butte de Warlencourt (7/10) – Lieutenant-Colonel A.D. Derviche-Jones noting in his history of the Battalion that 2 companies were almost completely wiped out - only 7 men survived. Casualties – 411. Via Mametz Wood to Albert (9/10). Entrained for Longpré (13/10) and from there transferred to the Ypres sector.

1/9th Battalion (Queen Victoria's Rifles). 169th Brigade, 56th (1st London) Division: On right of 169th Brigade's attack at Gommecourt (1/7). Casualties – 545. To Bayencourt (2/7), St. Amand (3/7). Later began tours of duty Foncquevillers sector, billets at Hannescamps and Bienvillers. Via St. Amand and Gaudiempré to Beaudricourt (18/8), Villers-l'Hôpital (21/8), Agenvillers (23/8). Entrained at St. Riquier for Corbie (3/9), to Happy Valley (4/9), Billon Farm (6/9) and from there took over Casement Trench astride Maricourt-Longueval Road. To positions near Leuze Wood (7/9). Advanced through Leuze Wood for attack on Bouleaux Wood (9/9) – objectives taken – new line at first named Victoria Trench, later Bully Trench. To Citadel Camp (10/9). Casualties for 2 days operations – 350. To Billon Wood (12/9), trenches south of Leuze Wood (13/9), occupied Loop, Fusilier, Cheshire and Combles Trenches (15/9)-(18/9). To Falfemont Farm (19/9), front line Combles (23/9). Attack on Combles Trench (24/9) – some gains made but counter attack forced withdrawal. From Falfemont Farm to Casement Trench (26/9), Méaulte (27/9), German Wood (29/9), front line Lesbœufs – Foggy, Shamrock and Fluffy Trenches (30/9), support at Hog's Back (2/10), Citadel Camp (3/10), reserve trenches south-east of Ginchy (7/10) and in evening into support at Hog's Back. To front line Lesbœufs (8/10) – attack on Dewdrop and Spectrum Trenches. To Bernafay Wood (9/10), Mansell Camp

(10/10), Treux (11/10), Picquigny (12/10), Limeux (21/10). Entrained at Pont-Remy for Berguette (23/10).

1/12th Battalion (The Rangers). 168th Brigade, 56th (1st London) Division: From Bayencourt moved forward to front line at Hébuterne (30/6). Attack on Gommecourt (1/7) – on left of 168th Brigade with 1/14th London on its right, Battalion entered German lines. Heavy fighting around Nameless Farm. Withdrew to Sailly-au-Bois. Casualties – 517. Carried out tours of duty in Hébuterne sector – billets being at Sailly, Bayencourt. To Halloy (21/8), Neuilly-l'Hôpital (23/8). Entrained at St. Riquier for Corbie (3/9) and from there marched to Vaux- sur-Somme. To Citadel Camp (4/9), Casement Trench (5/9), Maltz Horn Trenches (6/9), Sunken Road Trench near Guillemont (7/9), Angle Wood Valley (8/9). Attack on Ginchy Telegraph (9/9) – heavy fire from The Quadrilateral right company reached Leuze Wood-Ginchy Road – left held up by fire from enemy positions south-east of Ginchy. To Billon Farm (10/9), Falfemont Farm (14/9), Angle Wood Valley (16/9), trenches at Hardecourt (18/9), Angle Wood (19/9), trenches north-west corner of Leuze Wood (20/9), Chimpanzee Valley (22/9), Bully Trench, Leuze Wood (24/9), Via Chimpanzee Valley to Morlancourt (28/9), Happy Valley (30/9), trenches east of Guillemont (3/10), front line east of Lesbœufs (5/10). Failed attack on Dewdrop Trench (7/10). To Trônes Wood (9/10), Mansell Camp (10/10). Marched to Treux and boarded French buses and lorries for Belloy-sur-Somme (12/10). To Mérélessart (19/10). Entrained at Longpré for Merville (23/10)

1/13th Battalion (Kensington). 168th Brigade, 56th (1st London) Division: In support of 1/14th London for attack at Gommecourt (1/7) – leading waves did not reach further than No Man's Land. Casualties – 326. Via Souastre to Foncquevillers (2/7), front line Hébuterne sector (13/7), Sailly-au-Bois (18/7), front line (28/7), Bayencourt (30/7), front line (5/8), Sailly-au-Bois (11/8), front line (17/8), Bayencourt (20/8), Halloy (21/8), Millencourt-en-Ponthieu (23/8), Sailly-le-Sec (3/9), Citadel Camp (4/9). Moved to forward area south of Leuze Wood (6/9) – attack from wood at night met by German counter attack. To Casement Trench (8/9), to Billon Farm (11/9), Maltz Horn Farm (22/9), Morlancourt (28/9), Citadel Camp (30/9), Trônes Wood (9/10), Mansell Camp (10/10), Vaux-en-Amiénois (13/10), Estaires (23/10).

2/13th Battalion (Kensington). 179th Brigade, 60th (2nd/2nd London) Division: Arrived Prouville from Boffles and Nœux (29/10). To Vauchelles-les-Quesnoy (3/11). Entrained at Longpré for Marseilles (14/11).

1/14th Battalion (London Scottish). 168th Brigade, 56th (1st London)

Division: Moved forward from Bayencourt (30/6) for attack on Gommecourt (1/7) - on right of Division, its right flank close to the Hébuterne-Puisieux Road, Battalion suffered heavy casualties during advance across No Man's Land. German front line reached. Withdrew to British line during evening. Casualties – 590. To Sailly-au- Bois. Via Souastre to Foncquevillers and took over trenches facing Gommecourt Park (2/7), Souastre (6/7), front line Hébuterne (10/7), Bayencourt (17/7), Hébuterne tenches (23/7), Sailly-au-Bois (30/7), Hébuterne (4/8), Bayencourt (10/8), Hébuterne (16/8), Bayencourt (20/8), Halloy (21/8). Entrained at Doullens for St. Riquier and from there marched to Drucat (22/8). From Drucat practice attacks with tanks were carried out. Entrained at St. Riquier for Ville-sur-Corbie (31/8) and from there marched to Sally-au-Bois. To Citadel Camp (3/9), Leuze Wood (5/9), Maltz Horn Farm (8/9). In action near The Quadrilateral (9/9)–(10/9). To Billon Farm (10/9), Angle Wood (14/9), Leuze Wood (17/9) – operations cancelled and returned to Angle Wood. Relieved 1/5th London in trenches north-east of Leuze Wood same night – position on line of road running between Leuze and Bouleaux Woods-Combles Road. To Angle Wood (20/9), Leuze Wood (24/9). In action north of Bouleaux Wood (25/9) – party advanced southward along light railway to within 500 yards of Combles. To Falfemont Farm (26/9), Ville-sur-Corbie (28/9), Bernafay Wood (30/9), front line east of Lesbœufs (4/10). Attacked (7/10) – gun-pits and southern end of Hazy Trench held after hand-to-hand fighting and strong counter attacks. To Bernafay Wood (8/10). Casualties since (6/9) given in Regimental history as 531. Reached Fremont (10/10). Began move to Laventie sector (20/10).

2/14th Battalion (London Scottish). 179th Brigade, 60th (2nd/2nd London) Division: Arrived Montigny-les- Jongleurs (25/10). To Buigny-l'Abbé (3/11). Ordered to Macedonia – entrained at Longpré for Marseilles (15/11).

1/15th Battalion (Prince of Wales's Own, Civil Service Rifles). 140th Brigade, 47th (2nd London) Division: Reached Conteville from Vimy sector (4/8). To Drucat (5/8), Villers-sous-Ailly (20/8), Naours (21/8), Mirvaux (22/8), Franvillers (23/8), Bécourt Wood (12/9), front line High Wood (14/9) – forming up in Black Watch Trench. Attack on High Wood (15/9) – stiff opposition encountered during advance up eastern side – Battalion records note that just 150 men reached objective. Dug in just beyond the Switch Line. Moved forward to Drop Alley (16/9), Flers Line (18/9). Bombing attack on enemy position at junction of Flers Line and Drop Alley failed (19/9). Via Bottom Wood to Albert (20/9). Casualties for 4 days fighting at High Wood – 380. To Hénencourt Wood (21/9), Albert (29/9), The Quadrangle near Mametz Wood (30/9), Flers Line Eaucourt l'Abbaye sector (4/10). Attack on the Butte De Warlencourt and Warlencourt Line (7/10) – high casualties from

German barrage while advancing through Eaucourt l'Abbaye and machine gun fire beyond village. Attack failed. Casualties – 349. Battalion records note that more than half of the attacking force had never been under fire and had joined a few days before. Via Bottom Wood to Albert (9/10). Entrained for Longpré (13/10) and from there transferred to the Ypres sector.

2/15th Battalion (Prince of Wales's Own, Civil Service Rifles). 179th Brigade, 60th (2nd/2nd London) Division: Arrived Francieres from Auxi-le-Château (3/11). Ordered to Macedonia – entrained at Longpré for Marseilles (15/11).

1/16th Battalion (Queen's Westminster Rifles). 169th Brigade, 56th (1st London) Division: Moved up during night from St. Amand and assembled in trenches at Hébuterne (30/6). In support for attack at Gommecourt (1/7) – German front line trenches taken – small party led by officer of 1/5th Cheshire (Pioneers) reached objective at The Quadrilateral. Withdrew to British line. Battalion historian – Major J.Q. Henriques gives casualties as 600 out of an attacking strength of 750. To Bayencourt (2/7), St. Amand (3/7), front line between Foncquevillers and Bienvillers (6/7), St. Amand (22/7), front line (30/7). Major Henriques records that on (5/8) a German came towards the British line with a list containing the names of wounded and unwounded prisoners taken on (1/7). It was always the proud belief that not a single unwounded member of the Battalion was taken on the day and this was confirmed. The Battalion War Diary provides a good description of life, conditions and activity in the trenches at the time. Written in great detail, often even the smallest points are record. Such as the entry for (7/8) that notes a German staff officer observing the British lines wearing white kid gloves. To Bienvillers (7/8), 'D' Company and part of 'B' remaining at Foncquevillers for work carrying gas cylinders to the front line until (12/8). To front line (15/8), St. Amand (19/8), Sus-St-Légar (20/8), Villers-l'Hôpital (22/8), Domvast (23/8). Battalion marched to see old battlefield at Crecy (25/8). To Corbie (3/9), Happy Valley (4/9), trenches just south of La Briqueterie and about a mile to the north of Maricourt (6/9), trenches north-east of Faviere Wood (7/9). In action east and south-east of Leuze Wood (9/9)–(10/9) – attacks on Loop Trench and sunken Combles Road repulsed. Casualties – 307. To Citadel Camp (10/9), trenches north of Hardecourt (13/9), Angle Wood (15/9). Attack 5.50 a.m. (18/9) on sunken road checked by machine gun fire – only 3 officers and 90 other ranks remained unwounded by 10.00 a.m. Withdrew to Angle Wood. To front line (20/9), Falfemont Farm (23/9), divisional reserve at Casement Trench (24/9), Méaulte (26/9), trenches east of Lesbœufs (30/9), Citadel Camp (3/10), positions east of Trônes Wood (7/10), front line north-east of Lesboeufs (8/10), positions west of Trônes

Wood (9/10), Citadel Camp (10/10), La Chaussée-Tirancourt (11/10), Huppy (21/10). Entrained at Pont-Remy for Berguette (23/10)

2/16th Battalion (Queen's Westminster Rifles). 179th Brigade, 60th (2nd/2nd London) Division: Arrived Ribeaucourt and Domesmont from Villers-l'Hôpital (29/10). To Bellancourt (3/11). Entrained , at Longpré for Marseilles (15/11).

1/17th Battalion (Poplar and Stepney Rifles). 141st Brigade, 47th (2nd London) Division: Arrived Maison-Ponthieu (3/8). To Agenvillers (5/8), Brucamps (20/8), Montonvillers (21/8), Pierregot (22/8), Bresle (23/8), Mametz Wood (11/9). Took over forward positions at High Wood (14/9). On right of 141st Brigade's attack on High Wood (15/9). Severe losses of Brigade saw temporary reorganization as a battalion under Lieutenant-Colonel Norman of 1/17th. To Mametz Wood (17/9), Switch Line (18/9), Albert (20/9), Bresle (21/9), Mametz (27/9), Prue and Starfish Trenches (29/9). On left of 141st Brigade's attack on Eaucourt l'Abbaye (1/10) – checked by uncut wire in front of Flers Line. To Starfish Trench (2/10), Flers Line (3/10), Mametz (5/10), Franvillers (11/10). Moved to Ypres sector (15/10).

2/17th Battalion (Poplar and Stepney Rifles). 180th Brigade, 60th (2nd/2nd London) Division: Arrived Bernaville from Bonnières (29/10). To Bussus-Bussuel (3/11). Entrained at Longpré for Marseilles (17/11).

1/18th Battalion (London Irish Rifles). 141st Brigade, 47th (2nd London) Division: Arrived Neuilly-le-Dien (4/8), to Gapennes (5/8), Ergnies and Gorenflos (20/8), Flesselles (21/8), Molliens (22/8), Bresle (23/8). Attack on High Wood (15/9). Casualties – 223. To Mametz Wood (17/9) – back at High Wood same day. To Albert (20/9), Bresle (21/9), Bécourt (27/9), front line facing Eaucourt l'Abbaye (29/9) – unsuccessful attack on Flers Trench. Renewed attack gained some ground (30/9). In support for attack on Eaucourt l'Abbaye (1/10). To Fricourt (5/10), Franvillers (7/10). Transferred to Ypres sector (16/10).

2/18th Battalion (London Irish Rifles). 180th Brigade, 60th (2nd/2nd London) Division: Arrived Outrebois (28/10). To Vacquerie (29/10), Gorenflos (2/11). Entrained at Longpré for Marseilles (19/11).

1/19th Battalion (St. Pancras). 141st Brigade, 47th (2nd London) Division: Arrived Hiermont from Bonnières (4/8). To Noyelles-en-Chaussée (5/8), Gorenflos (19/8), Flesselles (20/8), Molliens-au-Bois (21/8), Bresle (22/8). War Diary notes training program in the area including a Divisional attack practice at Franvillers on ground set out to represent High Wood. To trenches Fricourt and Mametz Woods (11/9) – Headquarters at The Quadrangle.

Moved forward to support at Bazentin-le-Grand (Mill Street) (14/9). Attack on High Wood (15/9) – War Diary notes 2 tanks on Battalion front put out of action at 6.15 a.m. – one from a direct hit. Moved forward with 1/20th London at 7 a.m. (zero plus 40). Finding congestion in communication trenches Commanding Officer, Lieutenant Colonel A.P. Hamilton climbed out of the trench to lead attack and was killed almost at once. Relieved from captured positions and to Mametz Wood (17/9). Casualties since (15/9) – 316. To positions between Bazentin-le-Grand and Bazentin-le-Petit (18/9), old German line between Fricourt and Bécourt (19/9), Bresle (23/9), support trenches Bazentin-le-Grand (27/9), Flers line south-east of Eaucourt l'Abbaye (28/9). Bombing attacks along Flers Line and Flers Support (29/9). Attack on Eaucourt l'Abbaye (1/10) – leading waves held up by machine gun fire in front of German trenches and waited in shell holes for arrival of tanks. Later advanced through village to Le Barque Road. Relieved midnight (4/10) and to the Quadrangle. To Franvillers (8/10). Entrained at Albert for Longpré (14/10) – arrived (15/10) and marched to Gorenflos. Entrained at Pont-Remy for Ypres sector (17/10).

2/19th Battalion (St. Pancras). 180th Brigade, 60th (2nd/2nd London) Division: Arrived Mezerolles from Cannettemont (28/10). To Berneuil (29/10), Ailly-le-Haut-Clocher (3/11). Entrained at Longpré for Marseilles (18/11).

1/20th Battalion (Blackheath and Woolwich). 141st Brigade, 47th (2nd London) Division: Arrived Agenvillers (6/8). To Flesselles (21/8), Molliens-au-Bois (22/8), Bresle (23/8), Mametz Wood (14/9). Moved forward for attack on High Wood early morning (15/9) – War Diary notes 2 'armoured cars' on way up to assembly positions behind support line. One machine broke down and unable to move forward used its Hotchkiss and 6-pdr against enemy lines. Later – crew set fire to it and left. Advanced 11.30 a.m. – bombed down enemy trenches – 'cleared wood entirely.' Casualties – 263. To Bresle (21/9), Millencourt (25/9), Mametz Wood (27/9), front line (Cough Drop, Drop Alley) (28/9). Strong points and 100 yards of Flers Line taken (30/9). Attack on Eaucourt l'Abbaye (1/10) – Hassault held up until arrival of tanks. Later passed through Flers Line into village and on to Le Barque Road. Relieved and to Black Wood (4/10). To Mametz Wood (7/10), Franvillers (8/10). Entrained at Albert for Longpré (15/10) and from there to Yaucourt-Bussus. Entrained at Pont-Remy for Ypres sector (17/10).

2/20th Battalion (Blackheath and Woolwich). 180th Brigade, 60th (2nd/2nd London) Division: Arrived Heuzecourt (29/10), later to Yaucourt. Entrained at Longpré for Marseilles (19/11).

1/21st Battalion (First Surrey Rifles). 142nd Brigade, 47th (2nd London) Division: Arrived Barly from Maiziéres (4/8). To St. Aucheul (5/8), St. Riquier (6/8), Buigny-l-Abbé (21/8), Vignacourt (22/8), Villers-Bocage (23/8), Lahousssoye (24/8), Bécourt (11/9), trenches north of Fricourt (14/9). Attack on High Wood (15/9) – moved forward via Mametz Wood to Bazentin-le-Grand in reserve – later assisted assaulting brigades (140th and 141st). Attacked Starfish Line about 5.30 p.m. – advancing east of wood under heavy shell fire brought to a halt in front of objective. History of the 47th Division records just 2 officers and 60 men left out of the 17 and 550 that had gone into action. Relieved and to Black Wood (19/9), Millencourt (20/9). To Mametz Wood (28/9), High Wood (1/10), Starfish Redoubt (7/10), front line Eaucourt l'Abbaye sector (8/10). Unsuccessful attack on Snag Trench at night. Relieved and to Mametz Wood (9/10), Laviéville (10/10). Entrained at Albert for Ypres sector (14/10).

2/21st Battalion (First Surrey Rifles). 181st Brigade, 60th (2nd/2nd London) Division: Arrived Neuvillette from Estrée-Wamin (28/10). To Autheux (29/10), Berneuil (3/11), Villers-sous-Ailly (4/11). Entrained at Longpré for Marseilles (24/11).

1/22nd Battalion (The Queen's). 142nd Brigade, 47th (2nd London) Division: Arrived Barly from Magnicourt-sur-Canche (2/8). To Montigny (4/8), Oneux (5/8), Canchy (16/8), Vauchelles-les-Quesnoy (20/8), Bourdon (21/8), Villers-Bocage (22/8), Béhencourt (23/8), Albert (10/9), Mametz Wood (11/9). Attack on High Wood (15/9) – in reserve carrying ammunition through to forward area. Took over front line in High Wood (18/9). Relieved and to Black Wood (20/9), Millencourt (21/9). To Mametz Wood (28/9), High Wood (2/10), Switch Line (3/10), Starfish Line (4/10), front line Eaucourt l'-Abbaye sector (8/10). Attack on Snag Trench at night – forward posts established on Eaucourt l'Abbaye-Warlencourt Road. Relieved and to Mametz Wood (10/10), Laviéville (11/10). Entrained at Albert for Ypres sector (14/10).

2/22nd Battalion (The Queen's). 181st Brigade, 60th (2nd/2nd London) Division: Arrived Neuvillette from Izet-lès-Hameaux (28/10). To Candas (30/10), Brucamps (4/11). Entrained at Longpré for Marseilles (24/11).

1/23rd Battalion. 142nd Brigade, 47th (2nd London) Division: Arrived Remaisnil from Averdoingt (2/8). To Bernâtre (4/8), St. Riquier (6/8), Francieres (21/8), Vignacourt (22/8), Villers-Bocage (23/8), Lahoussoye (24/8), Albert (11/9), Mametz Wood (14/9), Bazentin-le-Grand (15/9) – in reserve for attack on High Wood. Attacked east of High Wood 9.25 a.m. (16/9) – encountered heavy fire – Battalion history recording that attacking companies ('A', 'C', 'D') never returned. Remains of Battalion (with 1/24 London) attacked Starfish Line early morning (18/9) – met strong fire from northern corner of High Wood - objective taken. Later enemy counter attacked – Battalion history recording that a withdrawal of 100 yards was forced followed by heavy bombing and hand-to-hand fighting until dusk. Relieved and to Black Wood. Casualties since (15/9) – 581. To Millencourt (20/9). Moved forward to Eaucourt l'Abbay sector (1/10). In action towards Flers Line (2/10) – attacked at 6.45 a.m. – heavy casualties from machine gun fire and withdrew. Relieved and to High Wood. Casualties – 163. In reserve for operations in front of Butte de Warlencourt (8/10). To Laviéville (9/10). To Albert (14/10) and entrained for Ypres sector.

2/23rd Battalion. 181st Brigade, 61st (2nd/2nd London) Division: Arrived Barly from Ivergny (28/10). To Outrebois (29/10), Candas (30/10), Ergnies (4/11). Entrained at h Longpré for Marseilles (23/11).

1/24th Battalion (The Queen's). 142nd Brigade, 47th (2nd London) Division: Arrived Mezerolles from Gouy-en-Ternois (1/8). To Maizicourt (4/8), Neuville (5/8), Neuilly-l'Hôpital (11/8), Vignacourt (21/8), Pierregot (22/8), Béhencourt (23/8), Bécourt Wood (10/9), High Wood (11/9), The Quadrangle (14/9), Mametz Wood (15/9) – moved forward for attack on Starfish Line. One company attacked with 1/21st London about 5.30 p.m. – advanced through heavy shelling with high losses. Assault checked and forced to dig in under machine gun fire. Other companies also suffered heavily in their attempt to reach objective. Renewed attack (18/9) – with 1/23rd London involved in hand-to-hand fighting until dusk. Relieved and to Millencourt (21/9). To Bécourt Wood (28/9), Eaucourt l'Abbay sector (1/10). Relieved and to Bellancourt (9/10). Entrained at Albert for Ypres sector (14/10).

2/24th Battalion (The Queen's). 181st Brigade, 60th (2nd/2nd London) Division: Arrived Barly from Beaudricourt (28/10). To Fienvillers (29/10), Mouflers and Vauchelles (4/11). Entrained at Longpré for Marseilles (25/11).

Hertfordshire Regiment (Territorial Force)

1/1st Battalion. 118th Brigade, 39th Division: Arrived Grouches (24/8). To Bus-lès-Artois (25/8), bivouacs in wood close behind Englebelmer (26/8), Mesnil (2/9). Took over line – companies at Fort Prowse and Fort Moulin. In reserve during 39th Division's attack north of the Ancre (3/9). To Englebelmer (12/9). Relieved 16th Rifle Brigade in left sub section Y Ravine (19/9). Relieved 1/1st Cambridgeshire in Hamel right sub section (3/10). To Martinsart (7/10). Relieved 17th Sherwood Foresters on right of Schwaben Redoubt (10/10). In support during successful attack on enemy portion of Schwaben (14/10). To Englebelmer (16/10), Senlis (18/10), Schwaben Redoubt (29/10), dug outs near Authuille (30/10). Relieved 12th Royal Sussex in centre sub section left of Schwaben Redoubt (1/11). Relieved by 17th Sherwood Foresters and to huts in Pioneer Road (3/11). Relieved 16th Sherwood Foresters left River sub section (8/11). Relieved by 12th Royal Sussex and to Martinsart Wood (10/11). To Pioneer Road (11/11), Schwaben Redoubt (12/11). Assembled for attack (13/11) – War Diary records that 'direction was kept and the Battalion had very soon taken all its objectives, capturing the whole of the Hansa Line and advancing to a depth of 1,600 yards – over 250 prisoners were captured and many Germans were killed.' New line consolidated and held until relieved during night (14/11). To Aveluy. Casualties – 147. To Warloy (15/11), Orville (16/11), Candas (18/11).

63rd (Royal Naval) Division

1st Royal Marine Battalion. 188th Brigade: Arrived Acheux from St. Pol area (4/10) and from there marched to Mailly-Maillet Wood. To Varennes (8/10), Fomrceville (9/10), Hédauville (17/10), Englebelmer (20/10). Relieved Howe Battalion in front line Hamel left sector (22/10). To Englebelmer (25/10), front line (28/10), Englebelmer (30/10), Varennes (31/10), Puchevillers (5/11), front line (7/11), Englebelmer (8/11), Varennes (9/11), front line (10/11). Attack on Beaucourt (13/11) – on left of 188th Brigade's assault – heavy casualties (including all 4 company commanders) soon after leaving start positions – small parties only fighting through to German third line. Relieved and via Hédauville to Puchevillers (15/11). War Diary notes 'advanced 490 strong, returned 138 – casualties 352. To Gézaincourt (17/11), Bernaville (18/11).

2nd Royal Marine Battalion. 188th Brigade: Arrived Englebelmer from St. Pol Area (5/10). To Hédauville (8/10), Englebelmer (21/10), Hédauville (31/10), Puchevillers (5/11), Hédauville (7/11), Englebelmer (11/11). Attack on Beaucourt (13/11) – advanced behind 1st Royal Marine Battalion – Divisional history by Douglas Jerrold noting hand-to-hand fighting in German third line – heavy casualties – small groups only continued fighting. Relieved in Station Road noon (15/11) and via Englebelmer to Hédauville. To Puchevillers (16/11), Gézaincourt (17/11), Bernaville (18/11).

Anson Battalion. 188th Brigade: Arrived Acheux from St. Pol area (4/10) and from there marched to Mailly-Maillet. To Hédauville (8/10), bivouacs east of Englebelmer (19/10), Hédauville (30/10), Puchevillers (5/11), Hédauville (6/11), Englebelmer (7/11). Attack on Beaucourt (13/11). Relieved and to Hédauville (15/11). Casualties – 322. To Puchevillers (16/11), Beaumetz (18/11).

Drake Battalion. 189th Brigade: Arrived Forceville from St. Pol area (4/10). To Englebelmer (8/10). Relieved 14th Hampshire in front line Y Ravine sector (16/10). To Englebelmer (17/10), Mesnil (21/10), Englebelmer (23/10), front line (27/10), Hédauville (30/10), Puchevillers (31/10), Hédauville (5/11), Englebelmer (6/11). Took up assembly positions in gulley in front of Hamel sector (12/11). Attack on Beaucourt (13/11) – more than half of strength (Commanding Officer Lieutenant-Colonel A.S. Tetley mortally wounded) lost during advance to first objective (Station Road). Withdrew to original enemy front line about 4 a.m. (15/11). Casualties – 196. Later moved via Englebelmer and Hédauville to Arquèves. To Doullens (18/11).

Hawke Battalion. 189th Brigade: Arrived Acheux from St. Pol area (4/10). To Forceville (6/10). Working parties to line south of Hébuterne. H.Q. and

3 companies to Englebelmer, 1 company to Auchonvillers (16/10). Company at Auchonvillers joined rest of Battalion (17/10). To Mesnil (19/10), front line Hamel sector (20/10), Englebelmer, (21/10), front line (24/10), Englebelmer (27/10), Hédauville (30/10), Puchevillers (31/10), Hédauville (4/11), Mesnil (6/11), front line (10/11). Attack on Beaucourt (13/11) – advanced 5.45 a.m. – leading waves cut down by machine guns situated between German first and second lines – survivors fought through to Station Road. Relieved and via Englebelmer to Arquèves (15/11). Casualties – 419, Divisional history by Douglas Jerrold noting that some 400 of these occurred within first half hour of attack.

Hood Battalion. 189th Brigade: Arrived Forceville from St. Pol area (4/10). To Mesnil and took over line Hamel sector (16/10), Englebelmer (20/10), Mesnil (23/10), Hédauville (30/10), Puchevillers (31/10), Englebelmer (4/11), front line (6/11), Mesnil (10/11). Attack on Beaucourt (13/11) – on right of advance passed through enemy front line – cleared dug-outs in railway cutting – later almost 400 prisoners taken at Station Road and Beaucourt Station. Withdrew via Hédauville to Arquèves (15/11). To Doullens (18/11).

Howe Battalion. 188th Brigade: Arrived Acheux from St. Pol area (4/10) and from there marched to Mailly-Maillet. To Varennes (8/10), front line north of Hamel (18/10), Englebelmer (22/10), front line (25/10), Englebelmer (27/10), Puchevillers (5/11), Hedauville (7/11), Englebelmer (11/11). Attack on Beaucourt (13/11) – entered first and second lines – heavy losses during next advance – just 1 officer and some 20 men reaching third line. Withdrew via Englebelmer to Hédauville (15/11) – at 11 p.m. to to Puchevillers. To Gézaincourt (17/11), Bernaville (18/11).

Nelson Battalion. 189th Brigade: Arrived Acheux from St. Pol area (4/10) and from there to bivouacs in Acheux Wood. To Englebelmer (8/10), front line Auchonvillers sector (16/10), Englebelmer (17/10), Mesnil (20/10), front line Hamel sector (21/10), Englebelmer (24/10), Varennes (30/10), Puchevillers (31/10), Varennes (5/11), Englebelmer (6/11), front line (8/11), Englebelmer (10/11), Mesnil (12/11). Attack on Beaucourt (13/11) – heavy casualties among leading waves during advance on Station Road – Divisional history by Douglas Jerrold notes third and fourth waves fell almost to a man in first and second German lines. Withdrew to Arquèves via Hédauville (15/11). Casualties – 342. To Gézaincourt (18/11).

REGIMENTAL INDEX